Also by Gérard A. Besson:

History:

The Book of Trinidad (with Bridget Brereton)
From Colonial to Republic (with Selwyn Ryan)
A Photograph Album of Trinidad at the Turn of the 19th Century
Scotiabank, The First 50 Years in T&T
The Angostura Historical Digest
The History of ANSAMcAL
The Cult of the Will

Fiction:

Tales of the Paria Main Road
Play Whe Diary of Dreams, Caprices and Charts
Folklore & Legends of Trinidad and Tobago
The Voice in the Govi
From the Gates of Aksum

ROUME DE SAINT LAURENT
... A MEMOIR

Frontispiece: "Mortals are equal, it is not birth, but virtue alone that makes the difference". Detail, French revolutionary print, Bibliothèque Nationale de France.

GÉRARD A. BESSON

Roume de Saint Laurent

...a Memoir

PARIA
2015

© Gérard A. Besson 2015

All rights reserved. Except for use in review, no part of this publication may be reproduced or transmitted in any form or by any means, electronic or mechanical, including photocopy, recording, any information storage or retrieval system, or on the internet, without permission in writing from the publishers.

 www.pariapublishing.com

Typeset in Poliphilus 12 point by Paria Publishing Co. Ltd.
and printed by Lightning Source, U.S.A./U.K.

ISBN 978-976-8244-21-5 (softcover)

Cover paintings:
Creole in a Red Turban by Jacques Amans (1801–1888), circa 1840
La liberté guidant le peuple by Eugène Delacroix (1798–1863), 1830
Battle at San Domingo by January Suchodolski (1797–1875), 1845

Frontispiece:
Les Mortels sont égaux, ce n'est pas la naissance c'est la seule vertu qui fait la différence, print, 1794

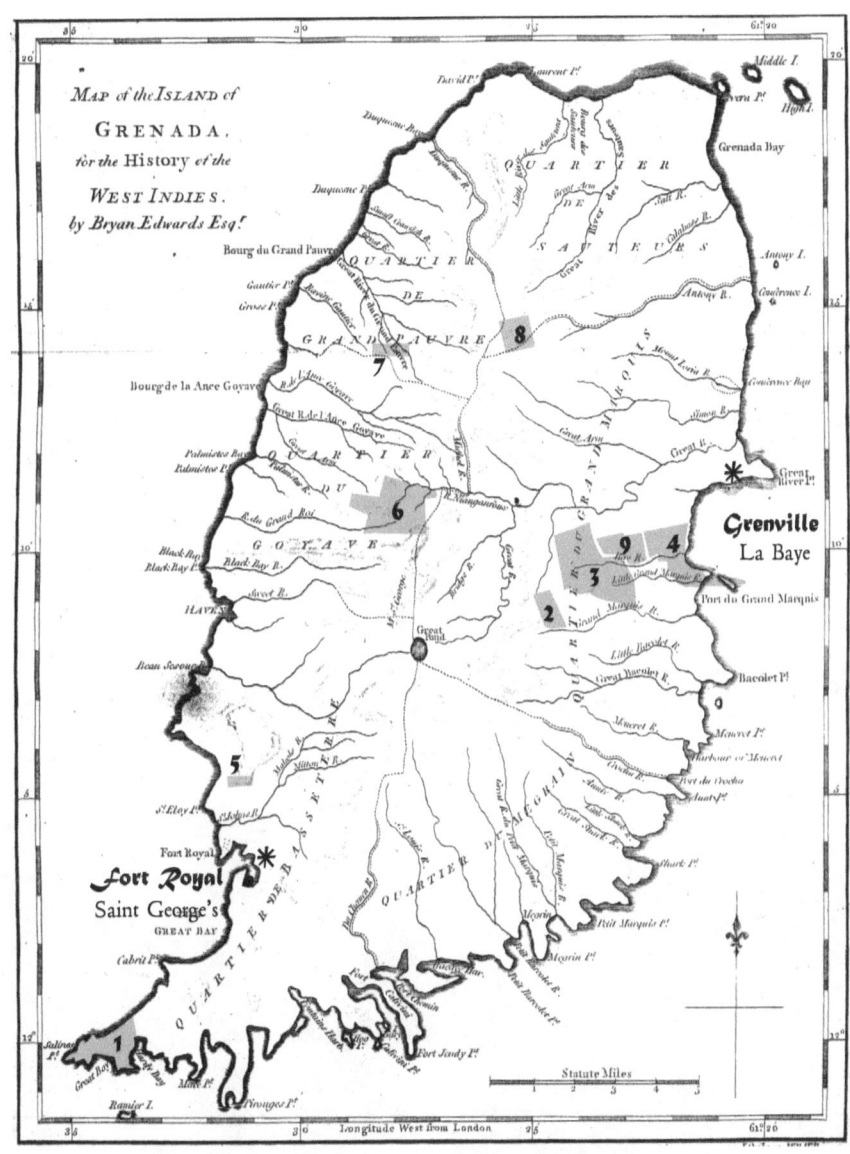

Plantations owned by Everard de Barras, father of Stanislaus de Barras: Point Salines:1, Balthazar:2, Belle Vue:3, Soubise:4. Owned by Marianne Roume née Rochard: La Fontenoy:5. Owned by Laurent Roume &Rosa, née de Gannes, later by Julien Fédon: Belvedere:6, Mount Saint Laurent:7, also called Mount Saint Laurent:8. Owned by Bathilde Chartier de Lotbinière: grand mother of Julien Fédon: La Digue:9. (Map from Brian Edwards 1807, shaded insets, Garvin Smith from Pinel,1763.)

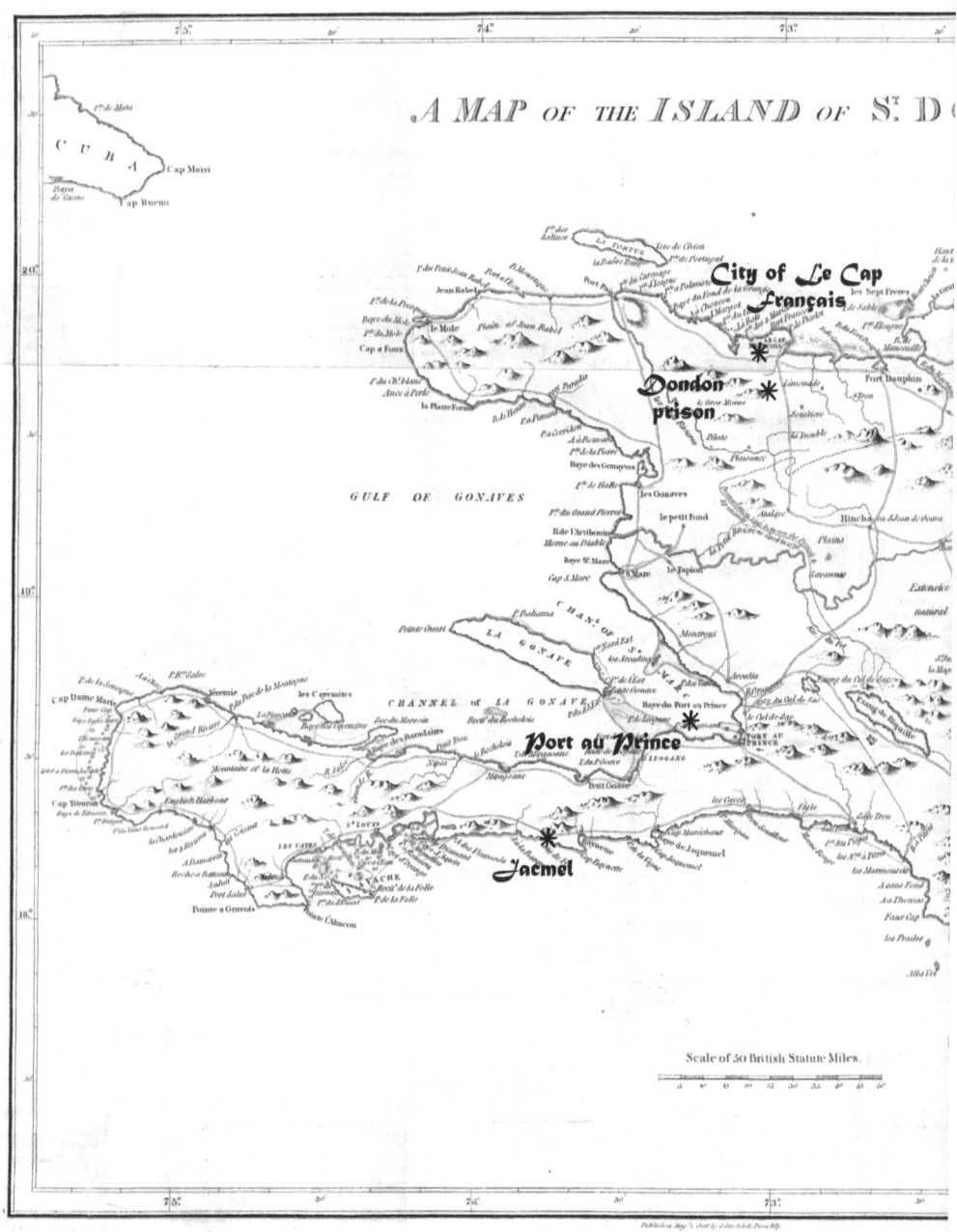

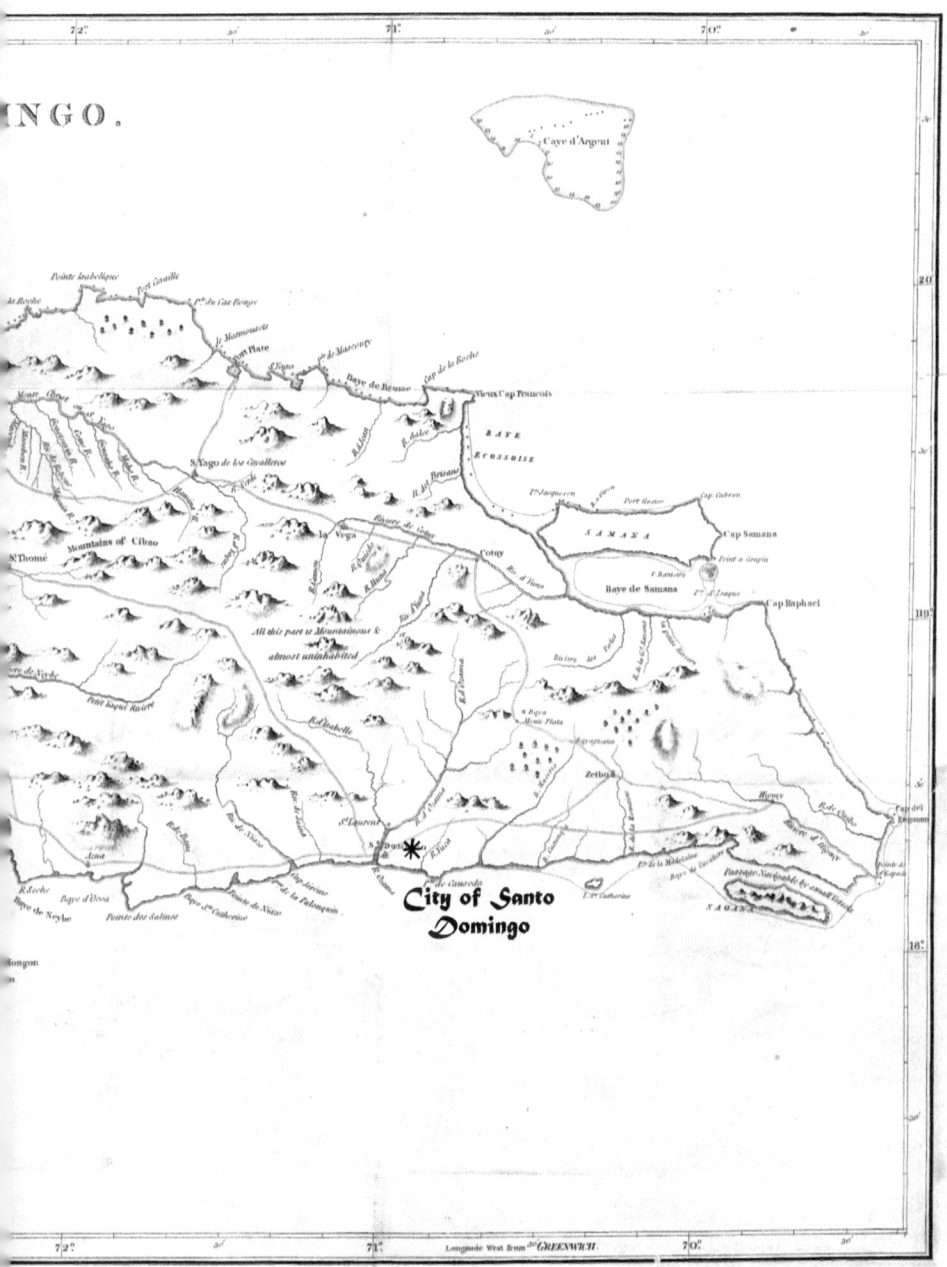

(from Brian Edwards 1807) Hispaniola: As Spain conquered new regions on the mainland of the Americas, its interest [in Hi]spaniola waned, and the colony's population grew slowly. By the early 17th century, the island became regular stopping [point] for Caribbean pirates. In 1606, the government of Philip III ordered all inhabitants of Hispaniola to move close to [Santo] Domingo, to avoid interaction with pirates. Rather than secure the island, his action meant that French, English and [Dutch] pirates established their own bases on the abandoned north and west coasts of the island. In 1665, French colonization [of the] island was officially recognized by King Louis XIV. The French colony was given the name Saint-Domingue. In the 1697 Treaty of Ryswick, Spain formally ceded the western third of the island to France.

IX

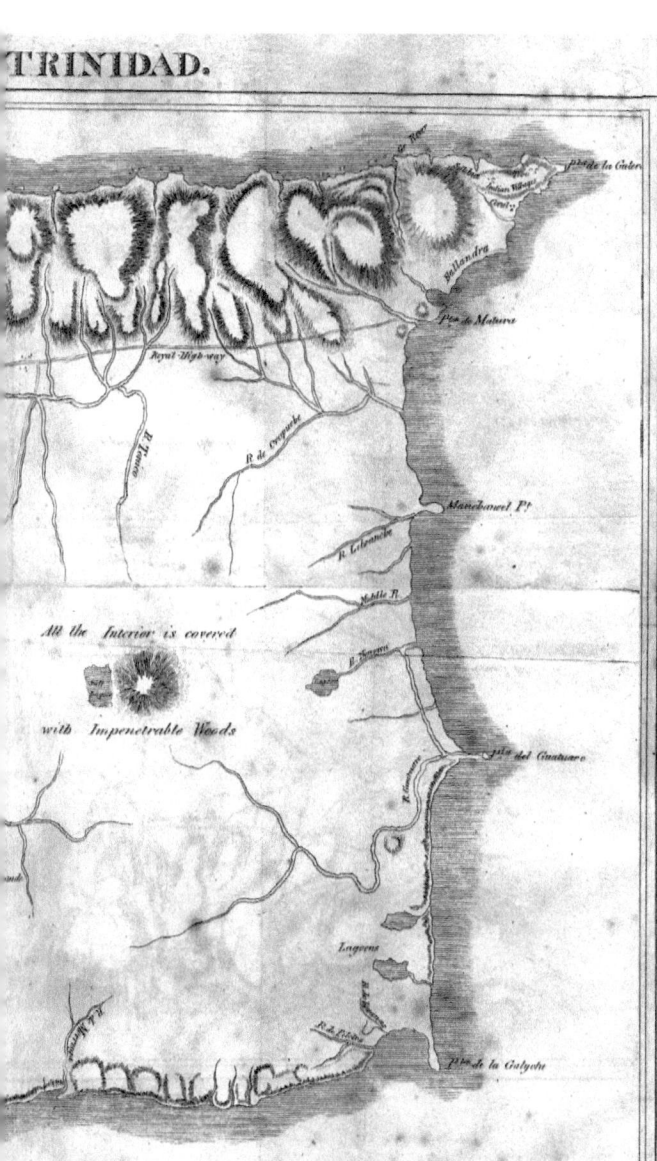

(Map from M'Callum 1805) Trinidad in this period was crisscrossed by what was called "Indian Footpaths". There was the Royal Road that linked the town of Port of Spain to encomienda of Arima and to the hamlet of San Fernando. Virtually the entire island was covered by what was called Imperishable Woods and was, to a considerable degree, impenetrable. The majority of the interior was unknown to the cartographer, and there were merely a few dozen plantations along the coast of the Gulf of Paria.

"Behold me then haled before this swift and bloody judgment-bar, where the best protection was to have no protection, and all resources of ingenuity became null if they were not founded on truth."

Thomas Carlyle, The French Revolution III, 34.

"It may seem unfashionable to say so, but historians should seize the imagination as well as the intellect. History is in a sense a story, a narrative of adventure and of vision, of character and of incident. It is also a portrait of the great general drama of the human spirit. That is why historians should attempt to enthral and inspire the reader in equal measure."

Peter Ackroyd, Daily Telegraph, 25 August 2011.

To

ALICE BESSON

PREFACE

The story of Philippe Roume de Saint Laurent as coloniser and as propagator of Trinidad's "celebrated" Cedula for Population of 1783, which brought scores of French Creoles and hundreds of their free black and coloured cousins to Trinidad, along with many thousand enslaved Africans, thus creating an instant population in an erstwhile virtually abandoned Spanish colony, is a well known and accepted narrative. Recounted *ad nauseam* over the centuries it has acquired the patina of myth. As such, little is known about the man who is supposed to have crafted the document that has been described by Professor of history Carl Campbell as the first constitution of Trinidad.

This work of fiction is meant to quicken an interest and lend some understanding to the period. Hopefully, it will give form and dimension to this somewhat shadowy historical figure and suggest answers to some of the puzzling questions concerning Roume's life; for example, how was he able to enter the political landscape of revolutionary Paris and gain the trust of the extremist regimes? And why, even though he had a career as a French administrator in Grenada, Tobago, Saint-Domingue and Santo Domingo during the turbulent period of the French and Haitian revolutions, he is not remembered publicly in Trinidad and Tobago or present in the pantheon of heroes who worked towards the liberation of the western world in the age of revolutions that witnessed the birth of the New World's republics?

Historian Olga Mavrogordato sparked an interest in Philippe Roume in us and others in the 1970s and out of that interest this book emerges. Thanks to the work done by Michael Pocock in the National Archives in Paris—which he generously shared with us—some of which he used in his own book, *Out of the Shadows of the Past*, we have been able to see beyond the outline of Philippe Roume's life as sketched by historian P.G.L. Borde in his *History of Trinidad under the Spanish Government*. C.L.R. James' *Black Jacobins* allowed us to get a glimpse of Roume's career in Saint-Domingue and in Santo Domingo, and from James Redpath's *Toussaint L'Ouverture—Biography and Autobiography* we glean that Roume "under a simple and modest exterior possessed much knowledge; was of a phlegmatic disposition and would have been inaccessible to the attacks of the factions, had not his ordinary fickleness called forth their efforts." Leon de Gannes was kind to share historical and genealogical information,

Curtis Jacobs' paper, *The Fédons of Grenada, 1763-1814* was an invaluable resource, as was the material sent to us by Ashley Steele. Michael Jessamy unearthed archival records, organised them and sent them on to us, and Ronald Harford made available hard-to-come-by documents, maps, etc., thank you very much, gentlemen. From Masonic records we learnt that Roume had a son, Maresse, born out of wedlock, and from other sources, such as Bryan Edwards' historical work, we understand that he was admitted to the Paris Bar, while Wenda Parkinson's *The Gilded African* tells us something of his relationship with Toussaint L'Ouverture.

We explore, from little known material, his links through marriage to the Lambert family of Île de Ré, famous for the South Sea Bubble, an 18th century financial collapse, and we lift the handkerchief of history by another corner to get an understanding of his relationship with a Grenadian mulâtresse, Marianne Rochard, the mother of his two daughters, whom he married in Saint-Domingue with Toussaint L'Ouverture as their witness.

Notwithstanding the fictional nature of the book we have followed the historical events of the period that shaped Roume's remarkable career as closely as we might. Every important element in the story is based on fact or some tradition, however tenuous, bearing always in mind the words of Michel Chevalier, French historian and statesman, who had this to say: "He who views the events of the past with the eyes of his time is very much exposed to a chance of error. Many a time, it is a panorama in which the objects are dim, because one is placed beyond the point of view."

I dedicate this book to Alice Besson. It was her generosity, not to mention patience that went way beyond wifely duty, that made it possible. Raymond Ramcharitar brought to bear his most critical faculties and Simon Lee his artful skill as editor. Bridget Brereton wielded her inflexible red pen and kept in check the wild excursions that historical fiction writers embark upon. Brenda Almandoz was kind to cast her careful eye. My gratitude to them all cannot be exaggerated. It is not without interest that this preface is completed on the 23rd of November 2015, two hundred and thirty two years, to the day, after the promulgation of Trinidad's Cedula for Population of 1783.

Gérard A. Besson
"Tall Stories"
23rd of November 2015

CONTENTS

MAPS

Grenada, Hispaniola, Trinidad	VII - XI
Preface	XII
List of Characters	XVI
Timeline	XX

BOOK FIRST

1:	Remembering To Die Paris, 1805	1
2:	Philippe Rose Roume & Calypso's Island	15
3:	Sir Laurence Lambert: The South Sea Company 1765	26
4:	The Marriages 1765	37
5:	André Fatio, The Beginning of the End Île de Ré, 1775	47
6:	Bertrand de Charras The Closing of Accounts, 1775	57
7:	The Surveyors, 1777	63
8:	Bertrand de Charras, 1779	78
9:	The Interloper, Balthazar Estate, 1780	83
10:	Trinidad's First Constitution	101
11:	The Royal Cedula for Population, 1783	110
12:	As One Door Closes, Another Opens Paris 1783 – Tobago 1786	130
13:	Sir Laurence Lambert Finding Persephone, Île de Ré, 1789	149

BOOK SECOND

14: Rue Saint-Séverin, 1790 — 192
15: Look! Stanislaus de Barras! Paris, 1790 — 227
16: The Fields of Mars & Venus — 250
17: Baton Changes Bout, Saint-Domingue, 1791–1792 — 256
18: The Stigmatised, Saint-Domingue, 1792 — 293
19: The September Massacres Paris, 1792-1793 — 318

BOOK THIRD

20: Meeting Chadeau & The Escape From Grenada, 1796 — 342
21: War in the Vendée 1793–1796 — 368
22: The Fall of the Incorruptible, 1794 — 389
23: Heart's Cut, Paris, 1796 — 398
24: The Admiral's Bones, 1797 — 433
25: Finding Calypso, 1793–1796 — 460
26: L'Anse Mitan, Trinidad, 1820 — 488

APPENDIX

Glossary — 493
The Cedula for Population — 498
About the Author — 504

List of Characters

Major characters:

Philippe Rose Roume de Saint Laurent, hero, Grenadian French Creole, coloniser of Trinidad. Served as Commissioner to Saint-Domingue and to Santo Domingo.

Marianne Katronice, also **Soubise Rochard**, heroine, free coloured woman, Grenadian with dual personality, diarist, Philippe Roume's second wife, illegitimate daughter of Thomas Rochard l'Epine and Ya Ya, also called Geneviève Katronice, born a slave.

Sir Laurence Lambert of The South Sea Company, grandfather of Françoise (Fanny), first wife of Philippe Roume, character behind the moneylenders.

André Fatio/Samuel Bosanquet, moneylenders working for the The South Sea Company.

Bertrand de Charras, Françoise's lover and Philippe Roume's mother's second husband.

Rosa de Gannes, Madame de Charras, Philippe's mother, wife of Bertrand de Charras, sometime lover of André Fatio.

Everard de Barras, Philippe's mentor and tutor, father of Stanislaus de Barras, Grenadian revolutionary, uncle of Paul de Barras (French republican general).

Françoise (Fanny) Lambert, Sir Laurence's granddaughter and Philippe Roume's first wife.

Shadrach Lazare, first mate on Funillière's ship, lover of Françoise (Fanny Roume née Lambert, Philippe Roume's first wife).

Henri-Christophe, childhood friend of Marianne, general in the revolution in Saint-Domingue.

Sarusima the Carib, Philippe's guide and Rosette's foster father.

Stanislaus de Barras, free coloured, illegitimate son of Everard de Barras and Azalia Pradine, a free coloured woman, lover of Marianne, father of Julien, by Rosette, eldest daughter of Marianne & Philippe Roume.

Julien Fédon, Grenadian revolutionary, Tante Mam'zelle's grandson by her illegitimate son Pierre (whom she had with a French overseer of her estate, Dieudonné Fédon) and Brigitte Cavalan, a free coloured woman.

Toussaint L'Ouverture, liberator of Saint-Domingue.

Jacques Chadeau, Grenadian revolutionary (Fédon revolution).

Minor characters:

Rosette, Marianne's and Philippe's eldest daughter, mother of Julien, by Stanislaus de Barras (lover of Marianne).

Manon, Marianne's and Philippe's second daughter.

Arthur Dillon, Tobago governor and Philippe Roume's friend.

Decima de la Forêt, Dillon's lover and Rosette's foster mother.

Papa-oncle Felicien, Marianne's avuncular childhood friend.

Mallie, Marianne's father's cook.

Paul de Barras, nephew of Everard de Barras, vicomte and Republican general, lover of Marie Josèphe Tascher de la Pagerie.

Captain Jean-Saint-Paul Funillière, pirate captain and Marianne's lover during her pirate period.

Tante Mam'zelle (Bathilde Chartier de Lotbinière), neighbour of Marianne as a child, grandmother of Julien Fédon.

Bob, a Negro boy, sailor on Funillière's ship (Robert in *From the Gates of Aksum*).

José de Gálvez, Spanish Minister of the Indies.

Vincent Ogé, mulatto from Saint-Domingue, "saviour" of Marianne and Philippe when they are attacked in Paris.

Doctor Franz Anton Mesmer, Swiss doctor and hypnotiser.

Maximilien Robespierre, republican revolutionary.

Georges-Jacques Danton, republican revolutionary.

José de Abalos, intendant of Caracas.

Madame Matilde and Doctor Maurice Lannes, "saviours" of Marianne and Philippe when they get attacked in Paris.

Manon Philippon Roland and **Jean-Marie Roland,** Girondins, friends and confidants of Marianne and Philippe Roume.

Dr. Edmond Saint-Léger and **Frédéric-Ignace de Mirbeck,** Roume's co-commissioners in Saint-Domingue.

Louis Antoine Léon de Saint-Just, infant terrible from the Nivernais, Marianne's lover.

Marissé Roume de Saint Laurent, illegitimate son of Philippe Roume.

Lys de Cayeux, woman with whom Philippe Roume has a son, Marissé Roume de Saint Laurent.

Jean Baptiste Bideau, St. Lucian, owner of the schooner *Botón de Rosa* (appears in *From the Gates of Aksum*).

Captain John Black, owner of the schooner *Swallow* (appears in *From the Gates of Aksum*).

Laure de Girardin de Montgérald, la Comtesse de la Touche, wife of Arthur Dillon, lover of Philippe Roume.

Marie Josèphe Tascher de la Pagerie, Josephine, cousin of Laure de Girardin, lover, and later wife of Napoleon Bonaparte, later Empress.

Napoleon Bonaparte, First Council, lover and later husband of Josephine, later Emperor.

Very minor characters:

Juan de Catilla and **Augustin Cramé,** Spanish engineers/surveyors.

Vandelle, Manon's playmate, a former slave in Grenada.

Jean de Pontieux, friend of Marianne's, colleague of Philippe Roume in Tobago.

Yzore Delpeche, dwarf, factotum of Jean de Pontieux.

Simon de Gannes, Philippe Roume's grandfather.

Wabo, Elisa, Samson, slaves in Grenada.

Curé Peissonier, a priest in Grenada.

Abbé Bertold d'Audain, Carmelite, Philippe Roume's religious teacher.

Manuel Falquez, Martin de Salavenia, Spanish governors of Trinidad.

Miguel and **Francisco Le Zama, José Farfan de los Godos, Alexandro Díez dos Ramos,** Spanish planters in Trinidad.

Louis Rosnay, attorney of Thomas Rochard l'Epine in Grenada.

Marie Alciñia Funillière, wife of Captain Funillière.

Melchior, Sir Laurence Lambert's factotum.

Abbé Henri Grégoire, Catholic priest and revolutionary, chief spokesman for Société des Amis des Noirs in the French colonies.

Pierre Pinchinat, mulatto ideologue from Saint-Domingue.

Jacques Pierre Brissot, a leader of the Girondins.

Léger-Félicité Sonthonax, commissioner to Saint-Domingue.

Victor Hugues, republican revolutionary, executioner in the Antilles.

Gilbert du Motier, Marquis Lafayette, commander of the National Guard in France.

Honoré Riqueti, Comte Mirabeau, revolutionary.

Camille Desmoulins, revolutionary and journalist.

Jean-Paul Marat, revolutionary.

Charles-Henri Sanson, executioner.

Julien Raimond, mulatto, commissioner to Saint-Domingue.

Jean-Marc Chavannes, revolutionary with Ogé in Saint-Domingue.

Cloudia de Payen, perhaps a lover of Stanislaus de Barras.

Cécile Fatiman, obeahwoman in Saint-Domingue.

Zinga, the boy with the obeah woman (appears in *Voice in the Govi*)

Captain Boucoud of the ship *Quatorze Juillet* to Saint-Domingue.

Jean-François and **Georges Biassou,** slave rebellion leaders in Saint-Domingue.

André Rigaud, mulatto leader in Saint-Domingue.

Desmaizeaux, majordomo with a stutter, **Cook** and **Bottle Washer** (deaf), friends of Marianne in Saint-Domingue.

Jeannot, a leader of the 1791 slave uprising in Saint-Domingue.

Boukman, Jamaican, instigator of the slave rebellion in Saint-Domingue.

Brudieu de Columbier and **Simon-Armand Lignière,** whom Roume deports to France from Saint-Domingue.

General de Blanchelande, Governor of Saint-Domingue.

Jean-Lambert Tallien, supporter of Marat, a revolutionary.

General Santere, commander of the Paris National Guard.

Louis XVI (Louis Capet), **Marie Antoinette,** king and queen of France.

General Jean-Baptiste Carrier, notorious killer.

Louis-Marie Fréron, journalist and politician, "saves" Roume upon his return to Paris.

Joseph Fouché, the "butcher of Lyons", who is with Tallien and Barras after the Terror.

Étienne Polverel, commissioner to Saint-Domingue.

General Étienne Laveaux, general in Saint-Domingue.

Vicomte de Rochambeau, leader of expeditionary force against Saint-Domingue.

Hyacinthe Moïse, nephew of Toussaint.

Jean-Jacques Dessalines, supporter of Toussaint.

Raimond and **Michel,** Roume's fellow commissioners in Santo Domingo.

Madame Villevaleix, Léger-Félicité Sonthonax' Negro mistress.

Edme Étienne Desfourneaux, French General in Saint-Domingue.

General D'Hédouville, agent of the republic to Saint-Domingue.

General Kerverseau, Roume's predecessor in Santo Domingo.

Colonel Henri Vincent, General Agé, staff officers loyal to Toussaint.

Don Isador Avalar, Spanish plenipotentiary.

Isobar of the Resurrection, priest at Santa María la Menor in Santo Domingo.

Pedro Antonio José de Sucre, father of Antonio José de Sucre, Venezuelan revolutionary with whom Marianne leaves her daughter Manon.

Jean Patience, Marianne's bodyguard in Paris.

Timeline of major events

1711   Sir Laurence Lambert's grandfather advances 400 thousand pounds to British Government.

1722   Collapse of South Sea Company, the South Sea Bubble.

1743   Philippe Rose Roume born in Grenada at Saint Laurent estate. Toussaint L'Ouverture born on the plantation of Bréda at Haut de Cap in Saint-Domingue.

1761   Marianne Katronice born, Stanislaus de Barras born.

1763   Treaty of Paris; Grenada is passed to England.

1764   Laurent Roume dies, first asiento held by the Lambert family expires.

1765   Philippe Roume's first trip to France, visit to Île de Ré, Philippe Roume marries Françoise (Fanny) Lambert, Rosa de Gannes marries Bertrand de Charras in France, return to Grenada.

1775   Sir Laurence sends André Fatio and Samuel Bosanquet to Grenada.

1776   André Fatio arrives in Grenada.

1777   Philippe Roume's first voyage to Trinidad, Bertrand de Charras leaves Grenada for the American wars.

1779   Bertrand de Charras returns to Grenada with Comte d'Estaing, reconquest of Grenada by the French, Rosa is ruined by Fatio and Bosanquet, acquires San Xavier in Maraval, Trinidad. Second raid on Île de Ré, Cornelius Bosanquet is killed by Sir Laurence while stealing twenty-four bags of gold guineas.

1780   The Romance of Marianne and Stanislaus begins. Philippe Roume kills Bertrand de Charras in a duel. Marianne becomes a pirate, until 1785.

1781   Fanny moves to Trinidad, Philippe returns to Trinidad, expedition with Sarusima into the hinterland of Trinidad, visits Venezuela for the first time. French take Tobago from the English.

1782   Philippe Roume returns to Venezuela, Rosa acquires several other estates and applies for land grant in Maraval, which becomes Champs Elysées estate.

1783   Philippe's second trip to France, issuing of the Cedula for Population 1783.

1786   Philippe Roume and Arthur Dillon arrive in Tobago.

1789   Samuel Bosanquet visits Sir Laurence, brings Bob the Negro. Fanny returns to Île de Ré, meets Sir Laurence. French revolution begins, Bosanquet rides to meet Funillière. Philippe and Marianne are in Tobago with Dillon and Decima, leave Tobago. Marianne's daughter Rosette (aged 2) remains with Decima de la Forêt.

1790	Philippe and Marianne in Paris. Soirees at Manon Roland, meets Danton and Robespierre and at the Jacobin Club, meeting with Stanilaus de Barras & Dr. Mesmer. Ogé leaves for Saint-Domingue in October, is arrested in November.
1791	February: Ogé is brutally executed in Saint-Domingue.
	August: Start of slave rebellion in Saint-Domingue.
	November: arrival of Philippe Roume and Marianne in Saint-Domingue, meeting with Henri-Christophe aboard ship.
	December: meeting of Philippe Roume with the slave leaders.
1792	Philippe Roume and Marianne return to Paris. The September massacre.
1793	War in the Vendée, Philippe Roume meets Laure de Girardin (until 1795).
1794	April: execution of Danton and Desmoulins.
	July: execution of Robespierre and Saint-Just. Philippe Roume and Laure de Girardin return to Paris.
1795	Fédon uprising in Grenada. 1798 Stanislaus & Fédon escape to Trinidad. Stanislaus goes to Güiria with Sarusima the Carib and Rosette, Fédon stays aboard ship and escapes to Curaçao.
1799	Philippe Roume and Marianne return to Hispaniola.
1799	Philippe Roume gets married to Marianne in Saint-Domingue, birth of their daughter Manon.
1801	Toussaint, promulgates an autonomous constitution for Saint-Domingue, with himself as governor for life.
1803	Toussaint holds Marianne and Philippe Roume in prison in Dondon.
1803	Philippe Roume, Marianne and Manon leave Saint-Domingue.
1805	Philippe Roume dies in Paris.
1806	Marianne returns to Grenada with Manon, moves into La Fontenoy, inherits Jean Pontieux's estate.
1806	Jacques Chadeau shows up at La Fontenoy.
1807	Sarusima the Carib comes to Grenada with news of Rosette, Marianne moves to Trinidad.
1808	Great Fire of Port of Spain in March, Marianne goes to Tucupita with Jean-Baptiste Bideau.
1820	Marianne and Julien row to Winn's Bay.

The regimes of Revolutionary France
The National Assembly / Assemblée Nationale May 4, 1789 -
September 30, 1791
The Legislative Assembly October 1, 1791 - September 20, 1792
The Convention September 21, 1792 - October 26, 1795
The Directory November 2, 1795 - November 9, 1799
The Consulate November 11, 1799 - May 18, 1804

BOOK FIRST

1: REMEMBERING TO DIE

PARIS, 1805

His breath came in short, rapid gasps. Wisps of consciousness floated like cobweb gently blowing in a shaft of sunlight, sometimes visible, sometimes not, anchoring memories that had not entirely lost their flavour. He tried not to let the phlegm rattle in his throat, as he knew it would make her feel that he was going. He was going. He braced himself, assuming in his mind a more dignified way of lying, and tilted up his chin, glancing along his cheek towards where his last official uniform was thrown across a récamier. Gold brocade, handsome with the dark blue twill, the hilt of his ceremonial sword, the Republic's golden fasces shimmered on the pommel.

His eyes were moist. He thought to raise a hand to wipe away a tear. He decided not to, as it would alarm her.

The cobwebs of his mind floated upwards and shone in the sunlight of recollection. He saw himself with her and their child, Manon, boarding the frigate *Révolutionnaire* at Le Cap Français. He had not said goodbye to Toussaint. He had written a letter to Bonaparte, advising against an expedition.

It was on the high seas that the first signs of illness were manifested. A wrenching pain, so sharp, so surprising in its intensity that it made him crouch and grab the gunwale for support as the battleship settled in the bosom of a long Atlantic roller to rise up, her bow breaking free. His face was cold with sweat. New York was behind them, France ahead.

He had been twenty-two in 1765 when he first saw France, a place strange, yet familiar. He loved it. It had been shaped by inherited memories. France was the land of his forbears.

He felt at home in Paris. His mother, recently widowed, had leased a house on the rue Saint-Séverin. They used it in the way people used townhouses when they really lived in the country or on islands. They were well connected. He met a girl in an enchanted circle of gaiety, charm, and Mozart. Her name was Françoise Lambert. Everyone called her Fanny. She too lived on the rue Saint-Séverin.

They were married that year and returned to Grenada to a house newly built on a rise, overlooking great beauty in the parish of Grand Pauvre, where their daughter Elizabeth was born and where other babies were born only to die, tiny things to be buried quickly beneath a copse of bois immortelle, inaugurating the graveyard on the plantation.

His marriage to Fanny had not so much failed as withered. His mother thought her extravagant. He knew she was unfaithful. He thought of his mother, remembered her as strong, perpetually enduring, the Marquise de Charras, châtelaine of the habitation Champs Elysées on the island of Trinidad. He preferred that memory. His own holdings there at Diego Martin; Fanny's estate at Ariapita. Such a long, long way from home. What home? Home in Grenada? Home in Paris? Home in Saint-Domingue?

Home in Tobago. With Marianne. He dreamt he had closed his eyes and saw her quite plainly, dressed in white, in someone else's clothes in the style of the previous century. She appeared to be in costume. He had almost laughed out loud. Dillon's glance contained him. A long-legged mulâtresse with auburn hair. Black eyes shining like licked stones, skin the colour of golden honey; young, in her early twenties, high-breasted, big-bottomed, toes splayed apart from walking barefooted in her young life, without a glance she strode

1: REMEMBERING TO DIE 1805

past him in the market at Port Louis. He remembered her. He had met her long ago, before everything changed. That night in Tobago he and Dillon, in court dress, had paced the front gallery of Government House in anticipation of the arrival of the Maréchal de Castries. There he saw her again as she passed through the garden in company of a group of girls and women. They were ogling the officers who sat smoking or playing piquet in the long gallery. A carriage turned into the drive. Two young slaves with torches ran before it. The other girls ran away. Not she. The brilliance illuminated her features, inflamed them; he noticed her slightly flared nostrils, he had thought them endearing.

The officers rose to attention. The governor descended to greet the Maréchal. His eyes remained locked with hers as significant events unfolded. During their Tobago years, a daughter was born to them in Port Louis. He named her Rosette in memory of his mother. Their other daughter, Manon, was born in Santo Domingo. She was named for Manon Roland, their friend. Together, they experienced the future of the world. Power passed through his hands, battles unrecorded were fought, won, lost.

The vision fled, as the opiate faded and the pain returned. He awoke before dawn to the musty smell of poverty mixed with sickroom odours. Marianne had climbed into bed with him for the warmth. There was no money.

The Parisian street sounds rose up with the melting fog. Sunlight entering with the morning's breeze. Shouts and whistles. Bells chiming. The thump of a broom on a carpet, the clatter and rattle of horse-drawn traffic. Life will go on without him. There was to be no future with her. He felt suddenly afraid. She stirred. He realised that the child was asleep between them.

The room had grown dark. All pain ceased. A cloud passing the sun. It will pass, he thought, then he realised that the darkness was for him. He felt so alone. I don't want to go now. Desperate. I want to stay a while longer with you. He saw her nod.

"Yes, I know, my love, I know," she murmured soothingly.

Philippe Rose Roume de Saint Laurent died in Paris, France on the 29th of September 1805.

Reading from my Memoirs at La Fontenoy Estate, Grenada, 1806

MY RETURN TO GRENADA. I could just make out the island rising and falling on the horizon. Bluish, cloud-shrouded and vague it appeared, a smudgy bruise of memory. I had been born there in 1761, I was now forty-five years old. I had not seen my firstborn, our daughter Rosette, for almost seventeen years. And there were other matters, grave and deadly, to be dealt with. These, buried in the furthest, deepest pits of memory must now be exhumed in the light of day.

A high tide running brought the Yankee clipper *Carolina* straight into the inner harbour of Carenage Town, Fort Royal (or, as it is now called, Saint George's). The anchor chains clattered, and the buildings rotated. My head swam and I steadied myself by gripping hard the fo'c'sle's railing. There was the fort, now it was gone, the hills were sliding to the right, there were new buildings on the Carenage going past, and so many people. The fort again, the English Union flag. I felt my stomach tighten with a slight pain on the right side. The ship swung about some more and stopped. All sounds returned.

I followed my mind and waited. It was almost dusk. In the wake of the afternoon shower the sky became golden; the huge red falling sun teetered on the brink of perpetuity, lighting us in a topaz glow as we embarked the longboat.

Not for me, this perpetuity. I feared that this move could mark an end of things. Immigration: a young Englishman, clean and handsome with a red moustache. "Returning home, Madame Marianne Roume?"

It took me a moment; I had not been called Marianne for years. The moment sufficed, a lifted red eyebrow.

"Oui."

"Bonne chance," with a cultivated English accent.

"Merci, Monsieur."

The smells of warm damp air, rum, cargo and them. Some of them were staring frankly, some were looking away. I was overdressed, as was Manon. The things, some cases and boxes, all his. Not the worst for wear.

"Take us to Monsieur de Pontieux. Come Manon, quickly, up, merci, yes, those and these."

The buggy clattered forward. I sat up straight and opened my pink parasol with a little pop and smiled for them to see. To Granby Street. The gates were closed.

"Ring."

The driver hesitated, sensing embarrassment, I knew that at a glance he knew exactly my situation, if not my identity.

"Ring."

Still he hesitated.

"Ring."

He jumped down and rang. I could hear it in the silence of that shallow space between the end of bird-song and the beginning of the night's serenade of a million unseen terrors.

"Don't ring again."

"Mama, are we seeing Papa's friend now?"

"Yes darling, look, someone is coming, look, there."

The great iron gates moved. Slaves in white jupé appeared to light the way up the long drive over which huge forest trees seemed to glower. Doubts about our reception stirred the most ancient suspicions, as the driver whoa'd the horse to a snorting, jingling, stamping stop beneath the vast, well-lit porte-cochère. A gust of wind lifted the branches and almost blew away my bonnet. I glanced up and smiled as my collar fluttered against my cheek.

"Jean, how very kind of you."

"Marianne, welcome, allow me, and this must be...?"

"Manon. Manon, curtsey."

"Oh oh, sea legs. Come. Up you go, come my dear, Yzore Delpeche will show you everything upstairs and serve you a light supper and we shall speak in the morning."

"HEAR THAT WIND, wrap up tight Manon, go to sleep my darling." Sleep. Jean de Pontieux's old house on Granby Street creaked as the *Carolina* had done in the Atlantic's weather, and in my head I swayed and rocked, still possessed of the motion of the ship and of the sea that we had endured for the sixty-seven days of the journey.

I awoke to a pink and gold dawn as gentle as the dew on the windowpanes, murmuring, "Life of my life, I love you." The memories of Tobago had returned to me.

As I strove to maintain the flavour of the dream, I readied myself and Manon to join Jean de Pontieux for breakfast.

"He acted as one inspired, Jean, about Tobago," I said, suffocating with rising nostalgia. I had come to know that nostalgia takes the past as its mournful subject, and I must learn to hold it at arm's length.

"Philippe was aware that Tobago was of little value to France." Jean de Pontieux's calm voice, a soothing anodyne.

"No one knew exactly where Tobago was. Tobago was known to be often lost, not always found," I told him. He understood. I had once sailed the Caribbean Sea.

1: REMEMBERING TO DIE 1805

This cautious natural philosopher. It was as though we were rehearsing a conversation meant to inspire my confidence.

In the old-fashioned living room I could see that examples of his skill as an amateur botanist. Ferns, in great variety, in shiny brass pots. Framed specimens. A herbarium. Piles of books next to a well-worn armchair. Glass cabinets and occasional tables filled and covered with gorgeous shells and rare quartz that sparkled in the sunlight.

"But he did not want the island to be returned to England," Jean replied, guiding us towards the French doors that led to a grey-and-white flagged inner courtyard where an iron table had been laid for breakfast, his dwarf Yzore Delpeche in attendance. "What he wanted was for France to keep Tobago and for him to get an administrative post there."

"Yes. He was in debt; Gálvez would never repay him for what he had spent out of his own pocket. Far less recognise him for the hazards he had faced while travelling to the islands, encouraging French colons to take advantage of the Spanish Cedula and to go to Trinidad and not to Louisana."

I was breathless now, wistful. I had to look away. These feelings came from what I no longer possessed, I knew that, they lay at the heart of this melancholy. . . yet.

"He was a resourceful one, your Philippe, and lucky too—his life was often at risk." Jean de Pontieux was kind. My babbling was embarrassing. I could hardly believe myself.

"He was able to persuade Luzerne at the Versailles conference that if Spain saw Trinidad as the lock for Spanish South America, then Tobago was its key." I told him what he already knew. "The Spanish government was about to promulgate his Cedula, to populate Trinidad. He had already persuaded their envoy to convince the French government to keep Tobago. Can you imagine, Jean, and he was then so young and inexperienced."

"People saw him as he chose to be seen, my dear, while he shifted his shape as circumstances required."

"Oh yes. At times, they saw themselves in him. I saw this in Paris. I saw him change there. He survived the September massacre, then The Reign of Terror, when everyone we knew was guillotined. Then the hazards of the war in the Vendée. We lived through all of that."

"Then there was Saint-Domingue."

"He is gone now, Jean, and there is nothing."

Jean de Pontieux was in his late seventies. He appeared fragile, with sharper features. His white hair, wispy and sparse, was tied at the back with a blue ribbon in a tiny queue. Seeing him in the morning light, I could still glimpse the handsome, dark-eyed scholar of our shared Tobago years.

Anxious, I enquired, "And Jean, what of Rosette? Is there any news?"

Soon after Philippe's death, Jean de Pontieux, responding to my letters pleading for information, had intimated that our daughter was not in Trinidad. Neither was she in Tobago with our friend, Decima de la Forêt, in whose care she had been left as a babe. As far as he knew, Decima had died some years before.

"When was this, where could she be?"

"Is Rosette lost, Maman?" Manon, my most constant companion, consumed with curiosity, listened to everything that was said.

"No darling, she is not lost."

"Just very hard to find, not so Maman?"

"Oui, moichè, very hard. Hush now, grown-ups are speaking, there you are, eggs, you can begin."

"I have no idea where she is, my dear," Jean said kindly. "More than likely, if she survived her childhood, she would now be living in Venezuela."

1: REMEMBERING TO DIE 1805

"Venezuela?"

"Yes, and most probably with someone, a protector, a husband even? Who knows. She would be no longer a child."

"But why Venezuela, Jean?"

"What is Venezuela, Maman?"

"Hush, I will tell you later."

"As a result of the upheavals in Trinidad following the English conquest in '97, a large part of the population was deported," said Jean, trying to give me hope, "especially the Black Jacobins, *sang-melés, les affranchis* and what have you." He waved a dismissive hand, "The English did not want to risk another Fédon style uprising there."

"And there has been no word of her, Jean? Nothing, ever?"

"No, my dear, not to my knowledge."

"Can we go on the ship and find her, Maman?"

"That she lives is my constant prayer, Jean."

"Don't cry anymore, Maman."

"No darling, I won't cry again. Jean, I must now have a place for us to settle quietly and live with the hope that we find her." I breathed deeply. Calm. I must not allow myself this emotional breakdown. "And I hope that L'Empereur remembers us with Philippe's pension," I smiled and looked at him fondly.

"You can go with Delpeche now, Manon. Perhaps he will show you the morocoys. You will show her the morocoys, won't you, Delpeche?" said Jean, smiling. "And when you come back, there will be cake."

"What are the morocoys, Maman? Can I have cake now?"

"When you return, it will be ready, go. Thank you, Yzore."

"This is for you, I hope you don't mind."

I had noticed a blue velvet bag on a silver salver that Delpeche had moved aside so as to place a basket with fresh loaves.

"And take heart, Marianne, we might still find her."

"If you don't mind, Jean, I prefer Soubise. I have grown accustomed to being her."

He smiled, his inclination ever so slight. Manon and the little man were already at the garden gate.

"On the contrary, Jean," I placed my hand on the soft velvet and felt the heavy coins within, "for this, I am very grateful. I have one hundred and twenty-five Louis d'or, and these." I took from a little straw casket a white linen table napkin, monogrammed with my initials, and opened it theatrically, to reveal a gold necklace set with emeralds and diamonds with matching ear pendants, over which Jean de Pontieux placed his own napkin. It was the last of my pirate treasure.

"I shall think of this as a loan, Jean, and when you can make an arrangement with regard to these, you must allow me to repay you."

"Whatever will suit you, my dear Soubise. I understand that Chantilly will be for sale."

"No Jean, Chantilly is too close to Grenville, you know that."

I glanced at him. Jean de Pontieux had been with us in Tobago. He had seen me let Marianne go, and Soubise come. He knew that and everything else—what had happened there, the massacre in '95 at Grenville with Fédon and Stanislaus de Barras—it irritated me and made me once more suspicious. I glanced at him again, banishing the frown that had crossed my mind. He had felt it.

"I beg your pardon my dear, do forgive me." He placed his hand upon mine, and I took it in my own.

"It is all right, Jean, those are my ghosts, all of them."

"There is La Fontenoy, the Chevalier Hersende de la Suse has removed to Trinidad. The house is in ruin, but there is cocoa, some coffee, no slaves, but..."

1: REMEMBERING TO DIE 1805

I held up my hand, "No slaves Jean, just somewhere where we can live in peace."

"Then La Fontenoy will suit you. It is close to Saint George's and overlooks the bay. The motto of the Croy family who financed de la Suse reads 'J'aime qui m'aime, vive Croy'."

"I like who likes me—I like that, Jean."

AND SO IT WAS La Fontenoy, a comfortable house once, now sadly dilapidated. Yet the levantine tiles were marvellous, with vibrant colours worthy of the alchemists. The rose pink wash on the outside and the paint-work on the inside were flaking, falling off or peeling away in every room. The façade was crumbling and roof tiles had tumbled into the garden that was surrounded by silence and consumed by the buzzing heat of noon.

Jean de Pontieux sent his domestics to cut and clean, paint and polish, and to restore the roof, the kitchen garden and the out-buildings. Furniture also appeared, oddments, the debris of other calamities. There was a young free person, half child, half woman, a chabine with gold eyes and skin, small negroid features quickly arranged in a broad face that expressed a gentle anxiousness and a willingness to please. Vandelle. I shall keep her near us. I unpacked our cases and the crates to find the carefully wrapped packages that contained my diaries.

Then, there were other things to unpack and put away— Philippe's things, my toilette, and the dresses I had worn in Paris, which he had admired me in. Some still held a hint of Saint-Domingue, a smoky pistachio residue, into these I had sewn my jewelry in those final days.

I opened wide the windows and in came the warm inquisitive wind seeking Marianne. Rigid with another bout of suffocating nostalgia, I stood staring across the recently repainted room at my reflection in a full-length looking-glass embedded in the moulding of a wardrobe. Seeing myself, I slipped my arm into a sleeve of one of Philippe's formal coats that I had hung on a peg behind the closed door. I passed that arm, now his, over my hair, my face, and shoulders. In the reflection, he held me. I searched the coat for his smell. It had gone. I fled the empty room, taking with me my old diary, to walk in La Fontenoy's unfamiliar garden.

THE NIGHTMARE'S NEST. Returning has evoked memories. The solitude. I would have to get used to that. The cacophony of bird-song after a shower of lashing rain. Fields of cane-in-arrow furrowed by a burning breeze. The heat. The silence. In the fierce incandescence of noon, ox carts travelling in slow motion. The sound of the lash, screams for mercy borne by that hot wind. Woodsmoke. The aroma of spices, church incense and candle wax.

The isolation, existing in past ruin. Deserted plantation houses, their empty rooms littered with the jetsam of a previous domesticity. I shall become accustomed to the changes that feel like the end of a performance. The seasons, wet and dry, I shall have to remember how they came and went, marred by hurricanes, frightened to death by earthquakes, punctuated by invasions. These always turned back the clock to the time when it all began, thus making things ever difficult for the children born in chains.

We were seen as intelligent animals. Our humanity discussed on deep verandahs in quasi-theological debates on the properties of the soul. This produced a false science amongst the planters, who spoke of us, of these topics, in our presence as if we were not there. In a manner of speaking, we were not, as it was yet to be determined if we were actually human beings, capable of moral choice, in possession of free will, or immortal souls. Those of us who survived created a way of life, carried forward in our collective grief, hidden in half-remembered traditions, secreted in a Patois of our own understanding, and embedded in a morbid mythology of our own invention. The lash, the forced labour in the fields, the

1: REMEMBERING TO DIE 1805

polite work in the big houses and the craftsmanship displayed in the estate-yards delineated the reality of our confinement. However, to explain our present affliction, we brought into being a fabulous, macabre parallel universe. A universe that existed in the privacy of the dilapidated barracks in which we still copulated, in the unworked cane-breaks and ratoons now inhabited by the fer-de-lance and in the desecrated churchyards, whose tombs and mortuary chapels we converted to other work.

This private life I knew well. It was constructed from the detritus, the rubbish heaps of that which was thrown away by the Grands Blancs. It was determined by words lost in the smell of cesspits, coal-pot smoke, bloody reprimands and the unanswered prayers raised to a misunderstood deity in the agony of boiling cane syrup. It was created by the misinterpretation of the iconography contained in the cartouches seen on world maps and was constructed from the shin-bones of unrealised lives, the rib-cages of devastated futures, the skull-boxes of redirected incarnations and, naturally, the soul-cases of undreamt sweet-dreams. Thus was made a nightmare's nest, in which the die of our fate was cast to become over the generations the subsoil of these islands. In this nightmare's nest were laid some awesome eggs.

All this did not prevent them from seeking us out. Some with lust, many with rage. Others in weakness, or even loneliness. From those wild penetrations came a new people, *les gens de couleur*. Before the original Grands Blancs, that is to say the real aristocrats, left, after Grenada was handed over to the English, they had commenced freeing their bastards. Something of the same order began with the remaining *gens de couleur libres—les affranchis*. Free-papers were being handed out. The remaining slaves now belonged mostly to these free, mixed-race people, *les affranchis,* who lived increasingly in the wreckage of that lost civilisation.

In those ailing years before the French Revolution, slavery and bastardy had produced exotic fruit. These soaked silently in the demijohns of familial envy. Thin-skinned and touchy as Ti-Marie, they were afflicted by the weaknesses of petty jealousies and absurd snobberies. Abroad, and easily confused, they became pets for a dissipated aristocracy, and after-dinner curiosities for the revolutionary parvenus of the café society of Paris. From there, a handful of these fortunate sons would return enlightened and politicised, caught in the momentum of world events. They were the harbingers of retribution, reckoning up the debts of past eras and sending in the account.

They went to France wearing their fathers' knee breeches and returned sporting pantaloons as pseudo sans culottes, enlightened Creoles and pretend Black Jacobins, overflowing with liberté, and a knowledge of all manner of wines, holding forth on egalité, on ideologies, on taffetas, tri-colours, laces, and truffles. Imagining fraternité while discussing cheeses or dried fruit, or women so white you could see right through them if the light was right. They had become experts on farm machinery, democracy, secularism, gunpowder, cannon fodder and all else that was required to change forever 'life in the tropics.' My story is about them, the children born in the nightmare's nest.

2: PHILIPPE ROSE ROUME & CALYPSO'S ISLAND

For PHILIPPE ROUME it had begun in his childhood. His first sense of himself was formed in his mother's imagination, framed in Belvédère's vast, seemingly eternal twilights. One of his earliest memories was of his mother Rosa saying, "We are of the blood of the princes of Brittany." He had been named for her, Philippe Rose Roume.

Rosa's father, Simon de Gannes de la Chancellerie, Chevalier, Ordre Royal et Militaire de Saint-Louis, was thus distinguished for loyal service to the crown. De la Chancellerie. For Philippe, it contained the sounds of a well-regulated carillon chiming within a castellated château.

Simon de Gannes, born into a family of soldier-administrators in Québec, had married thrice. From his first marriage, there were two daughters, one of whom was Rosa. Simon, in his prime, had been a strong, stern-minded man. He was one of the handful who, in the aftermath of the Battle of the Plains of Abraham, had made their way south.

Departing the ruins of fallen Québec in the winter storms of disappointment as an impecunious refugee, the veteran Acadian, together with his daughters, travelled first to La Louisiane and then to Grenada. In his looks and stature, Philippe Roume would grow to favour this grandfather.

His other grandfather was the first of that family to come out to the Antilles, he served as *Intendant* in the administration of Grenada. Not distinguished by the particle 'de', he possessed no ancestral seigneuries trailing after his name, lengthening it into mythical descriptions of a medieval countryside. His son, Laurent Roume, the man that Rosa de Gannes married at the age of fourteen, was twenty-five years her senior. Unlike his wife, he was from the clerical bourgeoisie who had become wealthy plantation proprietors, having taken advantage of the opportunities offered by their office in the French colonial service. Laurent Roume was a plain man who liked ordinary things. Rosa, however, made up for that.

From this marriage came three children, the eldest of whom was Philippe. He was born on the 13th October 1743 in Grand Pauvre on a plantation called Mount Saint Laurent.

Philippe Roume's father was a man of ledgers; a clerkly parsimonious accountant with gold-rimmed spectacles above pursed lips and poised pens. As a child, Philippe thought that his father's fingernails were actually blue; then he discovered that it was ink.

In Grenada, everything changed after 1763. The island was passed from France to England by the Treaty of Paris. Then Laurent Roume died in January of 1764. He left Rosa in possession of some two hundred and fifty slaves of all ages and conditions, and two thousand one hundred and five acres, representing six prosperous plantations: Paradise, Lataste, Trievia, Duquesne, St. Laurent and Belvédère, the latter being her principal holding and her home, with over nine hundred acres. Rosa de Gannes de la Chancellerie, as she would become once more, was raven-haired with dark fervid eyes. By nature she was gay and was possessed of a yielding grace.

Young Philippe, along with his brother and sister, grew up on the estates. He became a pupil of Everard de Barras who, early on, recognised the boy's potential. De Barras had been posted as the *conseillier du roi* to Grenada as a young man and was a friend and colleague of Laurent Roume. He saw that Philippe was quick-witted and possessed a keen curiosity, the discipline to study and a willingness to be taught. He provided Philippe with a classical education based on the trivium: grammar, logic, rhetoric, then geography, astronomy, arithmetic, music, geometry and later, Greek, Latin and some of the Romance languages.

"Your mother's head is full of legends," he told the lad, "and the *noblesse de chancellerie* is simply those who hold certain offices under the king."

He cautioned Philippe that he should not be presumptuous but accept the fact that he was little else than bourgeoisie.

"I know that your father and grandfather were *intendant* and *conseiller à la cour royal*, but you can take it from me that in France no nobility is recognised except that of the *épée*. Ours is a warrior nation, and it is only from the army that *La Gloire* flows."

He advised Philippe to mix with people of quality and to avoid arrogance.

"Pass your afternoons with the children of the Jacques de la Bastide and de Lagarigue, the girls," and advised him to acquire the art of kissing hands. "You will soon be accustomed to good manners and you will have, for the rest of your life, an air of civility, which will make everyone like you."

Philippe received his religious instruction from the Abbé Bertold d'Audain, a reclusive Carmelite with whom he wrestled over the more subtle distinctions between the philosophy of Aristotle in the Nicomachean Ethics and the Stoic philosophy of Epictetus with regard to *prohairesis*, "intention," or "moral choice." He grasped that it was this capacity that distinguished human beings from all other creatures. The Abbé, trained to contemplation, cautioned him saying: "The importance of *prohairesis* for Epictetus is that it exerts a power that allows people to choose how they will react to impressions rationally. Remember, Philippe, that what is insulting is not the person who abuses or hits you, but the judgment that these things are insulting. So when someone irritates you, realise that it is your own opinion that has irritated you. Try, therefore, in the first place, not to be carried away by the impression; for once you gain time and respite, you shall find it easier to make the right choice."

"Then by exerting their *prohairesis*, that is their will, or choice, people can choose rationally how to react to impressions?" asked the boy, wonderingly.

"It is a faculty impossible to be enslaved," responded the Carmelite.

Everard de Barras encouraged scepticism and intellectual discussion in the lad who had taken up residence at his home on Soubise estate, not far from Grenville town. This training was augmented, as time went by, with a regard for the work of the philosophers of the day who emphasized reason and individualism rather than tradition, and the works of those who would advance knowledge through the scientific method. At geography lessons, they would at times discuss the southern hemisphere of the Americas, its rivers, mountains and offshore islands, some of which were in truth parts of the continent that in ages past had broken away. Trinidad, the uncultivated island to the south, was one such island. It was described as a wilderness and as unpopulated since its discovery more than two hundred and fifty years before. Because of its proximity to Grenada, its pale mountains could be seen on a clear day. Trinidad evoked for Philippe a sense of mystery. On one such occasion his questions put to his teacher conjured the words of the poet Homer:

"'Far apart we live in the wash of the waves, the farthermost of men, and no other mortals are conversant with us.' Ogygia," de Barras said, pointing to the pale blue mountains that appeared to hover above the horizon, "it was the lost island mentioned in the Odyssey, the home of the nymph Calypso. She detained Odysseus there for many years."

2: PHILIPPE ROSE ROUME & CALYPSO'S ISLAND

Philippe's interest quickened. "Does not the etymology of Calypso convey to conceal, to hide, or to deceive?" he asked, his enthusiasm, as ever, keen.

"It certainly does."

"It is, then, a splendid name, don't you think, for a lost and mysterious island." He said this so earnestly that de Barras had to laugh.

"Oh, Trinidad is not lost at all," he answered, "it is purposely neglected. The Spanish conquistadors, Sedeño, Ponce de León and others scoured it for gold a hundred years ago. Finding none, they contented themselves by exporting the native population to Hispaniola."

"Is it then uninhabited?" asked Philippe.

"No. The natives still move easily back and forth across the Gulf of Paria to the mainland. It has an official Spanish presence, with a governor, a handful of officials, Capuchin missionaries and a few settlers. I see it as a place in waiting."

"Waiting for what?"

"The events of history, I suppose," replied de Barras. "The Spaniards have always put it about that it is a deadly place. Malarial, with vast lagoons. It is reputed to have huge anacondas, the largest in the world, man-eating cats and several species of crocodile, not to mention mud volcanoes, quicksands and boiling pitch. The truth is, they fear the machinations of the English."

"The English may well crave it. It is a large island, existing in a perpetual state of potentiality," said Philippe thoughtfully, "so well watered, it must be fertile, its soil not depleted."

"No. It is desired by the English because of its proximity to the Orinoco delta, the gateway to the Spanish Andean highlands. It has always been associated with tales of incalculable wealth. In times past it attracted Sir Walter Raleigh, the English courtier and explorer."

"Trinidad—the last unexplored island in the Caribbean Sea and home to the nymph Calypso," Philippe spoke gravely, as though pronouncing upon an omen.

"In truth. It has never been devastated or raped by war," replied de Barras. "It is barlovento, below the wind, below the hurricanes. It has hardly known the curse of African slavery. It is utopian."

"Utopia, that means the perfect place, not so?"

"Indeed so. That word comes from the English homophone eutopia, derived from the Greek for good, and place, the good place."

"The good place," Philippe Roume said thoughtfully, shading his eyes against the blaze of blue and the westing sun.

THE ROUME FAMILY TRAVELLED to Paris early in 1765, a year after Philippe's father's death. With Everard de Barras' recommendation, Philippe Roume, having been articled in his Grenada chambers for the required period of time, received from the Parlement of Paris the authority to practice law as an advocate. It also happened that both Philippe and his widowed mother were to enter into the holy state of matrimony while in France. They both met their future spouses due to the happy accident of living on the same Parisian street and, finding acquaintances in common, they discovered that they enjoyed similar taste in music, art and pleasure. Philippe, ensorcelled by his advancement, assumed the style of the *noblesse de robe* and elevated his surname to distinguish the wooded hilltop in Grenada where he was born, becoming known to history as Philippe Rose Roume de Saint Laurent.

2: PHILIPPE ROSE ROUME & CALYPSO'S ISLAND

Reading from my Memoirs at La Fontenoy, Grenada, 1806

MARIANNE KATRONICE, ME, MYSELF & THE DEVIL. I pressed the oldest journal to my face as I walked into the abandoned garden and inhaled memories of another time. In the lingering sea light of my homecoming, I yearned for them to flow into myself. My earliest recollections I had inscribed in these books, while I still knew only the surf smell of the wind at Soubise estate. This was my very first journal. The one my father had handed to me here in Grenada, before his death. In it were the descriptions of my childhood and early years. I shall not read them to you, instead, I shall relate what they meant to me. As they say, 'Tis distance lends enchantment to the view, and robes the mountain in its azure hue.' To begin: I, Marianne, was born in 1761, on Soubise estate, La Baye, Grenada. La Baye is the largest bay on Grenada's windward coast. It receives the easterly tradewinds that pour relentlessly out of an unimaginable vastness, bringing marauding corsairs, changing weather, bad news, and the dust of another continent along with old women, transported to this island as a result of their having been swept up in maelstroms on the Guinée coast. Everything in this bay leans away from those winds and is covered on its windward sides by a rust-red patina, a distinguishing blight that I associated with myself.

First memories. The sounds of white sheets snapping in the wind. The smell of hot muscovado, fresh cow's milk, and cedarwood shavings. Up there, blue sky, seen through a lattice of large green, red-orange and yellow almond leaves.

Of my grandma and my mamma. I heard how they had gone to the great house, Château Soubise, above La Baye. How they had stood at the main door, side by side, until the man noticed them. The man came to the door. My grandmother turned and walked away. My mother YaYa became Geneviève Katronice that day. Katronice had been my grandmother's only name. That was how people got names in those days.

Geneviève Katronice was a beauty, everyone saw that. Her voice as soft as a coo, with eyes that caressed you when they lingered. Her skin—a rich, dark, unblemished brown. My Papa was M'sieu Thomas Rochard L'Épine, he owned the habitation Soubise and all of us, toute moun.

I heard a story told, not to me, I was little, too little. But I knew it was about me. It goes: "Manman-à té ni yon gouôs jà à caïeli..." There was once a beautiful mother who had a pretty daughter whom she called Marianne. The mother's task was to fill a large jar with water for the house. The jar was much too heavy for little Marianne to lift, so it was the mother who went every morning to the river so as to fill the jar. One morning, when Marianne's mamma went down to the river, she filled the jar to its brim with water, but could not find anyone to help lift the jar onto her head. She stood there, crying out, "Can any kind Christian soul come to load me?" But no one came to help her with the heavy jar. The people at the river seemed oblivious to her cries. She called out once more, and pleaded. "Any good Christian souls here today?" Some blanchisseuses who were passing looked at her without seeing her, while others, standing in the water, helped each other with their wet linens and tubs. Soulless all, no one was aware of her presence. "Well, then," she said despairingly, "if there are no good Christian souls, are there bad Christian souls? Any bad Christian souls here today, who can come and load me?"

After uttering these words, there appeared before her a devil. She saw him coming, the ramiers taking flight through the wind-blown almond trees, directly towards her. She glanced about; nobody else was paying attention. She felt that she was not even there. The devil said to her with a voice that seemed to reverberate in her head, "These hereabout are not possessed of souls. If I load you what shall you give me?"

"Me, I have nothing!" The devil, who was tall and disarming, smiled wickedly and answered, "You have a child, what is her name?"

2: PHILIPPE ROSE ROUME & CALYPSO'S ISLAND

"Marianne," replied the mother.

"Give her to me, if you want me to load you... Y fau ba moin Marianne pou moin pé châgé ou." At this everyone laughed. That I remember.

Well, this given away girl-child grew wild. I was in everything: from the cooking pots in the barrack-yard to the kitchen of the château, where Mallie, who was chief cook and housekeeper, allowed me to lick the plates. She had been brought by that wind from Africa and was in charge of teaching the art of subservience to the ignorant domestics.

THE HABITATION La Digue bounded with Soubise estate, with the Grenville river flowing through them both. Soubise was the larger of the two. La Digue was one of those whose windmill's tattered sail had long since ceased to rotate. No hogsheads rolled in its yard, and if the conch shell trumpet called at day-clean, no one came, it was just the old henchman losing his mind.

I would often be over there where Tante Mam'zelle de Lotbinière, half-starved, half-crazy, perpetually in waiting, lived in the big room upstairs. I, as ever trailed by that wind, would tiptoe into the old mansion. The interior was an empty shell painted green. Shafts of silvery insubstantial sunbeams fleetingly illuminated the flight of insomniac bats, at which the big tomcat, Samothrace, would take flying leaps as they flitted in the draft caused by my sudden intrusion.

I would find her sitting up in a four-poster bed, as big as a hut, with a precarious tiara and big gold rings with glistening stones, red, green, white and blue. One on each bony finger, all tied with red thread to her thumbs, you know, so that they don't roll away.

"Come here little nigger, and see what I have."

It was always some oddity. That day it was a miniature, just a face, painted on a circular piece of porcelain. A strange girl, so white she was nearly blue, with large upturned eyeballs and short brown curls. I had never seen such a marvel. I climbed up on the bed and took the wonder from the crooked fingers. I placed it to my ear, closing my eyes and opening my mouth, you know, so as to hear better. Nothing.

"She does not speak, Tante Mam'zelle, Mam'zelle."

"No, she is dead."

"Oh, Miss Fifine is coming from Mustique today, she could make she talk."

"Y chè moin, y chè moin," croaked the old lady, "Oui! ou tout bel!—y chè moin bel."

"Oui, Tante Mam'zelle, Mam'zelle, she is very beautiful." Actually I was not sure. This dead girl with her upturned eyes seemed remote, obscure and blue.

"Moin ka allé, moin ka allé, I have to go now, Tante Mam'zelle, Mam'zelle."

"Come, take this." She placed in my hand a small copper coin. It was a picaioun, very nearly worthless, almost entirely effaced and worn quite thin.

"Merci, Tante Mam'zelle, Mam'zelle. What is it?"

"It is money, chile, l'argent, keep it, always keep it."

"Oui, Tante Mam'zelle, Mam'zelle, I shall keep it."

"Allez, allez, I must prepare for His Grace, M'sieu le Duc," she whispered, "he is coming this afternoon, I am his favourite, you know, allez, allez," and rang a little bell. At once a tall black man, dressed like a general with gold braid, white silk stockings, silver-buckled shoes and a powdered wig appeared, and with great dignity held the door open for me. I ran away down the stairs through the cobwebs and out into the sunlight of carefully preserved memories. Later, after I had crossed the Grenville Road and was walking through the almond trees, I opened my hand to see l'argent, there it lay in my little palm, small, round and brown. I raised my hand to my nose and smelt it, it smelled red. I liked that.

From the house above, I hear the girl-woman Vandelle ringing the little silver bell, the one given to me by Manon Roland on the occasion of our last meeting. It is inscribed: Liberté.

3: SIR LAURENCE LAMBERT:
THE SOUTH SEA COMPANY
1765

SUNRISE, SUNSET. Sir Laurence Lambert watched time as it travelled by observing the morning's shadows, barely discernible. Winter's cold sunlight filtered through the sunshades. These, grown yellow with age, gave the room a soft ochre tone. He had known open spaces as a boy where sheep, grazing in mustard fields, dusted by pollen, had their undersides turned yellow. Golden fleece. Then, hallowed halls and gothic stained-glass. Medieval bookworms. Stacks. The Form Master, Mr. Stacks, at Tonbridge School. Then, Cornhill and Threadneedle Street, Temple Bar and Charing Cross. The coughing smell of the City of London. There, he would later say, he grew to admire the perfidious nature of the English.

Sir Laurence would be departing the City of London hopefully for the last time. His recuperation after a fall from his horse had been protracted. He was presently awaiting his son, who had made arrangements for his return to France and to Île de Ré.

In 1711 his grandfather, Jean Lambert, had advanced loans amounting to some £400,000 to the British government at a time of its near bankruptcy. It was put about that it was to feed the Duke of Marlborough's soldiers, who were campaigning in the Low Countries during the War of the Spanish Succession. The loan led to the granting of a charter by the British Parliament

3: SIR LAURENCE LAMBERT 1765

which established a business venture controlled by his family: The South Sea Company. It was a fantastic joint-stock scheme that was meant to generate vast revenues for the British government and, in so doing, make possible the quick repayment of the loan. On the recommendation of the Chancellor of the Exchequer, Laurence Lambert, Jean Lambert's only grandson, was made a baronet.

His grandfather Jean had manipulated the unrealistic expectation of vast riches to be obtained from the sugar trade, and the presumed unlimited financial potential of the West Indies. The public's interest in the unimaginable wealth of the sugar magnates of England, men like Peter Beckford, Christopher Codrington and the Drax family, was harnessed to promote the sale of shares in The South Sea Company.

But when the Company's share price collapsed in 1722, great opprobrium was laid upon the Lamberts and their servants. The busting of the South Sea Bubble. That was more than forty years ago, when he, Laurence, was barely a lad.

Now, leaving London and returning to Île de Ré, Sir Laurence had three moves in mind. First, reinvigorate the dormant asiento. Second, the grand annual Portobello fair of Panama to be moved to a new venue. And third, to recover what belonged to them.

Them. By them he meant all of them. The living, the dead, and the unborn. He could not bear the thought of their mockery. He felt their reproach, silent but palpable, seen through the varnished sheen of their portraits on the stair. His great-grandfather, swathed in furs, displaying his richly mounted translucent chalcedony, Dianabad, a piece made for him by Dinglinger. And more especially, his mother. Her eyes, he could no longer endure. To home and another fresh start.

Here they were. He had encouraged them to believe that his infirmity had worsened. It amused him to see them act with such false solicitude. Playing the role of the sleeping invalid, he closed his eyes as his bedroom door opened.

"Uncle Laurence?"

"Sssssssssnooorrr-g,g,–g–Gug,gua. Haaaa!"

"He's still asleep."

"Sir Laurence, it is time. Sir Laurence?"

The sounds of blinds being quietly drawn. Sunlight, seen through half-closed eyes, spread and illuminated the shiny dust on furniture from a distant past. The desk, the solitary chair. The bed, its crimson velvet hangings, its wooden posts, carved by a guild of masters now extinct. Ledgers piled, some arranged, others filed, some in tatters, loose-leafed, pens, ink. An abacus in ivory and jet. The commode.

"Sir Laurence, it is time. Sir Laurence."

Lavender, sage, rosemary, artemisia and wild thyme. Time to go home.

"Marjorie? John? I was just dreaming of you both. Is it time to leave? Are we leaving?"

"Yes, Uncle Laurence, it is time."

"I shall miss London. Cough, cough."

"Now, up we go."

"Françoise? Where is Françoise?"

"In Paris, Uncle Laurence, she is in Paris, remember?"

HOME. Île de Ré, off the northern shore of the Pertuis d'Antioche strait in western France. A place where the air, cool and clear, is washed a clean blue. Low in the Atlantic, it received the westerlies as they poured across on their way to France unhindered, except for the thickets of kermes oak that shaded the standing stones, more than half submerged in the fragrant garrigue.

The foundation of the family rested on an insect of the order Hemiptera, the kermes scale-insect, from which a red dye, called crimson, was derived: this strong, deep red colour came from the dried bodies of the females of the species.

The family business. The family produced crimson dye for export. It operated as a bank, engaged in mining, traded in tapestries, wheat, soap, sugar, barley, oranges and wine, in horses and gold, guns, wool, boots, iron armour, and human beings.

As a boy he had explored the length and breadth of the island. There was not much of it, less than twenty miles in length and about three wide, with hardly a hill. Just mostly stones. A ring of standing stones about which a Merovingian king had built a monastery in the fifth century. The walls of the château fortress, where he was born, were built upon the remains of the monastery, and were hung with trophies of the wars that had swept this small, flat place.

Île de Ré became English in 1154 when Aliénor d'Aquitaine was queen. It had been part of her dowry. A triptych in the long gallery by Hals the Elder depicted Henry III of England returning the island to Saint Louis of France in 1243. Another huge oil by Cornelis Claesz van Wieringen, overwhelming the main hall, showed the island seized by Benjamin de Rohan, duc de Soubise, in 1625, who was later forced to give it back by Charles, duc de Guise.

The Lamberts of Île de Ré had prospered as a result of being traders and living on such an island where events offered opportunities diverse and far more propitious than the production of crimson dye.

JOURNEY'S END. Lavender, sage, rosemary and artemisia. Queen Artemisia, by Master van Rijn. In exchange for favours unmentionable, his great-grandfather had accepted this portrait of an imaginary queen who is on the verge of drinking from a poisoned cup that also contained her husband's ashes. Sir Laurence had it hung in his bedroom where he could watch her. Artemisia, wormwood. It was synonymous with calamity and injustice. When he was a young man, he associated this painting with the family's misfortunes.

SUMMERTIME. "Ah, here is Françoise." His granddaughter, called Fanny by her Anglophone parents, he thought her beautiful. And more. He often told her this.

"Absinthe?"

"Yes, thank you, grand-papa, I know I am. And look, I put on my best stockings to captivate you, grand-papa. Look!" It had always been their way.

"You have had my heart ever since I first saw you."

They spoke to each other as friends or as lovers might, with mock quarrels and rapprochements, bribes and surprises. They were confidants, who at times betrayed one another, only to be reconciled. This was one such occasion.

"You sold them, you promised you would never."

"But there was no money, Papa had none, and I needed money. You know that he is worse than hopeless."

"Hapless, yes, unfortunate man."

"Papa said that we lost everything when the bubble burst. Tell me about the bubble, grand-papa?"

She knew about it. It was their way.

"No, not everything was lost. It was a financial fiasco involving a venture that we had financed. What did you do with the money I sent you?"

"Paris is expensive, grand-papa, and we were drawing too much attention to ourselves, tradesmen at the door, letters from attorneys, our name in *Mercure de France*."

3: SIR LAURENCE LAMBERT 1765

"I don't care for newspapers. Those were your grandmother's diamonds, and Boehmer and Bassenge would never have paid you their true worth. You should have come to me, I would have dealt with them." He made a gesture of cutting his throat.

"And what do you have left to sell, mon cher petit grand-papa? Almost everything is gone."

"Not at all. Never everything."

She sat, dressed in white linen, on an Adraskan rug that depicted the Tree of Life with sensuous human forms, peacocks and birds of paradise. It matched her crimson hair and complemented her clear, white skin, her rounded arms, delicate neck and long thin feet, which were now bare for him to admire.

"My dear grand-papa, I have news. Before leaving Paris, I met a young man who was presented to my parents by Sire de Choisy, a colleague of a Sire de Barras of Grenada."

"Grenada. Mmm. . . absinthe?"

"Yes please. Mama likes him, Papa says I must get your consent. I want to marry him. Wait, he is young, well off, well born, and comes from the island of Grenada. A planter, with many estates producing sugar. His name is Philippe Roume de Saint Laurent, he is in Paris with his mother and his brother and sister. They have taken a house on the rue Saint-Séverin."

He scowled and thought: sugar. "That's where we live when in Paris. Where are they, is it opposite to Le Cygne de la Croix?"

"No, they are next door. Don't pout. I know you know that Bertrand would like to marry me, but dienst is dienst and schnaps is schnaps, that's German, remember, you told me that. A proverb; duty is duty and drinks are, well, drinks. And this is the time for duty. I shall always remember my handsome marquis, but I would not dream of marrying him. He has nothing. Shall get nothing. His father lost what little was left. Bertrand's only hope is a wealthy

Jewess. Philippe Roume de Saint Laurent is a rich planter. Do I have your consent?"

He appeared interested.

"I shall meet him. Invite them."

Never one long to dwell on issues settled according to her fancy, Fanny changed the subject. "Tell me about the bubble, grand-papa, the one that bust."

"Politics, my dear girl, is the root of all evil."

Fanny giggled and drew up her knees. Her grandfather often related to her the family's escapades; for these, she was all ears.

"The Whigs took full control of the government of England in 1715."

"Wigs?" One must prompt appropriately.

"The Whigs, a political grouping. They instituted constitutional monarchism in England and fastened opportunism to the absolute rule of the Parliament. We gave large bribes to parliamentarians in the Whig government to support the Acts of Parliament necessary to enable our South Sea Company. "

"Yes, grand-papa, the real rulers in England, you were saying, are the politicians."

"Yes, the politicians. . . they always muck up everything. They held a parliamentary inquiry into the collapse of the Company—but you know what? It was all theatre. Theatre, because they themselves profited while the going was good."

"We still control it, don't we?"

"Yes, yes, it was they themselves who gave us the monopoly to traffic in blacks with the Greater and Lesser Antilles and with all of South America. The whole of the south Atlantic! And the monopoly on the slave trade in the Spanish possessions."

"The slave trade?" This held a fascination for her.

3: SIR LAURENCE LAMBERT 1765

"In that commodity our family have always traded, from long times past. White slavery. Caucasian maidens, Jewish beauties, galley slaves for the Venetian navy, and Nubians, black as night, and what have you, for the Arabs, you know. But after the War of the Spanish Succession, that's when we got the monopoly to ship Africans out of Guinea, the asiento."

"The African slave trade is profitable, is it not?"

"Vastly. We were contracted to ship four thousand eight hundred blacks a year out of West Africa to the colonies in America. A single voyage from the African coast to the west carrying eight hundred Africans netted a profit of sixty thousand English pounds, or more."

"How did the English come by such an arrangement to ship slaves to Spanish colonies? Why did the English Parliament give us such a lucrative monopoly?"

"At the end of the War of the Spanish Succession, Spain ceded Gibraltar and Minorca to England and agreed to give to the English the asiento. A valuable monopoly, a slave-trading contract. The granting of the asiento was a part of the Treaty of Utrecht signed between them in 1714. The English had been in desperate need of money during the war. We loaned them more than four hundred thousand English pounds, mostly in bullion. We did this to garner political influence, and to make lots and lots of money for ourselves. We formed the syndicate that created The South Sea Company. The asiento was meant to be a bonus for taking on almost half of the ten million pounds of English indebtedness. They had the wars to pay for."

"Was it profitable?" She was actually interested.

"Yes it was. They paid us interest annually, at a rate of six per cent. They—the politicians—love to have their palms greased, but when The South Sea Company fell apart, they pointed their sticky fingers in all directions."

"All except at their own selves, not so?" Fanny said encouragingly.

"Bright you are, my child."

"But people bought the shares you sold. Didn't they know that they were taking a great risk? The south Atlantic is a wilderness. Those islands..."

"Greed. When people are obsessed with money, they take the most dreadful chances," Sir Laurence said, sipping absinthe and adjusting his gold-rimmed pince-nez.

"Yes, but it's all right, don't you agree? I think some greed is good. If you are not a bit greedy, how can you feel good about yourself?" she said, smiling brightly.

"Exactly, like absinthe. It was very exciting. Money madness gripped people in England! Alexander Pope, the poet, jostled and pushed with the rif et raf to come to the tables that we had set up on Threadneedle Street to accommodate all the greedy who wanted shares. Hogarth made an engraving. Have it here somewhere... The great and the good came. They pawned their jewels and sold off valuable land to get the cash to buy South Sea stock. Even members of their Royal Family! Then the entire thing collapsed. We were accused of everything under the sun: bribery, dealing in our own shares, giving loans to persons who had bought shares with those shares as security so that they could buy more shares. Merde! As though anybody has ever grown a vast enterprise without any of those measures!"

"What was the truth, what happened?" She regarded him closely as he hesitated. She saw the smile before he realised it, now here it comes, she thought, the old fox.

"The South Sea Company's money was indeed used to deal in its own shares. Only carefully selected individuals purchasing shares were given loans backed by those same shares to spend on purchasing more shares. Using advance knowledge—this gained by bribing politicians—of when the national debt was to

3: SIR LAURENCE LAMBERT 1765

be consolidated, we were able to accrue enormous profits from purchasing debt in advance."

"Speculation and fraud." She peeped at him, appreciating the candour that they had always shared.

"Isaac Newton, the magician, lost a fortune when the bubble burst: took it philosophically, saying that he could calculate the movement of the stars, but not the madness of men. Yet, some made fortunes. We have since restructured the Company in spite of all the ill will of the English public and their politicians. We own it; in truth we own more of it now."

"But the actual trade with South America, that never happened."

"No, not really. It was all in the shareholders' imagination. The trade in slaves did! Eventually. By the 1730s, the blacks of Jamaica numbered eighty thousand, and in Barbados between 1708 and 1735 the planters bought eighty-five thousand so as to move the slave population from forty-two thousand to forty-six thousand."

"The blacks are an excellent item, grand-papa. Such a turnover!" she said, seriously, wonderingly, her expression for a moment unguarded. The sunlight, streaming in through the tall slim windows of the vaulted hall, highlighted her magnificent head of hair, her lovely delicate features, the loose white peasant blouse she wore, and its contents, as she bent forward reaching for an orange. He so appreciated these casual gestures; he knew they were for him.

"It was a gold mine for the stock holders."

"Yes, grand-papa." Penitent. "So where did the money, the real profit from the asiento bonus, go, grand-papa?" Blue eyes wide, a child's.

"To me. Ha, and then, if I only knew, I wouldn't be here, ashamed to look these portraits in the eye! It was here, you know, in this house. All in gold, the profit from the scheme!"

"Where? Where was it?"

"In this house of course, below in the crypt."

"Gold doesn't just vanish like a soap bubble, grand-papa. Who stole it from us, didn't you ever find out?"

"I know, I did. I had brought it all here to hide it away from the English, for another day."

"Who took it, grand-papa?"

"In '59," he growled, "the English navy took what they could find. Hawke, the admiral, he arranged for an attack on us here on the island. They took away a little, but there was a lot more left."

"Shame on you, grand-papa. To let a fortune get away. And now I shall have to put myself upon the block. Traffic in my flesh! My marriage to Philippe Roume will facilitate a recovery. Dante's Divine Comedy is right, when it says:

> O *Avarice, my house is now your captive:*
> *It traffics in the flesh of its own children*
> *what more is left for you to do to us?"*

"Don't be impertinent!"

"Sorry, I am sorry, I should not have said that, it was..."

"Mean and stupid!" The little mouth, a rosebud.

His indignant look softened as he rose. He bent towards her upturned face and kissed her lightly on it.

"Smoothen your crimson feathers, ma chérie, I have many more golden guineas, they are downstairs, right there," he said, pointing, "in the oubliette beneath the crypt of the old Merovingians. I shall give a few to you for your dowry and you may invite your newest beau and his relatives."

4: THE MARRIAGES

1765

He was the first to wed. After a short engagement, Philippe Rose Roume de Saint Laurent took the hand of the Honourable Françoise Lambert, the granddaughter of Sir Laurence Lambert, Bart. But not before Rosa was pleased to accept, on behalf of her family, an invitation to visit the ancestral château-fortress of the Lamberts on Île de Ré.

She was charmed by the tasteful simplicity of a life lived amongst beautiful objects of great value and consequence, all reflecting the rich art and history—the high culture of aristocratic Europe. Rosa naïvely believed the Lamberts to be exceptionally well connected. Their baronetcy placed them within the ranks of the British nobility with connections to the Parliament in London and the City's banking interest. In Sir Laurence, she discovered a gentleman of the old school, one who was possessed of an eye for beauty, her own.

Setting out across the empty spaces of Île de Ré, the Atlantic's spring sky rolling high above, and dinghy sailing on the dancing waves—she was such a good sailor—Philippe and Françoise, or Fanny, as some members of her English-speaking family called her, fell in love. Chasing the sunlit showers that crisscrossed the undulating landscape, riding identical Charentais ponies, taking shelter beneath ancient, lichen-covered stone tables, they shivered with delight as they embraced. Roume so loved this crimson-haired, blue-eyed beauty, so young and unblemished, whose breath smelled of lavender and whose skin, delicate and glowing white, promised a rich ripeness hardly imaginable by those who had experienced only the molasses, sapodilla, and cinnamon tones of the islands.

He re-declared his devotion. Fanny found herself even more charmed by this handsome stranger than when she had impulsively accepted his proposal in Paris. Tall and bronzed, his calm, stolid disposition, so mature in spite of his youth. He was different, so un-Gallic. Wise beyond his years. He had been fashioned by a warmer sun. Philippe promised a life of adventure, a sensual mixture of fecundity and elegance in a place on the frontier of the New World. A Utopia, as he would frequently say. She saw herself with him in paradise. Having gained her grandfather's acquiescence, she blushingly admitted him to her charms.

TORCHES FIXED IN IRON SCONCES BLAZED red and orange, casting eccentric shadows to the wind. A silhouette standing within the vaulted porch-way, Sir Laurence Lambert awaited Philippe Roume, the man to whom his granddaughter had so impetuously promised her hand. From far away came the sound of the sea at Pertuis d'Antioche as it boomed and sighed farewells in perpetuity for souls long departed for the Outremer.

"Ah, Philippe, my dear boy, come sit and we shall share a little of this excellent calvados. We have it from our Normandy estates. Now tell me of your island, having explored my own."

Philippe, with an uneasy poise, appeared to the older man excitable and prodigal as he spoke to him of Grenada. He regarded him closely, the torchlight illuminating his clearly defined features and his youthful form. Young. Very young, he thought, yet intense, he searched for another word. Ambitious. Yes.

4: THE MARRIAGES 1765

Philippe described the dazzling sea, the mysterious mountain of water and fire surrounded by even higher mountains, often clothed with clouds. The rivers and cascades; the fields of waving cane worked by diligent blacks. The Great Houses, the society in which his mother moved with charm, and his own aspirations to increase the prosperity of his family. Sir Laurence, attentive, polite and curious, inquired into the thinking of the leading men of the island, and Philippe explicated, to the best of his knowledge, the thinking of Everard de Barras with regard to their fears of a future under English rule.

Philippe then spoke of another island, one that had always intrigued him. It was virtually untouched, he told him, still in its virgin state. A larger island named La Trinité by Columbus on his third voyage.

"You say La Trinité is uninhabited?"

Philippe explained that Trinidad was a Spanish possession that had been neglected for centuries.

"It has tremendous potential, Sire."

He had to think of the Greek word for warrior. Hero. No, not a hero. Then, Hermes, god of transactions and boundaries: the son of Zeus and the Pleiad Maia. Mercury, a messenger, perhaps?

"Potential. I admire you, my boy. And your people, the colons of the islands. Now that the perfidious English have taken away their birth-right, would they go and settle in Spanish Trinidad?"

"Yes, Sire, indeed, we have spoken of it. We dream of it. I dream of it."

"It would take a great deal of persuasion to move those who have long ago put their roots deep into the soil of other places, to remove to another island. Would it not?"

"Yes, indeed it would, but an urgent necessity, one that spells out survival, would accomplish this," answered Philippe, the warmth of the calvados rising.

"It would require a person knowledgeable and sympathetic to the needs of the colonists, one with great persuasive powers, to accomplish that."

"I could, Sire, I could do that. I, we, have been in preparation for such a move for some time."

"Indeed. For some time. I see that you carry the star of destiny, my boy. I see that clearly. The opportunity to implement your dream of settling Trinidad is presently some distance away, yet it can come, and when it does you shall do it. For Françoise, your children, and for your people?"

"Oh yes, Sire."

"Françoise will not come to you empty-handed. There will be a hefty purse to start your lives. And there is some other business that we shall talk about at another time. You are a principled young man, I can plainly see."

"I shall do my utmost to make Françoise happy, I promise."

Naïve. No. Mercurial. A salesman? The salesman! Sir Laurence smiled. He placed his hand, not without genuine affection, on Philippe's arm.

"Yes, you shall, and now we join the ladies."

PHILIPPE ROUME was not the only one who could lay claim to Fanny's affections. The confident and much indulged Bertrand had long set his heart on Fanny, notwithstanding her inferior social status. He was deeply disappointed by this development. He had been raised to get his way. It was his due, it was his right, as he expressed with rage, his refined features tightly drawn across his face.

"You, marry this bumbling islander! A provincial nobody. Ah Bon Dieu, you must have lost your mind, Françoise. Are you in

4: THE MARRIAGES 1765

love, or is the old man paying you to do this? What have I done to offend you?"

"He is no bumpkin, Bertrand. He is refined and educated. It is my duty, my grand-papa desires it. This presents an opportunity for alliances and the infusion of what the colonies produce in quantity, money."

He should know that, she thought impatiently, and understand that nothing would change between them.

"I shall never let you go. I shall follow you, I shall be with you there, or here, or in hell!" Bertrand exclaimed, with an appropriately melodramatic gesture.

"Look," she smiled, her deshabillé negligé revealing far more than concealing, "you will always have this, me. Come."

"Ma belle fille."

Seeing them together, Bertrand became convinced that Françoise, his belle fille, had indeed fallen in love with this provincial creature who obviously worshipped her. She would not vanish from his life, this he vowed to her and to himself. "There must be something in all this for me," he told himself bitterly, as he regarded the happy couple laughing, playing at masquerades in the big old rooms. Tearing his eyes away, he noticed Rosa walking on the terrace arm in arm with Sir Laurence, laughing at his sly obscenities. Her oddities he thought so original; her renditions of the earlier pieces of Chambonnière so delicately performed on the antique harpsichord. As she affected ecstasy in the firelight, her profile had aroused him, her dark curls falling over face. She looked, for a moment, like a gypsy, wanton. This led him to invite her to visit Château d'Angoulême in Angoumois, a vast pile that belonged to his mother's relatives, now more or less abandoned.

"Yours?"

"Eventually," he lied, "when I inherit the title, and everything else."

Suddenly, into Rosa's life came, for the first but not the last time, the thrill of clandestine love. This commenced with delightful outings, where gallant compliments came aplenty, all with a practised charm. All were well received and welcomed by Rosa with wistful lingering glances. He was young, too young, so small in stature, but vigorous, such a rider, so light, so poised. His black curls, small mouth, something vulnerable there, perhaps corrupted in his youth. At first, they had to be careful. What had commenced as a flirtation, merely an idle dalliance in the desolation of airless afternoon siestas, turned breathlessly into a heart-pounding distraction, urgent and commanding.

Rosa took charge and announced her decision. She, having taken him as her lover, would have him for a husband. As she saw it, for the young gallant to be accepted by the unsurpassed beauty of Grenada would be considered not merely "ton" or even "bon ton," but, in fact, be "haut ton."

The young people, Fanny in particular, were dismayed by Rosa's acceptance of Bertrand's proposal of marriage. Fanny assumed a vague and increasingly removed air, and was only interested in her own wedding plans. Sir Laurence understood his granddaughter. Philippe said that he was happy for his mother, keeping his true feelings to himself.

Bertrand was fifteen years younger than Rosa's forty, and exactly three years older than Philippe, who spoke of it to Sir Laurence, saying that he saw his mother's marriage as the acquiring of an older brother, smart, elegant, noble and French born. He is trying not to reveal his true feelings, thought the older man as he scrutinised him, standing at a casement on the last evening, illuminated by the shifting candlelight.

By the end of that eventful year they all returned to Grenada together.

4: THE MARRIAGES 1765

Reading from my Memoirs at La Fontenoy, Grenada, 1806

MEETING HENRI-CHRISTOPHE. I understood, ever since I was a child, that I lived in a coexistent universe; one which, naturally, involved raising the dead. I smiled to myself as I admired our daughter Manon's thin brown curls and the other, Vandelle, at play at my feet. In the soft lamp-light of La Fontenoy's sitting-room, I have been rereading entries in one of my diaries, the one in which I described my childhood recollections of times spent at Soubise estate in the 1760s. I had written these while living in Saint-Domingue, during a period that was shaped and coloured by my experiences there.

Raising the dead—this I witnessed. It concerned money. Inheritance, always a problem. Marie Saint-Cyr, a well-off *négresse libre,* had passed away. Her last will and testamentum had been registered in the High Court at Fort Royal.

In the fore-day morning of Marie Saint-Cyr's passing, with the rain beating so hard on the shingled roof of the house of mourning that everyone had to speak up to be heard, her goddaughter Ianté was seen with her ear to the mouth of the deceased. That raised an alarm and also the curtain on the spectacle.

"What she tell you?"

Me, Marianne, who was always there, somehow missed the rest of that conversation.

But I witnessed its consequences. "Fifine say she coming!" A short fat black woman was shipped in from Mustique that very day to speak to the deceased Marie Saint-Cyr. When she came, dressed as a man, she drew, with a lump of chalk, a tombstone with a cross upon it on the front door of the house of mourning.

"That is for Ghede Nimbo," she informed the air. "He is the custodian of the past, the record keeper of the final solution, and also the guardian of children."

She spent a long time with the dead woman; there were clouds of incense billowing from the bedroom window, the rattle of an açon, and some very disturbing singing. Then the words, "Receive this water and drink, and do not permit any evil to come whence you are setting out, and permit all the women of the household to bear children." Then came a roll of drums and a plaintive chorus. When Fifine came out, she appeared wrung. She, having conversed with the dead, interrogated the goddaughter Ianté.

"What your commère tell you?"

"She tell me she have a next child."

"Yes, she have children. She have Stéphane and Marie Paysette."

"Yes, but she say she have a boy, his name is Henri-Christophe."

Henri-Christophe? No one in the house had ever heard of him.

"What else did she say?"

"She say, everything have to share with Henri-Christophe."

"Where is Henri-Christophe?"

"He outside, she say, he by the old closet next to the guava tree. He dey, he waiting," said Ianté.

Well, everybody went outside, and there, true enough, was a boy, a big boy standing under the guava tree, waiting. You could see that he was waiting by the sense of impermanence about him.

"Ey boy!" called Stéphane, she was like a child herself. "Your name is Henri-Christophe?"

"Oui."

"You know Ma Saint-Cyr."

"Oui."

"How you know Ma Saint-Cyr."

"She is my mammy, Miss."

"So, who you belong to, boy?"

4: THE MARRIAGES 1765

"M'sieu de Favinières at Sans Souci."

Well, more confusion. "Bring him," some said, "let him see his mammy."

"Don't bring him in the house! You ent see he is a zombie."

"He is no zombie, he is a rude boy, everybody know he has no behaviour."

"Let his mammy see him," said Fifine, the lady from Mustique. That was when I paid attention to him, a coal-black boy of about my own age. As he came up the steps in the pouring wind our eyes met. He appeared detached, unfastened to affairs. I, naturally, followed him into the bedroom where the corpse was right there in the middle of the iron bed. As the boy walked towards the bed, I saw the corpse in her best going-to-market clothes sit straight up, her white kalandé well set tight on her head. With her eyes closed, she said out loud:

"Mi y chè-lá moin mené ba ou çé yche-moin, çé y chè moin!"

And with that, the corpse spoke up for half an hour. "Oui," she said, "look at the child I brought into this world," her Creole Patois heavy with her native Twi, the language of the Ashanti. "He is my child, you must take the money that I leave and buy him from M'sieu de Favinières, he and his father belong at Sans Souci. He have to go to school and be a book man, so that when he make man he will be a king like my great-grandfather." She told them, "Ianté will mind him," and with that, she done dead for the last time. Fifine, the person from Mustique, stayed behind and was the chief overseer. I never forgot that night in Grenville. "It have a dead girl in a plate in La Digue," I told them, but no one listened.

Next morning, sitting at the top of a flight of decapitated concrete steps of an old house demolished long before I was born, I was gazing through its vanished rooms towards the bay. There, the glassy light of the sun was so bright I could see the crystal-clear edge of the world where it met the sky. It came to me that what I thought in my head about everything was bigger than my mouth was able to say.

The transaction regarding the said Henri-Christophe's purchase and subsequent manumission was never concluded. And then at another time I heard that he had run away, shipped out as a cabin-boy aboard a Dutch clipper for Saint-Domingue, but not before he had come to me in the cocoa early one morning to invite me into the gully and to show me how he is make man.

That black boy was one of the eggs laid and hatched in the life-in-death struggle of slavery's nightmare's nest, don't doubt that.

5: ANDRÉ FATIO, THE BEGINNING OF THE END
ÎLE DE RÉ, 1775

Île de Ré, late summer, just over ten years later. The siesta attempted, failed. Sir Laurence, ever restless, a little greyer, a little sterner around the mouth, stepped out into the sunny atrium where servants had splashed the hot Florentine tiles with cool well-water. He walked barefooted through the warm puddles, stamping his feet in the largest of them. Sparkling droplets soaking the hem of the crimson robe draped over his angular frame.

"Master Fatio has come, Sire. And Master Cornelius Bosanquet awaits you as well." His major-domo, obviously awakened from his own siesta, stood blinking at the entrance.

"Yes, Melchior, yes, thank you. Show Master Cornelius into the tower library. I am sorry that they woke you Melchior. And bring in Master Fatio, ah, put him there. But, wait; I am not done. Before that, first fetch me a few bergamote oranges and a knife of course."

"Of course, Sire."

He would speak to his business partner Cornelius Bosanquet later. And he would not tell him much, if anything.

André Fatio gazed into his black deep set eyes, having glanced at his receding hairline, while trying not to look into the open robe that Laurence Lambert had pulled up and around his bony knees.

"And your father, he is well?"

"He thrives, my Lord. Praise God."

"Excellent, André." He paused and began to peel an orange. André sat calmly looking at him already enjoying its aroma.

"I require you to go to the Antilles, first to Grenada. My granddaughter lives there, married to a Creole for the past ten years. Grenada is presently held by the English. There is a rich harvest to be reaped there amongst the French planters who are always in need of money, living beyond their means. They are to be replaced by English planters who must now control the supply of sugar."

"Indeed, my Lord, they already prosper at Barbados, in the Leeward Islands, and of course Jamaica."

"You should take Samuel Bosanquet, our partner's son, with you."

"Yes, my Lord," said André politely, watching motionlessly as Sir Laurence peeled the fruit while deeply inhaling its fragrance.

"The asiento that was granted to our South Sea Company at the conclusion of the War of the Spanish Succession gave us thirty-seven years in the African trade. The period of confusion after that war gave an extension on the contract of thirteen years to supply slaves to the Spanish colonies, plus shipping five hundred tons of goods annually to the great fair at Portobello in Panama."

"That expired in 1764, if I am not mistaken."

"Indeed, André, indeed. In fact we received one hundred thousand pounds sterling from the Spanish Crown in compensation for the loss of our privileges in the slave trade."

"I take it that as Europe squabbled over who should be king in Spain, your perspicacity led you to support the cause of the Duke of Anjou?"

"At considerable expense. Whose son became Charles III of Spain! Illuminated by the new wisdom, I hear, André. Committed to stimulate economic and intellectual development. Bravo for us!"

5: ANDRE FATIO, ÎLE DE RÉ 1775

"I believe, my Lord, it is called the Enlightenment."

"In any event, the asiento has returned to us, we will be trading in Africans as the Compañía Gaditan for another thirty-five years. This in gratitude for services rendered to the Spanish Crown, or more accurately to Don José de Gálvez, who in turn owes us many a favour."

"Congratulations, Sir Laurence! Your generosity has placed the Gálvez family on the path of ascendancy in their colonies, and, if I may say so, expanded your capacity to realise significant returns."

"Exactly. But it will require manpower, André, African slaves. They do not grow on trees."

Sir Laurence placed the orange on the table, he had peeled it for the benefit of the aroma, and raised his eyes to meet André Fatio's. "We must raise between three to five hundred thousand English pounds to procure an ocean-going fleet of slavers. A modest sum in times of plenty, but alas..."

"And that is why you would like me and Samuel Bosanquet to go to the Antilles?"

"The South Sea Company must be refinanced, hence our entry into lending money on interest to French planters in the Antilles. They will take it and be in our debt. We shall foreclose, inevitably, then we shall sell their mortgages to the English. And we shall make the profit. A further profit will be had as we sell new Africans to the English. Mortgages. Difficult in the best of times. Chancy at the worst: What! We shall count on the worst. We need that money, it is one of my several initiatives, you understand, to fit out ships! The African coast, André, to the African coast! Money to pay shipwrights, money to purchase guns, rum, trinkets and rubbish in exchange for Africans who will be sold in the West Indies and the Spanish colonies for gold. It is a good business, the blacks are ephemeral, constantly in demand."

"What is Gálvez's role in all of this?"

"The Spanish island of Trinidad, is just south of Grenada. I understand that in return for our, ah, how you say, assistance there is to be a Cedula for population promulgated, in which my, ah, son-in-law, Philippe de Saint Laurent of Grenada, would be significantly involved. It is a plan of José de Gálvez. The idea is to encourage Catholics in the other islands to settle at Trinidad, receive lands, open up the forest to establish plantations, man the militia."

"So, if I understand correctly, your prize is to be the sale of slaves to these new colons in the island of Trinidad?"

"Why yes, certainly, André, that's what the asiento is all about. More like an extension on the margins. I am told there is a word for it in the Creole Patois of the Antilles, a lagniappe: what remains on the cloth after the grain was weighed is passed on to the purchaser."

"It is a risky enterprise, as it has to be taken to the planters of the islands by someone whom they trust. Is there such a person?"

"Yes, I believe that my son-in-law, Philippe de Saint Laurent, is the perfect person. He was the one who first opened my eyes to the commercial opportunity in the settlement of Trinidad, more than a decade ago. He said that a great many planters would support it. Now I have Gálvez, the plan will come to fruition. And, there is a society of some sort in Spain which sees itself as the catalyst for change in the Empire. It is time to act, André, it is time to renew the old covenant."

"As it pleases you, Sir Laurence."

"Give me your hand."

In a movement practiced, swift, the knife was passed lightly across Sir Laurence's palm and that of his partner's. Hands grasped. Blood mingled. A pact sealed.

"A bergamote orange, André, take one."

"Thank you, my Lord."

"You will be informed of the arrangements made for the journey, my boy. You shall be well taken care of, no fear."

5: ANDRE FATIO, ÎLE DE RÉ 1775

"Thank you, my Lord."

Parting from young Fatio with an artful smile, Sir Laurence ascended a spiral stair that led to an octagonal tower room, there to examine the rare and beautifully illustrated alchemical work, the Chrysopoeia of Cleopatra, and to discuss with Cornelius Bosanquet, his old friend and accomplice of a thousand transactions, the properties of the lapis philosophorum, the transmutation of chrysopoeia, and golden objets d'art into bullion as illustrated in the rare and much acclaimed works of Zosimos of Panopolis.

Sugar. Later that evening, alone, and wandering the old castle's corridors, he repeated the word over and over while appreciating by candlelight another of Claude Lorrain's paintings. A seaport, Delia at Delos, birthplace of Artemis and Apollo. Ruins, arranged in classical dilapidation, built on the sea. Men at work on the water's edge. In the soft, hazy sunrise there were ships coming in, or were they departing? It had been commissioned by Frédéric de La Tour d'Auvergne, duc de Bouillon, general of a Papal army. The Duke, unable to repay debts to his great-grandfather, had left it with him together with his bejewelled ceremonial sword that had been presented to him by Richelieu who had won him over to the King, along with a gold-inlaid armour by Negroli, which stood next to the oil. Foreign travel.

ANDRÉ FATIO'S ENTRANCE INTO Grenada's planter society the following year, 1776, was accomplished by his disarmingly pleasant manners and engaging personality. A handsome man with bright blue eyes, he had about him, the subtle scent of bergamote and, an abundance of raven-black hair. His conversation was amusing and his manners polished. To many Grenadians, he appeared to possess a "ton" of his own. In fact, he was Huguenot and Swiss.

André and his partner, Samuel Bosanquet, as agents of The South Sea Company, set about the business of accommodating the hard-pressed planters of the island by offering short-term financing at very attractive interest rates. They were able to save several proprietors the embarrassment of having their property sold at auction before the doors of the court, and gained the gratitude of the community. There were planters who harboured misgivings, because even as emoluments were passed about, foreclosures were effected and buyers appeared as if by magic from beneath the decks of the English merchantmen.

In the course of their first year in Grenada, both Bertrand de Charras and Rosa avoided the company of André Fatio and Samuel Bosanquet. They saw Fatio as someone in trade, a common man, a Protestant, and a bounder. As for Samuel, he was surely a Jew, thus especially to be despised. They were both Sir Laurence's venal creatures. This attitude was to change as time passed, prompted mostly by de Charras' need for money and by the groundswell of emotion generated by his loss of Françoise.

After a decade of marriage, Françoise and Philippe appeared serene. When she became pregnant and gave birth to a daughter who thrived, he almost died of jealousy, imagining their intimacy. Then he was secretly pleased to see that she could not carry other pregnancies to full-term. She lost her second, then two others, then became pregnant again and lost the child mid-term.

In his dread-filled nights he saw plainly how she had changed. His Françoise barely recognised his presence and never invited him to her boudoir. She had actually taken to treating him with civility!

Bertrand well understood that he was married to a woman who measured her social success by her advancement to the Marquessate of the realm. She relished being called Marquise de Charras, even though he could not inherit the title. As a Frenchman and an aristocrat, he scoffed at Rosa's pretensions and the notion that Philippe's connection to the 'noble' Lamberts of the United Kingdom conferred an aura of prestige. He knew them as money lenders, to be at best in contraband and most at home with piracy.

5: ANDRE FATIO, ÎLE DE RÉ 1775

In a rage of hate, he prophesied that she would go to them, begging, but he, never. He found that he could not bear to be in her presence and thought increasingly of leaving. Seeing her in this environment, she appeared to him as old, coarse and common, vulgar beyond amusement.

His wife's naïveté became a matter of complete indifference. She had not yet come to understand the true complexity of the ménage à trois into which she had inadvertently stumbled. Because of the eventual change in their conjugal arrangements, she had deferred introducing Bertrand to the family's complicated financial affairs.

Despite her inclination to live a luxurious life, Rosa had never been an idle person. She was well acquainted with the plantations in her possession. Insisting on managing their financial affairs, she gave the arduous tasks of ordering the work and the supervising and disciplining of the slaves to her son Philippe. She knew that large infusions of money were vital so as to finance sugarcane production. This invariably necessitated restocking the plantations with slaves.

In any event, Bertrand had no interest in sugarcane cultivation. Arriving at an understanding, he was pleased to be left alone and ungraciously accepted a modest stipend. However, he took to pretending that his wife's money was his and to pursue opportunities at the gambling table where he was not an expert and to seek creditors who were only too pleased to extend to him all the money he wished. As his indebtedness increased, in his malice-filled idleness, he plotted revenge on Françoise for marrying Philippe. He considered that a matter of honour.

Rosa too was in need of money. The necessity of financing the forthcoming crop was now considerably beyond her means. In trepidation, she felt compelled to broach the topic of mortgages with her husband. Taking pleasure he shouted "I told you so!" spitefully suggesting that a conversation with André Fatio could prove useful.

She never suspected that Fatio had already been approached by her husband without her knowledge. Bertrand's motives were increasingly driven by the anticipation of the exquisite pleasure which he would have in bringing ruin on the Roume family. Impoverished and at a loss, Françoise would come back to France with him where they would live, at her grandfather's expense, in perpetual pleasure.

Pressed by her husband and despite being warned by Philippe but trapped in the despair of her desperate situation, Rosa agreed to receive André Fatio at Belvédère. He inspected the land, the plantation, the buildings, the slaves and, as it would appear, Rosa herself. Impressed, he expressed a concern. Rosa's need was immediate. André's assurances of the benefits of English rule and the ease with which financial transactions could be accomplished were what she wanted to hear and she was amused by his attentions. She recognised at once, of course, that André Fatio's interest in Belvédère was concurrent with his desire to debauch her. The very thought brought on a warm flush that lingered into the night.

She chuckled quietly to herself as she stepped from her tub, the following morning, having glimpsed her full body in the mirror through the fragrant vapour of the basil bush-bath that she had taken on the advice of her old nurse Murcia for the pain in her hip. That André Fatio should continue to insinuate himself in a manner suggestive of intimacy, had continued to amuse her.

André Fatio, she thought to herself, thinks us provincial imbeciles. She smiled at her reflection in the glass that Murcia's daughter was holding up to her. The wet black curls caught in her eyebrows, bath-water running down her cheeks and her alabaster shoulders, round and firm. Statuesque, Bertrand had once said long ago, when comparing her nakedness to the Venus Anadyomene by Titian, a large oil, one of the many nude studies treasured by Sir Laurence at Île de Ré.

Her daughter was to marry Sire François-Ann de Mazille, and Rosa was obliged to pay, by law, Francisca's share of the legacy left to her by her father, Rosa's former husband. This was approximately one hundred and twenty thousand livres.

5: ANDRE FATIO, ÎLE DE RÉ 1775

"I WOULD ADVISE AGAINST IT," cautioned Samuel Bosanquet, when he heard that Fatio was about to advance substantial funds to Rosa.

Bosanquet was small and slightly built. Fair, with thinning sandy hair. His close-set dark eyes, appeared interrupted by a disproportionately large nose, were haloed by dingy circles from the time of his adolescence.

"Why?"

"It may go against Sir Laurence's intentions. In any event, de Charras does not have it in him to repay us."

"I would like to have it in her."

"That is not the point, André."

"Sam, dear Sam, if we do not advance the money, they will go under. They cannot last another season. I have already allowed them a line of credit, fifty thousand, and another tranche of one hundred and twenty to come. In any event, Sir Laurence would enjoy his granddaughter's return to Île de Ré. Philippe Roume is more interested in populating Trinidad than his family's affairs in Grenada. He may even have already served his purpose. This is, and will remain, an English colony. And I gave her my promise."

"You will ensure their failure. Sell their plantations to the highest British bidder. This surely will bring about unsuspected consequences. So be it, André. Remember, I warned you. This will be your undertaking, not the Company's."

"So be it, Samuel. So be it."

And so it was. André Fatio's continuing interest in Rosa's affairs led eventually to more, and even closer inspections of her assets, which yielded the results envisaged by them both.

Rosa, as executrix of the entire estate, in defiance of Philippe's warnings, desperate pleas and unprecedented tantrums, proceeded to mortgage all their plantations for ten years to André Fatio for the sum of £97,000. This was in addition to the other previous advances. She also signed over power of attorney to him personally. This she kept a secret from Philippe. André continued to see her and to allow her credit, but never enough to solve all her urgent needs. Then suddenly he stopped calling on her. As a consequence, by the end of 1777, she faced bankruptcy and ruin. She became panic stricken and avoided seeing Philippe. She was informed by post that André Fatio was in the process of foreclosing on her assets.

6: BERTRAND DE CHARRAS
THE CLOSING OF ACCOUNTS
1775

HE HAD BEEN against his mother's dealings with André Fatio. Instinctively he knew that such an association would be as disastrous as it would be distasteful and degrading.

Furious at what was becoming public knowledge, he found her one morning in a state of collapse, sitting at her desk, terrified at the unfolding consequences of her actions and decisions. She told him all. He regarded her dishevelled appearance. His alarm mounting, he could not contain himself.

"When you acted like a fool and married that ass de Charras, I said nothing!" he shouted, rising from his father's chair. "You are an idiot. I warned you, I warned you about Fatio, you vain and stupid fool of a woman. The man has had his way with you and ruined us!"

She had never seen him so angry. Alarmed by his appearance, she pleaded desperately: "My dear Philippe! What could I have done?"

"You could have left the managing of the estates to me, mother! To me! It was to be mine. But no! It was a part of your pose, the great châtelaine, the doyenne of this ridiculous place, you and your charms."

"Oh Philippe, please don't... we can still save Belvédère, we still have it, our home."

"For how long, mother, a year, two, three? They will take it, sooner or later! Within months of your receiving Fatio's money and taking him into your bed, we are ruined. We have lost everything, everything."

"Oh Philippe, I am sorry, you were right, I should never have received him, never seen him... forgive me I... my dear boy, don't leave, please, Bertram is gone from our lives and André, wait... we shall fight them in the courts."

He couldn't hear her for the noise in his head. Before she could finish he fled the room. Overcome by the thought that he had lost his inheritance so carefully garnered by his dead father and dreading a future that he could hardly imagine, he sought his old teacher Everard de Barras' help and advice.

"Did you tell your mother of your concerns?"

"I pleaded with her to end the involvement with Fatio. I found it debasing and embarrassing, I feared the outcome. I suggested to her that we abandon some of the estates and consolidate. She would not hear me."

"I understand."

"Yes, and so do I now." He hung his head to hide the tears.

"I shall see what can be done for your mother, Philippe. But as regards yourself, I would prepare for Trinidad, if I were you," said de Barras, regarding his former pupil with concern. "It is now time to look to a different future."

Some weeks later Philippe Roume and Everard de Barras met to discuss this different future. "Growth is the action of creative impulses," remarked the old gentleman, rising to bring greater import to his delivery. "One such creative impulse I would recommend to you, especially at this juncture. It is expressed in a society which

6: BERTRAND DE CHARRAS 1775

has come into being in Spain, Sociedades Económicas de Amigos del País. We understand that two leading Spanish scientists are on their way to Trinidad. One is a surveyor, the other, an engineer. Highly trained, highly placed, very influential in their navy, with connections to the Capitanía General de Venezuela in Caracas. According to what I understand, they would have sailed from the port of Cadiz just over two months ago.

"These are letters of introduction to them from associates of mine from happier days."

"These Spaniards, de Catilla and Cramé, are they also members of the Society of Friends of the Country, and what is that Society about?" enquired Philippe, his wish to please his patron actually tinged with curiosity, not to mention the sinking dread of the last several weeks having somewhat been postponed.

"I would imagine that they are and, you could think of the Society as a part of the reforms crafted by Spain's new Bourbon dynasty," the old man continued, speaking with an optimism that he hoped was contagious. "Nothing less than what you may describe as the Spanish Enlightenment, the Society is actually an arrangement, encouraged by the king, to diffuse and apply the principles of the scientific Enlightenment in her colonies, Venezuela being one of them."

"And also Trinidad, that fabled land of the nymph Calypso?" He had to laugh in spite of himself.

"Yes, Trinidad is a part of Venezuela," said de Barras seriously. "The organisation that has sent out these men was founded by Don Xavier, Conde de Peñaflorida no less; presently he is president of the Real Compañía Guipuzcoana de Caracas. They are in the cocoa-trading business. He is a free-thinker and philanthropist. On a practical level, as the war in North America draws to an end, a victory, aided by France, will change a great many things for the colonists in these islands. The Society's purpose, which becomes urgent, is to rescue their empire from decay through far-reaching reforms. They must guard against a revolution happening in South America."

"Would that mean the weakening of the Church?" asked Roume, smiling now, knowing well his mentor's views.

"Hardly. But promoting science is one of the goals, as are facilitating trade and commerce, modernising agriculture, and avoiding wars. These ideas stimulate improvements in the professions and the arts in Spain and in her colonies."

"I must say, I find it difficult to believe. Spain is not known for such liberal views," said Philippe, "it has lingered the longest in Europe in medieval ideas."

"The Enlightenment called it forth," answered de Barras, "and the Spanish king allows it, for the moment, while the Holy Inquisitors watch and wait."

"I am sure not for long, maestro. Trinidad is known as an unhealthy and dangerous place. The man-eaters visit it regularly in pursuit of a change of diet," said Roume, as he helped himself to a glass of claret.

"There are no man-eaters there, Philippe, they were exterminated years ago. Prepare yourself. There is money for this, raised by us and others who see Trinidad as the most viable option. See it as an expedition! The development of Trinidad will be our endeavour. It will be an adventure," said de Barras.

"De Catilla and Cramé are to make a survey of the island, you say?" The notion was appealing to him.

"The future beckons, my boy. But this is serious, we, all of us, must now leave this island, Grenada, it is over for us here. We must find another island and Trinidad is the last available."

"I think I will enjoy the change," said Philippe, pensive, as he thought sadly of his family's situation. That he must now make good. His brother, François, like their father, was a man who could

6: BERTRAND DE CHARRAS 1775

hardly stir from his chair. Now at the age of thirty-three, he, for the first time, spared a thought to concern himself with life, its meaning, and passing time and death. Time. I must find the time to make a fresh future. He looked up and nodded, smiling ruefully.

"Excellent, Philippe, excellent," said de Barras, looking closely at him, while placing a purse on the desk, "it will suffice; if not, there is more, but keep an account! Now, be off with you, my boy, I have some family matters to see to."

FANNY'S PERSONALITY, even before these events, had been altered by grief for her lost children and a sense of desperate isolation. Grenada appeared orphaned, teetering on the most distant perimeter of the world, soon to be trapped in the horrific nightmare of an uprising of the blacks. She had experienced this as a clear premonition. They said that it had happened before.

She had encouraged her husband to pursue the possibility of establishing a French-speaking enclave in Spanish Trinidad and had been pleased that he had plans to go abroad and to meet the Spanish officials there.

She fully understood the necessity, the growing urgency, for the planter families to remove themselves from Grenada. The change of government from French to English in 1763 had fractured a fragile accommodation between master and slave, it would never heal. She thought that she could see the rebellion incubating in their hearts. An age-old, deep-seated anger dwelt there, driven by the recent and unfamiliar cruelties perpetrated by the English. She knew that all would explode into a massacre.

The sudden indescribable silences that haunted Belvédère in the past months were reflected in the abandoned fields; in the distant mountains, where fires mysteriously appeared. Certainly it was suspected in their inscrutable minds and glimpsed in the covert glances of those who slyly served them. At times, these silences were interrupted by an audible chuckle. There were tensions and unfinished conversations stumbled upon in the pantry, as topics, assuming the commonplace, became obviously forced and false.

"Yes mistress, no mistress."

To bob a curtsy and to flee.

Yet, she was attracted to the English administrators and the officers attached to the garrison. One she had met previously during her grandfather's time in the City of London. She danced with him at Government House. She danced for them in the privacy of a secluded house that had been converted into an officers' club. It was good, she told Philippe, to be in favour with the future. There were men there who would see him well placed in that new dispensation. She would make sure that in the event that England kept Grenada, they would have a place. Indeed, Philippe received a seat in the new Legislative Council. The price? She assured him, it was no skin off her back.

7: THE SURVEYORS

1777

He was aboard a swift windjammer out of Bequia. The equatorial current, chased by a stiff following breeze, poured like the wind through the Galleons Passage, as the *Stella Maris* sliced the morning air.

Racing along the high cliffs of Trinidad's northern coast the world appeared a bowl of light. To port, sea-mist was rising in the sunlit air. Surf, bright-white, boomed in black caves with gargoyle faces. Tall, thick green wood, springing directly from the water's edge, climbed high to become one with a blue mountain chain, receding eastward. He had gazed upon it from afar since boyhood, imagining a naked girl called Calypso running through the forest. To starboard was the far horizon of the Caribbean Sea as it rose and fell, following with every rushing swell. His spirits soared. He stood bare-chested on the bowsprit and imagined himself as the harbinger of another future. Easterlies at noon embroiled the rolling waves, humming in the halyards and bellying out her snapping canvas.

He smiled and turned his face upward to catch the warming sunlight. Around him, the emerald sea brightened into a greener green, decorated by trails of clean lacy whitecaps.

A yellow haze appeared by late afternoon, a page in his life's story had turned. He believed himself to be empowered by the towering mountains of Venezuela's Paria peninsula, seen through the mist. I shall renew my family's fortunes. I shall make my fortune here.

The skipper signalled a change of tack and, coming about, the *Stella Maris* plunged through the narrow strait of the First Boca, sending shoals of iridescent carite leaping. The salt spray brought the aroma of fresh water and of the mammalian life of the Gulf of Paria. She slipped quickly past the shadow of Monos Island and away from Madame Teteron's lonely tooth to enter the wide gulf where, carried gently in the lighter air of a lingering sunset, she heaved to and dropped her anchor. After the turmoil of the day, he found the quiet expanse soothing. Beneath the gradually appearing stars, the schooner turned nervously with the remous, a curiosity for schools of nursing dolphins and copulating humpback whales.

He was to be met at the fisherman's hamlet, described on charts as Puerto d'España. This was set, he discovered the following morning, in a tangled mangrove and manchineel swamp, overlooked by giant ceiba pentandra. These flourished in an underbrush of head-high ferns, thorn bushes, and sea grape trees. The mangrove's smell reminded him that this place was given to epidemics. These had decimated the Spanish officials and hopeless planters who never numbered more than one or two score. Overhead, a vast congregation of high-flying vultures swirled in the rising heat. Calypso could never prosper here, he thought coming ashore at a rock-strewn estuary, looking about for the guide who, he had been assured, would be waiting.

Fascinated he listened in silence as Sarusima, grandson of the cacique Buchumar, the Carib guide and head porter who had been sent to receive him, related in a language invented by himself that his people called the area Coo-moo-cu-rapo, the place of the silk cotton trees. But to him, it was the dark green mangrove that dominated the muddy shore that defined the place, giving the appearance of a

7: THE SURVEYORS 1777

frontline where a contest raged, an antediluvian struggle between the far-reaching ocean and the stubborn land.

So unlike Grenada, this island appeared to him a place where the colonists, having reverted to savagery, survived, more or less, in a manner similar to the handful of abandoned Negroes who sat about the estuary in sphinx-like stupor. They were all ignored by the migratory tribal people, painted red and decorated with green and yellow parrot feathers. Going about in unabashed nudity, they appeared to move with certainty within a reality entirely of their own imagining. He would learn from Sarusima that they disdained to speak to the foreigners, believing them to be evil apparitions. They adored the land tortoises, called morocoys, the savage imparted, to which they whispered charms of banishment in the hope that they would lead the strangers away into the interior, where there were volcanoes of boiling mud to swallow them.

Mountains covered with imperishable wood surrounded the outpost. High up in the towering growth, he saw cascades gushing as they took the mountain trail. A profusion of grotesque orchids bloomed in mossy pockets of rot. Fiery flora appeared, to decay in a day, leaving a perfume that oozed into his dreams. In the evenings, giant sloths moved with an indescribable leisure amongst fluorescent blooms that appeared to come alive and take flight against sunsets, made ghastly with a screaming, squawking onrush of flocks of macaws, miniature parrots, and hundreds of thousands of scarlet ibis, whose flight, in such quantities, gave the impression that the tender gloaming was terribly bruised and bleeding.

PHILIPPE ROUME, Juan de Catilla and Augustin Cramé ascended El Cerro El Tucuche in the driving rain of an August morning and attained the high plateau by mid-day. They had taken the Carib footpath from the hacienda owned by Don Pedro de Le Zama at the base of the mountain's southern flank. By mid-afternoon the sky suddenly cleared, just in time for them to see the island displayed in sunlight. In the far distance, clear all the way towards the south, a vast landscape presented itself. An open plain, with savannahs to south and to the east, an undulating land covered by high woods above which a pale mist shimmered. They could make out lagoons and swamps, crossed by rivers. A virgin land. Roume, standing to one side of the others, experienced a deep sense of predestination. Could this be it, really? The promised land, dedicated to the Holy Trinity by the High Admiral of the Ocean Sea almost three hundred years ago. Untouched. Almost uninhabited. To his relief, he found himself happy to be rid of the dismay at the loss of his family's estates and the morbidity of mourning the end of his life. He could live again, here.

Brigadier Cramé, a tall Castilian with an eagle's visage, the expedition's surveyor, joined him at the precipice. The preparation of accurate maps of the Viceroyalty of New Granada was his assignment. He had, as the result of lying on the wet grass, dozens of tiny frogs, speckled gold and red, clinging to his beard and long hair, and to his coat and trousers.

"My dear Cramé, you are covered in golden frogs! It must be your destiny," laughed the youthful de Catilla, taking the telescope from his eye and passing it to Roume. "See, look to the south, there, is that a mesa?" As he took it, his fingers trembled, it was cold on the mountain. He glanced at Cramé, but he knew that it was his heart that had been moved by the wonder of seeing his boyhood dream, his lovely Calypso, laid out before him.

"Yes, there are two, perhaps three," said Cramé, the miniature frogs leaping in all directions. "Flat-topped mountains, tepuy, as they are called. One to the east, there, called Tamana, and that one, almost on the coast, Naparima. On the main, there are several that are known as 'houses of the gods' by the natives who consider them sacred places."

7: THE SURVEYORS 1777

"In the distance, southwards, another range of mountains may be seen. It is a fair land," enthused de Catilla. "Those valleys beneath us are fertile, they will yield aplenty. They are valuable beyond imagining with hardwood timber, but I believe that the greatest value in the development of this island is that, over there." He was pointing to the south and west where a very wide expanse of water filled the entire horizon. "The Gulf of Paria, almost landlocked and beneath the wind. It could harbour the fleets of the world. A commercial and maritime centre capable of attracting trade from Panama to the Amazon and beyond. And there is pitch at Brea to caulk all those ships. An industry in ship-building could commence, the timber is all around. See there, Roume, can you see the slip-ways and the new and burgeoning towns?"

"There must be fortifications on those mountains to the north. We must protect all this future wealth from the English raiders," said Brigadier Cramé. "32 pounders en babette," he chuckled, lifting his hands to his eye and sighting, measuring the angle of elevation, using an imaginary gunner's quadrant.

The wind had picked up again and already the rain was coming down through the mists in large cold drops. "See the city, Juan, Augustino, see the shining city by the sea, teeming with people!" exclaimed Philippe enthusiastically, it must be the altitude, he thought, laughing loudly. "See the avenues, its boulevards. And windmills too. Machines. There. And there."

"Come, you visionaries, get out of the rain, enjoy this snug hacienda. There will be roast beef, and I hear venison as well, for supper, all served by dancing gypsies," called de Catilla from the palm leaf-covered lean-to that their Carib guides had constructed close to a sputtering fire upon which an unknown creature was being turned by a near-naked woman, painted red, with blue and yellow feathers in her hair.

That night, as they lay in hammocks just barely protected from a torrential downpour, Juan de Catilla and the Brigadier, much impressed with Roume's passion and vision of the island's prospects encouraged him to put pen to paper.

"Write a report, Philippe, address it to me. Make it as detailed as it may be. Tell me your ideas, what you see as possible. I shall put it into the right hands in Caracas," de Catilla suggested.

Roume was heartened, his dread of the future much reduced by what he had seen of this Trinidad, the rich condition of the soil, those smiling valleys, windy and cool. Healthy. He had made inquiries from the natives that he met. "No," they said, "we do not have those ants here," they told him, "this is not like Grenada. We have big ant-eaters, tall as a man, they take care of those little fellows."

Returning to the colony's capital, San José de Oruña, he regaled the governor, Don Manuel Falquez, and his ferocious-appearing doña with the details of his journeys across the island, and that very day, he commandeered Falquez's desk to write the first draft of his report.

That evening, in the governor's ajoupa palace, next door to the perpetually melting daub and wattle-walled church that Sir Walter Raleigh had not burnt to the ground in 1597, the fifteen or twenty residents of the island's ancient capital listened in boredom and dismay to his excited talk of colonisation and development.

"I shall take as my own, three hundred acres in that large valley to the west. It is now in the possession of Don Diego Martino," said Roume eagerly. "I have spoken to him, he is in agreement." He laid aside a map showing the location of the Martino property, which he had roughed out in charcoal on the back of the parchment that declared his permission to travel in this Spanish territory.

"But does he own it?" tittered the governor's wife. She, an Andalusian heiress in her own right with medieval features and a husky voice, was wearing Chibcha emeralds set in Inca gold.

"It is unclear what he owns," remarked Falquez, refilling his own and Roume's goblet. "If you listen to these long-time residents, they own every inch of this island."

7: THE SURVEYORS 1777

"Do not discount that too readily, your Excellency," said the youthful José Farfan. "We have been here for a long time and have had to move about this island, from valley to valley, much in the same manner that the Caribs have done from since Adam was a lad."

"I could offer to you something close to the redoubt, on the port," remarked Alexandro Díez, "bounded by the Tragarete river, which for half the year is dry. It is partly planted in tobacco, with a fine house."

"Fine house, my eye," sniggered Farfan. "It has a graveyard on it! Don't touch it, my friend, the ghouls come out at six sharp along with the malarial vapours."

"Come and see what we have to offer in the Ariapita valley," chortled Le Zama.

"Ah, but do you own it?" shouted the company.

Roume's first visit to Trinidad lasted several months; it fired his imagination and invigorated governor Don Manuel Falquez, who had been pleased to entertain a person with such vision and diverting imagination. For Philippe Roume, his visions, in the opalescence of rummy evenings, projected on the giant forest trees, were already accomplished. He could see the ships off-loading their cargoes in the estuaries; he could hear the rumble of hogsheads on the imagined hard-wood wharf, and the tinkle of doubloons and Louis d'Or glittering in Trinidad's sunlit mornings.

Before parting, Don Juan and the Brigadier, with the governor's compliance, again extended to Roume an invitation to return to Trinidad. Coming ashore in a Grenada that no longer held for him a doom foretold, he reported to Everard de Barras what he had seen of Trinidad. The officers of the Spanish navy, he told him, were so impressed that they had suggested a memorandum so as to summarise a plan for colonising this beautiful island, pledging their support.

Juan de Catilla had assured him that Don José de Gálvez was the right official to address. Gálvez would understand the value of such a proposition to his own career, particularly the notion of experienced French planters settling Trinidad, bearing in mind Spain's lack of manpower in her provinces, and the urgent need to populate the island and arm it in face of an almost certain English attack on the only island that lay beneath the wind.

Reading from my Memoirs at La Fontenoy, Grenada, 1806

MARIANNE BECOMES SOUBISE ROCHARD. As a child growing up the wind simply blew. Where does it go when it blows, I wondered. Papa-oncle Felicien came to mind and I had to smile, as I looked at Manon asleep on the carpet at my feet. Although reduced in the rind of memory to the faintest fragrance, I could still see his old face. How his smile would emerge from its folds.

I wrote this entry describing him while we were in Tobago in November of 1787. I pictured him then, how he sighed as he walked. He was a *parrain*—a godfather, so to speak—to the newly arrived slaves who, in secret, he taught the manners needed to stay alive. Old, completely grey and neglected by the overseer, he was no longer allotted tasks. Papa-oncle Felicien was my main source of inspiration. He shuffled about, to be seen asleep by that pillar or even faster asleep against that post, or walking along the beach trailed by his instantly vanishing foot-prints as he attempted to follow the remains of the frothy half circles left behind by the beached foam. Sometimes I would join him on these windy walks. One morning I asked him:

"Where does the wind go, eh, Papa-oncle Felicien?" Without hesitation he answered, "Into the blue, moi chè."

I loved Papa-oncle Felicien, how he smelled of old tobacco, and often held his hand, it felt like holding a big plank of wood. To follow his meandering stroll that marked the extremities achieved by the thoughtless waves, was an outing that I enjoyed.

7: THE SURVEYORS 1777

"Chè cocott," he said to me one morning, and this made me very happy. "Chè cocott, what dey does call you?"

I immediately answered, "Dey does call me Marianne, Papa-oncle Felicien."

I looked into his face, looking down at me. His ancient eyes, large and round, reflected the distant sea's horizon and sky around us. The world in two globes. My head revolved.

"I am Soubise Rochard," I told him.

"Bon," he said, not uttering another word.

I remembered the way he looked, as he sat in the corner under two boulas and a gran tambour hanging from the rafters of his hut. From inside his shirt, he had taken a tiny drum and a little baguette, like a laylay-stick, with which he began to tap it. Offbeat to begin, then quickening into a skipping, tripping, happy-sounding rhythm, the words of which came to him as if by chance from a distance, at first in a raspy whisper and then, in the sweet low melodious voice of his youth. He sang:

Papa Llegba, ouvri barrier po'moin aogo ye

Azima Llegba uuvri barrier po'moin

ouvri barrier po'moin aogo - ye - e . . .

I sat and watched and listened from a shadow, and, all of a sudden, I realised that a strange and wonderful thing was taking place. Papa-oncle Felicien, notwithstanding his grey hair, grew young before my eyes! He straightened his body, looked upward and smiled, and to my amazed delight became tall and slim and shiny. His face, beaming, unlined now, was aglow as he smiled and sang and whispered to Atibo Llegba so as to remove the barrier that he may pass, so that when he would come back, he would salute the loas and thank the loa Ayibobo.

It was on a windy afternoon, as I approached the front steps of Château Soubise, that I realised that there were two of me,

Marianne and Soubise. Pretending that I was someone else, I was ready to run away, as one small foot went before the other, I was prepared to say, pointing, if asked where I was going, that it was *her* shadow that *she* was chasing, being afraid that if *she* lost it, *she* mightn't find it again, being so close to nightfall.

Mallie had her back turned. I saw us both, as we walked right through her reflection in the big mirror with the gold-leaf frame. No shadows showed in there.

"Aiè! chè, bò doudoux!
Doudoux ba ou poule-épi-diri;
Aiè! chè, bò doudoux!"

Rice and chicken, and kisses too! Because he had let me come into the wide gallery that very evening and stand by his chair, I had the run of the place. Mallie said that I was ten. In the mornings I was always there, early. As he took his petit déjeuner à la fourchette, he would absentmindedly reach over and put his arm around my little waist as I stood there in my tattered, religiously patched, spotless white dress that smelled like sea breeze. It showed up my golden-red skin, orange eyebrows, jet-black eyes, and hair. This all served to complement my narrow, round, high, furry forehead, turned up nose and oddly shaped lips that reminded him of his sister's daughter, or his sister herself, when they were young.

I ate out of his hand, out of his plate, so that he could not help but see me as his child, his daughter, his only family in Grenada. That was when the wind found out, and took it everywhere. No one ever treated me as a slave born to labour, born to suffer, chained to Soubise estate; I was Soubise Rochard.

I took to running on the tips of my toes, taking flying leaps to leave my shadow behind. I don't remember now, but I might have thought of it as belonging to Marianne, whom I wanted to leave behind. It didn't work; as I landed, we were stuck together again. Looking over my shoulder, I even saw her jump in beside me as I leapt into my bed.

7: THE SURVEYORS 1777

Everybody could see us, on an afternoon, after he had listened to the overseer, cuffed his domestics, signed the papers that the attorney had brought, and informed the cook what he, we, wanted to eat that night, as we walked out into the bronze light of the lengthening penumbra, the sea booming, the fishermen, in rows along the shore as they hauled in the vast semicircles of net, and, without saying a word, enjoy the breezy distances described in the spectacle of dry season sunsets.

I learned haphazardly to be familiar with the books he left behind in the wake of his loneliness. These I took in curiosity to him, convinced of their magic, and I would ask him to talk to them, as I had seen and heard him do, and he would read to me from them. I felt certain that books talked back to their readers in secret, and spent a lot of time on his big bed with several books open in front of me, speaking encouragingly to them and listening intently. Perhaps they only spoke French and could not comprehend Creole Patois? You see why I had to learn to speak good French.

"AAAA, BEEE, CEEE," that's how it went actually, and because I was well good for myself, I put it together, interjecting words of my own invention with such sincerity in their pronunciation that the listener believed that these words were in truth foreign, and that I was bilingual. To maintain attention I developed a sense of drama. I could mimic everyone and could be seen by all in my white tattered dress, putting on performances for him in the torpor of Sunday afternoons, in which the actions and behaviour of people on the estate could easily be discerned in pantomimes mimed to perfection that made not only him laugh to the point of tears, but also the sanctimonious Curé, Timothy Peissonier O.P. and the disdainful commandant of the Quarter, the gallant Chevalier de la Tocnaye. Not to mention the domestics, who told everybody that the little chabine girl had taken over Château Soubise. That was the year I shot up.

I stayed with Mallie in the stone-floored kitchen that was connected to the main house by a covered passage. I shelled peas, peeled provisions, stirred this pot, that pot. Mallie, whose intelligence verged on clairvoyance, was tall and as black as coal. She had a completely round, bald shiny head, and was covered with a labyrinth of tiny wrinkles from head to foot. "This is how you do this, girl, not like that, take it for you fadder," she said, her eyes as bright as a child's, her teeth, long and perfect, the colour of old ivory. The silver tray held his coffee.

The estate house, which was called a château, was large, two-storeyed, washed with white-lime on the outside and completely unpainted on the inside. It was built of cedar wood and furnished with French-crafted mahogany in various styles. One met a dining table with fearsome brass castors, surrounded by eight unfriendly chairs; passed melancholy sideboards, glimpsed into the tall, gold-leaf-framed, ever-patient mirrors, and explored the contents of iron-bound chests that surely held the sandy secrets of long expired explorers while admiring the chiffoniers, and dreamt in beds with turned, carved and spiralled posts. There were miniature altars covered with blue sateen and a lace cloth with a wide valance, holding votive lights, statues of saints, small bottles of holy water and a padded prie-dieu.

Everywhere, silver plate reflected wealth, and at night, the candle's flame caught and brought to life the melancholy eyes of ancestors long dead on other islands. Every morning we sat at a furious-appearing desk where I practiced drawing letters.

I remember paying a lot of attention to my reflection in the big mirror with the gold frame. It hung on a wall in the long room. There was me and me. Different me's. The me who had so many words for everything in her mind, and the me who could barely mumble dis, dat an' d'oder. I understood that as a difference. I kept an eye out for differences.

7: THE SURVEYORS 1777

One day I kissed myself in the mirror; it made me feel so alone that I never risked that again. Then I found a small hand mirror in an ornate silver frame in the closed up little room next to his. I took it to him.

"Can I have this, please?"

"Where did you find that?"

"Upstairs."

He looked at me long, I looked back; we looked at one another, long.

"All right, but do not touch anything in there again."

"All right," and for the first time, "thank you, Papa."

I saw him suffocating. He looked away, I looked away, I lingered, he caught the smell of my sea-breeze smelling white dress that was so small for me now that he told somebody to get some clothes for me, which they did. I got dresses that smelled of the cedar chest and some unbelievable underwear. Mallie started to arrange my hair on a morning, combing it out and plaiting it in an imaginative style, away from and around my narrow face. This showed up my bright fine features. Mallie did not tie it in kalendé; I grew up in a hat and with a bonnet.

I was hiding from my shadow one day in the closed-up little room, thinking that my toes were my mother's and my hands were his. I was divided between them. Me and me. I never saw them together. I saw my mother only sometimes in the house, where she behaved like the house slave, YaYa, and where she knew her place, which was in the back. This was when she was not upstairs with him. Only he called her Geneviève. I went everywhere, upstairs downstairs, meme bagai. I told people that my name was Soubise Rochard.

I also saw my mother en fête. As when my father as Maître Rochard had visitors from other plantations. Then my mother and other women as filles de joie, noted for their well-formed breasts and their lively spirits, would bathe at the river's mouth, salt and fresh, while drinking rum, laughing, splashing each other, shouting bad remarks, and then dressing themselves up in bright cotton jupé, plaid madras and foulard. They would climb the hill, singing, to the château to spend a night, a day, or even a week of carousing and having jolly times. On one such night of nights, I saw the captain of the mill, Wabo, the husband of Elisa from Balthazar, standing in the milk-white moonlight listening to Elisa's delirious howls. She was carousing and being jolly. Well the next month, a big mahogany branch hit Jean Babonneau, the overseer from Balthazar, who was supervising the clearing of a field, and killed him dead. Then Elisa take in with a belly working that almost killed her.

"Wabo is a bad nigger now," Mallie told me. "He Massa watch him good. De day he cuss the new overseer, Mr. Ross, he Massa order three hundred stripes, it skin him from shoulder bone to knee. He screamed like a woman. He Massa dash pimentade, with brine, pimentos and lemons into the gashes, Mallie said that was a remedy against gangrene. They put him in irons and make Samson hold him down and order Congo Ahab, un nègre de la Côte, to shit in his mouth. Then Wabo ran away. He is marooned now. A real bad egg. Oui."

The house training continued. "Clean your teet with this, girl," I was told. "Bite the end, bite it till it's a brush and rub it, rub it good on all your teet."

"Urrg, that stick taste bad."

"Yes, but you is to be a lady now, so you must have nice white teet. You must smell nice. Crush up basil leaves and thyme leaves, crush them, crush them, now, pass them under your armpit when you finish bathe, bathe in basil water, don't forget. When last you bathe? Eh? Ou ka paka behé."

I learned to cook. The house filled with the aromas of fabulous meals. Mallie taught me to mend, to sew. She tried me out with

7: THE SURVEYORS 1777

the red hot congo irons; that was a disaster for the clothes. I could make up the beds, lay the table, flowers, silver, plates, napkins, everything. I liked that, to make everything neat. I would polish the heavy silverware and napkin rings. And there was church. The Curé, Père Peissonier, took a personal interest in an unsuccessful attempt to purge my mind of my mother's saints. These had come from Ti Guinea with the original ones transferred to these islands in chains or carried by the wind across the rolling sea. Impossible, I knew that. I did what they all do. I joined the two. Holy Mary, Ezulie, La Sirène Yemanja, full of grace, the Lord is with thee, blessed art thou amongst women and blessed is the fruit of thy womb, Shango. I explained it to her, that is, myself. That it was all the same transcendent beauty, the woman that you yearned to express, that you knew you were sometimes, often, even when. . .

I made my First Communion, I loved the dress. My first pair of shoes. He would call me to serve him at the table. After which I would have to come in and sit up straight and eat, nicely. He taught me everything. He taught me to write my name, and laughed out loud when, after a great deal of spilt ink, he realised that all I wanted to write was Soubise Rochard in big slanting letters. All the dresses in the double armoire in the little room became mine.

8: BERTRAND DE CHARRAS
1779

He left Grenada with the rank of Lieutenant de Vaisseau as these events were unfolding. Bertrand de Charras was on his way to the Académie de Marine at Brest. There he would take command of the 16-gun corvette *L'Aurore*. This would mark the entry of France into the American War of Independence in 1778.

He returned to Grenada from the American wars a year later, covered in glory. In fact he arrived with the fleet of Comte d'Estaing in 1779, serving with a regiment of grenadiers under the command of Comte Arthur Dillon. He was a part of the invading force that defeated the English and returned Grenada to France. He was not unduly perturbed to discover that ruin had overtaken the Roume family. He had already spent his share of the arrangement made with André Fatio. Bertrand's obsession with Fanny had only deepened. Bertrand wanted her, she could tell; she imagined herself taking him half undressed and bathed in sweat. For Philippe and herself, however, everything changed with the reconquest of the island by the French forces. It was then that she became reckless about her affair with Bertrand.

8: BERTRAND DE CHARRAS 1779

SUCH MATTERS FLOWED in time; she longed for her own island. To be engaged once more in the capriciousness, the volatility of cosmopolitan life. Paris in summer. Her grandfather's world at Île de Ré. A world that Bertrand, enveloped by fresh sea air, brought with him on returning from the American wars. It came with the stamp of his boots, the rattle of his sabre, his superciliousness, his hypocrisy and unabashed lust.

She had married this man, Philippe Roume de Saint Laurent, in the springtime of her life, so rationally as a fanciful arrangement providing security along with adventure and travel. But the arrangement had unexpectedly become far more binding than a wedding ring. She failed to realise that she could not live with Philippe Roume without loving him.

Yet, she could not imagine living for the rest of her life in Grenada. The planters' compulsion to terrorise their slaves terrified her. Her fascination with the slave trade had passed. She saw them as ugly and stupid, as dangerous and unpredictable as the earthquakes.

After she had one of the domestics flogged, the one that resembled him most, Philippe had railed at her in a fit of anger, accusing her of adultery. She told him, with the bitterness of dismay, that she found her ability to sleep with him after he had taken that one, no doubt his grandfather's daughter, standing in the stables, before coming in for dinner, reeking of the mingled smell of horse sweat and her armpits, was the indication of her own tragic decline. That he took, when it pleased him, any of the willing, or unwilling, women on the estates, and then came to her, overwhelmed her with revulsion. The very idea of his intimacy with them was unimaginably repugnant. Their smell, their grotesque physiognomy, their coarseness, their gross hair, did he actually touch it?

"Do you kiss it? What an opéra comique."

He answered her shouting, she thought that he would strike her, that to be master here, first the women must be mounted like pawing horses in heat and made subservient. You had to cover them, conquer them and breed them, otherwise they would walk all over you. In the estate yard, there was the branding iron, the whip, the bloodhounds: these were the physical manifestations of dominance. For supremacy to be complete, the black woman, whose hysteria reshaped the submissive mind of black men, must be made subservient, docile, then rewarded with progeny. That his grandfather's daughter was his to do whatever he pleased with. That his grandfather's daughter ruled the women in the house and in the yard and that she was the final barrier that guarded them against the poisoned cup, the graveyard dirt, the mapepire zanana in your bed or the tarantula in your shoe. Yes, *they* had to see that *he* favoured *her* so that *she* would have power over *them*.

"You fear them! You coward!"

This was when he struck her hard across the face, sending her sprawling to the bedroom floor. Their lives had now entered separate trajectories. She could not stand the way he smelt, or help but find herself debased. She knew that she was abandoned, marooned. She grew to despise all these people. Oh, the idiocy of Philippe's mother, her absurd pretensions. Such a foolish woman to have married a person like Bertrand. And then to be defrauded by André Fatio, her grandfather's creature, whom she had seen oozing charm from every pore, oil his way into Rosa's life and into her bed. After the death of the old Chevalier de la Chancellerie they all appeared to have been cut adrift from reason.

In the lonely vastness of Belvédère she had been drawn increasingly to her former paramour. A diversion at first, in pursuit of companionship that was shaped by a common nostalgia and in the afternoon's humidity, by boredom. She did not think twice about resuming their relationship and remembered that she was impervious to guilt. She was now more woman than Bertrand could imagine, than Philippe would ever know again. She could wear them out. The consequences of all this she did not care to

8: BERTRAND DE CHARRAS 1779

confront. She took Philippe after Bertrand, he fresh from the stable, their respective odours rising against Belvédère's deep green sateen-covered walls. Her assignations led to more violent confrontations with her husband. She saw clearly how André Fatio and Bertrand had destroyed the family. She would return to France with Bertrand. Too many of her babies had died. That she could die here herself, alone, this haunted her unceasingly.

THE NEWS THAT CONFIRMED BERTRAND'S DEATH washed over Fanny, leaving her body rigid with grief. Incapable of speech, she stepped out of it and fled, a different model of herself, into the vast remoteness of Belvédère, to hide from Philippe Roume in its cobwebs, to become lost in the mildewed gloom of its ancient recesses, and to grow familiar with this new self and, in so doing, arrange to leave this ghastly place.

HIS MIND, AS HE strode briskly through Belvédère's fern-shaded verandah, was agitated by the imagined smell of gunpowder. The dead man's look of surprised disdain had stayed with him, along with that smell, ever since the morning when he had shot and killed Bertrand de Charras.

De Charras had to die, Philippe thought, as he crossed the billiard room. He had wronged his family, injured him personally and financially. There could not be any other outcome. He had sent Maurice de Pradine, as his second, to call on Bertrand de Charras. As the challenged party, it was Bertrand's right to choose the weapons; he selected pistols. Philippe had thought of harpoons himself.

Their meeting gave rise to the myth that Bertrand de Charras had sailed from Grenada aboard a frigate that carried his sailing orders and was never heard of again, vanishing in the cannon smoke of an unspecified naval encounter. In truth, his bones were unearthed from its shallow grave by feral dogs that had dug much deeper trenches in search of leather-back turtle eggs.

That it was the end of their marriage, he accepted philosophically. Neither he nor Fanny were the same people who had chased rainstorms across Île de Ré.

De Charras was the first Frenchman whom he had killed. The black lives he had taken were of no account. His feelings had to do, he rationalised, with weighing this lingering sense of guilt against the knowledge of the sin of taking a life. It returned him to the religious instructions of his childhood, those through which he had daydreamed his way. Sin was the act of contravening God's will. Killing was a crime. He came to the conclusion that he had violated a moral standard to which he subscribed and that he would prefer to deal with guilt rather than with sin. *Prohairesis*, it was his moral choice that Bertrand de Charras should die. In truth, he knew that it had only to do with jealousy, which was nine points of revenge. Returning to Grenada from Petite Mustique, where they had met, Philippe Roume discovered that Fanny had left for Trinidad. He hated the idea. Trinidad was his, what the hell was she doing there.

9: THE INTERLOPER
BALTHAZAR ESTATE, 1780

EVERARD DE BARRAS WAS well into his eighties, yet he walked erect and had most of his teeth; although it had occurred to him that he was a man from another time. He wished that he, too could be setting out for Spanish Trinidad. His thin hands trembled just a little as he drew towards him the bundle of papers to which he must now give his attention.

His elder brother had died at Fox-Amphoux. Matters concerning his interest in the Grenada plantations had to be settled with his nephew Paul, the new vicomte de Barras, who had entered the regiment of Languedoc as a cadet gentilhomme and who would need the income from the plantations for the upkeep of his military rank and the maintenance of his new status.

Sitting back in a chair that had crossed the Atlantic more than sixty years before, he sighed. The twilight of his life appeared to mingle with the melancholy hour. Turning, he watched Philippe, with whom he had spent the afternoon, from his window. He has the steady stride of the traveller, he thought to himself. Further on, beyond the garden wall, in the high branches of an almond tree, he could glimpse the long, thin legs of another young man, his son Stanislaus, who held a sense of grievance, a grievance that he understood. It was shared by many in Grenada. It had been made especially poignant in the wake of the English conquest of their island.

"I want to join," had been his earliest remembered words. "Join what?" his exasperated mother would ask.

He did not have the words; inwardly he hungered to be recognised, to be acknowledged, accepted, praised, comforted, scolded, even beaten, in the give and take of everyday familial discords, reconciliations and farewells that promise fidelity, in sickness and in death.

Philippe Roume was hardly disturbed by the boy's exclusion from the affairs of the de Barras household. He knew that Everard de Barras had acknowledged Stanislaus as his son and that he sent money to his mother. A short, slim roll of small silver coins wrapped in brown paper arrived from time to time to ensure that Stanislaus received clothes and schooling from Mr. Nesbit, the Englishman who ran a school for boys at Grenville. The neat wooden house on the estate ensured that the boy's mother was not dishonoured by indigence, nor disrespected beyond her condition.

As he neared the estate's stables, the groom already rushing forward with the rein, he asked himself, why this indifference for the other, imported from another place, now rooted in this, the New World? Why this poisoned fruit that robs us of all compassion? Of the Free Coloured people, he once said to de Barras, "They are the fruit of our passions," obviously not thinking of the older man's peccadilloes, one of which was presently hanging from the almond tree. "We seek only to satisfy our desires, they are the product of our brutality." And remembering the warmth of black girls with ramier's eyes, he added: "Even of a night of love."

But might they not, he thought to himself, as he turned his mount about and trotted towards the almond tree, those children of the night, be our redemption? Something, he could not remember what exactly, in his recent past had made him feel that his life was changing. He would lead this young man to a respected place in

9: THE INTERLOPER 1780

honest society. Stanislaus must be persuaded to leave his post in that tree by a gesture of benevolence. In an act that would exorcise—for this indignant, resentful, rejected one—the pain of future years. He felt that he could taste the pleasure of helping Stanislaus, of consoling him; for in so doing he would surely enjoy the *summum bonum*. . . "the highest good."

Looking up he barely saw the convulsed features, the tears of rage running, his mother's lips curled in anger. He did not see the green almond fly from the sweaty hand, but felt it strike his eye in a blinding flash of pain. As the animal reared, he fell backwards, down and down, he heard the words screaming through the red and yellow leaves.

"I hate you, I hate you, Philippe Roume!"

Stanislaus leapt to the ground and ran towards the gate. From thence, he sprinted up the dusty road and into a track that meandered through a long abandoned cocoa field, to vanish into a copse of old immortelles, where he flung himself upon the ground.

He stayed the night. Shivering with dread, he heard the nightmare's haunting call of the jumbie bird. His mother found him the following morning and took him home to abuse him in advance of the expected retribution. Everard de Barras arrived.

The boy, stumbling ahead, was taken by his father for a walk in the direction of Balthazar's great house. They walked past the almond tree and crossed the lawn, towards the broad flagged stairs. They sat in the front room in silence. The man regarded his son. The son speechless with hysteria. And after silence his father explained that he was to be sent to France to learn a trade, he was to become a silver-smith, or perhaps even jeweller, so that when he became a man, he would be independent. Stanislaus de Barras said nothing; he couldn't have, even if he tried.

He left, eventually, the house that he had looked at since he was big enough to climb the tree. He walked past it towards the dirt road, to turn left and take the track that was a shortcut to Soubise estate. He knew he would find in the morning's heat, a tall, red-skinned girl, who would be washing clothes in the Grenville river near to a cocoa field, where tiger-striped butterflies danced with duplications of themselves in a never-ending rush of wind.

Reading from my Memoirs at La Fontenoy, Grenada, 1806

STANISLAUS DE BARRAS: THE BOY IN THE ALMOND TREE. "I am not a slave." He said that to me once, long ago. "My mother is a de Pradine, a free woman."

I was looking at the drawing that he had made of me when we were both fifteen, maybe sixteen. I had written, in what I thought to be a decorative script, beneath the drawing, Soubise Rochard. I knew that he was not a slave.

The sweat of the cocoa shed was on him. His black curls sticking to his face. You had to look good to see the nigger in him.

He was not the first to show me how he is make man either. Around us, the buzzy heat of the day, the numbing silence of the cocoa field, the disarray of pairs of tiger-striped butterflies dancing in the wind. My disarray. In my mad disarray, I had clenched his body between my legs, hooked together at the ankles, and stretched them, squeezing him hard. I heard him groan and felt him enter me more keenly as I drenched him with my passion. Then it was his disarray, he moaned and called up something from somewhere and shivered, his face reshaped to an innocence that I was never to forget. I saw this and joined him in complete disarray that took me away to a place that I would seek, without success, with others for its indescribable outside of self-ness.

I could not have comprehended a word I uttered, had I heard, because there were no words as yet for all this.

9: THE INTERLOPER 1780

"My joyous flesh."

"What?"

And so it began. Stanislaus de Barras. He, too, was an egg that had been laid in slavery's nightmare's nest.

The unfamiliar feeling of tenderness had caught him by the throat and caused a sense of betrayal of something he could not name. His disarray had disturbed him, he forgot himself, becoming disarmed, and now there was nothing. I was laughing. Yes, at him.

"You're a stupid, red, chabine slave."

I jumped to my feet and cuffed him hard in the stomach. He doubled over, his face twisted, breathless, one hand pressed against his body while the other tried to grab me. I skipped away and stood there, leaves lifted by the wind blew about us, and watched him.

"I stupid? You stupid."

And with that said, I turned and ran through the fleeting shades of green and bright.

"That boy will put a baby in your belly, girl."

"What boy. Eh, who?"

"Stanislaus de Barras."

Mallie, she knew my every move.

STANISLAUS—I had always known him. A tall, thin boy, with a long face, a sad expression and negroid lips. He was a strange boy, full of sorrow and beauty. Something in his large brown eyes made him seem older than he was. There were times when he would come to me to show me his manhood; this excited me to the point of a dizzy breathlessness. He could be so desperate in his wanting me. He was the first man to reveal his true feelings. I would refuse to allow my flesh to stutter out a yes. But then I would storm his mouth, lay siege to his face, neck and chest, his belly and his beast.

After, we would find ourselves in a nest of leaves, fanning one another with the pieces of clothes that we had ripped off. I would open the nibbled fingers of his clenched hand, to pick at the dirt permanently embedded in his heart and mind lines. In his exhausted sleep, the rich odour of his perspiration, mixed in with that of the cocoa shed, aroused me. I would wake him, watching his wrinkled dreams depart, and I would see him see me.

He wished that he could go into another life with his dreams. He needed not say that, his defenceless face alone was sufficient. I knew everything. I understood, to the extent that I could feel my entrails stir. I could become crazed with his sadness. He would enter me again. Then, afterwards, our ability to speak would come dribbling back. His devastated world had intruded into my own hallucinogenic one, which was unequally divided between me and her.

Stanislaus once told me that from the time he remembered himself, he was conscious of Philippe Roume, who was much older than he. He saw him received in his father's house at Balthazar estate, become his father's ward, be where he could no longer set foot. He wished and yearned to go inside. How he longed to see inside that house again, to see his baby brother, his baby sister.

As a boy, and well into his adolescence, he could be seen up in a big almond tree all through the long dry-season days, sitting in the high branches, looking into the de Barras house on Balthazar estate. He was like me, a child of the estate. But he was a yard fowl.

Always barefoot, outgrowing his small boy's clothes, staring at the house, looking to see them, or at the gate, lurking, to see them pass, they never chased him away. He would intrude and boldly walk through their Sunday afternoon garden party, just for them to see him, hoping for them to call him over, just once, for a piece of yellow sugar coated sponge cake. They never did. It was as though he was not there. He must have thought about Philippe Roume a lot. There was a time, he once said, when he sincerely believed that he was his brother.

9: THE INTERLOPER 1780

Azelia Pradine, his mother, to whom Stanislaus always referred as de Pradine, replied, "Don't be a fool boy, you ent see that they don't want you? Stop going there every day. They will set the dogs on you."

But still he went, every day, to see his father, who hardly looked his way, and when he did, it was to tell him that it was time to go home. Philippe Roume was kind to him in an off-hand way, with a smile and a hello and an occasional treat.

He behaved like a good-looking, pass-for-white person as he became older, and grew into the type that they instinctively distrusted. But, on the other hand, he had something compelling and desperate, something that makes a person like me, who had been given to a devil, curious.

I was attracted to him because he was like a white boy, but wanting, so I gave him to me. 'Little Stanislaus, no one to love you, give yourself to me' was a song that I made up when I was in love with him, but I never sang that to him or told him that I felt sorry for him.

He changed. He became rough and angry and said that he hated them, and me. I knew what he meant. I didn't really hate them, but you see I could go inside Soubise estate house whenever I wanted to.

"THE MASTER WANTS to see you," said Mallie sternly, "he is lying down."

I was surprised to see my mother standing there next to the attorney, M'sieu Rosnay, who was sitting at my father's desk.

"To Guadeloupe?"

"Yes."

"When, oh, when?"

"At month's end."

And so it was arranged. My freedom and my mother's were to be given. Manumitted, we were no longer to be slaves. And to avoid having to pay the English government the £100 that this necessitated in Grenada, we were to go to Guadeloupe with Louis Rosnay.

Later, my father sent to call me to come to his bedroom. He gave me a book.

"It don't have anything in it, Papa, where have all the words gone?" I was shocked. I had never seen a book like this. It was completely blank.

"It is called a locus communis, a commonplace book. A journal or diary. For you to write your thoughts and observations in, for your… for *her* memories." He smiled.

He understood! It was for her, Soubise. A place to put all those words that blew about like leaves inside my wind-blown head. A book of memories, of course.

"Oh, thank you, Papa." I hugged him tight. That was how I received my first diary.

I took it for Stanislaus to see. Later on, he took it from me and, with a scrap of charcoal from his pocket, he sketched on the inside cover a line, a shape, and, with a nibbled finger, smudged them here and there, and I appeared.

"What you doing?"

"Making you more beautiful."

"Put it down. My mouth wants you inside it."

"Stretch out, be beautiful."

I told him that I was to go, leave Grenada, and go away to Guadeloupe. Even saying it to him seemed untrue. He just said, "All right," and nodded. I looked at him.

"Come close to me."

9: THE INTERLOPER 1780

I held his pale face up close, I felt his soft brown curls, I could see his skin as if magnified, so young. I needed his smell.

"I, too, am to be sent away."

"No, where to?"

"They said to France." It was unbelievable.

"To France? To do what?"

"I don't know."

He stood up, the afternoon sun blazing a halo about his head; he turned and walked away. Stanislaus de Barras was sent off to France to be trained as a silver-smith and to learn business.

I STAYED IN THE COCOA FIELD, sitting on a boulder in the river until the bird song faltered and the evening light began to fade. I picked up my book along with the washing and walked the long way home. Turning into the track that led to the kitchen, I saw that there were several carriages drawn up outside the front door. Curious as ever, I slipped inside. I shall never forget the day that I met him. Another one of those eggs laid in the nest of suffering. Like every egg, he was original, he had not happened before. But I had seen him everywhere. He was an egg of a different colour, a Massa egg, un oeuf maître. The sort of egg that I had been taught to curtsy before and say, "M'sieu Philippe."

He smiled and took my hand in his, my right hand, the one I kept in particular good repair, and, to everyone's amazement, in a motion that made my pounding blood rush to my head, he bowed, looked into my eyes, and kissed it. It went through me like the shock you get when you hit your elbow, you know, there! He smiled into my eyes. My mind went blank. To say I remembered what next, ha!

Philippe Rose Roume of Saint Laurent estate. I thought afterwards that everyone must have seen me so confused and speechless, but I did remember his clothes. A blue nankeen jacket, cream jean breeches, tall black boots, soft, with brown tops turned almost halfway down, a sea-island-cotton shirt, fine white lace, a funny little tan hat, never seen that hat before. This exciting friend of my father's would be entered and described in my new commonplace book, directly opposite to the charcoal drawing of me done by Stanislaus. His dark smiling eyes, black hair about his shoulders and a smell, just like the smell of that morning when I heard the sheets snapping in the wind. Looking back it was the beginning of time.

That was the week before we sailed for Guadeloupe. It was the day after my seventeenth birthday.

SON OF ASMODEUS. I had made a drawing of her, years ago in Guadeloupe while I was the Da for Captain Funillière's children. I looked at it closely.

"Who is that, Mama? Who is that old lady?" Manon, who had shot up, as they say, was as ever all questions.

"Oh, just an old lady that I used to know a very long time ago."

"Before I was born, Mama, eh, Mama?"

"Yes my darling, long before you were born."

"She frightens me, Mama."

"Yes darling, she could be frightening."

I hadn't seen this sketch in many years. I had enhanced it at Dondon in Saint-Domingue while I convalesced after Manon's birth. On that page, I had described how I had gone to see her, Tante Mam'zelle, just before I was sent to Guadeloupe.

Like a bird, I had landed on the window-sill and swung my legs inside the empty room. The front door had become difficult to

9: THE INTERLOPER 1780

open. The afternoon sun, slanting in, made my white dress shine. Like a soft whistle, I ascended the dangerous stairs and stood at her door, which was wide open. Inside, I could see Tante Mam'zelle, looking like a big old fish wrapped in a curtain. She appeared to be speaking to someone. Who? I listened. I could not hear a word. I moved to one side so as to see into the big looking-glass of her dressing table. All I could see was a rocking chair, it was rocking back and forth, back and forth, as though nodding, but no one was in it. Was it the wind? No, it had not followed me as it usually did. I stood at the door. Tante Mam'zelle looked at me and smiled a crazy smile, her bony ringed finger at her lips, "Shush," she whispered, and pointed at the rocking chair, "Eustache."

"Who?"

"Eustache Chartier, Sire de Lotbinière, my cousin, he is the keeper of the Royal Seals in Acadia. You better come back."

"Oui, merci, Tante Mam'zelle, Mam'zelle." And I curtsied low, as if before royalty, and rose and backed away. The rocking chair continued its back and forth nodding to Tante Mam'zelle, as if taking instructions. I tiptoed down the stair and flew out of the window.

The following day, I went back again, same as ever, through the window. This time, I heard real voices, loud, a man's, coming from upstairs. I could smell him, rum and horse sweat, man sweat. I could see them framed in the big dressing table mirror, like a huge moving picture.

"I want it now! It is mine!" shouted Julien Fédon. He was Tante Mam'zelle's grandson. Fédon was a dark-skinned man, with a long dog-like face, jutting teeth under a sparse moustache beneath which was his angry mouth. "Lancer is mine! I am planting it! Everything is changed! The English have gone; we are French once more. Now is the time. I must take this advantage. I want what is mine!" Rough talk, man talk, I knew that kind of talk; it was usually followed by blood.

Tante Mam'zelle, sitting up in her vast bed, was wrapped in the blue-black fur of some dead beast. "Not at all, fool! The English will return. You have nothing, only what I give to you."

"The estate is mine by right," he said. Tall and gaunt, almost as tall as the door, his whining voice, a misery to endure. "My father said so in your presence, do not deny it."

Tante Mam'zelle, her wrinkled face twisted with fury, her large isolated teeth demonstrating their startling resemblance. "My son was an idiot who said all sorts of stupid things in anyone's presence, he was a drunken fool who wasted everything."

"What else could he be! He was a bastard, born to you, mother of bastards, you wanted him to be what he could not be! Could never be in this blasted place!"

His angry voice, broken with anguish, produced hiccups and sobs, as his eyes filled with tears that overflowed to pour down his hard face, becoming lost in a straggly beard.

Tante Mam'zelle, flinging aside the black furry wrap to reveal a dress made of golden stuff, declared, a wizened finger pointing, "Pierre was my son. What passed between his father, Dieudonné Fédon, and me is my affair. I gave him life! I gave his sister life! He, an education in Paris! I gave him a trade to make a living. He was a bastard, yes, but he was a white man! He chose the barracoons! The niggers and your nigger mother, Brigitte Cavalan, to spite me! She, a Martiniquan witch! She put a wanga on him. Obeah! She and the Cavalans; obeah made him diseased and stupid. Oh yes, Brigitte Cavalan did not want him, or you, to have my name. My name! The Chartier de Lotbinière name. She wanted him and you, my grandson, and all the rest of you, to be Fédon, like your stupid, common father Pierre, old and foolish. Well, you became Fédon. And you are Julien Fédon, black, illiterate and cursed. There you are. There is nothing for you. General!" she called and was ringing her little bell. The black general appeared, resplendent in his gold wig and in full uniform with a musket, as if by magic, straight out from under the bed.

9: THE INTERLOPER 1780

Tante Mam'zelle, her ancient features venomous, one eye in one direction, the other lost somewhere in her head. "Get out, Julien, you shall get what you will get, when I give it to you."

The man hurled himself from the room, shoving me to the wall. I heard him wrench at the front door and heard it crash to the floor. Even then, I could recognise that Julien Fédon was yet another egg laid in the nightmare's nest.

I HAD HEARD Julien Fédon's anguish that day in Tante Mamzelle's bedroom. It was more than land that he wanted; he wanted her, his grandmother, to see him as the fruit of her womb. He knew what he was. But you see, he was limping, wounded in his manhood. He wanted her to see that, to sing 'petit po-po la pla dou-dou'. To look into the life that lived in his eyes, that was him, he, himself, not the shape of his nose, or the curl of his lips, or the texture of his hair.

All this had begun in a million other places. Secret places, ordinary places, dark places—such as the love-hate self-disgust of the mulatto bastard—that is a good place to look. Look, what you made in the belly of the virgin of the world. A child, a child born in the desolation of not being of this world. A new soul that came into a world that mixes up death with life in an ordinary way.

The hardships caused by the English moneylenders were also experienced by men of colour like Julien Fédon; this had made them desperate and as trapped as the slave population. With the sale of estates, the slave families were broken up. New owners, mostly the English, were afraid of them, so they were especially cruel. This was an old colony; we knew well the békés, the old French families, and they knew us. A great many of us were related, like me to the Rochards, or like Julien Fédon and Tante Mam'zelle, or Stanislaus de Barras and his father, all this going back for more than a hundred years. This little island was a cauldron, brimming with the intrigues of close relatives envying and hating each other. Now, war was becoming the answer.

ASMODEUS FILS; Julien Fédon's father, Pierre Fédon, received Lancer estate. Two French quarées, just over six acres. Tante Mam'zelle didn't give it to Julien. It went to her son, Julien's father. I could only imagine how this made Julien feel.

Mallie told me about them. She, Bathilde Chartier de Lotbinière, Tante Mam'zelle, Julien's granny, she it was who put him on this course.

"She was a bony woman-child once," Mallie said, drawing on her pipe, " and exhaling through her nose two identical columns of blue smoke.

Wide of mouth, thin yellow hair, surprising blue eyes, and a self-evading manner. As I would later describe her in my diary.

Tante Mam'zelle, ingénue, grew into a tall flat person and nobody noticed her. She had been taught to read and write French and English by an eccentric Scottish woman, who for reasons now forgotten had become her governess. They had, not by choice but by circumstance, left her alone. Some had died, others went to war and never returned. Had they been there, they would have sent her away to France or to Martinique to be married off. Failing that, a convent. There was no money for a dowry, but she had a name. Shy, she lived a dull, lonely life and, like La Digue estate, withered into peeling paint and faded prints and termite-eaten looks, with no one to talk to except the governess and the slaves, sharing a pipe of tobacco with cook on the back steps as the crickets sang their six o'clock in the evening song; until Dieudonné Fédon came from France to manage the estate.

Mallie was a child at La Digue before she came to us. She told me what she saw. I inscribed it years later as I imagined it, having

9: THE INTERLOPER 1780

experienced the desperation that drives hallucinogenic disorders myself. I have it here, I wrote it down. Here is what I saw. I saw Bathilde Chartier de Lotbinière assume the role of superintending manager, fore-manning the estate's affairs so that Dieudonné Fédon could come in, late or early, to report to her on everything that he was overseeing on that plantation that was not planting or reaping anything, except for the occasional sugar apples. These grew, by accident, in its more remote gullies.

"Be not afraid," she assured him, and sighed, the back of a thin transparent hand upon an even paler brow which was covered by a sheen of perspiration, "the isle is full of noises. Sounds and sweet airs that give delight and hurt not. Sometimes a thousand twangling instruments."

Dieudonné, never imagining the schooling she had received from her Scottish governess, or having heard of the bard, nor of his famed *The Tempest,* could not think of anything to say to that. He would sit awkwardly to eat the plate of food that she left out for him with a spoon. She, standing in the shadows of the silence left between the arriving boom and the withering sigh of the distant waves that caressed the great bay at Grenville, watching him.

Everybody knew everything, Mallie explained, relighting her pipe with a small piece of smouldering coal that she had picked up from the coal-pot with her thumb and forefinger.

Except them, as they entered the charmed circle of their own palpitating body heat. Bathilde Chartier's glance resounded like a bounced pew in an empty church, too loud, oh, bon dieu. His unworkable awkwardness. But he knew how she spent her day. Her invisibility at dusk, complete, except for the rustle of her anxious expectation. He knew she would take his empty plate, still warm, to the tub and wash it. He had seen her do this, from outside.

They, the slaves, had seen him, Dieudonné Fédon, seeing her, Bathilde, through the half light that the moon left behind, from the barrack yard, giggling, falling over themselves, slapping each other, tears of mirth bursting from their anguished eyes, dampening their aprons, their head rags unravelling, their one daily joy, her confusion. Mallie said that they saw her go through all the stages of her womanhood in one year, from maiden to nubile woman, to harlot, to mother. I had only known her as a hag. But it was, she said, the transition from maiden to harlot that was astonishing. To see a white woman in heat.

They would see him dawdle, gilded by the four o'clock sun, playing for time, his only possession. She, her eyes timid and indulgent, her turmoil a growing obsession. You see, he was just a common man, of peasant stock. She came from the race of the Frankish conquering aristocracy, and he had taken her unawares.

After a month or so, she saw herself as corrupted. A woman changed not by sin, the sin of fornication, but altered instead by the contamination of the habit of extremis, as her imagination was now dedicated to exteriorising fantasies embedded there from childhood. She played the role of reluctant harridan, compelled to punish him for misdemeanours occasioned in moments suspected, when she, caught in the spasms of lust, or even in the languor of subsidence that follows the earth-quaking climax, saw herself like a common peasant in the dirt. Like him. For this sin, she would hide him, naked, somewhere in the old place, then set out to find him, and he, erect, slipping through the darkness of the abandoned nursery, amongst the cradles, the bobbing rocking horses, the nutcracker soldiers standing at attention, the grinning harlequins, the staring antique dolls with rumpled hair, would slide from shadow to shadow. She would enter, her hands before her like a blind woman, her step light, her thin hair floating, rising on its own accord above her bony shoulders, and he would take her, standing, before the staring, unblinking glassy eyes.

Or, she might come upon him, unawares. Her eyes wild and alight in the dark like an animal caught of a sudden by the hunter's flambeau. Sometimes too in the rain in the devastated flowerbeds.

9: THE INTERLOPER 1780

With the slaves looking on. At times she became a valkyrie, a chooser of the hero dead. In this performance he would be a corpse, dead to this world, wrapped in a sheet-like shroud, laid out on a tombstone, sprinkled with dirt and camellias, sometimes with something rotting, like a toad or a dead crab, tucked into his funereal bandages. That grave, in the plantation's old mortuary chapel, marked the resting place of her dead governess.

"The house slaves saw the rot set in," said Mallie, drawing deeply on her pipe, her cheeks sunken, the fire from the pipe illuminating her nose holes. At first he had treated her as though she had gone mad. Then, he went mad too, they thought from fear, far madder than she, who was mad with lust. But when she became with child, then he knew that she had become possessed, he said so. It was too much to bear in silence.

In fear for his immortal soul, he sought out the priest, Curé Peissonier. An hour later he staggered from the confessional box grown torrid by the heat of his telling, sweating, and told all and sundry that the child was fathered not by him, no, no, but by the daemon. He took to reading the Bible, then to burning the liver, the heart and gall bladder of a fish caught for that purpose, the fumes of the burning organs having no effect. He, now familiar with *The Tempest*, referred to Bathilde Chartier de Lotbinière as another Sycorax.

"The succubus Agrat, daughter of Mahlat," whispered the lunatic, "it is she who mated with King David and bore a cambion, which is the offspring of a daemon and a human."

Bathilde became, in his deranged mind, the blue-eyed hag, the queen of the daemons, and one of four fallen angels of sacred prostitution who still mate with the archangel Samael.

And the Curé Peissonier cautioned him, "The cambion is the offspring of the incubus and the woman. This incarnation exists with absence of breath or heart-beat until it is seven years of age.

It is unbelievably heavy, too heavy even for a horse to carry, it cries like a child when handled."

Dieudonné whispered this, perspiration running wild down his head and along his emaciated body. I could see him in my mind's eye as Mallie spoke, knocking the dottle from her pipe. They took him away to Martinique, where he survived to a great age, locked away in a lunatic's cell in the city of Saint-Pierre. I was just a girl when she told me that story.

That story made the rounds. It is still told: a man on his way home finds a child, a baby that cries at his touch; he picks it up, it becomes heavy, heavier with every step, too heavy to carry any further. . . That baby was Pierre Fédon, Julien Fédon's father, poor Pierre. Poor Julien. You see why he did not take her name. The nightmare, life-in-death, had won her game. She had twins, a boy Pierre and a girl, Marie Pasqualine, she, they took away from her and then she died. All that remained of her was a painting of her semblance, as a child, on a plate.

I became fascinated with the story that Mallie related. You understand, because of my own condition. Marianne had been given to a devil when I was a child.

I knew them all, the Black Jacobins of Grenada, Ventour, Nogues, the Philip family, the Cavelan family, Charles Belleran; don't talk about Stanislaus de Barras.

10: TRINIDAD'S FIRST CONSTITUTION

HE RETURNED TO Trinidad the following year and came ashore with a hot swirling wind lifting a host of black vultures into a vast thermal high above the mud-flats in the mouth of a dry river to the east of Puerto d'España. His box and trunks had been heaped upon the embankment. He gazed at the ship's dinghy, already standing out to sea, with a sense of abandonment rising. He had to remind himself of the reason for his being here. Looking out towards the ship, he knew that he would want to leave this lonely and primitive hamlet as quickly as possible. Bracing himself, he turned and was startled by the gaunt Carib standing close behind him.

Sarusima communicated the news in his spattering of Spanish, informed by a choreographed performance, that was somehow hieroglyphic. The governor Falquez and his family, along with those whose acquaintance he had previously made, had all departed, in advance of the annual rains, to haciendas at Pampatar.

There were brigands in the Gulf, pirates at war. No ships, no boats, he must wait.

"Where are they? The people?"

What remained of the population were a few Spaniards too impecunious or too shy to leave the old inland capital of San José de

Oruña, and a handful of ignorant French planters long fixed in an irretrievable nostalgia. They were all prisoners, Sarusima assured him, of the numbing debilitation of those who existed in perpetual solitude, as a result of being invisible to him.

He must wait in a mud and wattle hovel with neither door nor window. A single room painted blue within. It held a broken bench, a string hammock and a pile of earth.

"How long?"

Of that there was no understanding. He thanked the savage for arranging his accommodation. It was one of a score or more that clustered about a redoubt, a deserted battery of three guns close to the embouchure. These were near to the small wooden whitewashed building which was used at times as a church. This was Puerto d'España. A place very different from Grenville.

Left alone in the rising heat, he could feel the approach of the suffocating paralysis of solitude. Not even the evening's breezes could dispel it. Fanny had moved to the island and had established herself at the Ariapita estate. In spite of their lives having changed so irrevocably, he had to make an effort not to go directly to her.

By evening, the two dirt streets of the hamlet were deserted, as its handful of souls took to their hammocks. This they did because by nightfall the place would be overrun by crabs, and casually stalked by caimans, grown bold and dangerous. These alarms could only be compared, as he would come to know, with the boa constrictors that one encountered in one's bed, or in the terrifying outhouse at the most awkward moments.

The nights, and these came on quickly, were filled with a cacophony of anonymous noises that emerged from the seemingly endless swamp. Sarusima taught him how to smear his body with the pulp of the red anoto plant against the mosquitoes. As his stock of tasso became uneatable he learned from the Carib to smoke anything edible on a boucan, to bake cassava bread, and to make use of the preservative

10: TRINIDAD'S FIRST CONSTITUTION

qualities of casuaripe, a thick black sauce concocted from the poisonous cassava root. This allowed him to preserve various meats in a pot that he kept on a low fire. It was a dismal place. Made more so with the rain as it came.

He was alone, except for the Chaima children whose heads, prompted by some obscure religious compulsion, were all deformed, bound between small, flat planks and who, like flies, gave him no privacy, as they were ever-present, sitting, staring at him, even as he slept or when he moved his bowels, prayed, or ate his frugal meals.

He was grateful for the company of the Carib, and relieved when Sarusima invited him on expeditions into the island's interior. Their first journey was to Tamana, a flat-topped tepui that he had seen from the mountains some years before. Sarusima approached it with the reverence accorded a sacred place. A story, told around a blazing fire while eating cascadoux with flat cassava cakes, described a time when the human race faced extinction. It was saved here in Trinidad by a couple, the last on earth, who ascended Mount Tamana and, eating the fruit of the moriche palm, ensured the survival of the universe. Later that night, Sarusima took him into a cave on the mountain's side. There, by the light of a flickering torch, he saw in the very heart of the mountain the petrified skeletal remains of this first man and woman.

As morning broke and great hosts of red-bellied macaws took flight, he could make out in his mind's eye what that first morning of creation wrote.

With Sarusima, Philippe Roume trekked through woods marked impenetrable on the old Dutch maps, using the footpaths of the ancients to go beyond the mangrove coast, crossing savannas and fording lagoons to the Atlantic shore. High above the tangled underbrush and across the land grew a monumental forest teeming with life. Philippe understood that in the rich alluvial of the forest floor, the roots of future wealth could be planted.

Early one morning, with thunderheads building like a boiling black dye ringing the wide Gulf of Paria, they set out on another expedition.

Paddling steadily southward, their eight-man corial moved swiftly as a shadow along the placid mangrove coast to arrive at the hamlet of Brea. Greeted by a delegation of caciques, the kings of the south, they were conducted into the hinterland, where a great occasion was to be celebrated.

It was the story of the hummingbird, after which the island was named. It was related, as a smoking pipe was passed around, by an ancient figure of indeterminable gender covered with dry banana leaves, twigs, feathers, and bones. It was interpreted by Sarusima, in a manner that suggested a first-hand account. Against the sounds of the encroaching night, the story, as it unfolded, was dramatised by dancers—young girls disguised as birds and plants, animals and spirits.

Philippe Roume saw in his imagination an earthly paradise painted in primary colours where only the largest and sweetest pineapples grew upon an expanse of golden sand. All about were exquisite jewels of light and air, which flew and hovered and drank to excess the nectar of a million blooms.

Then, as thunder rolled, shadows formed, encroached and magnified to show the menace of those who had come into paradise. Alarmed, he took this as a premonition. The killing of the jewels of light and of air. He knew, without telling, that these beauties in flight were the immortal souls of the people, who, upon their deaths, had returned to Iere as hummingbirds.

Against the backdrop of drums, the chanting of the children, the bellowing of the great conchs, the melodies of the flutes diminished as the insinuations of rattles and the hisses of the chorus intimated that an awful truth was to be revealed. Even as he watched, he felt the rumble of an earthquake and was about to rise when Sarusima put a hand on him and he sank back to the ground. Still the earth moved. Before him, the fire now belched forth smoke and a fearsome form emerged from it. The people about him screamed, some hid, others rolled upon the ground. Sarusima pointed, it was a shape at once hideous and

10: TRINIDAD'S FIRST CONSTITUTION

at once majestic, it seemed to be made of black light, and to have a vegetable quality, like a giant root, with the features of human form.

"Yúcahu, Yúcahu, Yúcahu," the people cried. "Yúcahu, Yúcahu," he heard himself shout.

There was a heat coming, rising from the earth, it rumbled and lurched. Before his eyes, with the reality of the nightmare, the black mass was forming all around, in the air, and on the ground; in mounting fear he rose to flee. Once again, he felt the hand of Sarusima.

"It is the zemi, Yúcahu, god of cassava," the Carib signalled and whispered to him, "be still and be humbled."

He sensed with a cowering fear a primeval power, one already old when Michael had imprisoned Lucifer. Yúcahu had come to avenge the destruction of the jewels of light and air by overturning the earth itself, causing them, the newcomers, to be swallowed in a convulsion of hot black and steaming pitch.

The following morning he followed Sarusima out upon a vast expanse. Black night captured in a bowl of light, it glittered as wide ponds and small eddies upon its surface caught and reflected the light of day.

"It is like a lake," he exclaimed wonderingly, squinting in the sunlight shimmering from the myriad pools of still water.

"Yes," said the other quietly, reverently, "it is our lake of pitch."

AFTER A PROLONGED PERIOD—at times he had no idea what day in the week it was—his clothes had started to rot and termites had gotten into his papers, he realized that he had grown a full beard. So convinced that doubt had diminished hope, that when he was awoken by a change in the atmosphere, he believed himself to be still asleep when he saw a flotilla of pirogues and large corials beached at the estuary close to the redoubt. As if by magic they had appeared. A very small red-painted Warahoon with a toucan on his head handed him a package wrapped in balisier leaves. In it was the summons he had waited on.

He travelled with them across the Gulf of Paria. They coasted the deserted bays and estuaries of the mainland, the heat palpable, the silence to make your ears ring, to eventually reach Güiria, a place even more desolate than the one he had left, and from there to take a schooner to the port town of La Guaira.

He was met there by a party of mountain men. These hijos de algo, 'sons of something,' were the progeny of the misogynist conquistadors who, in the early sixteenth century, had devastated the fierce inhabitants of this province.

Escorted by Don Diego de Losada, they took the mountain trail to Caracas, there to meet José de Abalos, Intendente, Governor and Captain General of the province and president of the Audiencia of Caracas.

Exhausted and relieved, Roume was received by the elderly Spanish Creole whose mild expression and low voice conveyed the authority of his position. Roume was charmed by the hospitality that was so generously offered. In truth, they charmed each other. Don José had read Roume's memorandum. They discussed it. The older man praised his vision. He told Roume that his timing was perfect, as the Societies of Friends of the Country were at present well positioned in the Cortes Generales to place before the Council of the Indies, these recommendations. He confessed that he had seen Roume's earlier draft and had assimilated some of the ideas contained therein into his own recommendations, to which these, Roume's further refinements, would be included in preparation of the final document that would be sent to Madrid.

For Roume the need to rebuild his fortune in a new land was urgent. He, for one, had lost his inheritance. Don José had a mandate, it was to create a population in Trinidad quickly, so as to defend a vulnerable entry point into the Orinoco river.

10: TRINIDAD'S FIRST CONSTITUTION

"A Cedula for a population," said Roume, excited as the wax dried on the parchment, "this is unique and historic!"

"Especially in its impartial regard for the mestizos, *les affranchis*, the free people of the Indies," remarked Don José mildly, regarding Roume.

"Yes, I've seen the new articles that have been added to the original document. They advance the situation of the *les affranchis*. It is original and will go to their heads. I suppose they will bring up the numbers that we need to advance development," said Roume.

"They, through the centuries, have been perceived by us as the living detritus of the colonial experience," said Don José, "and thought of as human merely to the degree that the European blood in their veins could be quantified against that of the African."

"Indeed, that is my experience. The men, if you can call them that, are sly and grasping. Dangerous. But the women are very beautiful."

He did not want Don José, whose respect he desired, to think of him as a person with narrow parochial views.

"Undoubtedly, this Cedula for Trinidad represents a shift in values uncharacteristic of these times," said the Don, "and yes, we need the free mestizos. They will become the bedrock of the new population in Trinidad and form the core of a militia. Men, even half-men," he glanced at Roume from beneath his thick white brows, "will fight for their land. Hold the island until we come."

"*We* will hold it, Sire," said Philippe, and then impulsively, and seeking to please the older man; "I believe that this Cedula will foreshadow the inevitable advancement that could even see the end of chattel slavery, eventually."

The older man smiled indulgently.

"Impressive, for an owner of many slaves, Don Felipe. Your humanitarian impulse for the purpose of establishing fairness for all people before the Law is laudable."

"But, are they all truly people?" he asked. "Truly human, do you think? From what I have seen. . ."

"Canon law, indeed holy mother church, has not established whether they are merely intelligent animals, not possessed of immortal souls," remarked the older man. "My own experience tells me otherwise."

"There the line is drawn," said Roume, thinking he had gone too far.

"We must reach beyond that line, my friend, and see the difference between what is perceived as a mere brute creature and what may become a crime against all humanity."

José de Abalos looked closely at the bearded, sharp-featured young man who sat earnestly on the very edge of his chair. A planter without a plantation, whom fate had turned into an adventurer, he thought to himself and wondered at the conflicts of the times. He will say anything.

"Don Felipe," said the older man quietly, "this work has exceeded my own expectations and that of those who seek universal enlightenment. On the other hand, it will dismay others who preside over the business of countinghouses. For them all blacks, free or enslaved, are merely creatures of labour, no different from an ass or an ox." He smiled kindly. "Nevertheless, it is to be recognised and you must be rewarded. His Majesty will know of it. I shall see to that."

Roume was gratified by Don José's sincerity and by his wish that this work would bring reward. This he took to mean actual remuneration, as it had indeed become an urgent necessity.

They grandly titled the document, "The Constitutional Charter of the Island of Trinidad." Don José, insightful, even intuitive, encouraged Roume to join an expedition that would make a journey through his vast Intendency, showing the flag and proclaiming the sovereign's majesty. In the months ahead Philippe Roume experienced a vast wilderness, unimaginable, a continent possessed of a horizon of towering mountains and snow-capped volcanoes; with savannahs,

10: TRINIDAD'S FIRST CONSTITUTION

immense and unnamed rivers so huge that they contained islands bigger than his own. The jungle, a great forest that had had its birth when the earth itself was freshly formed. For over a year he travelled from Caracas to the distant coast of the Guianas.

Sometimes at twilight in the flickering lamplight of his tent he would gaze at a map of South America, so vast. And that island, Trinidad, so small, it appeared to have been broken off, like a crumb, from the mainland. Leaving his tent, he would make his bed under the stars to experience another vastness, deeper and even more remote.

While walking on the shore of Lake Valencia, a steady breeze containing the icy chill of an Andean winter chasing the full moon, it came to him; his life, increasingly solitary, had now assumed a singular character, one that might even contain, he searched for the word—a destiny. The thought thrilled him. He would be a man of affairs, go to Spain, see the world. He felt the need for a woman, a real one, the Warao women were small and soft, hardly there at all.

The fleeing moon was overtaken by a dark onrush of clouds. No, he would not live in the dark alone. He remembered her, Rochard's daughter, he had met her at Soubise estate. In the distance a jaguar muttered. A premonition of sorts came to him as the moon reappeared. He had kissed her hand, it was a joke, and she had blushed and fled.

Purposefully he rose from where he had been sitting and walked towards the camp and the several fires. The jaguar had coughed again, closer. Looking upward he saw the great dark peaks arranged against the houses the zodiac, which in this awful isolation found their mirror image in the silent water at his feet that shivered, revealing the reflection of the windswept moon speeding by high above. I must look out for her in Grenada when I get back, he thought.

11: THE ROYAL CEDULA FOR POPULATION

1783

WITH CONVICTION, upon his return to Grenada from Venezuela in 1782, he made preparations to visit the French Antillean possessions. With the help of Everard de Barras he translated the proposed "Constitutional Charter of the Island of Trinidad" into English, Italian, German and French.

They despatched copies to Saint-Domingue where it was distributed through the network of Masonic Lodges. To whomever he met in the following months, Philippe Roume extolled the wonders of La Trinité—her size, the fertility of the soil, the expanse of the rivers that gave easy access to the interior. The promise of a Royal Cedula for population, he assured them, was an achievement without parallel in the New World. It was a jewel in the crown of an enlightened monarchy.

He preached it like a crusade. He spoke in churches, before legislative councils, in town halls, to families on plantations so isolated in the hinterland that they might as well be solitary islands, scattered on the mountaintops like a miniature archipelago, surrounded by an impenetrable forest that stretched from Caribbean shores to rugged Atlantic beaches.

These were places hardly visited, except by the wind. He spoke to lonely men living in plaçage with black women made free by

11: THE ROYAL CEDULA FOR POPULATION 1783

familiarity, and with their clinging, wide-eyed mulatto children, whose possessions were little more than a battered chest, a broken kettle, the Holy Bible and two or three pewter plates. He sought out and found deserted women and widowed, solitary men made callous by plantation living, all harbouring collectively a plethora of memories, mostly not their own. In isolation from the world, some had known incest and sodomy, rape and bestiality. They called to mind and described in detail the experiences of forebears in whose nightmares their own dreams recurred.

Most of all, they remembered the Carib wars, not yet over, even in settled islands. He understood. Their grandfathers, some still alive, and their fathers, even they themselves, had fought the warrior bands who defended to the death the sanctity of the petroglyph embedded in the flanks of the smouldering Soufrières, deep inside the forested interiors of their islands. Not a few had rotted in caves or on deserted beaches, made immobile by the poison left in their bodies, pierced by four-foot long arrows discharged by an invisible foe no taller than a boy of twelve. He assured them to the contrary, that in Trinidad, there were no man-eating Caribs.

He knew many of the colonists, knew of the miseries that they had endured. Some were indigent; others possessed means. Many were indolent, slothful and negligent, gone native, gone to rum, having forgotten who they were, but almost all had slaves. That was the important thing, labour.

He warned of the coming wars. He reminded them of the efforts made by their parents and grandparents to carve from the wilderness these plantations from which they profited, which they had defended against the pirate fleets. He cautioned them that the earth was now depleted on those lands, its fertility spent. The enemy would come, bloody and dangerous. That the hurricanes that had devastated their crops would return, and indeed they did. That the red ants would never leave. This was an opportunity to begin afresh in a virgin land that lay below the wind. Trinidad.

They came to him—some in secret, others pretending a bravado that he had to buttress. Every white man or woman would receive thirty-two acres of land, plus half that amount for every slave brought into Trinidad. But Roume cautioned them that to live in the land of the Holy Trinity, they must prove themselves to be Catholics and they would have to be prepared to swear the oath of allegiance to the King of Spain, who was of the house of Bourbon, a house to which they owed an age-old fealty.

Among them were the free mulattos, *les affranchis,* who appeared before him cautious, distrustful, unbelieving that such a charter could be granted to them, even if they were free. Free land for the bastard sons and daughters, for Massa's children?

"Yes," he told them. "Look, there it is, it is written in the fourth article. It says plainly that under the Law of the Indies, Free Negroes and coloured people, who, as planters and heads of families establish themselves in Trinidad shall have one half of the quantity of land as the whites, this, because there will be more Free Black and Coloured colonists than whites. And the lands allotted to you for each slave will be half of that given to the whites for theirs."

He assured both the white people and *les affranchis* that the fifth article stated plainly that after five years, *all,* all colonists, on their promise to stay and continue to live in Trinidad, would enjoy the rights and privileges attached to Spanish naturalisation, which would include the children whom they had brought with them and those born since. In consequence, they all would be admitted to honourable appointments in the administration and militia, according to their aptitude and ability. This article, together with the twenty-eighth, was of particular interest to the would-be colonists. It stated that all inhabitants had the right to petition the King through the intermediary of the governor. These rights also granted the facility to go to Spain, in person, for the purpose of obtaining relief from wrongs which they might have suffered.

11: THE ROYAL CEDULA FOR POPULATION 1783

Within five or six years, his work, the Cedula, would save the lives of thousands of people, free and enslaved, who would move to Trinidad with their families as the wrath of war and revolution swept through the Antilles. But it had cost him all his money. All he had, for certain. He had sold his plantation in Diego Martin, the proceeds of which he added to the money received from Everard de Barras and others.

ROSA WAS CONVINCED THAT THEIR TIME in Grenada was over following the recapture of the island by the French in 1779, as another battle for that island would surely be imminent. Thus, she set about the considerable task of removing the remains of her household to Trinidad and of creating a new life for herself in that strange and primitive environment.

In April of 1779, Philippe had acquired for her the small estate of San Xavier in the Maraval valley, just north of Port d'Espagne, comprising three fanegas of land, from Don Miguel and Francisco Le Zama. The title deed described her as Doña Rosa de Gannes, Marquise de Charras. She went on to purchase several other small estates in the Maraval valley, eventually owning it virtually in its entirety—a magnificent domain through which a river, shaded by enormous bamboo, ran. It was surrounded by high forest, virgin and valuable.

Rosa built a rambling wooden house with a thatched roof, whose porch was decorated with the cast-iron pillars salvaged from Belvédère. She erected a mill, boiling house and barracks for her slaves and planted a field of sugarcane.

To her mind, it was meant to replace Belvédère. *Élysion pedíon, Champs Élysées,* an afterlife. It came from the Greek poet Hesiod, she was pleased to say. Elysium—the Fortunate Isles at the end of the earth. She had heard from Everard de Barras that the poets described Elysium as having shady parks, with residents indulging in athletic and musical pastimes. She smiled to herself, looking around at the vast wild forest that surrounded the clearing, and imagined tennis and dancing at Champs Élysées.

Reading from my Memoirs at La Fontenoy, Grenada, 1806

I SEE A VAST . . . 1779–1785. I remembered leaving for Guadeloupe, I was eighteen, travelling together with my mother and Louis Rosnay aboard the schooner, *Crispin Wayne,* or perhaps it was the *Swallow*. I never saw my father again. He died within a year of our departure. Nor did I see Stanislaus de Barras, or Philippe Roume either, for many years.

I had discovered that Philippe was the owner of the habitation Mount Saint Laurent en la Quartier des Sauteurs, or the Parish of St. Patrick as the English would say. His mother, Rose de Gannes, was the proprietor of the fabulous Belvédère plantation as well as several others. He had spent his youth at Soubise estate when Monsieur de Barras was master there, years before I was born.

I had heard that he had been to Trinidad. I associated Trinidad with Terra Firma, the Spanish Main. To me, it was one and the same. An uninhabited island covered with impenetrable forest, the home of alligators and tigers that roamed its interior, snakes as long as a seine rope swimming in the swamps and slimy lagoons that covered more than half the place.

We had been told that man-eaters crossed over from down the Main whenever they needed a change of diet, so as to capture the Capuchin friars who had come out to the Antilles to create missions for the conversion of the very cannibals who hunted them through that impenetrable virgin wilderness that blanketed the island—all this to the accompaniment of bands of howling Alouto monkeys. After capturing the friars the man-eaters would preserve them in

11: THE ROYAL CEDULA FOR POPULATION 1783

wicker-wood facines strung high in giant Brazil-nut trees to fatten them for basting. It was said that Spanish friars tasted better than Englishmen or even blacks.

That place was not like Grenada, which was civilised, French, you know, with buildings built of brick, and hundreds of habitations.

Philippe Roume de Saint Laurent was a brave one. I would now pay more attention to Trinidad. I wondered when I would get to see his smiling eyes again.

In my young days in Guadeloupe, I told everyone that my name was Soubise Rochard. To capture her, I wrote and sketched what she saw into my new commonplace book. I commenced this on the day that they told me that my father had died. I was sad, but not for long. The news came with a little money and meant farewell to all I had known.

I, of course, didn't have much knowledge at the time. I was just glad, happy to be sent to Guadeloupe to receive my Free Paper. Basse-Terre was a windy town. I had been followed there by it, of course. What money looked like, how it was made and spent, I was soon to discover. My mother, once more YaYa, began the life of an emancipated black woman and became a marchande of boiled and roasted corn in the open market. Not long afterwards, I saw that I was blessed by being the sister of a coal-black boy, his eyes large and luminous. His father I never met, my mother I never saw again as I was put to work in the household of the Funillière family, to be a companion for, and to mind the children of, Marie Alciñia Funillière while her husband Jean-Saint-Paul was away being the captain of a fine schooner.

Well, let me tell you, that man was no saint. He invited me onboard and on the first morning out, quite early, beating up to Union Island in a drizzle, he had his way with me in full sight of the sailors. I put up a show, for them, naturally. I came to like him. I discovered that his main interest was piracy.

I was enthralled by the open sea and the freedom I felt while aboard a swift schooner. The air, salty and bracing, made me courageous. Once, we were sailing off Marie Galante with a brisk south-easterly quickening under a sky hoary with stars, the motion of the ship swift as she heeled on the tack that would take us directly to Basse-Terre. Suddenly, out of the dark, silhouettes of certain despair appeared. The Union Island bumboat flotilla. Fast ship's boats ballasted by boulders and rigged for speed. Pirates! It was I, sitting in the retroussé, staring at the stars who shouted: "Look! Look boats! Boats! Captain! Boats!"

They were upon us. I could see the wild hair, the black faces, the phantom-like forms leaning away from the gunnels. Some held grappling hooks, the one on the bow grasped a harpoon; all were prepared to leap. Jean-Saint-Paul swung the wheel about, sending the mainsail's boom crashing into those sleeping on the cabin's roof, sweeping them overboard. For the briefest moment I saw one, he appeared darker than the night, as he walked through the stars to hit the water with a shout. Careening crazily, our ship leapt and plunged through a wave that sent the sea pouring over her bow, drenching us.

"The flintlocks!" shouted Funillière. I threw myself through the small opening, missing the stairs and falling hard. The dingy light from the tiny whale-oil lamp hardly showed as it swung. There! The box. I braced myself, pressed it to me and opened it, the pistols.

"Soubise, take the wheel."

"Take the wheel?"

"No time to talk! No time to talk! Take it! Allez, allez!" And to a crewman, "Get the muskets! My God, they are dazed. Get the blasted muskets."

The wheel vibrated. The bumboats were gaining. He was priming the pistols; he rose and fired both; the harpoon man was flung away.

11: THE ROYAL CEDULA FOR POPULATION 1783

"Hold her steady, Soubise!"

Hold her steady? I could hardly keep my feet. And the wheel! It wanted to go the other way. He grabbed the musket and fired.

"Go about! Soubise! Take her about, allez, allez!!"

"What?" I shouted in utter confusion.

"Give it here."

He took the wheel and it spun around, the ship lurched, the boom swung about again with a great crash, and away we went. The lead bumboat was like a shadow. The crewman had reloaded.

"Fire, man, fire!"

A flash and explosion. Howling. The musket had exploded.

"Oh, merde! Take the wheel."

Oh, Christ, not again!

I watched him prime a musket and load it, the ship shaking and lurching, salty spume flying, and fire, taking the lead bumboat's helmsman in the face.

We got away, God damn it. I slumped to the deck, trying to catch my breath, I was shaking, hands, knees, and chattering teeth. But as relief slowly crept through me to mingle with the remnant thrill, it produced an intoxicating sensation of absolute delight. This feeling was to become as addictive as a potent drug.

He had lost five crew, with one blinded and another with a fractured shoulder bone.

By the following week, we were in the thick of it again. This time, an American sloop of war beating up from Dominica in search of English shipping.

"Hard-a-lee."

Just in time for a squall. Lost in the squall. By then, I had no qualms about the wheel. March was serene, with good prizes in the Grenadines.

"Kick'um Jenny!"

"Who?"

"Kick'um Jenny, a volcano beneath the sea."

"What?"

"Forget it, forget it, tell them to ease the jib sheets and take that line from the water, come on, move that big arse of yours."

He remarked casually, one morning, when I was shaving his head, that my height, my swaying grace, was similar to that of a fast sloop in open water. I was getting to like him.

"Look boss, what's that?"

"John Black's *Swallow*, Grenadian shipper, Irishman. Forget it, come here. Take the wheel."

We were becalmed. The drifting heat. The sea, clear as light.

"You know that only pigs and goats can see the wind," he said to me, as if I were an idiot.

"Oh? Look what I can do."

I put two fingers in my mouth and whistled three times.

"I'll give you a wind."

The east wind came and we stood away. The old devil, he loved to watch my backside as I strained to hold her steady. It was like that. He was such a powerful man. Large feet. Real wicked toes, claws, long. Everything about him was big, long, rough and hard. Bathing naked, leaping into the tepid sea, he, huge with square shoulders, his neck, when you could find it, was wider than his head. Bald, with cryptic tattoos on his torso, received, he lied, on the Barbary Coast. Covered with a fine mat of curling hair, his vast moustaches floated below his big red nose. Lovely man, laughing eyes, brighter than the sea, the sun. My skin turned the colour of dried tobacco. He loved that, the contrast between my sunburnt limbs and the rest of me. He told me, "this is the place for

11: THE ROYAL CEDULA FOR POPULATION 1783

you, Soubise my girl," his Marseillais accent thick with wine. He changed me. He taught me to sail, to shoot, to hold a dagger, use a cutlass. I became a pirate, had my hair cut quite close and dressed en garçon. We marauded, havocked and murdered. Murdered, yes: I shot a sailor, French I think, off Petit Mustique. My first. Shot him in the head. We took the schooner and her cargo.

A SCATTERING OF GREEN ISLANDS. Îles des Saintes, lilac valleys in sleepy shadow, you could smell them from afar, chive, thyme and rosemary; mist wreathing fast along the ridges at night and spangled with sunlight at dawn. Headland after headland. Their profiles like long-nosed alligators resting on the horizon. Cool and sheltered, curving to form restful bays. Martinique. Cloud-wreathed Pelée, fuming furiously by day, emitting a diabolical ruddy glow by night. Beaches with just green stones, only green stones from the size of boulders to tiny ones, even to the sand, green. Others, so white, so fine, like powder. Hot, hot, hot. Some bays are black, others made pink as a result of millions of conch shells ground to powder by the weight of time. Dominica. Carib island. We sensed their invisible presence high in the treetops.

"Why are the sailors going ashore dressed like monks and crossing themselves?"

"The Caribs love the taste of Spaniards, but not the taste of monks," he laughed, throwing back his head. "They ate a monk once and got the gripes so bad that they have never touched another." Liar, thought I.

We stood out to sea. North again as far away as Havana, and then eastward, bucking the Gulf Stream, boom hauled around to take every slant from the alizé. The sea seethed or rested as it hid the sunken reefs that carry names like the Coffin's Patch off Florida, or the Devil's Saw in the Dragon's Mouth, or the rocks off Redonda, the Mangler. Caught upon it, I saw the skeletal remains of a Guinée slaver. Out of Old Calabar, he said. Her ribs, bleached bone white against a ceramic sky. Her carcass broken. Masts shattered. Tattered shrouds dripping misery. Holds gaping black, emptied of a despair far more grievous than drowning in this turquoise sea.

Me, helming off Saint Giles in the lee of misty Marble Island. He, on the lookout, always anxious for a prize. Another violet sunset coming on. The sea running, waves like giant green horses smashing through the ringed cavities of cathedral rocks, booming; mist rising in the late afternoon sun changing everything to maroon, to gold. A colder wind in search of Marianne. There was so much to describe.

We dropped anchor in Canouan. Port Charlestown, small and quaint. He had a house there. And a woman.

"Look. Hear me! Forget it, I am sleeping on the boat." The sea was my life now.

He put the woman out. And bought me charms for my ears. Stirred by the guitars and the lush tropical setting, we strolled the docks hand in hand, everybody looking, what a lucky bugger he had turned out to be.

Marie Alciñia had long ago acquired another Da and I became first mate of a fine, new, two-masted sloop. We named her *Jacquetta's Revenge*. I had no idea who the hell Jacquetta was, but she was a good ship with a low silhouette and a shallow draught. She had yar, as I heard the Marseillais say.

I, me, Soubise, really—it was she who was filling up the common-book with sketches of leaping dolphins, giant turtles, driftwood monstrosities, and words and faces; his, mine, them, the scabrous crew, as he called the motley crowd of black boys and marooned men, the shipwrecked remnants of failed expeditions who, by joining us, were keeping their bloody hands in.

11: THE ROYAL CEDULA FOR POPULATION 1783

We had been in the Windwards for six weeks, laying in wait for a prize, when east of the Saint Vincent passage there appeared the blurred outline of what, at first, looked like a drifting wreck.

"What?"

"Sail on your starboard bow."

Me, "She has nothing but the pox, or worse."

"A schooner. Low in the water. Is she bound for Bequia?"

"Helms-a-lee?"

"Hard to port! Take the wheel. Ah—come on! Take the wheel. Pass the muskets! Tafia all around, allez, allez!" Rum always fired ferocity.

We came upon the gently rocking *Recovery of Cartine*, an ugly clump of a schooner, built small, riding on her sea anchors. Her sails, furled, resembled pocket handkerchiefs made of tow-cloth. But even before we hailed her, we were met with a determined shower of musketfire and scattershot from a swivel gun mounted amidships, and then, a culverin on her poop fired nails and spikes.

"Board her," Funillière commanded. "Allez, allez!"

"All hands! Ready, board her!" I shouted in turn. She must have something that they are defending.

Grappling hooks, harpoons and gaffs appeared. Aft, flat on my stomach, I took aim and fired my Pennsylvania long-rifle and hit an officer directing the loading the swivel gun in the face. Reloading fast.

"Fire the broadside, Master Lazare."

Five of the ten pieces of ordinance, all small French falconet four-pounders, roared simultaneously, sending a hail of grapeshot into her amidships and across her decks. Through the smoke, the return fire still came from a determined band of musketeers on her poop. They maintained a rapid fire, which was aimed at our gun-ports, picking off the boys who fired the four-pounders. We were now close enough to grapple. Another broadside sprayed her with grapeshot.

"Grapple and haul! Let's get her, over and up, allez allez!" And away he went over the gunwale and onto her deck, a pistol in each hand and a cutlass at his waist. As I watched from aft, I could see ten or twelve men, perhaps more, in close formation, fighting hard amidships about the forward rail. They were moving as a body to meet our boarders, who had managed to storm the *Recovery of Cartine's* decks with pistols blazing, bawling bloody murder, hacking, chopping their way through the defending sailors. These didn't seem to be putting up much of a fight. But there were also some who were more determined. Funillière was their target, naturally; two were at him, he was wielding an axe, when a section of rigging fell upon them. Rope and canvas, fallen spars a desperate tangle. Smoke, rapid fire. Funillière was waving his cutlass, forward, I could hear him bellowing, some of ours were dropping on her deck from the rigging. A man was falling from the crow's nest into the sea. Smoke, bah, stink pots of sulphur.

I reloaded, as another came at him. I shot him. Reloaded. Another got it in the eye. They really wanted him. Reloaded. The short and vicious fight was ending with Lazare severing the right arm of the foremost defender. Where's Funillière? The defenders were retreating onto her stern, the majority falling there to our cutlass men, more of ours, his surprise reserve as he called them, dropping from high upon them. Then it was over. Their colours, a Dutch ensign, were struck by a bloodied seaman. Where the hell is Funillière? With the Negro boy Bob, I clambered aboard. There he was. Lazare and I inspected the hold. Salt.

Funillière was interrogating the captain. There was no need, her captain pleaded, she was out of Liverpool bound for Barbados with a cargo of salt, out sixty-seven days, and destitute of almost every kind of provision. They? Passengers, they were volunteers, to take ship in Barbados heading to Virginia. Fighting men. They fought.

11: THE ROYAL CEDULA FOR POPULATION 1783

"They defended."

"There is nothing."

A survivor pleads.

"Where is it?"

"I know nothing."

"Take off his hand."

The survivor breaks free. He is dead, chopped in the head. Another pleads.

Too much blood. The decks are awash with it. Something must be hidden. I went to one of the last remaining fighting men. Defiant, a brave man, yes, that I could see, strong, he had been beaten about his body and face.

"I shall save you," I told him. "Tell it."

He tells it. "It is in his cabin," he said to me indifferently, pointing towards the captain, beneath floorboards that had appeared to me to be altogether too new when I looked. The captain claimed ignorance, salt, he insisted, still insistent, he had not paid attention to floorboards. He had not seen any leather bags. When he took the ship, he hadn't looked, didn't know. He said simply that he had been handed the ship at Merseyside by the agent of the owner and commissioned with instructions to find a crew and sail her towards Barbados, where he would rendezvous at these coordinates with another vessel. He said that he believed that we were that vessel and had opened fire when he saw us preparing to board him. I could see that the old geezer was lying to save his skin.

"And you fired on us," I said, wiping the sting of sweat from my eyes.

"I did, when I realised that you were pirates, yes." He was a man past his prime.

I gave the young man a drink of rum and asked, "Who was it, his name, the one who commissioned you and those men?"

"I do not know. I don't care about these fools. I wanted a passage to Barbados. The man who knew is dead. You killed him."

Funillière, "And you, captain, you were instructed to sail into these waters, 16º. 34' North and 60º. 30' West, and...?"

"Wait."

"How long have you been waiting?"

"I sighted the sun at sunrise yesterday morning and put out yonder drift anchors to hold her steady against the current."

"He knows that the other ship, which must be cruising in these waters, is on its way," said I, apprehensive of an imminent attack. "And if it wasn't for the light air, would be here already. It will take the rest of our lives to lift those floorboards and take aboard what is hidden in that cabin."

Did he hear me?

"Look, we have lost eleven crew, more than half, we don't know what's coming, let's go with her."

"Very well. Master Lazare, execute all the fighters and musketeers. Leave alive enough crew to handle a boat. There's Barbados, captain, now be off."

I could hear the order being executed. The young man rose to his feet and, without a glance, went out to his death. My God. So much for my word. With an armed escort and a pistol at his head, Funillière having very generously supplied them bread and water, for which they were 'monstrously grateful,' the captain and four sailors were ordered aboard a long boat.

They had not pulled away more than a hundred yards when I could see that they were in trouble, baling, sinking. Some swimming.

"Fire on them."

It was their boat. "Give me that."

Funillière took the gun from Lazare and fired.

11: THE ROYAL CEDULA FOR POPULATION 1783

The wind had risen.

"It was their fate. Their boat. If it is what I think that it is. This is a great bloody secret," I could see that he was serious, even afraid. "Nobody must know, certainly not them." He meant his scabrous crew. "I am taking them to Marie Galante with the *Jacquetta* and leaving you aboard here with Lazare and the Yankee, what's his name?"

"Cassius. Why do you go with them?"

"If I go with you on this pile of rubbish and send them back to Marie Galante, they will know that we have found a pot of gold. This way, they will only suspect it. Right? And take Bob the Negro. Keep Lazare near to you at all times.

"Lazare!" he shouted to *Jacquetta's Revenge*'s first mate, and quietly to him, "Make as if for Union Island, but take her to Trinidad. Anchor off the north coast at the bay of the caves and wait for me there, take the black boy and the Yankee," and taking his arm, "and if you smell a rat, kill it. I am for Marie Galante and will be with you in a week maybe two."

Then he looked at me, meaningfully. I knew what he meant. I primed and loaded the French pistols.

With a steady following breeze that had replaced the noon calm filling her jib, all others had remained reefed, I took the wheel of the *Recovery of Cartine* and made for the Galleons Passage. By morning, I was leaving Tobago abeam and was in sight of the mountains of Trinidad's northern coast. Finding the long sandy curve of the bay that was marked on the Spanish chart 'Las Cuevas' was to prove difficult.

"I'm taking her about, steady, Lazare, all hands to the foredeck. Allez allez!" The *Recovery of Cartine* handled well and responded quickly to the quickening easterlies that I was praying would hold.

"That's Paria Bay," said Lazare, the wind taking his dark hair in all directions, he knew these coasts, "the next big one is Las

Cuevas, if you go too high that one is Gran Tacarigua... there, there, that's the one, take her in."

We dropped anchor about half a league off the beach. A vast forest rose immediately from the shore and continued inland to where cloud-covered mountains loomed. Suddenly, a stillness. The light air that had brought us in dropped to barely a whisper as the sun slid inside a cloud. All around, the pale green water seemed a mirror.

He was earlier than he thought getting there. Ten days after our arrival, a lateen-rigged yawl was sighted by Bob the Negro. He had acquired her, cash on the barrel, at Capesterre-de-Marie Galante and had sailed her, single-handedly, on a course that brought him directly into the bay of caves. With the Yankee Cassius, Lazare and Bob the Negro ashore, he and I proceeded to examine the secret cargo that I had, of course, already had a look at. It had been concealed beneath the decking in the captain's cabin. Twenty-four large leather bags, each carrying a seal marked 'The South Sea Company'. We had struck gold.

"My God, this is a vast fortune. What are these?"

"English Guineas, freshly minted, there, the face of George their King. But I must tell you lass, this will change our lives. It will never be a secret, it cannot be concealed, for sure as day, someone will be coming after us and it. We can only postpone and hope that fate takes care of us and the pursuers. This must be hidden deep and we must go separate ways and disappear for a long while."

Later on, with everything returned in place, Shadrach Lazare joined us in the cabin. "You have been with me since you were a boy. Take this." He indicated a purse that contained some gold coins. "Take this, make your way over yonder mountains to the port of this island and find a ship and get to Martinique and lay low in the countryside. Here is some silver for the passage. Do not spend a gold coin, or sell a coin; they are all too new. There will be many eyes on the lookout. Your life will depend on your discretion, boy, and so will ours, be careful, very careful. I trust you. Trust me, we

11: THE ROYAL CEDULA FOR POPULATION 1783

shall meet again. Go now, and make ready for your trek. You leave in the morning."

And to me, reaching for a bottle of rum, after Lazare had left us, "You my darling, my sometime wife and shipmate. I know of an island in the Mouth of the Dragon that has a deep cave with many chambers. We shall journey there."

He was generous.

"Take it, Soubise, take it, you made it, take, take." He would give half.

"You are drunk. Go to sleep."

The following morning, I awoke to the calamities of the night. The Yankee, Cassius, while taking an evening dip, had been attacked and eaten by a shark. There were just his bloody breeches to be seen. The Negro, Bob, had jumped ship and there was just Lazare, the captain, and me. I took notice of a machete and a long-bladed square dirk, freshly washed, on the deck next to the backpack that Shadrach Lazare had prepared in readiness for his journey.

"But first we must store this all aboard the yawl. I hope she holds her seam. And then we scuttle this wreck."

We watched Shadrach sail the *Recovery of Cartine's* dinghy westward. He was heading for a bay called Maracas. There was a village there and a trail that led over the mountains to the island's capital, San José de Oruña.

"You are thinking that I should have killed him too."

"Yes."

"He was as a son to me."

"He saw me. He knows me."

"What does that matter?"

Everything matters. He had always been generous, I had given my share of the prizes to my father's old attorney Louis Rosnay in

Basse-Terre to hold for me. He had been amazed. I was amazed! After four years, or was it five, at sea, racing storms, outrunning the French, the Spanish, the English sloops-of-war, and the real pirates, I had gold coins deeply engraved from all over the world: Spanish, English, Austrian. I had no idea what it was all worth. Silver in quantity, too, large coins with the empress' profile, nice and new. And some beautiful things, golden things, jewels, objets d'art. But this hoard was a different matter.

THE FOLLOWING MORNING we sailed the yawl, perilously low in the water with all the gold aboard, into the Gulf of Paria. In the placid water a small scattering of islands appeared from the morning's mists.

"What's this place called?"

"It's marked 'Gaspar Percin's island' on the chart. There is an islet across the entrance of a cove that is called Winn's Bay. It's on the southern side of the island. The islet contains an entrance tunnel to one of several caves on Gaspar Percin's island."

"You know it?"

"I have been in them."

We made Winn's Bay by nightfall and spent the night in hammocks hung from scrawny trees above the rocky surface that covered the islet, the yawl made fast to one such tree. The following morning, he caught a quantity of jacks, which he fried in oil, we had these and soggy biscuits for breakfast. He straightway commenced to dig and remove the limestone boulders that blocked an opening that descended deep beneath the islet. This revealed a long tunnel that at high tide was filled by the sea, but at low tide afforded a watery passage into a chamber that was on Gaspar's island itself. With torches dipped in pitch we entered the chamber that without any other opening was blacker than night, and dripping with water. With great difficulty we hauled an iron box that he had brought

11: THE ROYAL CEDULA FOR POPULATION 1783

with him through the tunnel and into the echoing darkness of the cave, leaving quickly as the water rose above our knees. The heavy bags of coin were a different matter, these had to be divided up on board the yawl so as to make them manageable.

The following morning, as the tide fell, we reentered the cave and explored this macabre place with its strange and ghostly forms that seemed to come from its roof. These were repeated, growing from the ground. Stalactites and stalagmites, he explained. With anxious haste we searched until we found a cavern within the cave, high up above its high watermark. Into this we wedged the iron box. To achieve this, wood from Gaspar's island had to be cut to construct a ladder and to build a platform from which to work, so as to fill the chest with coins. All this took many days and nights, as the rising water would come rushing up through the floor and porous sides of the cave, causing us to leave quickly. Finally, some weeks later, having lived on fish and iguana, we commenced to reseal the entrance to the tunnel. This he did, replacing the large rocks and exploding a small charge of black powder, causing some of the boulders to become firmly wedged into the entrance.

THE FOLLOWING MONTH, we were once more in Capesterre-de-Marie Galante. Over the next few months he set about finding fresh crew for the *Jacquetta's Revenge*, inasmuch as the remnants of her former crew had all died, strange as it seemed, some from mysterious fevers and others from accidents, or from stab wounds received in sudden brawls.

I heard an old salt singing a shantey, I wondered with a pang if it was meant for me:

> *Laden with gold is the wind from the east,*
> *The best wind of all the four that blow;*
> *The girl that is born when that wind blows*
> *Want she shall never taste in all her life.*

12: AS ONE DOOR CLOSES, ANOTHER OPENS.
PARIS 1783 – TOBAGO 1786

He returned to Caracas in May of 1782, where he met Don José for the last time.

The Don was pleased to inform him that José de Gálvez, Minister of the Indies, had been informed of his work thus far, which had been reported to His Majesty's Council of the Indies. He advised Roume to take his case to Madrid as there was no telling how long the liberal views of the Economic Societies would have a voice in superior councils, especially as the American wars were coming to an close. He would be armed, he was assured, with all the appropriate letters of recommendation and an introduction to the Count of Abarca, the Spanish ambassador, a person sympathetic to the ideals of the Spanish Enlightenment, who would serve to advance their endeavour.

Returning to the almost empty roadstead in Trinidad, he went to see his mother Rosa at her hacienda in the Maraval valley. He found her sitting in her carriage beneath a strapping sandbox tree on the river bank, supervising the blanchisseuses as they sang in the rushing water. No, he had not seen Fanny, neither had she.

He was fortunate to embark a Dutch merchantman flying the imperial flag, and came ashore at La Rochelle, where he assumed the role of an impoverished French planter returning home. He did this, as he carried in gold, all the money he had left in this world.

12: AS ONE DOOR CLOSES 1783 - 1786

On impulse, he decided to go to Paris instead of making the long journey to Madrid. This change of plans was prompted by a conversation overheard between merchants in a tavern. They spoke of a great concourse of the leaders of the world which was taking place at the palace of Versailles where the treaties that would mark the end of the American Revolutionary War would be negotiated. Hearing this, he felt convinced that this would be his opportunity to meet the Spanish ambassador as he surely would be there.

GRATEFUL FOR THE letters of introduction, upon his arrival in Paris, he was relieved to know that Ambassador Abarca was indeed there and would receive him in his apartments, which were off the Galerie des Batailles on the main floor of the south wing of the Palace of Versailles.

"I have looked at the letters from Don José who recommends you, Sire de Saint Laurent, enthusiastically, and guides you to us instead of to your own embassy. I wonder why."

This portentous man, with a voice that seemed always to drop into a whisper, Roume thought, will judge me for himself no matter what is written there.

"In the words of the philosopher, 'Le mieux est l'enemi du bien,' Excellency."

"Indeed? . . .Voltaire. Mmm." Ambassador Abarca clicked his tongue once or twice.

A little breathless, in what he believed to be his best Castilian he continued, "To benefit from your office I seek your protection and your goodwill to bring to fruition the undertakings of Don José and many others."

"And these others would include yourself, of course?"

"Certainly, your Excellency, and all who support the stimulation of the economic and intellectual development in the New World."

"Please, go slowly, Sire de Saint Laurent."

Nodding and taking a deep breath, he went on, "I have with me, your Excellency, a manifesto that seeks an accommodation between certain French planters of the Antilles and His Most Catholic Majesty's government to settle in the island of Trinidad."

"I have read the proposals drawn up by José de Abalos." Here Ambassador Abarca paused to purse his lips, "I glean between the lines an ingenuity, an insight, not common in the correspondence of our governors. Tell me, Sire de Saint Laurent, what inspired my old friend to such heights of expression, approaching lyricism, by all accounts?" He clicked several times.

Roume appreciated Ambassador Abarca's irony and wry smile as the older man sat back and motioned to the others in the book-filled room that was embellished with gold-leafed baroque buffoonery and an infinity of reflections that he would listen to this young man from the French colonies.

Roume described the society that was to be created in Trinidad by the implementation of the Cedula. Stressing that this Spanish island, Trinidad, should not be left deserted, to fall prey to the ambitions of others, even if it had to be populated by French colonists. His description of the Gulf of Paria and vision of a great naval establishment at Trinidad stirred the ambassador's interest, as did the possibilities of mining platinum, a newly discovered metal, rarer than gold, that was to be found on the close-by mainland, a continent as vast as Russia. In closing, Roume expressed his urgent wish to meet Don José de Gálvez.

Entertained and pleased with the Creole's enthusiasm, the Spanish ambassador sought, that very day, to present him to his colleague, the recently arrived Gálvez. To his surprised embarrassment, Don José de Gálvez would not receive Roume de Saint Laurent, saying that he was familiar with Don Felipe's work and that he would be prepared to discuss the contents of the Roume memorandum only with the ambassador.

12: AS ONE DOOR CLOSES 1783 - 1786

"Reimbursement?" Gálvez had said to him, appearing more amused than puzzled, the ambassador recounted to Roume. "What for?" Gálvez had asked. "Don Felipe acted on his own accord."

"Did you?"

"I did," Roume answered, a sense of alarm in his voice. "We did, the responsible proprietors did. It was in the context of the initiatives encouraged by the Economic Societies of Friends of the Country."

"Which is a private consortium, albeit allowed by the Crown to exist—for the time being." Abarca waved his hands in an almost dismissive manner, pursed his lips and clicked his tongue twice. "Don José said that the Cortes Generales welcomed your enthusiasm, but there had never been any formal arrangements made with them to reimburse you for your travelling expenses. His words were, my friend, 'Don Felipe and his close relatives, his wife I understand, have already benefited from our generosity and, no doubt, will do so again from this Cedula.' Then he added, displaying, I thought, a hint of his origins, 'his wife's dowry, as I understand it, came with gold sufficient and a contractual arrangement to share in the profits of the asiento granted by His Most Catholic Majesty's government to her grandfather, Don Laurence Lambert. His Majesty's Cortes Generales is pleased with Don Felipe, we shall not hinder him in his further, ah—adventures.'"

The apartment suddenly became dark, as though an eclipse had commenced. Roume understood that he had been removed from the situation. Everard de Barras' words had come to pass.

The Spanish ambassador, noticing that his guest had blanched, continued evenly, so as to allow the young man to compose himself. "I am sorry, my friend. We are presently in the process of formalising the Cedula for Trinidad."

The realisation that there was no hope of reimbursement for the money expended, and that his work had been erased from official memory, fell upon Roume as a dead weight as he left the Spanish ambassador's apartments. Overtaken by glittering carriages and with gay laughter floating on the evening air, Roume rode his rented palfrey through the long avenue of plane trees towards the palace gates, to take the road back to Paris from Versailles. His immediate concern now was how to conserve what was left of his resources. He shook his head sadly, as the distant lights of Paris appeared beneath a cold ashen sky.

CAUGHT IN THE ENIGMA OF FORBODING he gazed through the rain-streaked window panes at the low clouds that almost touched the gables of the city. He was at the house on the rue Saint-Séverin that they, Fanny and he, had been presented with, upon their marriage, by her grandfather. He believed that he could never return to Grenada or even see Trinidad again. Despairing at the turn of events and angry to be dismissed as an adventurer, Roume was cheered only when he was invited to revisit Ambassador Abarca.

Once again in the ambassador's apartments, he was closely questioned on the overall condition of the islands in the southern Caribbean which, he realised, were imperfectly understood by the ambassador and others at the conference where negotiations had arrived at a crucial stage.

Abarca suggested that it was opportune for Roume to make the acquaintance of certain French ministers. On an impulse, he mentioned that he had read Law and been admitted to the Paris Bar and as such he was familiar with its nuance, as it related to property and indebtedness. He then went on to say that he was also knowledgable, in a general sense with English law. None of which was true.

At this Arbarca nodded gravely, saying that the future of the island of Tobago, which had been captured by the French from

12: AS ONE DOOR CLOSES 1783 - 1786

the English in 1781, was to be debated and this could present an opportunity for Roume to solve his most immediate problem, which was to gain a position.

His relief, so obvious, that the ambassador ventured a smile, as he went on to explain that Tobago should be in fact returned to England under the terms of the treaty being negotiated, but it was not in the interest of neither France nor Spain that it was. Retaining Tobago as a French possession, however, might be achieved utilising the basic principles of the Pacte de Famille, an accommodation existing between the kings of France and Spain, both monarchs being of the house of Bourbon. A proposal to retain Tobago for France, he believed, if succinctly argued, would be appreciated by the French ministers. He felt convinced that Roume should make such an argument to the Comte de Luzerne, a secretary of state in the French government and minister of the Marine Royale.

Through the following days that were turning into a lifetime, Roume waited, expecting the meeting to be announced at any moment. Discreetly, one afternoon, he was ushered into the anteroom of an obscure apartment in the palace. There, in the shabby light, he was quizzed by the Comte de Luzerne and the Maréchal de Castries, Minister of the Colonies, as to the actual, most recent state of affairs with regard to the economy and the composition of the population of Trinidad and of Tobago. Roume reported that the Spanish island of Trinidad was to be populated almost entirely by French-speaking colonists as a result of the work he had done over the past several years, which would culminate in the issuance of a Spanish Royal Cedula for the colonisation of Trinidad. He pointed out the close proximity of the two islands, and as such, in the current scheme of things, a French-held Tobago being a strategic move as well as a useful prize.

Regarding Tobago, one of the more knotty problems was the indebtedness of its inhabitants. To ameliorate this, Roume, having been coached by Ambassador Abarca, suggested a strategy that would enable the English planters to free themselves from the stranglehold of the London bankers' consortium. He suggested that a loan be raised. He could make the appropriate contacts with financiers from the Netherlands, who were virtually waiting outside the door, and who would consider repaying the London bankers what was owed to them for certain considerations in Tobago. If this could be achieved, it would reduce the burden of interest that had to be paid by the planter families there. The result would be more capital circulating.

He argued further, drawing from his own experience and knowledge of the geography of the area, that Tobago should be retained for France, for inasmuch as Spain perceived Trinidad, albeit with its growing French population, to be the lock that preserved her South American provinces, a French Tobago, by its very location, was the key that fitted into that lock.

Seeing that he had their interest, he rose from the table to walk to a large window that overlooked the most beautiful garden he had ever seen, now lit by thousands of lights. Turning, he said with confidence, "With regard to holding the island, it would require an individual experienced in the recent military operations in that part of the world. Such a one could be found in the person of Count Arthur Dillon."

"Who in 1778 sailed with his regiment to the Caribbean to campaign against Britain," agreed the Maréchal de Castries, leaning back into the large chair.

"Yes, he served at Grenada," Roume added smilingly, "where I had the honour to make his acquaintance."

Impressed by his analysis and by his insights, Luzerne agreed with the maréchal that he should make those intimations part of his proposal. He suggested that perhaps Roume de Saint Laurent, because of his obvious local knowledge, could consider taking up the position of Commissary-General in the Ministry of the French Marine Royale and in the administration of Tobago as Ordonnateur; this, naturally, Roume was very pleased to consider.

12: AS ONE DOOR CLOSES 1783 - 1786

Philippe Rose Roume de Saint Laurent, left Versailles now flatteringly referred to as chevalier. His creditors appeased, he was at last able to enjoy the Paris of his recollection at the house on the rue Saint-Séverin, while negotiating a line of credit for the colonists with certain selected Dutch merchant bankers in preparation for his new position.

He was formally appointed to the post of ordonnateur in April of 1786 and returned to Tobago with Arthur Dillon, who was replacing the Vicomte d'Arrot as governor. The Trinidad endeavour had been accomplished—financially disastrous for him, but successful for the French Creoles, who had prayed for it, and of course for the Spanish government, where it was felt that some its more urgent necessities had been met.

The phase of his life that had seen him as the coloniser of a Spanish possession and sometime judicial functionary in Grenada was over. His acquaintance with Arthur Dillon renewed, they sailed for Tobago aboard the *Océan*, 118 guns, arriving there on the 5th of December 1786.

Reading from my Memoirs at La Fontenoy, Grenada, 1806

JANUARY KISSES, 1787–1789. I took the stone path that wound its way through shady bird song into the garden, avoiding its shattered fountain and apotropaic herms. A battle had been fought here between Julien Fédon's republicans and the English. Skeletal remains persisted betwixt Grecian pitchers and bullet-spattered statuary along with belt buckles, eye sockets, broken swords and parts of minds, lingering, where in terror their brains had been blown away.

Perhaps I would read from my diaries today. There were ten or twelve of them, brimming with memories, some dripping with tears. My diaries looked like yesterday's bouquets, a salad of many memories with such a variety of souvenir botanicals turning to dust: leaf-pressed mementoes, unsent letters, spent.

There were one or two volumes that I had tied up tight with twine. You understand. Some leaves must not be seen. Get away, get gone, blown into the blue. Hiding from the wind, I shall visit them all some day. Perhaps even set some free, like prisoners of war, to return to the trees that had borne them.

It was on the 14th of January 1787 when I saw Philippe Roume de Saint Laurent again. He, too, was one of those eggs in slavery's nightmare's nest. A Massa egg.

We had dropped anchor in Rockly Bay, Tobago, so as to escape the worsening seas and to wait out contrary winds. Tobago had now become French. I came ashore, it was twelve noon. I saw him in the market. My heart leapt. He was so tall and handsome, so earnest, I wanted to abduct him on sight. Our eyes met that night, as Le Maréchal de Castries arrived at government house. I had gone there along with some Tobagonian girls, drawn by the smell of an ox turning on an open pit, the faerie lights in the trees, the sound of the military band, the crowd that we had followed and Marianne, who wanted to see if she would feel the same way, on seeing him again.

The following morning on the wharf there he was. In company with a party of gold-braided officers, he was walking briskly through the crowd of scruffy slaves and grimy porters, drunken sailors, guileful melusines and other mermaids, sirens, harpies and the many nymphs such as Decima de la Forêt that haunt waterfronts all over the world.

My God! He was coming directly toward me. Where to run? This must be an arrest. Perhaps they have apprehended Funillière. Who had advised that I should stay aboard *Jacquetta's Revenge* since it was safer for me to be at sea.

Aboard, we had a cargo of ball and powder already paid for, to be landed at the Tobago Cays; not to mention other undeclared necessities for marauding. He was now before me, the accompanying

12: AS ONE DOOR CLOSES 1783 - 1786

officers could hardly contain themselves. They were all drunk!

My hand in his, he doffed his hat and kissed it. I snatched it away. The man has become a fool, I thought. Not me. Already a crowd. A coach clattered up, a footman cleared a path.

"Step this way, Marianne, if you please. The governor and the maréchal await us."

"Marianne? Who is Marianne? What foolishness," I said. "Be off, I am a free woman."

"Come, Marianne, please. What I say is true."

I could see sincerity in his eyes, and something else. Oh, my heart was in my mouth.

"Come, Marianne, please, what I say is true. Don't you remember me?"

"Of course I remember you. You are Monsieur Philippe Roume of Saint Laurent estate."

"Yes, exactly. Come, Marianne," the hand again.

"Go with the man, girl!" shouted a hoarse voice. People were shoving; a child had been put upon someone's shoulders to get a better view. A crowd was forming. I didn't want a crowd. The officers and the footman had cleared a way, people were laughing. The horses were stamping. Naked sailors were looking out from brothel windows. Shouting. Advice coming from all sides.

"Oh, damn. Decima, come!"

She looked about her.

"Yes, come."

I grabbed her by the arm, Now the carriage.

"There, up you go."

With Decima de la Forêt hysterical and Philippe Roume joining in with her, I thought, as the carriage turned up Government House Road, this man might serve my most urgent need which was to get out of the life at sea and, find a new protector. I joined her in playing the part of the hussy, thinking anxiously, he must not become déniaisé, as they say, made wise to my most terrifying vulnerability, which was the burden of that gold. It had taken the joy out of pirating. It had altered my life, our lives. Funillière had become a merchant once more at Basse-Terre and Marie Alciñia's most faithful husband and soon the father of even more children. I knew that he would be making plans to return home to Marseille with his share of the gold. Would he keep his word and leave mine waiting in the sea cave beneath Gasper's island?

REMEMBERING TOBAGO, 1787. We saw Dillon as he strode towards the house, the smell of woodsmoke rising, the sound of his officers' laughter playing at bezique in the high white-painted verandah. He smiled and waved. We listened as he took the stair quickly. He must have heard the tinkle of the crystal chandelier; the wind was rising. He turned the large shining knob in the tall white door and stepped into the cedar-scented, darkened room. It closed behind him, without a sound. It contained just a bed, large with turned posts of a rosy island wood, the same tone as Decima's skin.

She had been with me on the night that the French maréchal came to see them. She said, later to me, that she had taken Dillon in at a glance. I believed her, she was possessed of the cunning that women sometimes manage to maintain when they do not love a man to distraction. Not me.

We had this brand new, white-painted house, with shiny brass doorknobs, big brass locks and hinges all to ourselves. Servants, liveried, brought food on silver salvers and prepared the beds for us to romp upon.

"I am no saint, eh," I said to him that very first day, "I am a pirate woman, you see me here, you don't know me, I could rob you. But you're sweet, you are a doux-doux."

12: AS ONE DOOR CLOSES 1783 - 1786

We made love then and there, he handled me in a thrilling and exciting way and I could please him, delight him and exhaust him. And because I could see that he, a master of men, the owner of people like me, with whom he could do what he pleased, marvelled at me, I assumed an air of careless frivolity. My smell, he said, was like fire under corn roasting, sparks flying, snapping in the wind. "Pax!" We held each other as tight as we could, finding no shelter from the great tide that was rushing past to vanish into the blue. I became as vulnerable as a cocoyea broom. The ties that bind it at his command.

Speeking of Dillon he said, "He is the fifth generation of his family to hold the rank of colonel in the regiment that bears his name. His people," he said, wonderingly, "are Irish aristocrats who have allied themselves to the French throne, serving as statesmen and soldiers."

I smiled deliriously.

"Service to the crown of France, which I too serve," he said, taking my arm to stand at the window, "has brought Dillon to this island in the contested west." I nodded and nodded, while looking at the Guinea slavers that turned at anchor in Rockly Bay. They were discharging their cargoes.

"Not without splendour," I told him, as the wind rose to caress me, pointing to Tobago's cannons, temporarily silent, facing an orange ball sinking quickly into the still, warm sea. I wanted him to know that I, too, could appreciate the subtleties at play in sunsets. The following week, I sent for my trunk. The first mate and crewmen arrived grinning.

"Mind your damn business. Inform the captain that I have a new berth. Take her to the Tobago Cays and keep the appointment. Then, if you are still alive, make for Basse-Terre."

Jacquetta's Revenge sailed without me. I sent a note saying that I would follow later. I never did. Jean-Saint-Paul Funillière, dear friend, lover, fellow buccaneer—adieu. My spoils, the money, the objects d'art. I made sure I got hold of those.

He talked to me as if we had known each other all our lives.

"Look, my treasure chest, look. See my jewels. When I was a small girl I was given to a devil, you know that?" There, now he knew almost everything.

He closed the lid and kissed me. Everything we ate tasted better as a wave of sensuality overwhelmed the house. His official papers. I read them, the instructions of the minister—"*Memoire du Roi pour servir d'instructions au sieurs Compte de Dillon, Gouverneur, et Roume de Saint Laurent, Ordonnateur de l'Isle de Tobago. 30 July 1786.*"

I would record his words, in my words, as I would come to dream his dreams, in my dreams, forever. I was in no doubt of that. I was twenty-six. 'In Tobago', I would write in my commonplace book at the top of each page every morning. This, I kept; she, Soubise, kept, scrupulously. I could see that this great man, this white man, wanted me. I had come into his life at a moment of vulnerability. He was wounded by circumstance, I would come to understand, while naïvely having lived others' dreams. This, I would realise, was his greatest weakness. He had been disarmed not only by the infidelities of his wife, whose name was Fanny, stupid name, but also by the chicanery of those who had robbed his family in Grenada of virtually all their worldly possessions. I could see that he could see that I was ignorant of such matters and insufficiently impressed.

"See," I told him, "how the wind, my wind, caresses my book. Look how the pages lift and fall. Like a mouth telling of what it contains."

I told him that ever since I was a child, I believed that books could talk. That books were alive.

"Look, its leaves flutter, calling out the words that flitter like leaves in my windy head."

He laughed. "What does it tell?"

12: AS ONE DOOR CLOSES 1783 - 1786

"It tells the story of the wind, naturally, from whence it comes. What laughter it has heard, which butterfly it has carried upward."

"Whose tea it has cooled!" he smiled.

"The smell of laundry it has dried, and a little bit of cat pipi too, eh?" I added, he laughing.

I told him that I was no longer Marianne, I was now Soubise Rochard. He smiled and said that he had realised that.

I wondered at our shared coincidences. Thomas Rochard L'Epine, my father, bought Soubise estate from Everard de Barras. I lived in the house that Philippe Roume had known as a boy and as a young man. He would tell me about his days there, where he received an education. I didn't mention Stanislaus, nor did he. Recalling Soubise estate house made me feel that Philippe and I were joined, our lives entwined, because we had shared Soubise. Philippe and I had slept in her beds, and experienced her intimacies. And Stanislaus de Barras, he too, was conceived on the estate, more than likely in the very bed in the master's chamber. Soubise, La Digue, Belle Vue and Balthazar estates were all arranged, almost bordering, near to Grenville Town. That was where the French Revolution in Grenada would begin.

⚜

IN THE MORNINGS Philippe would meet Dillon in the high-ceilinged, mahogany-furnished office, tall black Tobagonian flunkies in powder and knee-breeches waiting inside every door, dressed in blue and gold livery, their bare feet, freshly oiled, gripping the highly polished floor.

At a long table was a large military map of the island. They were planning the building of the windward road, a spectacular work that neither of them would see completed. It would involve hundreds of slaves over the next five years and would link Port Louis, or Scarborough as it would become, to Tyrell's Bay and beyond, and would facilitate the development of the rich river valleys, whose names reminded Dillon of the English countryside. Their zeal and enthusiasm naturally created enemies, as it interfered with the corruption, laziness, and the pursuit of self-interest endemic in the colonies.

Dillon came to appreciate Philippe. He very much valued his loyalty to the French crown. Roume as ordonnateur, together with another advocate, Jean de Pontieux, adjudicated over the island's Anglo-French legal system.

As a Creole, a descendant of Europeans born in these islands, Philippe had an understanding of the land, the planters, the climate, and the blacks. Dillon hadn't realised that Philippe was hardly a European. The salt of the Caribbean Sea ran in his veins, that we, Philippe and I, understood things differently and, that Philippe's imagination contained a great deal of my own.

"Through your ingenuity and energy, my friend," said Dillon, praising him, "you have created opportunities for the establishment of a French population on the Spanish island of Trinidad. Bravo. Now tell me about it."

"The corsairs returned with fabulous stories of islands in the most distant west," Philippe explained. "My own forbears came to the Antilles in search of these islands. They were martlets, the fourth sons, as described in heraldic lore. Birds without feet, forced to fly, to flee, forever."

"I know, it is the imagination of travellers and of refugees," answered Dillon.

"And of colonists and of all who have ever felt the claustrophobia of being left behind," said Philippe.

They spoke of the Cedula of '83. That was when I understood that Trinidad's Cedula was a very particular document when it came to dealing with people like myself, compared to what governed other islands.

12: AS ONE DOOR CLOSES 1783 - 1786

"It gives civil liberties and privileges to *les affranchis, gens de couleur, sui generis*, I did this for them," boasted Philippe, his eyes bright, his expression earnest. He wanted Dillon to approve of his ideals, to see him as a grand seigneur, a feudal lord and to perceive him as paternalistic, looking after his people, us. "It guarantees, under the Law of the Indies, that *les affranchis,* black or mulatto, would receive, upon swearing oaths of allegiance and fidelity to Spain, grants of land, gratis, in perpetuity."

"Spain wants Trinidad to remain Spanish." Dillon said this coolly, disinterestedly, he really didn't care about these islands, *La Gloire* lay elsewhere.

"Truly, in retaining these lands in extended families for two or more generations, the foundation for familial wealth is laid. Men will fight to keep such lands," said Philippe. He felt keenly about his resettlement scheme, in spite of having been so deceitfully encouraged by Laurence Lambert.

"That they, *les affranchis* would be treated with equality as time passes," said Dillon gently, "is a great privilege. Original." He understood that all of this was dear to Philippe.

"Trinidad will be a different place, Arthur, different from other islands in the Antillean chain. The majority of its free population are *les affranchis,* African or mulatto."

A different understanding of the world lay between them, I could see that. Philippe and I had woken up to the sound of the jumbie bird. Listened to the creation of dark melodies, but Philippe had never before cared for the *gens de couleur,* before he met me. Here he was claiming that he had brought about the Cedula because he wanted to save us. I knew that he had always seen us and the black people like furniture or dogs, or the rain, to be used, avoided or ignored. Yet, I imagined that there was something about being here, in Tobago, his practice on the bench, his work amongst them, the slaves, and living with us, the way we were, that this had made him change and see us differently.

I thought at the time that I loved Philippe; the truth was that I was very relieved to have as a protector a powerful man. I was far more concerned with my own security and future survival to be capable of that degree of selflessness that love requires—however temporary—without which there is no love; quite apart, I was young and too inexperienced to be able to appreciate his genuine qualities. But although I did not love him yet, I was, then, in love with him, a very different thing; his strength, his beauty, the certain suddenly serious tones of his voice, how that made me feel, even in memory.

He spoke bitterly to Dillon of the treachery of the Spanish Royal Court in his Trinidad affairs. He told him how he had come to understand, finally, the role played by the Spaniard, de Gálvez. A role assumed in collusion with Fanny's grandfather, whose South Sea Company held the concession of the asiento to supply slaves to the Spanish colonies. It was not about land, really, it was about slaves. The entire island of Trinidad would be mortgaged to Sir Laurence; its economy would be controlled by him through his pawn and likely successor, André Fatio. Laurence and André. Just as they had done in Grenada, they would do in Trinidad. Create an illusion of wealth for the greedy and take the profit for themselves.

HE TOLD ME that he wanted me in his life. To be with him always. We sat close together in the windy gallery that overlooked Rockly Bay.

"My little chabine," he whispered into my windblown ear, "you have to find a place too."

I am no chabine, I thought as I nodded and nodded. I heard him say, like a prayer:

"Little lamb, who made thee?
Does thou know who made thee,
Gave thee life, and bid thee feed . . .

He said to me that after their first daughter Elizabeth was born, his wife Fanny became with child every year and that she could

12: AS ONE DOOR CLOSES 1783 - 1786

not carry any of them to full term. I told him that it was one soul who was trying to make its way into the world, coming back each time. He said she could not take the climate. I thought to myself that she had discovered the potency of thyme à manger, an effective herb when it came to causing miscarriages. He was to tell me that after the death of their third daughter, of whom he was not sure that she was his, he could no longer bear to sleep with her. He said that he had killed a man. That it had been a matter of honour. Retrospective jealousy, thought I, as I felt him twinge at that most absurd of self-inflicted tortures. But men say all sorts of things at times such as these. We were together when he received the news that Elizabeth had died in Trinidad. This made him suffer and I shared in his grief.

I was the ordonnateur's Madame; Decima de la Forêt, the governor's. We dressed the part with colourful head ties, Breton lace and gold. This was called plaçage, that is, living with white men in the islands. The perpetuation of the white race in the New World was enshrined in the purity of the blood. This demanded inviolability of the white womb—a notion that naturally prohibited penetration by the men of colour. This caused white women, who stayed in the shade all day, to possess dominion over all conjugal preferences. No Othello could cohabit here. Our daughter Rosette was born that year. He named her for his mother.

REMEMBERING GRENADA. Belvédère was the most revered of habitations amongst the French in these islands, and certainly the largest and most impressive in Grenada. I encouraged him to speak of Belvédère, it was where he had grown up. I entered his dreamscape crafted from the pollen of childhood memories and saw it, as he spoke, with my mind's eye. It appeared worked in fine embroidery, scented with French vanilla and eau de cologne, haunted by the sounds of silence, fading, the slow tick as a great pendulum passed over the echoes of children's voices, shrill, he and his brothers' and sister's, as they went running, to vanish through enormous rooms.

The Great House, with lilac shadows, built of yellow brick and white coral-stone, shimmering in a green night, surrounded by dark forms. Ancient moss-covered forest trees through which flew giant raptors. All serene but for the lonely call of a solitary bell-bird far up in the cloudy peaks of Grenada's highest mountains.

Inside, upon pale cedar partitions, the legendary ancestors were displayed in lifelike portraiture, captured in elliptical gold-leaf frames. Dark, polished floors reflected sepulchral furnishings carved from solid logs of mahogany, dazzling brass-work, vast thrones and breath-taking love-seats. Upon moist walls were trophies of arms displayed in memory of epoch-changing wars. All spoke of an unfathomable power, inherited privilege, and the patina of incest perpetuated for generations.

The chivalric allegiances of those who had eaten of the lotus tree, who, forgetting friends and home, had lost all desire to return to their native land in favour of living on the extremity of the world, were displayed in the sixteen quartered arms, carved in granite, above the main door. Upstairs, taken by a flight that swept like a woman swirling in a dress of marbled silk, the surrounding galleries opened onto suites named for the colours of the rainbow in Arabic. These were decorated with the imagination of a habitué of the harems of the Grand Turk. From a distant ceiling hung a fantastic, many-tiered chandelier festooned with garlands of Bavarian crystal and made macabre by the bleached skulls of the slaves who had built Belvédère more than one hundred years ago. Belvédère, it began and ended there.

13: SIR LAURENCE LAMBERT
FINDING PERSEPHONE
ÎLE DE RÉ, 1789

THE SOUTH SEA COMPANY'S REAL GAINS, its true profit retained, came up to something more than six hundred thousand pounds sterling. Bank of England notes were legal tender and their value floated relative to gold. The challenge was to convert this paper into bullion. This, his grandfather and father achieved to some considerable degree, before and immediately after the collapse of the Company in '22. In his time, he had been able to convert a large quantity of Bank of England notes into guineas—nowhere near to the final figure in the ledgers, but a handsome collection of freshly minted gold coins. These he brought home and had converted into bullion, that is, almost all of them. Certainly not those early machine-struck guineas considered by connoisseurs, such as himself, to be the finest gold coins ever minted. Those beauties he had kept apart in twenty-four leather bags.

It was, in all, a handsome return; not taking into account the interest received on the original four hundred thousand pounds gained from the loan made to the bankrupt English government in 1711 or the profits from the African slave trade during the expansion of the sugar plantations in Jamaica, the Leeward Islands and Barbados. Sir Laurence's father, Jean Lambert, had reckoned that this, along with the Portobello fair, to be the family's largest windfall ever.

"The bonus," Sir Laurence muttered, remembering the slang word that had been newly coined, in his day, by the office boys and articled clerks in the City of London.

From the terrace he could make out the southern extremity of the inner court below. From there came the sounds of neighing horses, stamping hooves and the bustle of arrival. Samuel Bosanquet had returned from the Antilles. Ostensibly the partner of André Fatio, he had been, however, mostly otherwise occupied. The disappearance of the *Recovery of Cartine*, he had been made to understand, could cost him his life.

"My dear Samuel," said Laurence Lambert, "I am so glad you have come. Sit, no, first take your shoes off outside. Cat shit. Melchior!" Pointing, pointing. "Cat shit." It made his nose twitch. He looked about him. There, the tiny vial that contained the essence extracted from the bergamote orange, some drops upon his cuff.

"Sit, there. Melchior, absinthe. Take some Samuel. Now, what news of Françoise, my granddaughter?"

"Thank you, my Lord. Your granddaughter is alive and thrives, my Lord, she, I understand, is near, she should arrive within the hour." He knew not much else and the little he knew he was not sure that Sir Laurence would not want to hear, at least from him.

"Well? Well what?"

"Her plantation is called Ariapita, it is just west of the capital, it thrives, my Lord. She has had constructed a large residence with the appropriate appurtenances."

The idiot seems lost for words, he thought, or is holding back something. He looked away from the squirming person who sat before him, he had felt to strike him, hard, on the ear.

Samuel Bosanquet was the grandson of one of the syndicate's first employees. He had killed him, himself, on the day they had stolen his gold. The problem had always been the gold. In these quantities, it becomes a lodestone. Because gold attacks, it draws

13: SIR LAURENCE 1789

like a magnet, takes by the nose those whose noses are attuned to the aroma of rumours babbled in the bilges of rotted wrecks and repeated in waterfront binges. Seamen know and see all that passes and repasses the counter-tops of the docksides of the world. Gold hears and sees all things.

He always secured the château himself. It was a secure place. The main hall, once a Romanesque chapel in Merovingian times, had been rebuilt over the centuries into a blockhouse: high curtain-walls with towers oversaw the island's flat wind-blown plain; there were few openings. It looked inward upon a colonnaded atrium of Gothic origin, surrounded by cloisters. Everything else faced the sea. With men on guard at all the gates, on watch from the walls and at sea, Sir Laurence supervised the furnace in the oubliette, the deepest of the labyrinthine dungeons in the heart of the old fortress, where the spinning of gold coins and other golden objects into bullion was taking place. These, to be stored even deeper than the vaulted sepulchres of the Merovingians.

ON THE MORNING THAT THE GOLD WAS TAKEN, he awoke with a start before dawn, dazed from a sleep that had been induced by exhaustion to find Rosemounde, whom he took to bed for the sport and for the company, gone. Her absence was alarming. He sprang from the bed and stood in the silent dark. Nothing. That night, he had selected to sleep in the octagonal tower where the walls were thickest, the windows narrowest, and the floors of stone. As he turned towards the faint light coming from the alcove's casement he almost fell over her lifeless body. The lamp showed her handsome face distorted, frozen in the grimace that the poison had induced. On the table stood a pewter jar that contained wine. Wine that he had been too exhausted to drink when he had fallen into bed. He stood still and listened. Nothing. Quietly he got into his clothes and boots, took the already loaded brace of pistols and his sabre, and stepped into the hallway, listening. Nothing.

But it was not nothing. In the light of the almost gutted torch, the first sentry was dead at the bottom of the stair. He crossed the armoury and entered the inner stairwell that led to the dungeons; there was another body. The wine. Someone had poisoned the wine. He felt sick with fear. The dark was absolutely still.

They were loading bags, it was his gold guineas. The iron door to the crypt was open. He could see that. Then he saw him: Cornelius Bosanquet, he was directing the removal of the leather bags that contained the prized gold guineas. The thieving dog. He called out and ran to him. They met in the light made rosy by the torches that were held high by Bosanquet's people. Cornelius was never quick on his feet and was dead after merely a shallow thrust and a weak parry.

Another's blade pierced him and a blow to his head sent him sprawling into a dark and painful place that he was condemned to for several weeks. These were the last things remembered. It was a disaster. His most treasured collection, the guineas, gone. Cornelius was dead and there was no one to say who had taken it away, or to where. That's why he had kept Cornelius' son Samuel in his employ.

CORNELIUS BOSANQUET believed up to the moment of his death that he was merely exacting his due. Like dominoes in a row, the London banks had tumbled in 1722. When the Worshipful Company of Goldsmiths found that they could not collect loans made on the Company's stock, ruin was piled upon ruin, as the nobility contemplated suicide. Parliament was reconvened in December and an investigation commenced. Reporting, it revealed widespread fraud amongst the Company's directors and corruption in the Cabinet. Among those implicated were Jean Lambert, John Aislabie, the Chancellor of the Exchequer, and all the other directors who were impeached for their corruption. The House of

13: SIR LAURENCE 1789

Commons found Aislabie guilty of the "most notorious, dangerous and infamous corruption," Cornelius' father was imprisoned. By then, Jean Lambert had died and his grandson, Sir Laurence, had left London.

Cornelius, too, had served the syndicate. That made two generations of his family. He had not met the infuriated investors. Neither did he have to flee for his life, as his father had to, when the office of The South Sea Company was overrun by a London mob intent on killing him. A resolution had been proposed in Parliament that bankers be tied up in sacks filled with snakes and thrown into the Thames.

He, however, had been the scapegoat and villain, called liar, thief and dog of a criminal, as had his son, Samuel, because it had been their duty to remain and continue the Company in London. He had managed to escape an attempt on his life and was still held as a suspect that could be dragged before the Commons or London's Criminal Bar and indicted for grand theft.

Then came the news. Sir Laurence had created a new Company called Compañía Gaditana de Negros from which he, Cornelius was excluded. He, who during and after the Seven Year War had maintained the asiento, kept the slave trading business highly profitable, as well as the Portobello fair, while Sir Laurence licked his wounds ensconced on Île de Ré. Through all this he faithfully remitted to the Company what was its due and kept its accounts. Then he realised that he was not to be included in the new venture.

Cornelius made the arrangements and arrived with a raiding party. The *Recovery of Cartine's* crew and captain knew only that they were bound for Barbados. His son Samuel, who was in Grenada at the time, was to meet it and take the guineas to some deserted island where it would be turned into bullion.

His thoughts returned to the young man who sat before him.

"Speak up, Samuel."

And the tale unfolded, he thought this must be a yarn, one that matched the absurd ruminations in the novellas of de Noailles or even the epistolary tales, *Julie, ou la nouvelle Héloïse* of Jean-Jacques Rousseau. That Bertrand de Charras should have met his end at the hands of Philippe Roume had been predictable. But that André Fatio should have become obsessed with the idea of ruining the Roume family because he had been taken in and then rejected by a woman old enough to be his mother, was ludicrous. Yet André had filled his quota. Kept his accounts and remitted accordingly to the Company's bookkeeper, and received his due. He could not listen anymore.

That drama turned tragic was normal. Roume. He had not become distracted by his domestic affairs, he had kept up the recruitment of colonists. We have reaped the rewards of his work. He did not do that for us, he did it for himself. As expected, there were debacles created by the colonists. Dislocations by the war fought in the Antilles. We now have almost all the gold we need to refit the ships. Roume.

Sipping absinthe. "Roume. What of Roume?"

"He travelled to all the islands, even to the English possessions, my Lord... In search of more Catholics. He went to Caracas, to the Audiencia."

"Did he meet the minister of the Indies, José de Gálvez?"

"Not to my knowledge, my Lord. But he did go to Paris at the time of the treaty."

Your knowledge. "Where is he now?"

"He has left Paris, my Lord, he is by now, my Lord, the ordonnateur de l'île de Tobago."

Some sort of legal functionary.

"You say that Roume is in Tobago? What is he doing there?"

13: SIR LAURENCE 1789

"He is the Chief Judge, my Lord. Appointed by the Comte de Luzerne three years ago."

"I see. Tell me, Samuel, give me an estimate, how many Africans would be required to develop this new island Trinidad? Bearing in mind that those brought in to do the work of clearing, felling, and putting in the first crops will be dead in the first two years . . . tell me, twenty thousand?"

"Very likely, my Lord."

"That would give us five to six years. Under the terms of the asiento we may ship, what, four to five thousand a year."

To get anywhere close to that estimate the Company must control at least seven or even more ships at sea as well as others on contract. José de Gálvez. José de Gálvez was the man implementing the Spanish Bourbon reforms which would not last even his lifetime. Hmm, my own lifetime, he thought.

"At the grand peace conference in Paris, England lost most of her North American colonies. My Lord may care to encourage Don José to accelerate the colonisation of Trinidad. My Lord?"

"Yes, yes, I care to. He can do as he likes. Roume, he too has served his purpose in offering the Trinidad Cedula as a viable alternative to the French Creole planters."

"Who were ruined in Grenada."

"Poor dears. Lost their lands, now they have another chance in Trinidad."

"Where we shall sell them more slaves to open up the island to commerce, my Lord."

"And mortgage them again. Commerce. I shall set up the new trade fair there. No more Portobello in Panama, Samuel. Who in hell wants to go to Panama when they can go to Trinidad?"

"Indeed, my Lord."

Now to important matters.

"Samuel. My gold. Where is it?"

"My Lord, the money was taken to Trinidad by a man, Jean-Saint-Paul Funillière, the owner of a vessel. He was in the company of a black woman."

A black woman! The very idea that a woman could be black struck him as absurd. . .

"And! And?"

"This is what we know, my Lord, this is what the African has told us. The boy, the cabin boy. He escaped on the night that Funillière slaughtered the crew in Las Cuevas Bay, my Lord. At Trinidad. He saw the sacks of gold in the captain's cabin. The guineas, actually, the gold, your gold. . . my Lord. I brought the boy, a Negro, called Bob, with me."

"Who? Why?"

"He knows about, about," he dropped his voice, "the gold. He must speak to no one else."

"Rubbish, you should have killed him."

"I could not have, sir."

"He saw it."

"Yes, my Lord."

"Kill him."

"My Lord, he may be a way to the gold, my Lord. He may be of use to us . . . you. He could lead us to them, to her."

"Where's the boy? Bring him forth."

He had never seen a Negro close up. He was surprised at his appearance. He had expected a savage. The comely nature of the dark brown suede-soft youth who stood before him pleased him. Light blue nankeen jacket worn with cream kidskin breeches, white blouse and cravat, stockings, buckled shoes. Bosanquet had outfitted him to make an appearance. Toady.

13: SIR LAURENCE 1789

"Come closer boy, I want to examine you, closer."

The youth stepped forward into the light that came from both the fireplace and the lamp on the desk at which he sat.

"Bend, I want to touch you."

He felt, with his ancient speckled hands, the smooth contours of the youth's dark face, and then passed his hands over the thick mat of black hair. He did this while keenly regarding the lad's physiognomy. Pleasing, in a way handsome. The clear whites containing black eyeballs that looked evenly back, searchingly, into his own. He has a nerve. His hand cupped the young man's chin, while his thumb passed gently over the full lips. He saw him hold himself steady, despite an almost involuntary reaction to draw away. He noted that the expression in his eyes had changed, had hardened. Umbrage. Silent, but palpable.

"Tell me everything. Sit there, yes, pull it closer, closer. Yes. You can go. Yes go."

"Very well, my Lord."

Hesitating, verging on lingering.

"Go! Damn it."

Stockinged feet shuffling, hardly making a sound. The door closed softly. Click.

"What is your name?"

"Bob. Bob, Master."

"Tell me everything."

A pirate captain and a black harridan, slatternly and fearless, she a termagant, in her lunar wanderings, adrift amidst islands, sailing between heaven, earth and hell. He had to think of Selene, Artemis and Persephone.

"The pirate captain, Funillière, what of him?"

"I do not know, Master."

"You say she has power over him?"

"Yes, Master."

"A brawling, quarrelsome woman, is she?"

"Yes, Master."

"And they seized the ship as she lay becalmed off Barbados?"

"Yes, Master."

"You saw the gold, yourself?"

"Yes, Master."

"You say she sailed the ship herself to Trinidad's coast of caves where the crew was slaughtered by Funillière."

"Yes, Master."

"Her name? What is she called?"

"Soubise, Master."

"Soubise?" wonderingly to himself. Hecate becomes Soubise in the Antilles.

"You can recognise her, you can find her, you shall lead us to her."

"Yes, Master."

"You will find her. She is there, in the Antilles?"

"Yes, Master. She is in Tobago."

The myth, it came to him. Descent, loss, the search and the ascent. With the main theme the ascent of Persephone.

"Whether she be on the sea, beneath the lunar tides or, in the bowels of the earth."

"Master?"

". . . . ."

"Master?"

"Find her."

"Yes, Master."

13: SIR LAURENCE 1789

He regarded the boy, Triptolemus, the primordial man. No, no. King Memnon, the Aethiopian. Father of Thor, ancestor of all the Germans. A black, that pleased him.

"I shall put you in the care of my people and you shall point her out and they will bring her to me, and for that you shall receive a golden ear of corn."

"Thank you, Master."

"Melchior!"

"Sire?"

"Absinthe, another. Ask Samuel to rejoin me, and show Master Bob to his quarters. And see that he is prepared to travel when our agents from Bordeaux arrive."

"Yes, Sire."

"Thank you Melchior. Now to Funillière. Please admit master Samuel."

"Sire."

"Samuel, where does Funillière come from?"

"His family lives in Guadeloupe, but I have been told that he has returned to his native village of Callelongue, close to Marseille, my Lord."

"See first our factor in Bordeaux, hand him this. Go to Callelongue, find Funillière. Discover whether he has my gold. Our people from Bordeaux will aid you in putting the question. In the event that he does not have it, Funillière must be killed, he must not return to the Antilles."

Sir Laurence passed him a sealed document.

"Thank you, my Lord."

Samuel Bosanquet knew that he was a hostage, held against the possibility that knowledge of the treasure in gold, stolen by the accomplices of his dead father, might somehow come to him.

Sir Laurence had preferred to keep him close and treat him as his ward, the orphaned son of an esteemed colleague, as opposed to creating in him yet another loose end. The captain Funillière, he might well point the way for him to retrieve the treasure for himself.

"Melchior."

"Sire?"

"My granddaughter, has she come?"

"Yes Sire."

"Please, conduct her here to me."

"Sire."

THE WOMAN WHO STOOD BEFORE HIM was recognisable only because she reminded him of his mother. Sir Laurence had not seen his granddaughter Françoise for almost twenty-five years. He has hardly changed, aged or anything, she thought, as she entered the small round tower apartment that her grandfather occupied on cold autumn days. Regarding her, he had to think of the Moirai, the three Fates. Atropos, the eldest, the cutter of the thread of life.

"My dear, how lovely you are, a woman at last."

"Ravaged by life, I see you are thinking."

"Kissed by experience is what crossed my mind, come, kiss me, here," he pointed to his lips, "sit in the light, close by, next to me. Now, tell me everything."

What she spoke of had only to do with death, grief and loss. He noticed how the lines on her face framed her feelings. Elizabeth, her daughter, born in 1766, had died aged twenty, in her blossoming, two years ago. She made a gesture, so helpless that he felt her loss. There was a miniature of Elizabeth. She saw he could not look at it. She placed it on the table at the side of his chair.

She could not sit still and spoke, her clothes large upon her, ill-fitting and old fashioned, obviously uncomfortable, while pacing

13: SIR LAURENCE 1789

the room's circular floor. How thin and flat she has become, but physically strong, he thought.

"And your husband?"

"He has nothing to do with us, with me. He is in Tobago. He has a black woman, she was born on Soubise estate in Grenada, her name is Marianne Rochard, she calls herself Soubise. Perhaps he had her all the while. They live with the blacks and become like them."

"The nature of their cruelty is not unfamiliar."

A Soubise in Tobago, with Roume. Can that be the same one? Surely.

"Yes. At first it disgusts. Then you find that it comes naturally. You are free to kill them out of hand. The entire place is poised, perpetually, on the brink of unimaginable violence."

"So too is France. Weak and debauched; the dynasty has failed. It will fall. I don't give it a year."

"And then what?"

"Paris is hungry. Haven't you seen the starvation in the countryside? A peasant's war will commence. We shall be targetted, it is inevitable." He waved his hands over his head. "All this will be gone."

"And where shall you go, we go?"

"To London. To meet André Fatio."

"Is he to be the heir?"

"According to my will, and only if you agree to marry him."

"I see. Does he know your plans?"

"Of course not. It all depends on you."

"And my father?"

"He has already received his due. The family continues with you."

"I am well over forty."

"Then you better hurry to London. In any event, you have nephews. When all of this is over, I may well be dead, but the assets are safe. I shall show you. Now speak to me, tell me everything. I want to know everything."

FANNY LAMBERT, since departing Grenada, had lived in Spanish Trinidad. She had not been able to find herself after Bertrand's death and postponed the decision to return to France because of a lack of will. The person that she became, the one that she caught a glimpse of while in the prison of insomniac nights at Belvédère in its final months, she had failed to recognise. She was no longer a match for her indomitable grandfather, she thought, and believed that she had become someone who had failed the promise of their prime.

Fanny's decision to set up residence in an environment such as Trinidad's and take her daughter Elizabeth with her had been prompted by a desperate urge to get away from Grenada. She had grown to despise the remaining French colonists. Those who could not leave through lack of money, nerve or vision had formed a circle of envious spite. The place, ever since the English had taken it, had grown increasingly oppressive.

She abhorred the sly vindictiveness and abysmal ignorance of the mixed-race people, in whose faces she could now recognise the white families from which their bastardy sprang. They smelled of obeah, the sorcery of these islands.

As for the seething hate and secret anger of the slaves, this frightened her.

She grew to believe, in some misguided, possibly crazed manner, that the urge to get away to Trinidad was rooted in the idealistic notions expressed by Philippe Roume in the early days of their marriage. Trinidad, uncultivated and uncivilised and unsullied, was in a manner of speaking, a paradise.

These feelings had mutated into an inconsolable despair. In any event, she could not remain in Grenada. With Belvédère gone to

13: SIR LAURENCE 1789

the English speculators, she would have nowhere to live. Added to this, she learnt from André Fatio on one of his increasingly infrequent return visits to Grenada, that her grandfather had in '79 lost a fortune, his prized collection of golden British guineas, in a second raid on Île de Ré. She felt that she was really marooned in the Caribbean.

Hitherto, notwithstanding Philippe's indifference, she could rely on her own resources. These were not inconsiderable, as her grandfather had continued to send to her, through the course of their marriage, sums of money, usually Louis d'or as well as British guineas. Philippe had moved into a townhouse in St. George's, he expressed neither love nor hate towards her. Even his indifference was indifferent.

Nothing was a secret in Trinidad either. Fanny had always been informed of Philippe's visits in the months and years after she had set herself up at the Ariapita plantation. He knew that she was there. He never came to her. The plantation that had been granted to her by the Spanish Crown, some one hundred and thirty acres to the west of the town, offered respite, albeit temporary, where she could rearm and reequip so as to face them all.

The Ariapita plantation occupied a plain that rolled gently southward from the foothills in the north towards the mangrove shore. Heavily forested, it was overly watered by the Rio Ariapita that during the wet season flooded the south-western extremities of the estate. She built a new house, tall and square, its lower storey constructed from river-stone and the ballast bricks that arrived from Europe in the half empty ships which came for the hogsheads of sugar being produced in ever increasing quantities by the new estates.

Her twelve slaves were all Africa-born men, young. She did not want to face the sly demeanour and cunning ways of women and those who thought that they knew her well. She saw personally to the clearing of the land around the house, extending it regularly with every dry season for four years. She planted vegetables in what was called a provision garden, comprising mainly roots; yam, cassava, sweet potatoes, corn and bananas along with a wild variety, called moco fig. These she sold as food for slaves to the surrounding plantations and in the town.

She kept at bay all suitors and accepted no invitations offered to her by the Spanish colonial administrators or the planters' wives. She knew well that Pico de Lapéyrouse and Benoît Dert, her nearest neighbours, were friends of Philippe's, and avoided them. She lived alone in the house that she had furnished simply but not inelegantly. Elizabeth died within the first year of a burning fever that consumed her will to survive. Now there was nothing left of their marriage. She was sustained by this isolation until Shadrach Lazare arrived at her gate.

She supposed that she had always wanted a man. After the first year of living alone, sleeping alone, sleeping the sleep of the physically exhausted, she had grown once more accustomed to her body. Remembered it. It commenced with a ritual bath that she had acquired the habit of taking in the dark, in a room adjacent to the one where she slept. She would wash them all out of her hair, out of her armpits, out of her crotch, off the soles of her feet and especially from between her toes. A private act of cleansing body and mind. An act that reignited a passion that she believed had left her forever. Then one morning he was there.

"Hey! What you want?"

"Work."

"No work, go away."

"Yes, there is work. The fields are large, they are stealing."

She knew that the slaves were stealing the provisions grown on the estate and were selling them, bartering, whatever.

"When they steal, they will kill."

13: SIR LAURENCE 1789

Yes, she knew that. She had seen the change in them. At first they were cowed, thin and convinced that they too would be eaten like the provisions. From different tribes, they could hardly speak to one another. Now they had found strength in her preoccupation and in their numbers. She needed a man around.

"Are you white?"

"Maybe."

"What do you want?"

"Food, a place to sleep, money perhaps."

"Have you ever been an overseer?"

"No. But I can frighten them. Beat them, kill them if necessary."

"Come."

He came. She could not tell if he was mixed. She did not care. He moved into the stable. They rode about the estate together. She could see that the slaves resented him. He beat one of the thieves one night, woke him from his cot and beat him with his fists. He did not tell him a word. Just beat him bloody. The next morning he beat him again. The following week, as he was coming in from the fields, the same slave whom he had beaten hurled a wooden pole at him. Thrown from a tree, it knocked him off the horse and into the river. Before he could catch himself, the man was upon him with an axe. He defended himself with the pole, shouting for help, other slaves stood by looking on. The fight was to the death. He defended himself with the pole against the axe. Hardly a match, as the slave swung and swung, shattering the pole, he falling back. The others were on the river's bank laughing.

She heard his screams and calls for help and got the gun. With trembling hands she loaded it. She had shot corn-birds so she had some experience. She ran out towards the river, there she saw the fight. She fired at the slave and missed, hitting another one on the bank. It caused a distraction. This allowed Shadrach Lazare to take the advantage, they were now struggling for the axe, each one holding on to it. She could think of nothing else but to run into the water and bring down the gun on the slave's head as hard as she could. He fell forward, this allowed Shadrach Lazare to seize the axe and bury it into the back of the slave, deep into his body. The river ran red. The other slaves ran away. He went after them, found them, tied them up wrist to wrist between two trees and beat them with a horse whip till they bled and fell into a mangled heap, weeping and begging for mercy.

They were all sold cheaply to a French man called Begorrat who had a reputation for harshness. With the money, given to him by her, he bought six middle-aged men from two different planters at the slave market at Fort San Andres. He demolished the old barracks and with their help rebuilt it with much better accommodation for the new men. This all happened at the start of the dry season.

One hot night, after her ritual bath, she went to him in the stable, he was sitting at the door.

"Come with me," she said.

"No," he answered.

She stood there, the half moon backlighting her near nakedness. He got up and, taking her by her wrist, led her through the stable to one of the stalls that was filled with papra-grass, fodder for the animals. He threw down a horse blanket. She understood that she had to lie down like an animal, while he stood there looking at her. In the flat moonlight everything appeared in shades of grey. His eyes, sunk so deep, were invisible, like holes in his head, his profile, as he looked over his shoulder, was harsh and broken, she saw his front teeth, she had not noticed before that they protruded. He was pulling his smock from his trousers. She could feel his unseen eyes on her as he knelt at her side and raised her nightdress, she lifting herself, so that it came up beyond her breasts to under her armpits in a bundle. She put a hand on his arm and felt his taut muscles. He was shaking. He was looking at her, she felt to hide and started to

13: SIR LAURENCE 1789

draw up her knees when he parted them wide, bending to look. He was smelling her, sniffing softly, this evoked in her an undulation that started in her stomach and rippled down like twirling twin flames. He was upon her. She pushed at his trouser tops as she felt him fumble at his fly. He prevented her. Why, she wondered. His naked flesh entered her as he pinned her down, holding her hands hard on either side of her head. His rumpled head of hair fell on her face. She smelled rum on his breath and as she found his mouth, she could taste the tang of black tobacco. She was insensible, yet heard the wild cries she made, like singing something half in tune. Then it was over. Too quick, this was too quick. She held him as he tried to rise. He was breathing hard, panting, as though he had run a great distance. Wait, she thought, wait. She held his quivering body. She felt him let go, as he became soft and began to slip away. No, she found his mouth and moved so that he could remain there. She felt him rise and arranged herself for him. Then something fresh, new commenced, she slid away, he let her, she removed his breeches, taking them down and around his hard bony feet and sharp-edged toenails, and then threw away the nightdress and straddled him. They could hear the horses, restless, snorting and shifting, in the stalls. She could smell them, smell him now. He smelt of leather and wax, carbolic soap and something poor. She closed her eyes and rode him through swirling currents and cataracts, changing tides and rolling waves of exquisite rhythms, broken into by her wild singing, till he became rigid and bucked and arched himself and snorted like the horses, and now that the moon had found them, she saw him clearly, he was smiling. She had never seen him smile.

He never came into the house after dark. He would take her in the river or in the fields at night between the furrows bearing produce, ground provisions. Only in the day, he would take her sometimes unawares from behind in the house, pushing her dress up her back, he liked it with some clothes on, furtive she thought.

She saw herself return. She thought that she might become pregnant, she didn't care, but didn't. In his eyes, she saw herself as she was, older than he by eight or ten years. Tall, still crimson-haired, small sad breasts, thin, long-limbed and freckled. The freckles were new, they had suddenly appeared. First across her face like a spattering of red paint, then down along her body like a rash. She stood upon a chair to see them all in the oval looking glass that she had hung in her bathroom. The tuft of red hair between her thin thighs. He had asked her, it was their second night in the stable, if she had red hair down there, she had answered no, purple feathers. He laughed and laughed. It was the first joke that they shared and was kept as a conversational memento.

Then one day he came to her, she could see that he was in earnest about something. What? Her heart was in her mouth, suddenly, she thought that he was going to leave. No, no. He said, I have something to tell you and to show you. Something for us. What? Where? I shall have to take you somewhere. Where, she was so relieved she laughed and laughed and pushed her hands through her red hair, her face appearing, shining, expectant. Then he told her. It was a treasure beyond belief. A fortune in new, beautiful, golden guineas. Golden guineas! She suspected at once. How? He told her then that he had been a member of a pirate crew, that he had been there when they boarded a schooner. He had been with them, the captain and the woman. Yes. They gave me some. See. He showed her a leather purse that he wore beneath his blouse, golden guineas. She recognised them straight away. They were hers, her grandfather's. He said that he had come to her to work so as to be safe because of them. Yes. She understood that, gold was always a problem. And that he loved her. She gazed at him. Yes, he believed that he did. This was their future, he said. Yes, she nodded. Yes. She smiled. Yes. She had found her grandfather's gold. Yes, she loved him too. And would go away with him to New Orleans. Oh yes. He would show her the gold tomorrow.

13: SIR LAURENCE 1789

Tomorrow came too soon as usual with them. She awoke to find him putting provisions into two saddlebags, horses already saddled. They rode west along the bridle-path that took them through the coconut plantation where a few indentured Chinese worked in solemn isolation. Men without women, he said, as they cantered through. What is this place called, she asked, her animal huffing and pounding the sandy way. Cocorite, they called it. For the palms. She had not asked and he had not said where they were going.

He halted at a bend where the road turned north into Don Diego Martin's plantations, he dismounted and helped her down and they walked the foaming horses down a track through the sea grape and the mangroves to the sea. There, drawn up on the mud flats, was a dinghy. "Get in," he said, hitching the horses to a low-hanging branch of an old mango tree. "Where are we going?" "To sea," he said, simply. She got in, thrilled at the thought, she had not been sailing in years. He pushed the small craft off and jumped aboard. Working quickly he got the sail up and, taking the tiller, headed out into the soft light air. The noon sun was hot, she took off her blouse and the wind caressed her as she caressed him to his delight.

They sailed quickly westward towards the cluster of small islands, bypassing these they tacked towards the larger of some other islands. The shoreline had slipped away and the mountains appeared tall and green and stern. The wind shifted as they were rounding the point of the larger island. He pointed to where he had lain hidden and had seen them sail the yawl that contained the treasure. He had seen them all along, as he had followed them along the coast and into the Gulf.

She could see the vastness of the Gulf of Paria now, the view to the south showed the length of the island and in the distance, a flat-topped mountain on the coast. What is that? Naparima it is called. How far away? More than twenty miles on the King's Royal Road. The governor has built a town there, named for the Prince of

Spain. What's it called? I forget. As the sun turned westward, the mountains of Venezuela loomed high and blue. He tacked the boat in towards a bay that contained an islet at its mouth.

"Where are we going?"

He smiled. They tied up to a small tree on the islet. "We will hang two hammocks, here and here and build a fire there." And so it was done. That night they made love in one hammock until the rope slipped and they fell upon the hard stoney ground where the morning found them. He was busy, she could see, removing stones, rolling boulders, straining away at large, unmoving rocks, some of which were half buried in the rocky soil, with an iron bar that had lain at the bottom of the dinghy. "What are you doing?" Still he would not say. Then she saw a hole in the rocks that led down into a rough low passage that the noon day sun showed to some advantage. "Come," he said, "we must do this quickly before the tide rises." She, now quite thrilled by him, by this adventure, entered the tunnel. Bending low, she held on to his shirt from behind, as all light vanished and there was nothing but pitch black all around. "Wait, do not move yet or straighten up," he whispered. Struggling to get a flambeau lighted using flint and stone. At last the darkness wavered into view, it was an enormous cave, she could barely see about her but rather felt its vastness and the water that was cold around her calves. This is terrifying, she thought and said, shivering and holding on to him. "Let us leave, I am afraid."

"Come, it must be here somewhere," he said, he was looking for something, waving the flambeau about.

Around them clustered strange elongated monkish shapes that in the shifting yellow light appeared to move and flash and hover, throwing ghastly shadows. Overhead, she could make out the sharp and threatening points of others that looked as though they could drop and impale them. It was a scary place. The dark was threatening, the echoes of their voices eerie, the air was old and stank of something yet unseen, and still he worked his way along

13: SIR LAURENCE 1789

the walls that dripped and in some places ran with sea water that was coming in.

"What are you looking for?" she called, afraid, feeling the echoing silence falling in on her. "What?"

She saw him in the shallow light looking up into what appeared to be an opening and took the flambeau from his hand, as he sought to get a foothold. Above them she could make out the edge of an iron chest.

"Yes. Yes," she said, holding the light above her head, she could see that he was seeking a way to reach the ledge upon which the chest was placed. As she glanced nervously down into the rising water she saw a gold coin shimmer, then another. As she bent to pick them up, now certain what this meant, she lost her balance and the flambeau fell from her hand into the water and all went black. Her heart was racing as intuitively she knew that this was indeed her grandfather's gold. They stood there for a long time not daring to move while working out in their minds the direction from which they had come.

All right. "Come," he said, she was strangely calm as she sought and found his hand and they started off, bouncing into the shapes that now, in the absolute dark, glistened and sparkled with bright silver and green dots. Phosphorescent and cold, they seemed to blend one into the other. Round and round they went, their hands numb with cold, the water rising to her thighs, where, where, is it? The tension turned to panic. Where is it? She felt to flee, to run, where? She turned and stumbling fell into a hole, the dark water rising, coughing, the salt had got into her eyes, her throat, she coughed, and found an edge and scrambled up. "Where are you?" She called, her voice not her own at all, there was no one in the darkness, no one. Where was he, she waded about. Her hands waving, she called and screamed. No one answered. Then she saw it. A lighter shade of dark, the small waves were running through. She stood at the entrance to the low tunnel, looking back, shouting.

"Shadrach!"

To no avail. No answer. No Shadrach. Only the darkness and the rising, lapping, hissing water drawing away and returning, rising, rising past her waist, cold and salty, stinging her eyes as it splashed across her face, her lips and into her mouth. She coughed, panic had overtaken her. She struggled out of the rocky passage, and bruised and cut from the sharp rocks she climbed, blood running down her arms and legs, up onto the rocks.

It was late afternoon, still the very same day. That amazed her. She stared with shock back down into the foaming pit of the passage, the sea, white and black, it came, swilling, churning, filling up. She was not out of her senses. No, she knew what had happened, he had drowned in there. She also knew what she had seen. And she was alone again.

She spent the night wrapped in the hammocks and with the morning light she pushed as many rocks as she could into the opening and sailed the dinghy to Cocorite, where the horses, tethered, had waited. She knew that she must now leave this place. She had to get to France, to Île de Ré, to her grandfather.

"YOU SAW THE GOLD?" he asked, leaning forward, the tower room now become dark. "The man took you there for it. He would have given it to you?"

"Yes. He would have. There were gold guineas in the water. Several, they must have fallen from the chest, or perhaps had dropped when it was being filled. It would have been too heavy to be lifted into a place so high above if it had been filled with coins."

"Yes. I suppose."

"What shall we do?"

"Get it. I have already dispatched someone to find the woman, Soubise. She is in Tobago with your husband. Bosanquet went to

13: SIR LAURENCE 1789

find the man who stole it with her, a captain. Now they both must be caught and killed, they must not return to Trinidad, either of them, before we set sail to get what is ours. Which will be soon, very soon." He sat back into the shadows, "I must send to London for André."

"André?"

"Yes, I shall need help, I am not as I was. A ship to make the crossing, men, the right men. Trust. Men whose trust cannot be bought. My men. Melchior!"

"Yes, Sire."

"Melchior, go to Samuel Bosanquet, my order is now to arrange the death of the captain."

"Yes, Sire."

SAMUEL BOSANQUET was overtaken by Melchior at the port of Pertuis d'Antioche with his new instructions. As was his custom, Samuel travelled lightly and alone. His insipid appearance would at the end of his journey augment his costume. He would be dressed then as a pilgrim, with a broad-brimmed grey hat and a full-length felt cloak, seeking passage to the shrine of St. Stephen, there to pray at the reliquaries of the martyr which were preserved in the Church of St. Stephen in Jerusalem. His journey from Île de Ré on the Atlantic coast to the village of Callelongue on the Mediterranean would take just over three weeks. He travelled at first by coach and then rode in company with others through the wine countryside to Bordeaux where he had Lambert business to attend to. This business entailed engaging men who at various times had performed specific tasks for the Company. In this instance, a party of them were to repair to Île de Ré, thence travel to Tobago in company with the black boy, Bob, who would identify the woman, Marianne, who sometimes called herself Soubise, and kill her. Another group would meet him at Callelongue for the purpose of executing Funillière.

Samuel rode on towards Toulouse and then southward towards his final destination. As he travelled, he was surprised and increasingly alarmed at the tumult and unrest in the hamlets and villages, the towns and even the cities where he stopped. In some areas the people he saw about him were desperate, dangerous, many apparently starving. They spoke of la Grande Peur and indeed, fear was in their faces. The droughts of the previous year. The terrible winter frosts. The harvests had been disastrous. The storms and floods had wiped away what little was left. Unrest, since the worsening grain shortage of the spring, was now fuelled by rumours of a plot arranged by the aristocrats to cause a great famine so as to starve them to death. Peasants and town people were mobilising in many regions, arming themselves, often to mistake each other's intentions and to meet in deadly encounters. Across the land, the great seigniorial estates lay abandoned. Farms and fields neglected. Rural life had ceased as the folk deserted the villages and fearful peasants armed themselves in self-defence to hide in the forest.

All the talk in the inns where he stopped was of the great convocation called by the king for the assembling of the three estates of the realm, an estates-general. When he arrived at Marseille, the city was in an uproar. When asked his name, he said that it was Pierre Funillière in the hope that someone would say that they knew a person by that name. He made his way to the waterfront and found an inn that catered to pilgrims seeking passage to the east. There he found people avidly discussing the storming of the great prison in Paris. He portrayed himself as pious and made inquiries about ships and trustworthy captains. Funillière, he had heard of a captain by that name. Voyages to the Outremer were an industry, he was assured.

News of the upheavals in Paris rippled slowly across the land. Almost no one knew what had happened in the capital or what had

13: SIR LAURENCE 1789

caused the storming of the Bastille. What was understood was that a thin edge had been gained in an iron-clad, iron-fisted regime and that confusion, un-met, unrestrained, had reigned. That mutinous gardes françaises had joined the masses, that in provinces across the country the people were storming châteaux, expelling the servants, chasing away the seigneurs and burning the title deeds, all generated a giddy sense of devil-may-care.

No one believed that they were really participating in the end of the world. It was the moment to express the pent-up rage and the naked anger of a starving people. Not a few were actually crazed, hallucinating as a result of eating of ergot, a fungus that grew on wheat and in bread that in good years would naturally have been thrown away, but in bad times was consumed.

He saw them, bands of the crazed, weeping, praying, seeing spirits, the virgin Mary, the archangels, dead parents, popes and daemons. Skeletal men and women in tatters looking like the walking dead appeared out of the forest. Matted hair, toothless mouths, grasping hands, the foul breath of starvation, with calloused feet black with filth, they appeared in the drawing rooms, in parlors, in bedrooms. Some tore down tapestries and shattered Meissen porcelain figurines. But mostly they were simply in search of food and gorged themselves at dinner tables suddenly deserted.

He awoke one morning to find Marseille festooned in blue, white and red. Flags, new, hung from every building. Bunting and pennants fluttered. It was a beautiful sight. The August sky, so blue. The wind coming off the ink-blue Mediterranean carried a warmth that was born in far-off Africa. He leaned out the window, below were crowds of people dressed in these bright colours, waving, calling one and all to join them, and children too, and soldiers marching irregularly with beautiful women on their arms.

Amongst the throng rode cavalry, their horses decorated with blue, white and red tricolour cockades. These tricolour cockades were everywhere. Young girls flung them from baskets into the crowd.

In the distance along the street he could see wagons surrounded by cavalrymen. The crowd was shouting in a vast chorus a chant that went "Liberté! égalité! fraternité! Freedom, equality, brotherhood!" A man was reading out loud something he could hardly hear, then the voice rose above the tumult, he heard him say: "Liberty consists of being able to do anything that does not harm others."

Then the wagons came into plainer view. There were people in them, aristocrats by their look. Old men, and women, children and young men. The crowd around them was not throwing cockades but filth at them. People in the balconies around were emptying their chamber pots upon them. As he looked, he saw that there were more carts in the distance, also filled with notables. Boys and young men from a military school, all shackled together, walked in rows, beaten by men with rods and sticks.

The uproar was now beneath his window which overlooked a square. The aristocrats were taken off the carts and with kicks and blows were herded into the middle, where the men and boys were placed to one side and the women were taken away. All around was confusion. He saw a cavalryman draw a sword and slash a man across his face, to the crowd's roar of encouragement and approval. A slaughter commenced, as horses were ridden into the huddling band of screaming people.

My God, this is murder! He felt too terrified to move. Pruning shears and scissors appeared, they were shearing off their hair, their noses and their ears. Already he could see ropes being looped around the branches of the trees. The noise too, was horrible, he placed his hands over his ears but still it came, made grotesque by the arrival of a military band that was playing jaunty medleys and circus songs as the first bodies kicked and defecated to cheers and great applause.

Shots rang out and a different regiment was seen. Hussars charged into the screaming mass and panic reigned as the mob bolted in every direction, leaving the blue, white and red sashes, bunting and tricolour cockades to mingle with the blood and filth.

13: SIR LAURENCE 1789

That night there was a battle for the city. By morning the rescuing hussars had fled and the flags of the revolution were everywhere. Too afraid to leave, he stayed inside and watched the ferocious gaiety. There was the sensation that the very gravity of the earth had altered. That the principles of things had become rearranged. He gasped and yawned and rubbed his aching, sleepless eyes. He was starving. He was not alone, the hostel was now overflowing with people. A woman and several children had come into his room. He felt afraid of them and cowered. The following morning, the door was kicked down. It was the men from Bordeaux. They had come for him, they laughed at his condition. They threw out the woman and her brats and gave him beef and bread, apples, wine, he drank and became hysterical. They beat him into silence, for what he was ranting. No Sire Laurence here, now or ever. Look, they said, we know that you are here to find a man who has a secret. A secret that Laurence Lambert desires, give it, a name, or we shall start with your nose and end with your balls. For good measure we shall take off an ear. The stinging pain, the blood, it was only a very small piece of ear and he told them all he knew, which was more than they could comprehend. A captain Funillière you say, citoyen? We shall find him. Where? Callelongue. Have you ever seen him? No! no! no! never. Still, come with us. They were a bold and fearless bunch and, with him in their midst, they entered the swarming city streets and headed for the docks, stopping along the way to drink the wine of the harvest. Callelongue! Where is that place? There, just two or three miles, over there.

Arriving, they found a village built about the rocky cliffs that overlooked an estuary. They began a shout. Funillière! Funillière! Bring out the traitor. Others took up the cry and many bold men came forward crying, I am Funillière. Some were old, others too young, some had never been to sea. The one you seek is there, and there he was, Jean-Saint-Paul Funillière, armed with pistols, a brazen blunderbuss, and a cutlass in his waist. The man who had stolen the gold, his father's gold which was somewhere over there, in the Antilles.

"Who calls Funillière?" the man demanded, facing the wavering crowd, in the midst of which stood the Bordelais.

"We have come for what is ours," they shouted, "come let us take down the hoarder. Reveal your secrets, tell us all and everything." The wavering crowd surged forward, his wife appeared, she too was armed, and his sons, strapping versions of the father.

The pistols fired and two fell at Samuel's side. Another pistol appeared and fired, a man went howling to his death, and then a brazen blunderbuss fired and scattered shot about. He felt the pepper of hot metal slash across his face and a terrible pain enter his mind as all receded into nothing. He later learnt that the Bordelais had killed the captain and had been killed themselves. An old man had taken him to a house where they took a week to remove the bits of metal from his face and body. He had lost an eye. But he had not lost his money belt, no one had imagined that he would have such a thing. It was a revolution, he learned. And that the Parisian militia had taken the city.

Reading from my Memoirs at La Fontenoy, Grenada, 1806

GOVERNMENT HOUSE, TOBAGO, 1789. In this diary I recorded our final months in Tobago. We had joined Dillon for petit dejeuner at a table that overflowed with dispatch cases. These were newly arrived from France and told of riots and upheavals in the capital. Holding up a copy of the *Mercure de France,* Philippe said in a dismissive tone, "The so-called democrats are circulating the activities of a new society, Société des amis des noirs, in Saint-Domingue and Guadeloupe."

"What is that?" I asked. "Les amis des noirs, now that sounds interesting, eh Decima? Decima!" That girl was so vague in the mornings.

"It is a subversive grouping in Paris, instigated by the English, meant to destroy our economy by emancipating the slaves," said

13: SIR LAURENCE 1789

Philippe with a smirk. "A Society of the Friends of the Blacks. It emerges from them trying to find their conscience after their atrocities in the last war. The parliamentarians in London will use it for political gain. But, it will affect the planters here, nothing will keep it from the slaves. The very idea of friends of the blacks will be enough to create a rebellion."

"This is for us, les amis des noirs," said Decima, her sleepy voice melodic. "We have it already," she said and laughed with a certain slyness and, "this is not for them, the niggers, this is for *les affranchis,* like me and you, Soubise."

"A lot of chabine men want to be friends with white people," I replied, joining in with her la-di-da voice as I prepared petit dejeuner for Philippe.

"Well, they will get friends." She rose and left us, having heard her baby crying.

While Dillon dozed and Decima snored, Philippe wrote a speech to be delivered by him at the Port Louis High Court. A flowery declaration of loyalty to the King. It might have been the last panegyric of its kind to be delivered by a French public servant in the Antilles.

Arthur Dillon returned to France in September of 1789, travelling on the same ship that brought the news of the storming of the Bastille by a Parisian mob. He had been elected to represent Martinique in a grand gathering that the king had summoned, the Les États-Généraux.

Dillon did not resign his position as governor of Tobago. He simply passed it on as an acting position to the Chevalier Jean-Jacques de Jobal, the commander of the garrison, a person of such insipidity as to make you sick.

"I am sorry, Monsieur, but you and your little friends will have to vacate the house."

Jobal's astounding announcement came the very morning that Dillon sailed for France.

"By all means, Monsieur, my friends and I shall vacate the premises with haste," said my Philippe with such panache that I heard Jobal's surprised intake of breath, an acquaintance, an interpreter in the court, who had trained as a surgeon, Dr. Edmond Saint-Léger already stepping away.

We were standing on the jetty in the rising wind, the ship with Dillon still in sight. The parade had been called to order. The band, instruments flashing, blared. The march from the jetty to the barracks had commenced. The farewell delegation was milling around. Some were coming over. A numbing sensation was overwhelming me, headfirst. My ears were stopped up, my skin was tingling, my mouth had gone dry, I felt Philippe's hand on my arm just above the elbow. He was turning me away as a fury in me rose. I glanced over my shoulder, Jean-Jacques de Jobal had been joined by his wife and a company of officers, they were congratulating him. At my side, Rosette, our child, was saying something to Decima de la Forêt, who was taking her hand. The carriage was there; we entered, all together. We moved into the surgeon major's quarters at Fort Saint Louis.

That the Bastille had been breached by the citizenry of Paris and that the king and queen had been disturbed to the extent of their appearing in their nightclothes was amusing, to me at least. The news also contained a declaration—the Declaration of the Rights of Man and of the Citizen.

"What the hell is that?" I asked.

"It's rubbish! But it may mean the end of absolute monarchy," Philippe answered.

That night, I awoke to find Decima de la Forêt bending over to touch my shoulder. Philippe was asleep next to me. In the magenta glow of the candle flame, I saw her face, eyes wide, her finger on her lips.

13: SIR LAURENCE 1789

"People are in the house, wake him. We must take them by surprise, yes."

"The children?" My mouth went dry.

"Locked in. I came through the window from the gallery. Here, the pistol case, wake him."

"I . . . listen, a noise," I whispered, "On the roof, listen—Philippe, Philippe," I said softly in his ear, passing my hand through his hair.

He was awake. He thought it was for love. "Decima is here, there is someone inside, quiet, here, a pistol, it is primed, careful," my hands were shaking.

"Downstairs, now, listen, on the stairs. . ." she whispered, blowing out the candle and the lamp that burned low on the small table at the bedside.

Not a sound.

A figure at the window, I fired. A man cried out and fell with a crash on the shed below. As the door was thrown open, Philippe fired. Through the pistol's smoke, I saw a man falling backward, stumbling onto another; tumbling noises on the stairs, a whistle outside, several whistles; the sentries. The bloody sentries, where were they?

"There was a carriage outside. Down the drive. The one you shot out of the window is dead, I think," he told me, he appeared amazed.

"I am a pirate, remember," I told him. "Who the hell were those people?"

"Jobal's people, or thieves, or both," he said, I could hear in his voice that he wanted me to be calm. "We must be careful."

Thieves. I did not believe that. My instincts told me that they were after me. Me, because of the gold at Winn's Bay on Gaspar Percin's island. I felt my stomach clench. I must tell him.

The following week, at the courthouse in Port Louis, Philippe said to Jobal impatiently, "Those men, there, are being insubordinate. This is a court of law. I shall not stand for that sort of behaviour. What has happened here, Jean-Jacques, is a flagrant disregard of authority."

"Your own?" asked Jobal maliciously.

"Yes, as an officer of the court and of the realm."

"What is the realm, Philippe? Where is it? Who is it?" Jobal and others had disrupted the court. So it began.

Jean-Jacques de Jobal was, soon after the departure of Dillon, under the influence of the tradesmen and small landowners, the Petits Blancs of Tobago, who saw themselves as victims of Philippe's judgments. They portrayed Philippe as a royalist servant of the old regime. Indeed, he was—but scrupulous when it came to the law.

"Citoyen Roume, I shall not countenance your banning fellow citoyens coming here from Martinique."

Jobal had received a communiqué that in Paris rioters had taken the entire royal family along with what was called the National Assembly to Paris in a grand procession from the Palace of Versailles, led by buffoons, dwarves and crazy women. Now the chevalier had turned citoyen.

"These are French people, they may travel where they like." Jobal was pacing the corridor outside of the First Court, his voice, loud, was meant to carry to the sentries, the secretaries, the clerks, the slaves, and to the people in the street.

"Those people are insurgents, most of them felons," answered Philippe quietly. "All this will be destroyed. Don't you see that, Jean-Jacques? The upheavals are in France. It can still go either way."

"It will go in the direction of the will of the people," said Jobal with the arrogance of the come-lately. "The question has been asked, what is the third estate? Everything. What has it been until

13: SIR LAURENCE 1789

now in the political order? Nothing. What does it want to be? Something. Those people want to be something."

Sometime later on, it was the morning of the Mardi Gras, Philippe said to him, "Captain de Monferand has reported what could be interpreted as a mutiny of the Compagnies de Mallet and de Cordelier at Bacolet." Philippe was calm, his voice firm and even, he understood that things had changed with Dillon's departure. He demanded from Jobal, "You must go to the fort and enforce discipline!" I stood in the doorway and trembled. "Here, in these islands, order, discipline, must prevail. Any kind of breakdown will rouse the slaves to take the opportunity and revolt."

Jean-Jacques de Jobal, pretending to ignore him, walked to the window.

"There is talk of establishing a local People's Assembly. That must not be allowed, Jean-Jacques. Control of the colony must not pass into the hands of those people. That would mean a massacre. People are leaving. The English merchants have gone. Out there people are rioting, listen."

From the street below came the sounds of shouts and of women screaming. Someone was blowing a conch shell.

"Good, good! The English can go to hell! You have been reported to the National Assembly in Paris, citoyen Roume. A petition has been sent to Paris: seven hundred names demanding your removal. And the People's Assembly has been formed, it has met. That petition is its first act."

Just then, coming from the direction of the port, bellowing shouts were heard. People left their offices and ran to the windows, a noise, loud like a roaring, was plainly audible.

"Fire, fire, look fire!" someone shouted. I could smell the smoke, acrid, a burning in the throat.

"Fire—Jean-Jacques, call out the troops, now! The Guadeloupe Rangers have disembarked," shouted Philippe. My God, why does he not just kill this fool and take over the place, take command of those loyal troops and officers and march on the others? It seemed beyond me.

"Run the idiot through, Philippe, let's take the place over," I shouted into his ear. I saw him hesitate, his hand on his sword's hilt.

"He can't, he does not have it in him." Jobal stood before us in his dishevelled uniform, his hands on his hips, his silly face in a lopsided grin, his small unshaven chin sticking out. He turned and strode away.

The fire was a disaster. It burned its way across the town, devouring the old wooden thatch-covered buildings. It lasted for two days.

Power in Tobago had slipped away from Philippe. There were just two, perhaps three, royalist officers who stood by him with their handful of loyal troops. Edmond de Saint-Léger also stood by him in those tortuous times. Philippe had come to trust him. A long-time friend of Dillon's, he had delivered our daughter Rosette.

Now, citoyen Jobal ruled Tobago from the governor's mansion, where he held a court of bankrupt planters, grasping merchants and drunken soldiery. In the meanwhile, in the streets, the people, *les affranchis,* black and mulatto, many illiterate, had taken to wearing the tricolour and were pretending to read the Declaration of the Rights of Man and of the Citizen at impromptu streetcorner meetings, inserting their own wishful thinking with regards to notions of democracy and equal opportunity.

I took to carrying a primed French flintlock in my basket. Balls and powder-flask prepared. One morning, the children in and out of the fountain, I said to Decima, icy fear gripping me, "We are being watched."

She said she knew, or thought we were, looking away, pretending to inspect the weather.

13: SIR LAURENCE 1789

"It's Jobal and his people."

"No, it's not."

"Who, then?"

I didn't answer. She glanced at me. My past. I have to tell Philippe everything.

That night Philippe was saying, "News from Paris has reached Saint-Domingue. What happens there could affect us in these islands, from Trinidad all the way to Cuba."

We were sitting, looking at the rain from our cottage at the fort. Before us, Rockly Bay had all but vanished as a huge cloud debouched its contents, turning afternoon to twilight. Worried, I was about to tell Philippe of the gold that was hidden on Gasper's island and my suspicions with regard to the recent incident when Edmond Saint-Léger joined us.

"What do you mean by that?" I asked Philippe instead.

"There could be great pressure on the National Assembly by the extremists to extend 'rights' to the colonies, as they are called," said Philippe, I could see that he was not entirely sure of what he spoke. "They will use the disturbances in Paris as a device to isolate the moderates for their own ends. This will be opposed by the planters, the shippers of slaves, the merchants, the banks. Look, Soubise, this is a huge economy that involves tens of thousands of people. They do not give a damn about slaves, or liberté, égalité, fraternité and all that, all they want is power and money for themselves."

"Whether the monarchy continues as absolute or as imaginary, they don't care," agreed Saint-Léger.

"But isn't there the idea that the planters, the colonists, the rich people, have the ear of the king, so their interest will be carried forward?" I asked.

"I rather suspect that the king will soon be worried more about who is in control of his head than who has his ear," said Saint-

Léger. He had been drinking rum and there was something wrong with his hands.

"Of course. The Paris mob wants a revolution. Wants it to come here, to get control of the sugar estates in the islands, to get hold of the wealth," said Philippe. "They will raise the mulattoes with this talk of friendship to wrest power from the planters, take the plantations, keep the blacks as slaves and be rich or richer. One way or the other, everything will change."

"The revolution in these islands is not for the slaves," I said, thinking, it was for men.

"No. Not in these islands. It is a contest between the political clubs in Paris," Philippe said.

"In the short run," said Decima, who had joined us as well, her voice as ever holding a hint of laughter, "I have come to announce supper, we have executed Monsieur le Coq, he is now citoyen le Stew."

The following morning I was almost abducted, as I walked to the bluff that overlooked a gully on the eastern side of the fort. This I did from time to time for the exercise. I saw a man coming towards me; it was as though he had come out of the ground. A swarthy man, like a Spanish Creole. I turned to run as another, who had come from behind, held me about my waist. I screamed as loud as I could and kicked and fought with my feet, trying not to let the other grab hold of them. As I was dragged away and towards the gully, I could see people, other women, officers' wives, looking over. I screamed, dug in a heel and hurled myself backward. I felt him stumble in surprise, he tried to catch a foothold, but we were going over. Pushing hard on the ground with my heels, I accelerated the backward fall. As over we went, I saw a young black man, his face seemed familiar, then, two soldiers came running towards us. We all landed in the bushes below. By that time, the soldiers had arrived. I heard the one who held me say, "I shall come for you," and they were gone, through the bush and down the hillside.

13: SIR LAURENCE 1789

Even then, right there, before the soldiers pulled me from the bushes and up the hill, I knew for certain what this meant. This was not Jobal. This was about the gold in Winn's Bay. They had found me.

I had to tell Philippe, but I didn't. I put it off. He gave me a guard, a cornet from the Vendée, and strict instructions not to leave the house alone. Then, less than a week later, the tragedy of a too early, out-of-season storm struck Tobago. For four days it ravaged, uprooted and damaged everything throughout the length and breadth of the island. Plantation houses, factories and barrack rooms were all destroyed; their occupants blown away into the sea.

When we emerged from hiding in the gunpowder magazine at the fort, we could see the havoc that had befallen the island. In the harbour, twenty merchantmen and three Guinée ships with their live cargoes, along with several inter island-schooners, had all been sunk.

"Let's go to Trinidad," I said to Decima, putting an arm around her waist. I had to get out of Tobago, Trinidad was quiet, deserted; I felt to hide.

The following day, we could see a frigate riding at anchor amidst the desolation. The *Quatorze Juillet*, 74 guns, on her maiden voyage and carrying his summons from the Comte de Luzerne, the minister for the colonies. It stated simply that Philippe's presence was necessary in France to reply to the complaints of the English mortgagees in Tobago.

"Look, forget it. Forget them. Forget the, what is it? National Assembly in Paris! Let's get out of here. We could be in Trinidad in seven hours, five," I told him. I was desperate to escape from these people. Even as I spoke I knew that it had become a choice, the ship or them, as they would be sure to find me in Trinidad. To France, then, but I knew that it could mean death for him or worse, jail in irons for life. And God knows what would happen to me.

"No, not at all," he answered, "no question of going to Trinidad." He had struck a pose, the magistrate, the important man, fearless in the face of absurdity. Fool.

"What the hell is the matter with you, man? Since Dillon left you, you get stupid or what?"

"No, not at all."

"No, not at all, no, not at all. Is that all you can say? Eh? John Black's schooner is in Plymouth Bay. Trinidad or Grenada, choose!" I could see that he had come to a decision, I had to be sure that he wanted me with him.

"Marianne, pack your things." His voice was even, as though he was saying what he wanted for dinner. He did not want to go alone, I could tell. "Get the child ready to leave for Trinidad with Decima and her children. I would advise that you, Decima, go to Plymouth. Here, take this." He handed her a purse with money. "Be careful of John Black, he would want to take it all."

Calling me Marianne, I knew that he was becoming irritated. But as I gathered together what came to hand for the journey, I understood that I would be safer on board a warship bound for France than on this island or on any island in the Caribbean Sea. There was no question of taking Rosette on that journey of uncertainty.

"I have written this note to Picot de la Peyrouse, he will take care of Decima and all the children. Come, Marianne, all this nonsense is now over, we go to France."

"Decima, say! Speak up! Tell him that he is making a fool of all of us," I heard myself say, while thinking otherwise.

Her face bore the expression of an alarmed tightrope walker about to lose her mind.

Then he looked at me and said evenly, "Do not be afraid, this change is an opportunity for us, you and me, to see the world. Yes,

13: SIR LAURENCE 1789

the world is dangerous, it's dangerous everywhere, look around you. A king once said, 'Paris is worth a mass'. Well, I think Paris is worth a try. Fanny and I, we have a house in Paris. Now pack properly."

So, I obeyed. I kissed Rosette and hugged her close and looked long at her sweet face, as fair as his, her sad black eyes and soft, wispy hair. My baby. Adieu. I would not see her again for many years. I closed my ears to her crying and, with my eyes, I directed to Decima a plea to guard my child.

I saw the swarthy man again. Our eyes met as I was about to board the frigate's boat at the quayside. He was standing amongst a crowd of sailors. Fear gripped the pit of my stomach as he and the black man backed away into the crowd. The black was Bob the cabin boy, now grown.

In the ship's overladen boat, we were rowed out under guard. Jean-Jacques de Jobal was on the harbour wall to see us off. The sea around was dark and angry throwing up flotsam and corpses, many still shackled to planks of wood. These and others floated about and smacked against the boat and the shattered masts and tangled halyards of the wreckage. So many swollen, bloated black bodies. They had been aboard the slavers.

We set sail into a red and gold sunset, a fresh wind rising, behind us, claps of thunder in blue-gray clouds sent squalls filled with a cold rain across the misty Tobago hills which were slowly receding.

So ended our Tobago interlude.

The Declaration of the Rights of Man and of the Citizen (French: *Déclaration des droits de l'homme et du citoyen*), passed by France's National Constituent Assembly in August 1789, is a fundamental document of the French Revolution and in the history of human and civil rights. The Declaration was directly influenced by Thomas Jefferson, working with General Lafayette, who introduced it.

BOOK SECOND

14: RUE SAINT-SÉVERIN

1790

Reading from my Memoirs at La Fontenoy, Grenada, 1807

VIVE LA REPUBLIQUE. Lord, what a journey. I, a pirate woman, had been to sea, but this was more; it was a waste, vaster, deeper, always moving further, heaving, pitching, raining danger and excitement all around. A floating fortress, high above the water, out-racing the Atlantic storms of June. Sitting here on my bench at La Fontenoy, looking out on a calm Caribbean Sea, how I remember that experience. I had made a drawing in my diary of views from the quarterdeck of the *Quatorze Juillet*, as seen through her rigging. On board, we were not kept as prisoners, but we knew that we were not travelling on our own volition.

One night he quietly said, "look at me," the sound of the ocean outside rushing by, "look at me." I saw him in the penumbra of the cabin's swinging lamp-light; in profile, strangely coming and going.

"Marianne, I must tell you, I have no interest in real life."

Alarmed I asked, "what do you mean?" I took his hand, as I tried to find his face in the shifting dark and light.

"Life and death are much the same, they are the hazards of a chance that cannot be avoided. What I want, what I want to be, is something stranger, more deadly than real life. I need a purpose

14: RUE SAINT-SÉVERIN 1790

for this life, a meaning. For me, it may be in the heart of that upheaval taking place over there, in France." He was searching for the words. "I can only exist for those who believe in me."

"I know that." In truth I hardly knew anything.

"You can withstand the brutality of this world, of real life, and be strong for me when I am weak in what lies ahead. I shall need you."

What could I say? This man. Me. I looked at him for a long time studying his dark averted features with the cabin's lamp light passing and repassing. What had appeared to be little more than chance, I could see was, in truth, a place where inner destinies connect. He had already forgotten our daughter, our previous life, as well as his own. For a moment he was Philippe Roume, and in the next he became a thing that excited and intimidated me. That eye. It fleetingly appeared. It was filled with a passionate sweetness, like the eye of a dragon or a jaguar, courting its mate. I took him to me.

To Charleston, and four months and some weeks later, into the Bay of Biscay, to Bordeaux. The *Quatorze Juillet* breasting the low rolling waves. Top-gallants billowing, we raced towards the vast Gironde estuary. Blistering-cold crosswinds chased white cirrus across a brilliantly blue sky. Currents competing, causing quick-running tides, eddies, and slack waters. The wide river seemed to run upstream, while sparkling waves with white caps raced in the other direction. Gulls hovered at the level of her gunwales until overtaken.

Bordeaux. The port. Immense buildings lined the quay, emerging almost from the water's edge. So many ships alongside, a forest of masts, bowsprits and spars, a jungle of guys, halyards and stays. Beyond a city, bewildering, so many spires. A babble of shouts, shrill voices and the thud and rumble of barrels, rolling money, coming, going, sea birds shrieking, stevedores running, the aroma of red wine.

Huge mooring lines flung out to be pulled shoreward by smaller ropes into the hands of dozens who hauled together as the huge ship swung slowly, obeying the call to land.

Everywhere, the aroma of wine. So many white people, hungry-looking, haggard, sick, eating rubbish. But, there a black, there another, eh, eh, runaways, they must have escaped; and Chinese too! I had never seen Chinese, so strange. How this place was cold! I had on a lot of clothes. I felt stuffed into a bag of clothes; gloves, must get gloves. My teeth chattered, my fingers hurt.

Officials.

"Citoyen Roume, I see you style yourself de Saint Laurent. To what degree of the defunct aristocracy do you belong? A foreign prince, a debauched count, a vacationing chevalier? Or are you, as it is stated here, a suspected traitor to the revolution?"

Our handlers, naval officers, stood aside, deferring to the civil authority. Strange. I had grown accustomed to their air of command.

"I am a servant of the state, called upon to give an account of my stewardship during the period of change, citoyen. As to my style, that was the custom in the Antilles during the previous regime. My crimes, such as they are, will be decided by the National Assembly."

"And the woman?"

"She is my wife."

"Her papers?"

"Lost at sea."

"She is a black. Free or slave?"

"That is now of no consequence. She is a citoyenne."

"I am a free woman. This is my manumission paper. I am not his wife. He is my lover."

At this point, all assembled could not help but laugh.

14: RUE SAINT-SÉVERIN 1790

"The voice of the plain truth. Pass, citoyen Roume, and pass, citoyenne Rochard. They are now your prisoners. You may take them away."

We were not prisoners; the naval authorities had been instructed by the National Assembly to bring Philippe Roume from Tobago to Bordeaux. There being no one to meet us, our guards, an ensign and two midshipmen, were detached from the ship's company to escort us to Paris. Philippe was to be treated as a witness before the National Assembly.

The great docks of Bordeaux. Around us on the quayside, there was a great commotion as our belongings came ashore. We were to be taken to one of the inns that lined the harbour; the rain began in earnest. I was surprised to learn that it was after eight at night; even with the rain, it was light. I felt sick with the cold and had a fever. I stumbled with every step, as the motion of the ship was still with me. Philippe took command of our guards and they became our guardians.

The inn was commodious and smelt of rancid washing and rotted fish, but was heated by a large fireplace. We enjoyed several glasses of warm wine; then hot mussel soup and delicious bread, fresh from the oven. Some patrons stared as we ate.

"What are they doing?"

"They are dipping bread into sea water."

After the Spartan meals aboard the *Quatorze Juillet*, all this was extravagant luxury. And the beds. The fireplace in the room, smoky and warm. To sleep.

I awoke with a start. I was alone. In a wave of panic, confused, I looked about for Rosette. My God, what was I doing here. Collecting myself I stepped outside. There he was with the naval officers. We breakfasted all together. News. I learnt that every day there would be news: a revolution is about change, rapid change. The news from Paris—and all news came from Paris, because the city of Paris was in charge of the revolution—was that the Assembly had written a constitution. This, with the leaders of the city's mobs looking on, making sure that there was no backsliding. The king? Will there be a king? Yes. No. Yes. Philippe could not imagine the world without a king.

"Yes, there must be a king."

I understood, even then, in my own way. Without a king, the loss of the hallucinating effect of the monarchy will bring about chaos. It will take time to transfer the sentiments of loyalty and, importantly, legitimacy, from the monarch to the state.

The other news was that the Assembly had seized all the property of the Roman Catholic Church. What! Yes. The National Assembly voted 508 to 346 to nationalise ecclesiastical property. This was valued at three billion francs!

Outside, from the crowded street, came an uproar. A crowd was chasing a group of men and boys. Caught, they were beaten, clubbed to death right there. Another crowd came up singing; everyone wore something blue, white and red. A group of women, they all looked old and mad to me, shouted and screamed obscenities from toothless mouths. What was going on? The revolution. Stones were hurled. The inn's panes of glass were broken. A larger crowd gathered outside. The women shouted and gestured towards the inn where we cowered, it had something to do with us eating there. We were traitors to the revolution. The naval officers were alarmed. We went to the back of the place; the person in charge showed the way and we hid in a small room that was locked from the outside and the inside. Dark, there were rats. The biggest that I had ever seen. Rotten onions that stank. Things were so different here, everything was so otherwise. The day went by.

Then night came. Someone brought food. Then a hammering on the door, my heart was racing, Philippe too was afraid, I could tell. The naval officers had returned. It was early morning. The news was that soldiers from all over France were to gather and travel to

14: RUE SAINT-SÉVERIN 1790

Paris to celebrate the previous year's storming of the Bastille. We were to leave with the contingent departing from Bordeaux, or be lynched by the mob that had been swarming around on the lookout for the enemies of the people. Us.

"Come, the time is short, dress in these uniforms, quickly."

We changed into the uniforms and kit of the revolutionary guards of Bordeaux. Philippe, a lieutenant, handsome; me, a drummer person, boy, man, woman.

"The money? Do you have the money?"

Yes. He had the Louis d'or. I had what I had. Dangerous. He wore his in a large belt around his waist. I kept mine close to my body. We left everything behind and joined the throng that was growing quickly to the thousands. Bands played as the sun appeared. Cannon boomed. It was carnivalesque. Wagons and gun carriages, handcarts and boys riding bareback on spirited mules. Flags. The revolutionary blue, white and red tricolour was everywhere. Rosettes. I got one from a grenadier, another from a pretty boy. A view over vast distances, the wind cold. We too were moved by the high spirits of this glorious new age, as flags were unfurled against a sky rich with the momentous event in the making. To Paris we were heading.

The swaying, creaking cart in which we travelled had cost a quantity of silver coins, the horse that drew it appeared on the point of expiring. Philippe had taken up his role as an officer, naturally. He had a horse. He had been introduced to other officers. They laughed together—haw, haw, haw. Now everybody was important.

All around were the gaunt features of starving people dressed in layers of ragged clothes, their feet wrapped with cloth into which straw had been stuffed. All were thin, skeletal, with the foul breath of the hungry. That I would ever see white people in such a state! Philippe explained these people were not white. They were French people. It was only in the Antilles that people were white. The trees in long rows, too, were gaunt and full of crows. All black. The army and its following of walking skeletons was spread across a wide swathe of country and swarmed over it like ants, overwhelming everything: farmhouses, tiny hamlets, churches without doors, burnt-out châteaux.

The atmosphere of unreality only increased. Bands of men rode wildly about with large tricolour flags; some carried whips, others cudgels. They drove the slackers, the lag-behinds, those who would desert. I did not see a chicken, or a cow, or a pig, except for when they were to be eaten. The horde, as it surmounted a rise, would espy a town and descend upon it. If the defenders bolted the gates, a detachment of the army was formed into an assaulting contingent and opened fire with cannon; then, they stormed through and burnt the place! Alarming, terrifying sounds of clash and anguish.

We moved on, along drystone walls and tracks, across waterlogged meadows. Night came, pitch black except for the campfires. Crowds of people, farm folk by their appearance, came begging. We had nothing, we could buy nothing; we, too, were starving. All we had was gold, and that must not be shown.

We hid in the cart most of the time and went to the military encampment at night for food. All shared in the misery of this hellish trek. What was I doing in all this? I told Philippe that we should have gone to Trinidad or to Grenada; but no, duty first. Duty, my arse.

He lay wrapped in blankets, sweating away a fever. The young midshipman had gone in search of a physician; he never came back. I met an old woman who spoke Creole-French and had lived in Dominica, she promised to concoct a tisane. I gave her one of a pair of silver bracelets. She came back with a half bucket of chicken soup with potatoes, and something dreadful smelling in a little bottle. He drank it and slept for two days, during which a thunderstorm unleashed hell's own fury on the countryside. He began to look like them. Not me.

14: RUE SAINT-SÉVERIN 1790

We, the army of the Gironde, that's what we were called, had been joined by another, even bigger, more miserable army from Marseille. They had a song, La Marseillaise, or as it would be known: "Chant de guerre pour l'Armée du Rhin".

> *Arise, children of the Fatherland,*
> *The day of glory has arrived!*
> *Against us tyranny*
> *Raises its bloody banner*
> *Do you hear, in the countryside,*
> *The roar of those ferocious soldiers?*
> *They're coming right into your arms*
> *To cut the throats of your sons and women.*
> *To arms, citizens! Form your battalions,*
> *Let's march, let's march! Let an impure blood*
> *Water our furrows!*

The sun came out for the first time in years. He was better. The old woman brought us more chicken soup. I could see him change. He was becoming as one with these people. We Creoles are so easily swayed. Never see, come see. Days had turned into weeks. The old woman, her name, I shall never forget, was Louisa Perché, brought more food; I gave her a gold ring. We bypassed villages and small towns; the people were different now, less primitive, less starving, but all desperate. We were surrounded by violence. Fights erupted and spread, causing deaths, provoking the National Guard to intervene with more violence. Night. One must be on guard.

As the sun came up, the campfires' smoke blending with the fog burned my eyes. People were still asleep all around, on the ground, under the wagons, stumbling about, relieving themselves.

I made out what appeared to be a vast encampment beyond the fields in the distance. I had not seen it there the previous night. Later I discovered that it was the Parisian National Guard that had marched out to meet these armies and to escort us into the city. I no longer had to dress as a man. I arranged with Lousia Perché for some clothes, no problem in this madhouse that was called a revolution. We entered a manor house that had been deserted by its gentlefolk and had been looted for valuables by the revolutionaries, where we found wardrobes still full of dresses, hats, shoes, gloves, warm coats and valises.

I shaved him clean and trimmed his dark curls that he wore in a long queue. Philippe acquired a hackney-coach driven by a jarvey, an ancient person, deformed and polite. We entered Paris with the naval outriders and joined the crowds in the Champ de Mars. They had arrived to make camp and celebrate the first anniversary of the fall of the Bastille, with what was called the Fête de la Fédération. The place swarmed with armed men. Flags, so many. The tricolour was draped across everything. Orators were declaiming, drummers drumming, pamphleteers handing out knots of ribbon, blue, white and red, the tricolour cockade and revolutionary tracts. There were bands of smelly ragged boys begging, touching and pulling as we made our way to an encampment in the city centre. This place, the people, they smelled very bad. The city. Tall houses, huge buildings. Statues of men on horseback. Everything covered in black soot. Rubbish all about, long ago picked over, and over again. Stink. Shit and pee. Dead people left to rot.

The naval officers made arrangements for us to be accommodated, at our own expense, at a rooming house on one of the boulevards. Philippe had not told them that he owned a house on the rue Saint-Séverin; in any event, he was to appear before a tribunal at a moment's notice. Well, many moments passed as days went by. We familiarised ourselves with our surroundings. Philippe remembered the city; he had been there twice before. He purchased several slim green bottles of eau de cologne against the bad smells and also bought himself new clothes. These came with sateen sashes in the new republican style of blue, white and red. The change was underway. It would now go into rehearsal in his private mind and, to my surprise, I realised that he was altering his way of speaking,

14: RUE SAINT-SÉVERIN 1790

for as his old self departed and his previous links of loyalty to the king, the monarchy and to France as he imagined it, ended, he was acquiring the vocabulary of the revolutionaries.

Quatorze Juillet 1790. Fifty thousand strong, the soldiery of France marched into the Field of Mars, an artificial hill in the centre of the city. Rank upon rank, file upon file, they arrived, to the amazement of the hundreds of thousand Parisians who had created the hill with their bare hands in just a few days. They marched with arms displayed, with banners and flags, with marching bands, drum-majors flinging gilded batons high to catch the golden Parisian light, to the endless cheering and delight of the citizenry. A magnificent procession, singing the lusty songs of their provinces, they paraded past the king, who raised his hat in salute. We saw him. They shouted, "Vive le roi!" Then everyone heard a mass, sung by Bishop Talleyrand-Périgord, with two hundred prelates in attendance. General Lafayette, as captain of the National Guard of Paris and confidant of the king, took his oath to the constitution. Then a cannonade of hundreds of guns sounded a salute and thousands and thousands of Parisians all over the city who were not even there raised their hands towards the Champ de Mars and made a pledge to uphold the ideals of the revolution. We naturally joined in.

Across the country, as these guns sounded, they were taken up by other artillery brigades, as church bells sounded the tocsin, signalling that the world had changed. We stayed to join the feasting, and shared in the wine and food and music that came on in an endless procession as the prelates of the Catholic and Protestant faiths embraced and kissed one another as Christians and as brothers. A sight never before imagined, as we were assured by all.

As we made our way from the parade, I noticed that wherever we went, to enjoy the wine, to admire the fountains, to take a pee in the shrubbery, we were being followed. I became alarmed. This was a city in chaos, where we could be killed by accident, mistaken for someone else, a victim of misguided revenge or just happy murder. I remembered Tobago with a pang of fear.

"A man is following us," I whispered.

"Where?"

"Don't look round. I have a knife."

"You have a knife?"

I had a knife. With an eight inch blade. I had taken it from the kitchen of the house where I got the dress that I was wearing.

"Into this passage. Come here, kiss me."

"You are mad, there is no one."

Yes, there was. As we stepped into the dark, I saw the figure pause, waiting to follow, giving us a moment to move on, or make love in the shadows. Like a cat, I pounced. Caught by surprise, but practiced, he caught the arm that held the knife and turned me about, my arm up my back, holding me above the waist, dragging me out into the street. Another man was coming up. I struggled and freed my arm and stabbed at the hand that held me. I felt it enter and heard a cry. Philippe swung in with a punch that caught the man holding me in the jaw; this sent us both staggering out further into the street, right into the path of a carriage. In a matter of seconds, I found myself between the stamping hooves of the startled horses as the man, who had released me, was already making a swift getaway. The horses, thankfully not travelling at speed, were brought under control by Philippe and the coachman, and I was able to emerge from under the coach where I had rolled to escape being trampled.

A cultured voice enquired, "Are you all right?"

"Are you all right, Marianne?"

"Yes, I am, my arm and hand, I think I broke it . . . aaheee that really hurts, Philippe, oh, it hurts."

"I beg your pardon, Madame, Monsieur, please allow me . . . I am a physician."

14: RUE SAINT-SÉVERIN 1790

As it turned out, my bruises and bumps were superficial and would pass, but I had sprained my wrist very badly, and this would require a careful bandaging, which the good doctor was happy to do.

"Please allow me to be of assistance. I live on the rue des Francs-Bourgeois, just a short distance, come, that wrist must pain you something terrible."

Up and into a warm and comfortable coach that contained the aromas of fine cigars and off we went, my painful hand and arm throbbing. Doctor Maurice Lannes lived in a well-appointed house with his wife and daughters, young, but not children. We were made welcome and treated kindly by Matilde Lannes. A handsome woman, embonpoint, well nourished, as the English would say, and charming. My wrist, now bandaged tight by the good doctor, was still very painful; we talked in candlelight. They gave us brandy. She was worried by the turn of events, she had thought of leaving the city, but tied to her husband, his practice and, as it would turn out, to their friends who were intimately involved in the events of the day, she had become one the favourite hostesses of the Girondins.

Philippe, after introducing me as Soubise Rochard, calmly told our story. His story. "So we await the pleasure of the National Assembly."

In one hour they were treating each other with the respect of colleagues, having recognised in one another that ineffable quality possessed by white people who have been bred to a peculiar code of behaviour inculcated from birth, which, of course, is a mystery to people like us. In addition, something had passed between them, a signal or token that they both recognised.

"My dear Roume, if you would allow me, it would be my pleasure to introduce you to my friend and brother, Jean-Joseph Mounier, he would be pleased to welcome you to harmony at Les Neuf Sœurs."

"Nine sisters?"

"A fraternal order, my dear Soubise," explained the doctor.

"That does not admit women," added Matilde Lannes.

This was how I discovered that Philippe belonged to the Freemasons.

"And Georges Danton," continued Maurice Lannes, "has a special interest in meeting those who come from the colonies. He is an advocate for the abolition of slavery, while supporting equality of rights and universal suffrage."

"Yes, of course, I have heard of Georges Danton, we of the islands support freedom for the enslaved and equal rights for those who live in the half light between freedom and the tyranny of prejudice," said Philippe, taking my hand in his. So not true. This was news to me, I thought, smiling dazzlingly. The recreation of himself was underway. He would, in the ensuing months, change in a manner that seemed not merely to modify his personality as much as effect an alteration of his very nature.

"Coming from the colonies, Danton would be interested in what you have to say, I am sure," said Madame Lannes and, leaning towards her husband, she told him meaningfully, "and so would Maximilien de Robespierre."

"He is an outstanding personality and a frequent speaker in the National Assembly, voicing many ideas, enlarging upon the Declaration of the Rights of Man and upon constitutional provisions, often with great success," said Doctor Lannes earnestly. "He has a great following and is now recognised as second only to Pétion de Villeneuve. He is the leader of the extreme left; 'the thirty voices', as Mirabeau has called them."

"Yes, yes, my dear." And to us, "These men are patriots, they are the deputies, they all sit together in the National Assembly and will no doubt be pleased to meet you," and in a conspiratorial voice, "we ourselves must take a hand now. If we want things to stay the same, things will have to change."

14: RUE SAINT-SÉVERIN 1790

"And Jean Marie Roland and his wife Manon as well."

"Of course, mon cher."

The following day, Philippe met and reported to the committee designated to address colonial matters. This was chaired by Jacques Brissot of the Girondins. This group held sway in the National Assembly. Brissot was reputed to be a man whose dreadful power was derived from his ability to rouse the common people of the city to paroxysms of violence. Philippe later explained that the meeting, as it appeared to him, went more like a briefing of the committee of what was taking place in the French Antilles than an examination of his tenure in Tobago. There was no question of Philippe being taken to task as a result of having been reported to the former ministry dealing with colonial affairs that had been headed by the Comte de Luzerne. The Chevalier Jean-Jacques de Jobal? No one there had heard of him.

The house on the rue Saint-Séverin had not fallen into ruin, as much as it had been abandoned. This we discovered as we explored its many rooms that were filled with dislocated furniture, admired the parquet flooring, antiquated chandeliers and eventually reveled in its comfortable beds.

Philippe, beneath this newly assumed modesty, was knowledgeable. He expressed himself fluently, with tact and impartiality. Life here had effected a change in his physiognomy. His features, still drawn from the journey, had become sharp and more pronounced, particularly when he went unshaven. He possessed the actor's gift of being all things to all men. A born Creole. This mercurial quality would cause him to be vulnerable, as we would discover. However, it also saved our lives.

I told him everything about the treasure in gold hidden away in the cave beneath Gasper's island. He sat quietly and listened. "Someone has talked," he muttered. "They have gotten hold of your friend, the captain, and he has probably died keeping the secret. Now they are after you."

"Funillière dead, you think? My God. What shall we do?"

"Stay very close to our new friends, I suppose, and be on the alert. We could also draw them out."

"Draw them out?"

"Of course. Turn the tables on them, catch one. Make him talk, say who sent them."

VIVE LA COMPAGNIE, PARIS 1790. That we had been followed there had alarmed me more than the trepidation of existing in that uproar and confusion. I could not bring myself to step outside. Not he, as an advocate he was more concerned that as of August 16th the parlements, which for the French were provincial appellate courts, were to be abolished.

It had been one year since the commencement of the revolution and there was an atmosphere of fear all around us. Random violence in the streets claimed as many lives as starvation did. I saw it all, day after day. The mobs. They would attack with a blind instinct those whom they perceived as enemies of the revolution, and bludgeon them to death. As for the nobility who were seeking to leave the country—they would have money, valuables—they too would be ambushed and killed.

An alarming event unfolded a few weeks after our arrival. I had noticed a person, a man, poorly dressed, hungry-looking as they all were, huddled in one of the doorways of the street where we lived. He was always there. Always on the opposite side. Looking at him for hours on end from the window, I had little else to do, I realised that he was being fed. Irregularly, but fed. In this place where food was as precious as gold, this man had a person, different people, bring food for him. A loaf of bread, a sausage, a bone, a jug of wine during the day, even at night. I had been followed to France. He was a watchman. He was on the lookout for me.

14: RUE SAINT-SÉVERIN 1790

I could see him day and night. He was like a taste, a lingering smell of something burning. I was fed up of being kept a prisoner.

When I explained to Philippe what I had come to know, he replied, "Let us catch him or kill him. Now. At once," his voice low and unemotional. Peering through the wrong end of a telescope, as it now appears, I remember how we left the house some nights later, down through a back stair that led to a courtyard. There was a wall, low, up and over, that was easy. I was dressed in my drummer's uniform. We pretended, to ourselves, to be thieves. It was exciting. We stole through a maze of backyards over walls and gates, through a black drizzle punctuated by yellow lamplight, until we were back on the street where we lived. It was now dark, the night redolent with smoke and the contents of chamber pots. I had my knife and a short sword that Philippe had found in the street. Philippe was armed with a rapier and a length of lead pipe.

We had been drinking the wine that was a part of our disguise and were a little drunk as we came staggering up the empty street. The fellow, huddled in a doorway obliquely opposite to the building in which we lived, must have heard us approaching. He must have sensed something, because he jumped to his feet. Philippe was quick with the length of pipe, which he threw hard at the man like a spear. The man parried it away with a long staff, and with almost the same motion drew a pistol and fired at Philippe, and missed. The shot rang and echoed in the deserted street. For a moment the blaze of the discharge lit up a face which I had come to know. At once another man with a long blade in hand appeared from the same hole. Oh, merde. This is bad, I thought. Philippe had drawn his blade and was advancing quickly, with me circling out to the left. They had drawn together standing side by side, the sound of a sword being taken from a metal sheath was heard.

"Let her go," said one man, his voice low, almost conversational, "it is she whom we want."

"Do not concern yourself. She will be put to the question," said the second.

"All she has to do is answer," said the first.

Just then, as if on cue, a gust of wind blew up behind us. I felt it cold about my ears. In a split second, through the dark upon dark, I saw the man nearest to me raise his hand to his eyes and I sprang, flying, I am sure. Looking back, I was like a daemon that night, the knife coming down with all the strength of my youth. I felt it slice across and enter some part of his face and we tumbled, he falling back with me on top, stabbing that face again and again. I must have pierced an eye as this man screamed and could only think of getting away. In a darkness so thorough that only the blades could be seen flashing in the dim light, I strained to see and to escape the one who was attempting to escape me, while I tried to drive the knife into an arm or hand or slash him with the sword. Howling, screaming, the wet smell of hot blood all over me, I made one last attempt and hacked him on the head. As he fell, I could just make out, on the slippery cobbles, the man that Philippe had engaged, he was lunging for him, swinging the heavy sabre. Then I saw a body bent over, then over more, falling, a blade giving the briefest flash in its line of exit, the sound of another as it rang and clattered on the cobbles.

"Away, now, Marianne, come on. Go-go!"

Shafts of lamplight were emerging from solid black walls as doors opened. People were running up the street. We turned into the wind, and ran through the debris of the revolution, the scraps of posters, blowing leaves, and the vituperative pamphlets that drove the mad anger of their day. That they would make a fight for it, for me, came as no surprise. I had their gold. I would do the same. Well, now we could only find safety in the revolution as these, or others would return.

It took several days before I could bring myself to leave the house disguised as a workingman. Amidst the never-ending uproar, a sifting of the French way of life was underway. A change where power would reside in individuals supposedly representing the

14: RUE SAINT-SÉVERIN 1790

citizen body. What remained in the sieve was going to be thrown out, that to me was certain.

I jotted down descriptions of what I was seeing. I drew the faces around us. So many were distorted with the sheer effort to enunciate the new ideals of equality, so original that fresh facial expressions had to be employed for this different vocabulary. In the boredom of waiting for Philippe, while watching the street outside, I sketched rooftops. Chimney stacks, in charcoal, pouring black smoke into the cold, low, grey sky. Drawings of pointy, high-pitched gables, as seen through the drizzle. Steeples, spires, the winding narrow streets that frame ancient façades, the blackened stores and workshops in the dark alleyways of old Paris. Drainpipes too, and the little guttersnipes, haggard children, hungry little faces glimpsed from the window in the ever pouring rain.

There were so many leaders. Obscure men, who from one day to the next, acquiring different personalities, stood in the street in tattered clothes and shouted, with people crowding round to listen as pamphlets were handed out. Then suddenly they would become executioners. Nothing becomes more dangerous than when it is written down and set free as fliers. Leaflets, they get blown away to fall into people's heads. If you do not have the power to stop new ideas from getting away, your time has passed. If you do not have a better idea, it is time to go.

One day I listened to a toothless man read a proclamation on a street corner. I heard him say as he handed out leaflets: "No laws concerning the status of persons should be decreed for the colonies except upon the precise and formal demand of their Assemblies."

Philippe said that the crisis of this revolution evoked genius. Listening to the speakers, often women, I could hear how they shaped the opinions of the people, whose opinions informed the leaders, the deputies from the various regions of France in the National Assembly. Every day is a decisive day in a revolution. I heard of the women's march on Versailles, it had occurred in October of the previous year. These women of the Parisian slums, I saw them, came to know some, all were vile, all stank to high heaven and were violent and obscene beyond sailors. Philippe thought that I was putting us at risk to discuss such dangerous matters with people in the street. Then another thing I heard about was the king's prick. He had a problem with it, Madame Lannes explained. Men always do, we both agreed. This little king had no guts and probably a tiny prick, you know like the little ones you see on fat baby angels. He solved the problem, eventually. But by the time he did, his wife had grown accustomed to other forms of entertainment. His wife should have been the king, all the women I met were of the same mind. If she had not been a foreigner.

Matilde Lannes, I will always remember her as smelling delightfully of sachet, insisted that I meet a woman whom she described as the first citoyenne of the revolution, her friend and confidante, Manon Roland. She was the wife of the distinguished Jean-Marie Roland. We were cautioned, no more Madame and Monsieur, it was now citoyenne and citoyen. Jean-Marie Roland, we were told, was a leader of the Girondist faction.

Manon Roland's salon was held at her home at the Hotel Britannique, "aut delectare aut prodesse est" said Matilde Lannes. Philippe, and me as Soubise Rochard, attended this, our first soirée, he in a well cut blue frock-coat with culottes to match, a cream cravat, worn high, white silk stockings and neat black shoes with silver buckles. Oh, to see such a thing, to be in such a place! The atmosphere of unreality only deepened. I forgot to breathe. The beauty of everything: the mirrors—the gilt-edged room contained so many of them. The lights—it must have taken a thousand candles to maintain such a brilliance. So many paintings crowding the walls and hundreds of books, flowers in pink and gold settings, crystal candelabra glinting rainbow colours. A fire, blazing away. Madame Roland was a beautiful woman with the gentle smile of a spinster, or perhaps a young nun, and the inquisitive eyes of a songbird that had grown accustomed to houses. Her perfume told

14: RUE SAINT-SÉVERIN 1790

a different story. She was so interested in us. I was dressed in the finest frock found in that house that we had raided while coming up to Paris, and wore some of my pirate woman's looted jewels, the collar of emeralds and diamonds with ear pendants to match.

Madame Roland had never met a person like me. She was fascinated by my breeding, and I by hers. We spoke about books. I told her that as a child I thought that books spoke, but in secret, only to those who would tell no one. I noticed that she regarded me more closely. She too loved books, she said, and did feel at times that they were filled with life. I told her that my father had read the plays of Racine to me. First, *Les Plaideurs,* a farce, then *Esther.* This, he thought useful for young girls.

Manon, as she insisted that I call her—we were already using the familiar tu—had read the lives of the saints and felt that she might become a martyr, which she eventually did. Hers were wealthy people, her father a famous engraver. She was educated and the men she knew considered her a remarkably intelligent person, for a woman. So articulate and refined. She said she had disturbed a lot of people: I told her frankly that I had been born a slave, Marianne Katronice, but that I had become Soubise Rochard as I explored my reflection in the gilt looking-glasses at Château Soubise in La Grenade and that I had been manumitted by my father. There were a great many like us both, she assured me, who, upon reflection, had decided upon another reality for ourselves and believed that they were the future of France, of Europe if only they were free. Education gave them an understanding of nature, of scientific phenomena, of the workings of the universe. All of this had reduced her acceptance of God and of Christianity, and led her to perceive divine providence as another act of nature. I really liked this woman, with her small serious mouth. I wept a little as I spoke to her of Rosette, depicting Decima de la Forêt as a paragon of selfless virtue, which of course she was not.

"I understand fully," she nodded and smiled, as I told her of my own experience in understanding where the wind went. Taking my hands in hers she said, "As Racine wrote, 'The gods quell the winds for their journey. . . .' into the blue, naturally, ma chère," then looking into my eyes, "*Iphigénie*? no, no dramatic tragedy will be in store for you."

How wrong she was. That night, I met so many people that I thought the world must be changing for the better pretty fast. Madame Roland introduced us to Georges Danton, the leader, as we had heard, of one of the popular political clubs. Philippe had already made the acquaintance of several of its members, and it had been decided that he, because of his reputation in Tobago and his knowledge of the islands, would be invited to join them as an expert from the Antilles. She said that I, as a *fille de couleur*, was an asset to him, particularly with the work of a group called Société des amis des noirs. Just as I was beginning to tell her that I too had heard of that Société, supper was announced and in we went, arm in arm. We must have made a wonderful sight, as we were greeted with applause: me big and bronze, a prize asset, and she petite and light as air. As we dined in the lights of those hundreds of candles that shone softly upon the white napery and glittered amongst the slender stems of crystal glasses, I saw reflected in Philippe's eyes the transformation that I had previously noticed now actually in motion. Illuminated thus, he blended with the company and conveyed the impression that he understood that the past had to be cured by stern surgery. He had crossed the Atlantic.

Even as I admired what I thought to be the light of the Enlightenment in his eyes, Manon was telling me that the people wanted freedom to choose their rulers and their religion. People held deep resentments, mostly against the bishops with aristocratic pretensions. These resentments were shared by the rural clergy, many of whom lived in pious poverty.

"Jealousy?" I asked. Manon answered yes, that was one of the reasons for this revolution. She went on to say, "The Church property that was expropriated is being made available to the peasantry."

14: RUE SAINT-SÉVERIN 1790

"They will never give it back," I said.

She smiled and replied, "They will fight to keep it to the last drop of their blood."

"If the king had been paying attention, he would have known that if he took away half the Church's treasure and gave it to the farmers, he would have been much loved by them," I thought aloud.

"And by all of us. The third estate," she spoke as if we had shared a thousand confidences.

"What is that?"

"Us," she answered, "the people. We are bled to death by taxes, while numerous exemptions exist for the nobility and clergy. It was the Abbé Sieyès who remarked, 'What is the third estate? Everything. What has it been until now in the political order? Nothing. What does it ask? To become something'."

"Marvellous," I said, clapping my hands, "this country belongs to all of you."

"Easier said than done, ma chère. But tonight we celebrate the fall of the Bastille," smiled the lovely Manon.

"This is why a revolution is underway," said Jean-Marie Roland, who was sitting opposite us. He was possessed of a remarkable narrow physique, a long face and an almost bald head. I liked his eyes. He was saying, "To create a republic that is of the people, by the people, for the people, the Declaration of the Rights of Man and of the Citizen defines the individual and collective rights of all the estates of the realm as universal. Its first article declares that all men are born and remain free and equal in rights. And that means a great deal to them, the sans culottes."

"Why are the common people called the sans culottes?" I asked him in a whisper.

"Culottes are the fashionable silk knee-breeches of the nobility and bourgeoisie, look around you. The poor, the farm labourers, the peasants, the people who work with their hands, they wear pantaloons, trousers."

"Then why are these men here not wearing pantaloons?" I whispered.

"They will, eventually, I suspect," he answered quietly.

Hopelessly ignorant, I was curious to know how the new government worked. Jean-Marie Roland explained that there was a substantial minority in the National Assembly intent on keeping the monarchy. This minority occupied the right section of the hall; they were conservative by inclination. Then, there were the ones who called themselves Girondins; they sat on the left. They were for change, an end of the monarchy. In the highest benches on that side sat a faction called the mountain, the Montagnards, the radicals of the Jacobin Club, who would do away with all previous forms of government and institute something as yet undefined. In the middle were those who could not make up their minds, and they were called the plain. The whole was comprised of some seven hundred and fifty-five men, of whom four hundred were lawyers. Philippe would later say that it would appear that the lawyers had succeeded the priests in the control of France.

I would come to learn that some of these revolutionaries, who were all deputies of the Assembly, representing the provinces of France, attended Madame Roland's salon to sharpen their ideals, to make deals and to discover each other's secrets. Then, rising from the table, they would go into the streets and the political clubs, leaving their refined manners and culottes behind. Donning the red revolutionary Phrygian cap, tricolour sashes and tattered pantaloons, they would become rabble-rousers, haranguing the crowds in the broadest dialects of their provinces.

Philippe appeared forceful but dignified, gaunt, but handsome in his new clothes. He entered confidently into the animated discussions of these important and dangerous men and would also change into pantaloons to join them in the streets. He was different

14: RUE SAINT-SÉVERIN 1790

in his manner from them though. He was from the islands; they were from France.

I often sought the company of the women from whom I was learning many things of great importance. Manon made me a present of a pair of perfumed gloves. Philippe and I made a splendid couple in those circles of the ideologically undifferentiated. We were like cousins trained in the same manner, born and brought up to function in unison. Instinctively responding to each other's unspoken word, moving unhesitatingly to support one another with a glance or a touch. He had already learnt to survive among people whose weapons were smiles, who always moved indirectly, manipulating at least one step removed from their victims.

On another occasion we met Maximilien Robespierre. 'Maxil' as I came to call this prissy, articulate little man who came up to my armpits. Philippe said quietly to me in Patois that his stature was his only concession to brevity. I noticed, with revulsion, the greenish veins that showed through his very white skin and his small, girlish hands. Whenever Philippe spoke he listened closely to his every word. I asked what or who were the bourgeoisie, Robespierre answered that it was comprised of mostly lawyers, bankers and crooks. This brought about great shouts of laughter—it appeared that this company was mostly comprised of these.

"Then," I said, "in my opinion the king should have given the bourgeoisie everything. Make them officially the parvenus that they want to become so badly." I was speaking far too loud.

"We voted today on the admission of six deputies from Saint-Domingue. They understand that the colony cannot be on the outside of the revolution," remarked a stern-faced Danton.

"Do they?" Philippe declared in a loud voice, and turning towards the glittering room, continued, "We are from the Antilles, we must be on guard lest we lose the fruits of freedom. The news from the colonies should influence the decisions taken here. These deputies, whose interest do they represent?"

No one replied, although I thought I heard Manon murmur something under her breath, that sounded like, "the present company."

"That of the aristocrats of Saint-Domingue, the royalists, and those who own the wharves and warehouses in Bordeaux and Marseille. We understand that there is great division in the colony," Philippe continued, looking around the room. "The commanding officer, in Saint-Domingue, Mauduit, was captured by a mob of illiterate white women. They castrated him and dragged his body through the streets. With this, we have an understanding of what is to come." How does he know that, I wondered. He looked about him, this last had caught their interest.

"The governor of Saint-Domingue writes that a mulatto rising in the Artibonite shows how royalist sentiments are arranging themselves since the promulgation of the March decree, which turned mulatto rights over to be adjudicated by the Colonial Assembly. What can we expect? Political, like religious opinions, can never be completely changed without the use of violence. Every new government is at first compelled to be cruelly stern. Sometimes even unjust, so as to coerce those who neither desire, understand, nor consent to innovation. Saint-Domingue must be guided into the reforms desired by us in this company."

I saw his face, still marked by travel, bushy brows somber, handsome in the mirrored lights. Vanished was the youth who played the role of the coloniser whom Gálvez would not receive here, in Paris, in '83. Then he had been a royalist, a supporter and servant of the crown. Philippe Rose Roume de Saint Laurent who did not demur the honour of chevalier, but now . . . citoyen Roume before my very eyes.

"Wider horizons are just beyond the point of view," he was saying. Citoyen Robespierre paused in mid-discourse to listen.

"Liberty is strong food," Philippe continued, "democracy needs a strong digestion. When public safety was in peril, the people took

14: RUE SAINT-SÉVERIN 1790

power. There will be battles and massacres and other Bastilles will be taken. The old pestilential world will be burnt up, bloodshed and despair the price. These are but the hammer and the chisel at work. What is being carved is a future. What is being created is the destiny of the unborn. Who will perform the task of democracy through all its baleful stages? We from the islands, where there are those who would fight for freedom, we plead for a strong hand to raise her banner to wrest tyranny from the remnant royalists in Saint-Domingue. For these jewels set in that distant sea must always be a part of the new France, democratic, republican and free, and never go to England which is where those nine deputies from Saint-Domingue would take us. Now is the time. Vive la République!"

To those patriotic ideas, Robespierre could not but raise his glass and others did as well. Someone close by said quietly, "Sincere enthusiasm is the only orator who always persuades." Another added nodding, "It is like an art, the rules of which never fail." I searched the expressions and saw a few averted smiles answered by the knowing smirk of the sophisticate, but I also saw the nods of approval, of acceptance. The islands would get a strong hand; we got Victor Hugues.

Philippe, so volatile, was welcomed into the company of these audacious politicians and was invited to join their club. What he needed was an appointment of some kind though, as money would run out in this chaotic city where it cost a fortune to exhale. There was no one to extend credit to a Creole, even if he did have the collateral. Which he did not. We would come to understand how timely his discourse had been that night. They did indeed want Antillean men to take their revolution westward.

MEETING VINCENT OGÉ & DOCTOR FRANZ ANTON MESMER. I left my jewels for safekeeping in the care of Madame Lannes and some days later Philippe and I, disguised as her servants, ventured once more into the Parisian night. We met a rainy drizzle on the cobbled streets. These reflected on their medieval sheen the shapes of those who hurried in search of public denunciations, their footfalls harsh and ominous. A clatter of cavalry, dark-red coated riders with glinting sabres, went by. Urchins, now liberated in a dispensation unimaginable, ran in packs, their shouts echoing shrilly in the narrow alleyways. We avoided the violent language that was hurled like boulders at those whose walk or dress betrayed the now reviled class.

The streets were ruthless. The people, grown savage with hunger were vicious with unleashed revenge, they had become merciless in their actions, because there was no turning back to the previous desperation.

Beneath a lamplight haloed by the drizzle, we came upon a gang of enraged youths who occupied a park, they challenged us to admit, on pain of death, that we were their brothers and sisters in the revolution.

I felt Philippe feeling for the rapier that he wore beneath his coat. I reached for the reassuring weight of my own weapon. Then I heard something familiar above the shouts of rabid vileness spewed by those enraged: someone said in Creole Patois something like, "Hey black woman, how you find yourself here? Go back to Saint-Domingue where you come out from!"

I searched the crowd of jostling angry boys and there, yes, the sallow face, the negroid lips, the cataplan of a nose, a mulatto man, short, bulgy-eyed and stupid looking.

"Hey black man!" I shouted back in Patois, "tell your béké comrades to go to hell and look for white people to kill and leave we in peace."

"Where you come out from? Eh?" He was under my chin, his monkey face grinning. He was glad to see me.

"Where you come from?"

14: RUE SAINT-SÉVERIN 1790

"I from Saint-Domingue. What are you doing here? Who is the white man? These fellows will kill you. Come, come."

He had my arm. I shouted to Philippe who had heard and understood, "Let's go."

"Hey, hey, make way. This is my countrywoman. Make way, look out, move away garçon, this is my country woman, move away," he said all this while pushing and thumping the students who still milled about. "What's your name?"

"Marianne," I shouted.

"Marianne means liberty and reason over here, the portrayal of the goddess of liberty!" He looked closely at me and then shouted, "Make way for Marianne!"

We made our way out of the band of rowdies with Vincent Ogé—student-activist, political theorist in the making, rabid Enlightenment philosopher, as he thought of himself, certainly a republican-revolutionary and free mulatto of Saint-Domingue, who was sojourning in Paris at his mother's expense.

He presented us with red liberty caps, called Phrygian caps, these were to become synonymous with republican liberty. As the night progressed, I noticed that many women wore swords.

PHILIPPE ARRANGED TO HAVE some young ruffians, sans culottes, loyal to Robespierre, stand guard about the house on the rue Saint-Séverin. I bought myself a cavalry sword, huge and heavy. Philippe guffawed out loud when he saw me trying it on. It was strapped in its scabbard to my waist with the appropriate belt. I had walked about the bedroom naked with it on for him to admire. I would not venture out without it. I noticed that the sword, together with the tricolour cockade pinned to the red Phrygian cap, drew approving glances from other women and rousing cheers from the sans culottes.

ROUME DE ST. LAURENT ... A MEMOIR

Danton and the others would visit us at the rue Saint-Séverin. One evening he arrived with an older man who, although very much a part of this noisy crowd, stood apart. I was told in a whisper that this was Doctor Franz Anton Mesmer. I heard someone remark, "sinister." Swiss, said another. His work had wrought spectacular results. Because of his experiments with something called animal magnetism and his ability to alter his patients' state of mind, he had achieved fame in revolutionary circles.

Mesmer appeared to be as one with the talkative Girondin politicians and the argumentative students who swore and shouted animatedly into his impassive face. He was at ease with the militants too, who grew more convincing and assertive as they gathered about him. His approval was important to all of them, it would appear. There was Philippe; he was speaking to this Mesmer who had been here a moment ago.

We had to be cautious in the revolutionary milieu that had now overtaken our lives. Strangers—and they were all strangers—could prove deadly. It only required a hint of suspicion. A word misinterpreted would be followed by denouncement and imprisonment, which could easily end in being a passenger aboard one of the morning's procession of tumbrels heading for the Place de Grève where a new killing device, a guillotine, was being experimented with.

As the evening wore on, I noticed that Doctor Mesmer often stood in close proximity to Philippe. "He is a great man," Robespierre remarked to me au passant, while turning to explain to Danton that the revolutionary mood had heightened to become one of concentrated dread, which could become rampant, terrible and uncontrollable. "Just wait." They both laughed, falsely.

Roume turned away, seemingly fatigued with the vernacular of perpetual revolution.

"Citoyen Roume, I see that you tire of the banality of casual murder, especially when it comes with the hilarity of the vengeful,

14: RUE SAINT-SÉVERIN 1790

indeed celebratory, crowd." Before us was the enigmatic figure who seemed to have walked in our footsteps all evening. "Allow me a moment of your time."

Roume took the proffered hand and felt a familiar grip which he returned. He looked at once at ease. Doctor Mesmer, with a practised ease, took my own in his and raised it to his lips, I felt but a hint of breath. We stepped away from the circle that was arranging itself around Robespierre and Danton and found ourselves standing at a window that overlooked the narrow rue Saint-Séverin.

"I understand that you both are of the New World, Creoles of the Antilles. Not so?"

I was not surprised by the man's knowledge of our origins. There were few, if any, secrets in the revolutionary circles of Paris.

"I am indeed, we too would sacrifice the first fruits of the Tree of Liberty, as an. . ." Philippe paused.

"An offering of aparche, the first fruits, the most pristine portion of the harvest. I believe that was the word that eluded you." Mesmer had completed Philippe's sentence while glancing upward through the misty window pane at the darkening sky. He looked at Philippe Roume.

"Except during times of war," Philippe said, he seemed to be pleasantly surprised. Meeting someone with whom he could casually exchange remarks that recalled his classical education was a welcome change.

It did occur to me, as they spoke, that Mesmer may be one of the many . . . before I could formulate my final thought, Mesmer turned to me and, looking straight into my eyes with an ironic expression said, "Yes, I understand there are many, ah, charlatans and other dangerous men on your path and, in truth, they are already lost." And, back to Philippe, "But not you, Philippe Rose Roume de Saint Laurent, you are not lost at all. Indeed, you have been found."

"Found? By these here, who would change the course of the history of the world?" Philippe scoffed somewhat uncomfortably, thinking maybe we should now smile and walk away, except. . .?

"No, by one who can alter time. I offer choices, Philippe Roume. Select a future," said the doctor, raising his hand and passing his thumb along his fingertips as if he offered a pack of playing cards splayed out as a fan.

"I wonder why that makes me think of the triangles of Archimedes," replied Philippe. I looked closely at Mesmer who was, it appeared, about to take his leave, as a black tricorne had appeared in his hand and he was now wearing a cape, lined with dark maroon silk. An ebony stick with a gold knob was in his other hand.

"You saw the triangles in the imagined pack of playing cards splayed apart in the shape of a fan and thought, as a Maçon, of the spiral stair in your second degree. It reminded you of the unfortunate death of Archimedes and you wondered how your own would be? That is natural," said Mesmer, pulling on his gloves.

"Why, yes, I suppose. If one could safely select a future that would guide one away from a terrible or lonely death, one would," said Philippe, looking out the window with an expression not so much of despair, but more possessed of that indeterminable melancholy of those who have lived past middle age.

The doctor regarded him seriously as though studying a patient or a specimen.

"I would wish to die surrounded by loved ones," Philippe added.

"To be fore-warned is to be fore-armed. It would require making a journey. Shall we?" asked Doctor Mesmer, smiling and lifting his cane.

14: RUE SAINT-SÉVERIN 1790

LATER THAT NIGHT, as we prepared for bed, Philippe related what had happened to him as we stood at the window with Doctor Mesmer. It seemed like a dream, as he described it. Philippe said that he saw himself at a tropical port crowded with battleships. Handed on to the quayside, he was met by a delegation who conducted him with great ceremonial, he in a palanquin borne by huge blacks through a street paved with large square stones. People were waving from iron balconies. Those walking beside him were dressed in judicial gowns, while others wore academic robes. A military band followed with a martial tramp, loud and uniform. The jingle and clatter of cavalry was overtaking the procession. These people would enhance only their situation, he knew that without being told. I must not be taken in, he said to himself.

Philippe recalled that he could hear Spanish being spoken crudely, men were shouting obscenities, horses were stamping, a violent quarrel was taking place. He could not wake from this dream in which he felt trapped. In a panic he thought, I must wake up. "Damn it," he said, sitting up in a large bed. No this was not a dream. This was real. Marianne was not there, neither in the bed nor in the room.

"Marianne!" He looked about. "Where are you?"

It was a large room, brightly lit and painted white, with dark carved furniture. Swords hung on the walls. Trophies of wars.

"Marianne!" he called aloud, and swung out of the bedclothes to stumble on a rug as he ran to a window. He heaved at the bar and pushed it open.

"Marianne, what's that?" he exclaimed, "that, that!" pointing, as he turned away from its glaring brightness. From below he had heard a fearful noise. A clash of arms. He ducked his head. "Marianne!" he shouted.

Something had been flung through the open bedroom door. A blazing brand. He ran quickly and emptied a jug of water over it. Shouts of fighting on the stairway. He was under attack. The swords, he turned towards them. Men in pain were crying out, voices of command. The smell of burning, smoke filled the room, hot air rushed in.

He saw himself again; he was sitting at a large table, ink, pens, seals, paper. Dispatches and reports were lifted by the wind. Close by, an open window. Outside he could see, if he cared to look (and he did not), the city that he had almost single-handedly defended against a concerted attack by the English and black rebel armies. It was on fire. Blast them all. Now this.

"Marianne, Marianne," he shouted, "where are you?"

Stay or flee? The window. Below in a courtyard a thatched roof already on fire. There she was with a black stallion.

Choose. Jump or stay. "Jump now!" she shouted.

"What's this?" Where did that dream go?

"Get out! Do not enter here!" he yelled.

"Philippe Roume!" demanded a black man, dripping with sweat, blood from a head wound running down his chest, others filling the room, black bearded faces under helmets taken from decapitated palace guards, dressed in their looted uniforms. Ludicrous people, breathing heavily, heaving in plundered winter coats.

"Philippe Roume, I am commanded to take you. Come. Go."

"No."

"What?"

"No."

He could hear the sound of crashing timber and feel the heat of a close burning fire, the house was ablaze.

"Jump now!" she was shouting.

"Damn it, no, I am the master here. . ."

"Come, now!"

14: RUE SAINT-SÉVERIN 1790

"No!"

"Take him, Bazu, carry him, take him!"

"No."

"Grab him." Slippery, foul sweat, nuugg...

"What did he say?"

"Get off nigger."

"Come on, you old ass, owwee, the fucker stabbed me! Hold him, Petite-Jean, watch that... oh shit, don't stab him... oh damn! Look what... do not stab him Bazu, oh damn it! Now he's dead, what shall I tell them, you fool! You fuck! You killed him, get out, get out, the roof is falling—to the window..."

He felt a stab go into his neck and hot blood rush down his arm, his nightclothes soaked. The smell of blood, he choked on the smoke that was filling the room, another stab to the gut, that will do it, gaaar, the smoke, now everything will burn, "Damn them all to Hades!"

"Then nothing," he said to me, we were sitting together on the bed, a look of awe in his eyes, "in the distance came a pinhole of light, getting bigger, vague forms in white dresses. So this is what it's like, a smell of lilies," he said wonderingly.

What I remember of that encounter, during which Philippe had stared out onto the street below, was Doctor Mesmer saying to him, "Welcome back."

"When I thought of Archimedes, I did not mean to have myself killed!" Philippe had said quietly to the doctor. He was quite pale and with a shaky voice that was tinged with barely suppressed anger. I knew him well, my Philippe.

"They killed me! Damn it! It hurt, it was like..."

"Death. Did you choose?"

"Yes."

Doctor Mesmer said, "Archimedes died during the siege of Syracuse when he was killed by a Roman soldier, despite orders that he should not be harmed."

He then chuckled and suddenly appeared quite light-hearted, and said something, a word, which I couldn't catch at all.

Philippe, now in bed, appeared weary and in need of sleep. I took his hand and asked, "What was the word he said to you before he left?"

"*Prohairesis.*"

"And what is that?"

"A Greek term for moral purpose, making the right choice. I must be cautious."

His eyes were already closed as he explained: "According to a Greek philosopher named Epictetus, nothing is properly considered either good or bad, aside from those things that are within our own power to control, and the only thing fully in our power to control is our own volition, *prohairesis*, which exercises the faculty of choice that we use to judge our impressions. I was taught that as a boy."

And then he fell fully asleep, and I suppose that I did as well, dreaming of this strange Swiss doctor with the black cane and the white gloves...

15: LOOK! STANISLAUS DE BARRAS!
PARIS, 1790

HE SAW THE TURMOIL OF THE REVOLUTION as an earthquake in which they could perish, which nevertheless accorded him an unaccustomed position in the consideration of strangers, one that he did not actually merit, but one that thenceforward he would have to live up to. That notion excited him and sharpened his determination to survive. Their meeting place was on the rue Saint-Jacques, not far from where they lived on the rue Saint-Séverin. It was frequented by the revolution's most ardent defenders. A political club, one of several in the city, it was properly referred to as the Society of the Friends of the Constitution, but, because of the name of the street on which it was situated, it was known as the Jacobin Club. Before the revolution of 1789 it had been a Dominican convent.

The Jacobin Club of Paris played the ambiguous role of both stage and audience in this most original of political dramas. The throb of news, which was the grease that eased the wheels of the revolution, was the vibrant undertone that inundated its overheated air. A revolution thrives on instinct, the instinct that translates the word on the street into the brawling debate of the legislative process.

The former refectory hummed with revolutionary fervour that night and appeared to glow in the fierce light of dozens of torches that blazed above the crowded red-covered tables. The ubiquitous tricolour dominated. The revolutionary song, the Ça ira was being bellowed. The line *"Les aristocrates à la lanterne. . . Les aristocrates, on les pendra!"* with especial relish.

This evening's gathering had been dominated by the radical faction of the Club, the Montagnards, until the arrival of a noisy crowd that overwhelmed them all and silenced even Manon Roland and those others who were elaborating on instances of revolutionary justice. They had news: the royal family had been arrested! Then they sat down and ordered pot-au feu and wine.

"Arrested! My God!" Manon exclaimed with surprised alarm, already understanding the political implications of that event.

"They fled the Tuileries dressed as cooks and butlers," declared an old man with a blackened face and the shredded clothes of someone who had survived an explosion. He emptied Roume's tankard and belched with a grimace. "The very next day, the king was recognised and arrested at Varennes. They are in Paris now!"

"Arrested by a postmaster," confirmed a dragoon, removing his shako and unbuttoning his tunic.

As the place erupted at the news, to their surprise there appeared someone whom both Roume and Soubise recognised at once, but it was Marianne's heart that leapt and raced. Of all people . . .

"Stanislaus de Barras in Paris. Coming to eat at the Jacobin Club at three in the morning," thought Roume out loud.

Stanislaus de Barras had seen the two before they had noticed him and was, in fact, equally taken by surprise. Marianne! In company with Philippe Roume! Here! He moved quickly to one side and merged with others about a wine cask, where he downed a mug of Muscadet. Vincent Ogé, with whom he was acquainted, staggered up, and taking him by the arm, dragged him to where Roume and Soubise sat. Roughly making room, Ogé proceeded with enthusiastic introductions. This of course produced a potpourri of awkward moments in the imaginations of the three, only eased by Stanislaus when he in turn presented them to Abbé Henri Grégoire, a Catholic priest and revolutionary.

15: LOOK! STANISLAUS DE BARRAS 1790

"What will become of them?" asked Marianne, addressing the old man with the blackened face in an attempt to allay her distraction.

"The Assembly will no doubt provisionally suspend the powers of the king." Abbé Grégoire answered before the old man could say anything, "He and the queen will be placed under guard." he smiled with a note of condescension. "The Société des amis des noirs is seeking to legislate the equality of all *gens de couleur* in the French colonies, and Abbé Grégoire is our leader and chief spokesman," Ogé proclaimed. "He is urging the granting of wealthy *sang-melés*, free-born men like us, the right to vote in the colonies."

"We, the mulattoes, have a part to play in the future."

Stanislaus de Barras had addressed both Roume and Soubise with such an easy familiarity that it conveyed the impression that they were merely carrying forward an earlier conversation.

"The king, the king. . . ," the old man was trying to say.

"Forget the king," said the Abbé. "Here in Paris these well-off mulattoes, the products of slavery's hot houses, are coming to truly comprehend the potentiality of their fateful condition."

"Really?" muttered Soubise, noticing that he possessed almost feminine features.

"This will necessitate a recasting of history!" shouted Ogé and, before he could continue, Roume added, "Which is now possible, inasmuch as France is in the process of self-creation, a recasting of her past."

"The membership of the Société," Stanislaus was saying casually, "will make the issue of equal rights for well off coloureds the leading colonial question before the National Assembly. Our French colleague, Léger-Félicité Sonthonax. . ."

"You look like a white man," said Soubise, staring at his rosy cheeks and mass of brown curls, so fashionably arranged.

Ignoring her remark, Stanislaus continued, ". . . has on behalf of the Société written petitions. From the very outbreak of the revolution we claimed Rights of Man before the Assembly." He regarded Roume. "Rights of Man," he said softly, staring directly into the eyes of the interloper who had once, long ago, taken his place.

Stanislaus de Barras too had become a different person, far removed from the boy in the almond tree. Ten years in Paris had given him a voice and it would appear a cause. This thought was shared by both Roume and Soubise as they glanced at each other. The word "denouncement" had crossed their minds. This fool could have us killed.

"Congratulations, you have become a republican I see, Philippe Roume de Saint Laurent," Stanislaus said, passing his hand over the tri-colour sash worn by Philippe and so obviously savouring saying his name. He sniggered, in spite of himself.

"Yes, I have. And compliments to you as well, Stanislaus. Show me your company and I shall tell you who you are, as the old saying goes," replied Roume. The thought that he would have to kill this arrogant ass had already crossed his mind.

Smiling, Manon added, "Many an aristocrat has pledged his sword to the revolution, my dear."

"Indeed," replied Stanislaus, "for survival. When times change it is prudent to change with them. And you are a prudent man, Roume de Saint Laurent. Marianne, I see that you too have changed, but you did that a long time ago. How is Soubise?"

"Time changes everything, Stanislaus," Soubise replied steadily, "as it has you. You think you have power because you have the ear of the powerful. Just remember that time is longer than twine, and anyone could find themselves at the end of a rope in this revolution." He was too smug for words. Paisley vest and all.

"Thank you, Soubise, I know that I can always count on you for the plain truth," Stanislaus said and smiled, looking directly into her eyes. "Excuse me, I see Victor Hugues."

"Who?"

15: LOOK! STANISLAUS DE BARRAS 1790

She sensed that she was being watched and looked around and met the eyes of Louis de Saint-Just, a mauvais garçcon whom she had seen, and, avoided at a soirée chez Roland, to whom Manon appeared to be saying something earnestly.

"Stanislaus de Barras, my God, where did he come from?" mumbled Marianne, turning away, her heartbeat in her ear, loud and steady. "Straight from hell," answered Soubise. De Saint-Just, she saw, was looking at her with a triumphant expression of scorn and cynicism.

To Roume, the role of the Société des amis des noirs in recruiting these young mixed-race men would serve only to ignite the wrath latent in their beings. They would understand that they could take the islands for themselves. As this crossed his mind, he saw that they had been joined by the extremist, Victor Hugues.

"The monstrous nature and the absurdity of prejudice," the Abbé Grégoire was saying quietly and urgently to Roume, "is what these free, mixed-race men are beginning to understand, on a deeper level."

"Estimating the merit of the children of the same parent by the colour of their skin is a prejudice which stifles the voice of nature and breaks the bonds of fraternity asunder," cried Ogé, he appeared on the verge of tears.

"A heady challenge," Soubise said thoughtfully to the Abbé, "now that the old world is ending."

"Yes, citoyenne. A new understanding is in the offing," Victor Hugues responded harshly, shoving Ogé aside, and sitting across from her. His stringy black hair falling over his florid face, which already contained the grimace of an angry outburst. "A fresh interpretation of history must now be written." His voice rose, "For the people of the future who would know nothing of our inhibitions, of our embarrassing past, replete with humiliations." He regarded Roume.

"All that is required is the overthrow of the whites, and Massa's day will be done." That was Ogé.

"You say nothing about freeing the slaves," said Soubise. "Why not?"

"The African will free himself. It is human nature to be free. In doing so, he proves himself human," said Victor Hugues to her, bending close. She, not flinching, stared back into his yellow-rimmed, fighting-cock eyeball.

"Proves himself to whom, you?"

Disregarding her he went on, "African slavery, and what that means for those who know it, is offensive. Africans are not imagined to be a part of this European transformation, which has entirely to do with the renouncing of this vile race of kings and their profiteering sycophants." Hugues was now bellowing above the noise, but still addressing her. "Slavery must be denounced, otherwise all this," striking the table top with his fist while waving his other hand, "is a farce, just another war to replace one ruler with another, here in Europe."

"From Saint-Domingue," the Abbé said, "comes the report that there are disturbances. It may become a great uprising."

"It will commence. The north will rise, it will sweep into the cities!" shouted Ogé.

"That will be curbed," responded the Abbé.

"Free the African, declare universal freedom and all will rise and throw the English into the sea. I, for one, will take an army of sans culottes to the Antilles and free the blacks, guillotine the rest, and all this will end!" Victor Hugues shouted, his rough voice hoarse from the habit of abuse.

"It will take," the Abbé continued, not paying any attention to Hugues' interruption, "a fresh interpretation of the truth to prove that Africans are possessed of immortal souls."

"Souls, rubbish," said Hugues loudly, "how do you know that *you* have a soul? That's the foolish talk of priests so arranged to keep the likes of you distracted, you idiots."

15: LOOK! STANISLAUS DE BARRAS 1790

"The Société," said Stanislaus de Barras, he was now at the Abbé's side, "is dissimilar from the humanist emancipation movement in England. In revolutionary France, this Society is political."

Hugues jumped to his feet, his voice even louder than before. "This Société is led and protected by Danton and Robespierre. Its sole purpose is the exportation of the revolution to the Caribbean. These two are hypocrites," he pointed at Vincent Ogé and Stanislaus de Barras, "they just want to replace the whites with themselves." He appeared startlingly dark and gaunt, his features twisted with the vehemence of his feelings. "Left to me, you poseurs and all of your ilk would be executed tonight." And, turning to Soubise and then to Roume, "and you two dilettantes alongside them." At this, ramming on an old black hat, he flung a dark cape about his shoulders and left the room with the rowdy students slapping his back and parting before him.

"Who is he?" asked Soubise.

"Victor Hugues came from Saint-Domingue some months ago, he is, ah, ardent in his commitment to the revolution," replied Manon who had rejoined the gathering.

"As I was saying," Ogé interrupted, "the Amis des noirs have succeeded in having an amendment tabled at the Assembly in March of this year, which asserts the equality of free-born coloured men of property. It read 'all the proprietors. . . ought to be active citoyens'." A note of relief was in his voice, Roume noticed, helping Soubise with her coat. Victor Hugues was unnerving.

They separated as morning, bleak and windswept, dawned. The Abbé Grégoire, Stanislaus de Barras and Ogé were all unanimously convinced that this National Assembly's vote would enfranchise the *gens de couleur libres*.

As for Stanislaus de Barras, it infuriated him that Roume now had Marianne. Son of a bitch, she is mine, he thought.

ROUME DE ST. LAURENT ... A MEMOIR

Reading from my Memoirs at La Fontenoy, Grenada, 1807

AN OPEN DOOR, PARIS 1790. I felt the cool wind, so precious as it came to me. It promised an early petit carême and seemed to contain a clamour of voices, a hushed but fervent crowd, all jostling to be heard.

In these foreshortened tropical twilights, I am haunted by what I did, or didn't do in Paris in those years. Stanislaus de Barras. It was as though the sight of him had woken up an aperçu of forthcoming events in me, in Marianne. The same instinct to take him, keep him, returned. The exciting threat of urgent sex became intriguing and felt imminent. So intoxicating, it made my heart race then, even as it quickens now. Our glances had clashed and ricocheted above the noisy crowd that night in the overheated light of the Jacobin Club's cellar, where we could hardly make each other out. Then, at other times, in other places, I would frantically search the drawing rooms and salons to catch a glimpse of him. Our eyes would meet and a thrilling quiver would shoot up my spine. Oh no, no Marianne, no.

"Mortals are equal, it is not birth, but virtue alone that makes the difference," proclaimed Stanislaus de Barras in a voice long grown confident in the use of cliché. I glanced at him and thought, look at him. My heart leapt. I could smell the heat of the cocoa field and see the tiger-striped butterflies tippling in pairs. Already he had entered my dreams. I stared in wonderment at this well-spoken, handsome man who smelled of violet cologne and was confidently holding forth in Madame Roland's drawing room, with the admiration of the likes of Robespierre and Danton beaming down on him. So clean with his creamy cravat worn high up beneath his closely shaved chin and in his well-cut short maroon coat.

I wondered if he approved of me, my style, my perfume. He was expounding as a result of Philippe's enquiries as to the authorship of the Declaration of the Rights of Man and of the Citizen.

15: LOOK! STANISLAUS DE BARRAS 1790

"It was based, Marianne, largely on Lafayette's draft," said Stanislaus, searching my eyes, my mouth, searching to find me. We had not yet spoken personally. All our conversations were couched in revolutionary reference.

"Who is Lafayette?" Too many names.

"Lafayette had an ancestor who rode with Jeanne d'Arc to Orleans. Saving dynasties runs in his veins," said Robespierre who had been listening. He looked at me with an appraising expression.

"Have I met him?"

"No Marianne," Stanislaus said, glancing slyly down my décolleté, "I don't believe you have. He is the commander of the National Guard. He supported General Washington in the establishment of their republic. He is a patriot. As I was about to tell you. . ."

"She prefers tonight to be known as Soubise," said Philippe, smiling disingenuously.

I wanted to tell Stanislaus that I was no longer that other person, in the same way that I understood that he too, was no longer the bastard gazing from an almond tree, longing for his father's spongecake. That we were no longer the people we had been then. That he and I were no longer something of an arrière-pensée.

"Oh yes, I know. I remember Soubise, it does suit you much better than Marianne," he smirked. "Although Marianne is now popular here, she is an allegory of liberty and reason."

Oh my God, he is going to take my hand! He didn't.

"You were being trained to an apprenticeship, not so?" asked Philippe in Creole.

"Yes. As you know, our compère is kind and most generous to all his sons," answered Stanislaus in French, his voice and manner containing his freshly minted disdain. "I was apprenticed with the silversmiths Sellier et Fils. They, appreciating my inclinations, allowed me to read Law instead." Turning, he continued, looking at me, "It was at the estates-general where the revolution actually began." He was behaving as though Philippe wasn't there.

Vincent Ogé, fairly draped in the colours of the revolution, then joined us. He appeared better by day, I thought, as he gazed at Robespierre—unctuous, an attachment quite obviously reciprocated. These two, Stanislaus and Ogé, were Robespierre's creatures. Robespierre knew, Philippe had told me, something that many here did not understand, which was that the coloureds from Saint-Domingue possessed a third of the wealth of that colony.

Stanislaus. His piercing eyes and my own mad imagination had completely unhinged me. So quickly. My God. Why? My cheeks were on fire. For that? So long ago. With her, Marianne. I must compose myself before someone notices. I glanced at Philippe; he was now engaged in conversation with a person whom I had not yet met.

I leaned towards Robespierre, hoping this would signal to Stanislaus that my attention had been drawn elsewhere.

"Yes, but Lafayette's problem was the Paris mob, wasn't it?" I said and looked about, avoiding Stanislaus' eyes. "It was too big. Too many people. Too many intellectuals reading Voltaire. You know, at first I had no idea that this was a person, I thought it was a tonic or even a pastime, like alchemy or necromancy or something you were forced to learn or did in secret." This caused a laugh. I was so relieved, I surreptitiously rubbed my drenched palms on my thighs and felt a sweet tingling in my lower stomach. Oh Christ, first my mind, now my body, betraying me.

"In Paris," said Stanislaus, looking straight at me. His dark eyes burned holes into my imagination, "in Paris, the people marched on the Bastille." I knew about that. I managed to hold his gaze.

"Yes, I know," I chirped, "it is an old jail in the middle of the city. Last July, they took it over."

"There was no one to stop us." He smiled, shrugging an arm to show off his lace cuffs, while holding himself up and looking about.

15: LOOK! STANISLAUS DE BARRAS 1790

"This was followed by a march on Versailles, which forced the king, the queen and the royal court back to Paris; that was in October. An insurrection of women. All that year's undigested events."

Undigested events. Oh my God. My heart skipped a beat. That's what this is.

"The people, the sans culottes of Paris, possess an absolutely free press and as such live in a state of perpetual rumour concerning the actions of the queen," that breathy, soft voice went on. We now seemed to be alone in the room, just he and I. His earlier comment was surely meant for me: we were the "undigested event."

"Wouldn't you like to be away from Paris, my dear? Perhaps return to a life in the providential isles of the west?" asked Manon, taking my wet hand. "But, alas, we are all prisoners of our own devices."

Absolutely true. Manon, such a sensitive woman.

"All that was a blind addiction to faith, to ignorance," continued Stanislaus, suddenly so close I could smell him. I felt faint.

"But most of all, the people of Paris wanted food. They wanted bread. They marched to Versailles to demand it." I had to get away.

Manon smiled, "Ah, the zealots of the islands, they will take the message of the revolution to the new world.—You know him?"

I nodded. There was nothing I could say that would not lead to revealing the cause of my confusion.

"'March now,' Marat told them, 'to the National Assembly and demand food at once. . .' They did, we did!" This Stanislaus said while staring at me, at my décolleté.

"The revolution is not only for them," said Manon, "as they believe. A great many things will never be the same. Women will no longer be second on life's list of living creatures." She looked at me, her expression meaningful, and went on to say, "I intend a Declaration of the Rights of Woman and the Female Citizen, my dear."

"What a thought, so original, mmm... d'un bel esprit," muttered Robespierre.

"The revolution is influenced by the philosophy of the Enlightenment," Stanislaus was informing me. He was close—we were almost nose-to-nose.

"Yes, I know."

"These ideas were expressed in the Declaration of the Rights of Man and of the Citizen, which was a statement of principles, ideals, a lists of wishes for the human race." He was speaking in a low, meaningful manner, talking about politics in the voice of love, wretched man.

"You half-educated mulattoes here in France must see this as especially meaningful," I answered, with a self-conscious indifference, while flicking something imaginary, him, off my dress, my mind.

"Perhaps you have grown tired of the ennui of everyday love," whispered Manon, and turned her lovely smiling face toward me, while taking my arm. We were moving away from him. I was already missing him. "Flirtatiousness is fundamental to a woman's nature, but not all put it into practice because some are restrained by fear or, by good sense," she fluttered her little fan. "Our comrade, Robespierre, has influenced these young men who now form the inner circle of Société des amis des noirs. Especially Victor Hugues, Ogé and de Barras, they have become his protégés. They vie for his favour, jealous of his every glance."

Flirtatious, me? Was I being warned? I was like a passenger aboard a departing ship. Wavering, I heard myself say, "They are insecure in their roles, they do not know their place, they slip between the truth of their yearning for their white father's world and the reality of their failings."

"Perhaps. Robespierre has dispatched Hugues to Rochefort, there to implement revolutionary justice, I hear with exemplary success," her voice was almost lyrical.

15: LOOK! STANISLAUS DE BARRAS 1790

"Oh, Hugues, he is the worst kind of *sang-melé*," I agreed, "almost a white, he is no friend of the blacks. He has impressed Robespierre and the others, impressed himself on them. Shaped himself in hatred to become the scourge of the royalist planters in the Antilles."

"Hugues' indoctrination, I saw to it myself." I glanced at her, this was no chaste virgin patroness of the revolution! "He was in the political clubs then, violent and angry. I took him to the streets of Paris. The Abbé cheered him on. Robespierre came to see how he could arouse him to revolutionary fervour. To rouse the mulattoes, to demand voting privileges for the men of colour, whether by persuasion or force, he had to be trained. Form an army, murder the Grands Blancs and take the islands for France and the revolution."

"Friends of the blacks. Is there no talk of freeing the slaves?" I asked.

"No, these rights cannot apply to them."

"Why?" I asked, although I knew what the answer would be. I needed to hear it so as to remember the difference between us.

"Rights, human rights, cannot apply to them. Soulless, they have not the faculty of choice. And anyway that would mean a collapse of a significant part of the economy. France cannot afford to free her blacks. What they want is to make the system of slavery more secure," said Manon, her eyes twinkling in the candlelight, looking at Stanislaus who had been left behind after all. "Amour, toux et fumée en secret ne sont demeurés."

"What these thin-skinned fellows desire—as wealthy mulattoes, as pass-for-whites—is equality with the whites," I told her, not wanting to respond to her hint that love, smoke and a cough were all hard to hide, "to be equal to their half brothers and sisters, to marry their white cousins, and produce whiter children." I had spoken too loudly in my disorder. Damn it.

"To gain acceptance, recognition and dignity, especially in this milieu," Stanislaus said this knowingly, looking at me.

"To share in the political rights in the islands would mean that they must not forget their slave mothers, learn to ignore the ignobility of bastardy, forget the embarrassment of Negro features and hair and leave behind the mulatto African rivalries," my mouth was even dryer as I blurted. "But no, they want to push out the whites, both Grands Blancs and Petits Blancs. Take their place. Become the new aristocracy," I ended breathlessly.

"Everybody can now be what they were not." Speaking in a quiet voice, he placed his hand on mine. It was cold and damp. I felt it tremble. "The world is now a different place; this radical, social and political upheaval changes everything, for you, me and them."

He was so beautiful.

"The biggest problem, for me, is to stay alive. Especially now," I said, feeling something like vertigo. I was struggling to catch Philippe's eye, to smile sweetly at him and let him know I was still his. As I searched for my love, I felt Stanislaus' gaze piercing into me. I dared not turn to the see his face, he was like spirit, a jumbee; I couldn't get him out of my mind.

Where are the brooms? My God, will this night ever end? I remembered the old Antillean superstition of turning a broom upside down when you desired your guests to depart. I would have turned over a thousand brooms to see these people vanish. All, except Stanislaus.

"Cherchez la femme?" Manon whispered, she was now smiling conspiratorially.

"What?"

"Congratulations, ma chérie. You are a woman being sought by a man. No?"

"No." I turned away from her and there was Philippe.

15: LOOK! STANISLAUS DE BARRAS 1790

"Young citoyenne," a newly arrived person called Mirabeau was saying to me, grimacing, "you desire representation proportionate to the number of free inhabitants. The Free Blacks are proprietors and taxpayers, and yet they have not been allowed to vote. I agree it is a transgression of the Declaration."

"Instructed by the Declaration of the Rights of Man and the Citizen," said Philippe, his tone echoing Mirabeau's, "coloured colonists have realised their humanity; they have risen up to the dignity the revolution has bestowed upon them; they have learned what their rights are, and they will use them."

I turned to regard Philippe, who was at my side and was speaking in his calm voice. Not a hair out of place and no angry, pulsating veins protruding from his forehead, so different from these hardened, angry men. At that moment, I appreciated him. Manon had not taken her eyes away from us. She understood, I could sense, and I shrugged as she smiled.

"And as for the slaves," continued Mirabeau, "either they are men or they are not. If the colonists consider them men, let them free them and make them electors and eligible for seats; if the contrary is the case, have we, in apportioning deputies to the population of France, taken into consideration the number of our horses and mules?"

My God. Where are the brooms?

SOME WEEKS LATER I heard Ogé say that he was returning to Saint-Domingue to start the revolution there with or without the support of the National Assembly.

"I stand before you tonight, and therefore before the people of the Caribbean Sea, as the representative of a principle, of a cause, and of a defeat. I need a declaration!" Ogé's tongue was heavy with wine. "A document. What shall I write on, what shall it declare?"

"I know exactly what you shall write," said Robespierre unerringly to his protégé, "write this, here, now, here is paper. Roume, a pen and ink. Thank you, thank you. Now write this, address it to the President of the Assembly in Saint-Domingue, this is where you shall commence your great work. Write! Write this, now: 'A prejudice, too long maintained, is about to fall. I am charged with a commission doubtless very honourable to myself. I require you to promulgate throughout the colony the instructions of the National Constituent Assembly'. . ." I stopped listening.

Amongst much applause, the evening ended, late as they always did. Saying farewell to the Rolands we, together with all the men of rage, left. Our loud talk, echoing in the stairwell, was carried into the street. I had not caught Stanislaus' eye as he kissed my hand and held it in his, causing me to remove it while turning away to say au revoir to Robespierre, who now seemed to be ever watchful. Ogé appeared pleased. Bowing towards me, he almost fell over.

We waved, turning towards our waiting carriage and saying good night to all.

BY THE FOLLOWING WEEK, towards the end of August 1790, we heard that Vincent Ogé was preparing to leave Paris in disgust as there was no final decision by the National Assembly on the position of *les affranchis* in Saint-Domingue. As for the liberation of the slaves, there was no question of that, because abolition would be detrimental to the economy. Coming from a family of slave owners, Vincent Ogé could not but agree with them.

The nine Grand Blanc delegates to the National Assembly from Saint-Domingue had voted against the dreams of the Société des amis des noirs of enfranchising the *affranchis*, thus setting in motion the revolution in Saint-Domingue and, eventually, the Fédon uprising in Grenada. That the revolutionary notion of liberté, égalité, fraternité might not include the mulattoes, although so ardently supported by

15: LOOK! STANISLAUS DE BARRAS 1790

the Abbé Grégoire and many others, struck Ogé in the heart, with all the old familiar emotions of betrayal.

Burning, I could see, with the rage of unrequited esteem, Ogé left Paris with the title of lieutenant-colonel in a German regiment, and with the star and sash of the Order of the Lion, which had been purchased from the Prince of Limbourg by the Société des amis des noirs.

Imagine, a revolutionary needing to buy a chivalric order from a petty prince so as to give himself stature so as to start a revolution in his homeland!

"PHILIPPE, YOU HAVE to leave behind this Freemason business," I hissed, "haven't you noticed that the conversation has changed?"

The National Assembly, after the king's escape attempt, had evolved in October of 1791 into a Legislative Assembly. Philippe, as capricious as ever, also changed. He became as one with the embroiled men around us who were caught in this Pythian madness during those evil days. Their wicked speech was now rearranging their once pure humanitarian impulses. A new and different reality had arrived. In truth, all this had to be harnessed so as to manipulate the hysteria of the people for their own survival. The people of Paris must be moved from riot to massacre and eventually to regicide. It was the only way to live and ride out the storm. Nevertheless, to see them, these Girondins, in the mellow light, and listen to their euphonious tones in Madame Roland's salon, to hear their manicured tête-à-têtes and to smell the suppressed burps of champagne doux, was not my only diversion, as Stanislaus was never out of sight.

"THESE ARE LAWYERS and professional men. They are the bourgeoise; visionary, yes, but also the errand men for the street," I said to Philippe rather loudly. Living in this condition of perpetual uncertainty had produced in me a state of anxiety that could quickly turn to anger.

"Some take money from the king as well, some from each other," I hissed at Philippe, "as they vie to discover who could be more terrible with each discovery of revolutionary truth and fervour. For how long, eh?" I was preparing myself to meet the lions, the jaguars, the tigers of the Parisian revolutionary salon.

"I feel that I am a foetus in the womb of real politics," I said to him in an insolent voice, as we entered the carriage that would take us to Manon Roland's. "For sheer duplicity, betrayal and viciousness, these men are the masters. Robespierre finishes it off with spiteful righteousness, second only to Danton's. As for Lafayette, they can't stand him. As Robespierre would say, il m'est suspecte. The people, those people there, in the street, will sweep them up and all this away."

"Shut up. You will be overheard."

I leaned back into his arms, as the carriage swayed and moved forward into the agitated hum of the crowded street.

Oh, this poor man. We must leave this place. They can't hold it. I must leave this place. Stanislaus, this mad, mad obsession. There is nothing but fear here and death haunts us. I must get us home.

Everard de Barras had done his work well. He had shaped, in the youth placed in his charge, an outlook as elastic as that of his revolutionary contemporaries. Philippe understood that to survive, to live another day in bedlam, he had to become as merciless as those with whom he supped. I would watch him waiting, drinking the air like a wild beast, scenting the shifting miasmas. This would allow him, upon meeting the firebrands in the streets of Paris, to speak their violent language, be as passionate and as violent as they, be as merciless a killer as the next man. It was not a difficult undertaking; we of the slave islands understand how to live without a sense of humanity. Sans humanité, as an old song goes.

15: LOOK! STANISLAUS DE BARRAS 1790

Through the icy drizzle of the truncated evening had came the announcement that in February of 1791, Vincent Ogé had met his death in a manner so horrendous that it shocked even the hardened murderers of Paris into renouncing the nine deputies representing the colonists in Saint-Domingue. Camille Desmoulins, a journalist who published *Histoire des Révolutions de France et de Brabant,* a satirical weekly, had brought us the news of Ogé's death.

"Did you not expect that?" I was again suddenly furious. "What did you think would happen when he went back there? You actually believed that those people, those rich white people, with a lot to lose, would allow some little black man with a big mouth to come back and start a rebellion? Eh? You think they care about us?"

Philippe regarded me with a look of disdain which hardly masked his angry impatience.

"I believe that I am to be asked to go to Saint-Domingue. I understand that the Viscount de Blancheland is to be appointed governor general. Robespierre desires it and the idea is supported by Danton and Mirabeau. I have asked that Edmond de Saint-Léger be included. Remember him? He was in Tobago with us."

I stared at him, speechless. "Are you mad? Those people will kill us, as they killed Ogé. If you think Paris is a desperate place, can you imagine over there? I said we should go to Trinidad, or return to Grenada. No, no, we had to be in Paris, where duty called, no more real life! My God, man. What of Rosette? Have you forgotten her? She is somewhere, suffering terribly, alone, mistreated."

The fire of my rage was now sputtering into self-pity. I could see that my mentioning Rosette had touched him, but he continued to look through the carriage window at the gathering dusk, his manner grave, at the squalled, gloomy, rain-washed streets with hungry people hurrying by. He had become a colder man, less caring of me and my feelings. Not at night though, when the last of the endless stream of visitors had left. Not after Stanislaus had kissed my hand for the second time.

Where did le bon chevalier go? Men, I had come to understand, live in the several different compartments that comprised their minds, preoccupied by isolated events that are isolated, one from the other. Philippe's mind now occupied the fortress of the revolution.

"I understand that a play has been written about Vincent Ogé, where he is portrayed as a hero, a martyr to liberty," I heard someone say as we entered the now familiar house: the lights reflected in the gilt mirrors, the crystals glinting wth the candle flames, the burble of the crowd swelling about . . .

"Antillean planters are attacked in the streets," someone replied and sniggered.

"Charles-Henri Sanson waits patiently for us all," said another. Sanson was the official executioner. Vincent Ogé had not died for the revolution in vain. After the disastrous events in Saint-Domingue, the French legislature passed the reforms urged by the Abbé Gregoire and others in May of 1791, giving free-born mixed-race men of property, born of free parents, the right to vote in Saint-Domingue. Naturally, the colonial deputies from Saint-Domingue, outraged by this, all withdrew from the Legislative Assembly.

It would have been fortunate for the blacks in Paris if these men, Robespierre, Danton and Gregoire, instead of bewailing their existence and magnifying the extent of the sins of their fathers, had applied their talents in considering the best practicable means of educating them. But they had other objectives. Their aim was not to reform, but to destroy—to excite convulsions in every part of France, especially her colonies. The ill-fated Vincent Ogé became the tool and was, afterwards, the victim of their rabid ambitions. Poor fool. I looked at this man who stood next to me, stern-faced, resolute, already artificially assuming the posture of the ruler, the commissioner, a leader of men. In sight, a destiny imagined, the archetypal Creole, the Antillean man. My God. In Saint-Domingue!

15: LOOK! STANISLAUS DE BARRAS 1790

The details of Vincent Ogé's death held, for me, a fascination filled with fury, dread and suspicion. I was drawn to the macabre naturally, having been given to the devil. I found them in the journal *La Chronique de Paris*.

It told a baleful tale of betrayal, ineptitude and wishful thinking. Both he and someone called Jean-Marc Chavannes were eventually captured. They were taken to a public square at a place called Le Cap Français, where they were tied to a great wheel and beaten to death with huge hammers. My God. They had been taken by a force of white militia and black irregulars; among these, I read with disbelief, was Henri-Christophe.

In the furor of another evening at the Rolands, the contentious factions of the new Legislature gathered. The assembled reflected the divisons seen on the Paris streets that very day. Following the news of Ogé's appalling death and the killing of so many of his mixed-race followers, those assembled here became convulsed by argument. Blame was hurled like thunderbolts at members of the faction of the predecessor body of the Legislative Assembly for falling under the spell of the planters, represented by the nine deputies from Saint-Domingue. They were now condemned as bigots and racists, betrayers of the principles of the Declaration of the Rights of Man in their refusal to accept that those rights extended to the Free Blacks. They had condemned Ogé and his comrades to death at the hands of this reactionary body of self-seeking planters who were all royalists.

In the midst of this uproar, in the tobacco smoke-filled rooms that contained the damp smells of sodden rugs, was Stanislaus de Barras. Was he to be the next sacrificial lamb on the altar of the French Revolution?

Passionate in argument, eloquent, boastful, encouraged by the deputies, encouraged by me, to my surprised delight. I loved to drive him to extremes, see the red blush mount his face, his eyes wild, and me wild too with wanting him. All I could think about was the feeling of something opening deep inside of me, primeval fluids pouring. What a swamp. I must shave my armpits, I think I thought.

Naturally, everything we did, consciously or without thinking, served only to heighten our lasciviousness, which grew like an unseen presence transmitted by the invisible energy that passed between us. Oh, to suffer under the passion of love, delight one moment, despair the next. The mad exasperation, followed by a giddy topsy-turvy. To touch. The pit of hopelessness opened when I overheard Mirabeau say to him, "If your sweet charmer endures your assault, at this rate, she may detain you fifteen years blockading her, and concede when you are sixty-five, and she old enough to be a grandmother." They laughed together like men, har, har, har, then Stanislaus said, "I do not say that the pursuit of a particular woman is not a pleasant pastime, as any other kind of hunting. Only for my part, I find the game won't run long enough. They knock down too soon, that's the fault I find with 'em."

"The game which you pursue is in the habit of being caught, and used to being pulled down," said Mirabeau.

"But Cloudia de Payen is gorgeous, not so?" said the other.

"Well, she passes close to the snare, but does not take the bait. Perhaps I should increase the wager, eh? What do you think?"

They laughed again, har, har, har. Cloudia de Payen! I felt the tears in my throat. That blasted fool, fool! I turned and fled the room to find myself. I don't know how I found myself in a passage that ran down the side of Madame Roland's pantry. A scullery maid stopped to ask I can't remember what. As I hurried to somewhere where I could catch myself, I heard him behind me saying something in a muffled, breathless voice. I could only think of hiding my stupid self, oh fool, fool, he is only playing with you; he has other game to hunt.

"Go away, go, oh, no."

He held me close to him, the passage became smaller, the pale yellow lamp dimmer, his mouth was everywhere, his hands were

15: LOOK! STANISLAUS DE BARRAS 1790

finding me. I could choke with happiness. I laughed aloud, thinking the causes of love and madness are one and the same thing. I found him right where I had always done, right there, oh my love, my joyous flesh.

16: THE FIELDS OF MARS & VENUS

HE UNDERSTOOD THE URGENT NEED for them to leave Paris. Even as he spoke to Georges-Jacques Danton of his appointment to Saint-Domingue, he heard the uproar from the close by Champ de Mars turn into the sounds of a battle. The two were standing at a window in Danton's apartment watching the stampede that had commenced as the result of the advance of the National Guard, which had fired several volleys into the crowd and had charged with fixed bayonets, followed by a detachment of heavy cavalry.

Just then Camille Desmoulins, the journalist, burst into the room to report that the Assembly had issued a decree declaring that Louis XVI would remain king under a constitutional monarchy.

"Jacques-Pierre B, B, Brissot," he stuttered, "is advocating the removal of the king, listen to this," he was waving a tabloid sheet. "In this he says. . ."

"No time for that, Camille," said Roume, glancing at Danton and down into the street, "the radicals down there are massing to overturn that decree, come, we must be there. They do not want a monarchy. If that decree is not overturned at once, we shall be dead by tonight. Come, into the streets!" They were then joined by others, who, bursting in, came with the report that the people had been fired on.

16: THE FIELDS OF MARS & VENUS

"Who is in charge?" demanded Danton.

"Lafayette, he is with the, Na, National Guard," replied Desmoulins, stamping his foot angrily, his speech impediment enraging him.

"First he is a damn traitor, now he massacres the people!" shouted Danton.

"Lafayette could turn this to his advantage," said Roume impatiently, speaking into Danton's ear. I must guide this to suit myself now, he thought. "Lafayette with the Guard! For God's sake man, now that they have been bloodied with the death of so many citoyens, they could alter events . . . come on!"

Before he could finish, Danton grabbed him by the arm and hurled himself through the door, down the steep stairs and into the street, followed by Desmoulins and the others. The narrow street into which they rushed clamoured and surged like a trapped and angry tide. The Parisian mob had long grown accustomed to the delirium of unchallenged power. Shouting, flailing about him, Danton made his way through the melee, the others following.

All together, they forced their way into the middle of the largest gathering to where a group of women swathed in the tricolour were standing on carts at an intersection where four streets met, waving the tricolour and calling on those who thought only of saving their skins to stand, to fight and die for the revolution. Danton was thundering, "To me, to me, Paris is the heart of the rightful and naturally constituted centre of free France!"

"With steel and bread!" Some where shouting. just then, above all the din could be seen, further up the street, the tall shakos of the detachment of cavalry with lances at the ready in formation, preparing for another charge. "We will not survive a charge!" shouted Desmoulins into Roume's ear, "L, let, let's grab that idiot and get to hell out of here."

Ignoring him, Philippe Roume, a fury rising in him, standing at Danton's side, took up the rallying, shouting above the abating noise, "The light of liberty shines in Paris! We must not falter and fall before reactionary traitors. Overturn the decree that keeps Louis Capet on the throne!"

"To me! To me!" Danton's bellowing voice rose above the pandemonium, as the women and boys who were still about them called upon the cowed to take heart. Flags and banners began to appear as the growing mass rallied round the speakers.

"That was not a counter-revolution," Roume called out to the milling crowd. "Your blood that has just flowed is as yet another offering to the cause of freedom of the fatherland! Citoyens, we shall return to the Champ de Mars!"

In the mid-afternoon, the army of the people of Paris was marching back towards the Champ de Mars, where they were met with an even stronger and more determined force under the Marquis de Lafayette. Again, Roume harangued the crowd, commanding them not to disperse and pleading to overturn the decree that would keep the king in power. And as before, paving stones were hurled at the guardsmen. Roume could see the unease in the ranks turning to outrage, then to fear. The National Guardsmen had been augmented with fresh recruits, young men brought in from the countryside. He and Danton were at the fore of the crowd. Some who were not hurling boulders at the troops were chanting 'Down with the king!' while others were singing revolutionary hymns. Danton stood forth and, taking a large parchment from his bosom, read aloud a proclamation that demanded the end to the monarchy.

This brought cheers and shouts of, "Death to the king death to the queen!"

There were wild screams, becoming even louder, as paving stones hurled by those in the rear in the direction of the National Guard fell amongst the ones in front of the crowd, breaking heads and causing

16: THE FIELDS OF MARS & VENUS

elements of the mob to surge back into the ranks. Notwithstanding, Danton continued, now hardly heard above the noise.

Roume noticed that his discourse had caught the attention of some guardsmen who were shouting at the crowd to be silent.

Those about him screamed or cheered and, lifted by the sentiments that they thought they had understood, surged forward. At once, Lafayette, along with his aides, kicked their mounts and cantered along the ranks of the nervous men who were sweating in their uniforms.

"I am not going to die here," Roume said aloud to himself, just as he saw the order given to fire a volley above the crowd. The simultaneous discharge of more than one hundred and sixty muskets at such a close range deafened him. He could see Danton's robust form walking briskly towards where Lafayette was just managing to calm his skittish charger; already the order to reload had been given. Ignoring Danton, Lafayette raised his sabre and, even before he could lower it, shots were ringing out from the ranks of the nervous men. With those shots fired, the undisciplined troops, as they had done earlier in the day, fired indiscriminately into the crowd, reloading to fire again as rocks, paving stones, and even furniture were hurled into their midst.

With the breeze of bullets whizzing by, Roume, along with the others, found shelter in a grove of trees at the edge of the park. Lafayette had lost control of the men under his command. Hideous screams could be heard above the noise. Already the dead were appearing on carts, dragged and pushed by the wounded, as hundreds streamed past, running, falling, being trampled, the fear of death overwhelming their righteous raving. Women and boys were attempting to rally the bolters. Some were piling debris and carts into the street to create a barricade, while they harangued and pleaded with the crowds to turn around this retreat. Roume could see, through the thickening smoke, the young guardsmen fixing bayonets in preparation for the order to charge. That did not come, as the mass of people, now regrouped, surged forward from every avenue, street and alleyway, overwhelming the officers on horseback and scattering the confused guardsmen. The three, along with several others, made their escape through the maze of side streets that eventually led to the Seine.

Reading from my Memoirs at La Fontenoy, Grenada, 1807

I SAW HIM ARRIVE at the house on the rue Saint-Séverin as a person who had returned from the dead. It was my thirtieth birthday. This man is getting too old for this, I thought. He appeared haggard and was covered in dust, his coat torn, he had lost a shoe. All he could say was, "The monarchy will not survive. Danton is for me. I have his support."

"Ah, Bon Dieu, save me. Protect me from what I want," I said aloud, standing at a window, looking for a star, the moon or any augury, even those that I could not see, to wish upon.

THAT FATEFUL NIGHT IN in Paris, overtaken by lust for that fool, Stanislaus, overcome by the life we were living in revolutionary France, I had placed myself in the position of a woman enslaved to her joyous flesh. I saw Stanislaus every day. We fell upon each other in desperate moments of backs being turned, in the breathless spaces of cupboards and on the landings of attic stairs, as we closed our eyes to servants scurrying by, their cheeky laughter a promise, perhaps, of their complicity. In my solitude, which only existed in the dread of insomnia, I heaped coals of fire on Marianne's overheated, joyous flesh. My God. How could you do that? I was consumed by lust for this man. A powerful sense of my true being, one that I had never shared with anyone else, came back to me. It was formed by the secret that we shared in a manner previously unimaginable, for it made me free to act.

16: THE FIELDS OF MARS & VENUS

Desiring his strong, hairy body, his luminous eyes, his nutty-flavoured breath I could do anything. These feelings, my actions, could bend my destiny and distort my fate. Yet I would arise, my mind in disarray, from the warmth of the bed shared with Philippe, to meet Stanislaus in the dark-black of back-stairs, our bodies hot, our breaths combined to freeze together. I knew that this was stupid. I had become shallow, a schemer and a liar who would do anything to find him, right there. I could not see in the heat of passion, the thrill of the postponed guilt, the get-away-this-time excitement that left me shaking, that the only thing that I lived for could take away our lives. That was the dark horse I was riding. I thanked God, that morning, when we eventually sailed for Saint-Domingue.

17: BATON CHANGES BOUT
SAINT-DOMINGUE, 1791-1792

Reading from my Memoirs at La Fontenoy, Grenada, 1807

SAINT-DOMINGUE. We sailed for the capital city of Port-au-Prince and entered the long narrow channel of St. Mark, which teemed, to the point of catastrophe, with a wild farrago of shipping. Some, like ourselves, were seeking cautious ingress, while others, veering dizzily into the crosswinds of the harbour road, were fleeing under full sail the fires that had enveloped the port. It was the 29th of November 1791.

Philippe and his fellow civil commissioners, Edmond de Saint-Léger and Frédéric-Ignace de Mirbeck, had been dispatched to Saint-Domingue as representatives of the National Assembly to restore peace, to enforce subordination and to impose the rule of the revolutionary government on this, their errant colony.

Ships escaping the firestorm had brought us reports of the extent of the slave revolt and of massacres while we were still on the high sea. On August 21st, all the slaves in the north of Saint-Domingue had risen as news from France arrived telling that the servants there had overthrown their masters. The uprising had commenced at a place called Lambé and was still continuing unabated when we arrived in November.

17: BATON CHANGES BOUT 1792

This appeared to have given the signal. One Jean-François and another called Biassou had emerged as the leaders of a rebellion. The northern plains, Plaine du Nord, from Jean Rabel in the east to somewhere called Hincha, was now in revolt. The Petits Blancs, that is to say the poor whites, were murdering the mulattoes throughout this northern countryside. All this was so worrisome that through the night, I fought a rising hysteria in the stuffy cabin, until I could no longer breath.

Coming up on to the cool smoky deck in the ruddy sunrise, I climbed into the rigging seeking fresher air, only to be made ill by the sight and smell of the disintegrating corpses betwixt the anchored hulls of prison ships and abandoned slavers, the decks of which, as we slipped past, were lined with the skeletal spectres of the ones who could only stare and wave farewell. All around, the mountains were tinged to an awful dark by a red-brown smoke, as fields of cane burnt and the forest blazed.

Port-au-Prince had burned out of control for some days. More than half of it, as we could see, was nothing but a blackened ruin. Cracked and broken walls, isolated columns, fallen chimneys, heaps of yellow ballast brick. Black charred posts, their insides smoldering, sent out live sparks to snap in the pale dawn. Already, in the distance, there were more fires.

There before us, we were informed, another dreadful massacre was taking place. We were advised to put to sea again. We did, and sailed for the island's former capital Le Cap Français. On the way we saw entire towns ablaze, surrounded by burning cane-fields and smouldering hillsides. We came to understand that the massacre in Port-au-Prince had been occasioned by a referendum—over what, no one was able to tell us. In any event, as the polls closed, a riot commenced and the mulatto troops, led by one Rigaud, who was said to be the natural successor to Vincent Ogé, were burning the city as they retreated.

ROUME DE ST. LAURENT ... A MEMOIR

After the death of Ogé, the civil rights that had been granted in Paris to the free people of colour born of free parents by the decree of 15th May, 1791, had been repealed by the National Assembly in September of that year. Thus the question of the status of persons of colour was handed back to the local assemblies. Ogé's mulatto rebellion and subsequent death in February of '91 had mutated into this vast drama. It became one of the several causes that would shape this catastrophe.

The commissioners, along with the ship's captain and several eyewitnesses to the massacres who had come aboard, gathered to discuss the unfolding events. By the close of the meeting, it became clear to me that several wars were being waged. Various groups comprising royalists, Grands Blancs—that is to say, aristocrats, wealthy planters and merchants—the mulattoes, the Petits Blancs, many of whom were, or had been, indentured criminals, and the hordes of African slaves, were all contesting for the domination of Saint-Domingue, the French half of the island of Hispaniola.

The refugees spoke of the depredations perpetrated by gangs of maniacal slaves, originally inspired by a Jamaican called Boukman and another named Jeannot. They told of the fires, rapes and killings they had witnessed at the hands of the blacks. More than two thousand dead in a mere five weeks. Starvation and famine, we were assured, would follow the destruction of the farms and the killing off of livestock—already there was cholera. The commissioners were advised that twelve hundred families had lost all their possessions and that close to two hundred sugar factories had been torched. It was in this manner, while still at sea, that we were being prepared.

When news of the rebellion had come to Paris, to the National Assembly, no one had imagined anything on this scale. No one who had not lived in the Antilles and seen the violence meted out to the Africans could conceive the nature of the nurtured hate, the thirst for vengeance in the hearts of the blacks. It was out of that naïvety that the civil commissioners had been dispatched to

17: BATON CHANGES BOUT 1792

Saint-Domingue without any military support. Philippe and his colleagues held no military rank, nor were they in command of any kind of force; their authority was vested in the revolutionary government in Paris.

"You have to give the impression that you three are the forerunners of a formidable armada," I said to him later that day, as he sat looking hopeless on the edge of the bunk. We had hardly spoken for weeks. "Look at me, now you must appear strong."

He nodded.

"Go and tell the others."

There will be thousands of lives lost here, I thought as I walked the deck, along with those of the last two hundred years of misery. Columns of smoke rose. So many scaffolds were plainly visible through *Quatorze Juillet*'s telescope. I reeled away in horror from the close-up sight of naked bodies, sometimes two or three suspended from the same scaffold. After days at sea, coasting the shoreline, we finally rounded the cape of Le Cap Français and dropped anchor a mile or more away from the city. We were inundated with news of more atrocities, this time perpetrated by roving bands of desperate mulattoes, many of whom were *affranchis* who had, it was said, gone insane. I fled the captain's cabin where we had gathered after hearing the report of an incident where a pregnant woman, a planter's wife, had been gutted while her children were chopped to bits, their body parts flung to the hogs.

We could not stay here. This was certain death, horrible death. Feeling faint, my head pounding, I found myself on deck where a cool late afternoon drizzle brought some relief.

Standing at the ship's gunwale and gripping her wet shrouds, I looked on at what was taking place below me. Amongst the surrounding clutter was a small craft, a pirogue, it had brought us demijohns of fresh water. Kept under the watchful eyes of the mariners on deck, it had been made fast to our bowsprit and had drifted abeam. A burly black man with a pointed head, dressed in white—tall and strong, looked up and away and looked up again at me and, to my surprise, smiled and waved a huge hand. 'I know that face,' I said to myself.

"That man, there, there," I told Philippe, who had joined me, pointing, "that fellow, the big one, I know him, he knows me. Call him, bring him up, bring him aboard."

"Someone you know? Are you sure? That could prove interesting, useful. . . I say, Captain Boucoud, that man, the big fellow in white, could we have him up? I would like a word with him."

This was how I renewed my acquaintance with Henri-Christophe. He was anxious to tell us about the rebellion, how it began, who started it. He had been there, he told me. By then, we were sitting around the captain's table. We were all curious to hear what Henri-Christophe had to say of the uprising, he being a Grenadian, as I explained to the commissioners who had drawn up stools. At least that was how I represented him to both Philippe and the captain, not saying that I had known him in my youth when we were both slaves.

"But first what of Vincent Ogé?" I asked. "I read that you were there when he and his brother were captured by the soldiers sent by the colony's authorities."

"Ogé? A deluded man he was," replied Henri-Christophe with a shrug, making a face that indicated he thought little of him. "The mixed-race people are full of anger and despair, caught in the mill of this revolution. They will be ground to dust. Ogé was the wrong man. He did not even have the wit to die like a man for the sake of his memory." His voice, a deep bass rumble, was even and detached.

"What do you mean, die like a man?" asked Philippe.

Henri-Christophe regarded him scornfully, as if he preferred not to speak to him and said, "When the sentence was pronounced,

17: BATON CHANGES BOUT 1792

he implored mercy and wept like a child, abject, pitiful to see. I was not there, but it became known." He shrugged and looked at me. "He promised to make known great discoveries if his life was spared. He said that he was in the possession of an important secret that none but he could communicate. The judges granted him a respite of twenty-four hours. But it was not made known to the public what was divulged—if it was anything of importance." He laughed softly from somewhere in his large body and went on, "His secret, if he had one, died with him. Oh, how he howled as the iron hammer struck bone, as the executioners took turns to break him into pieces. But he was dead before the job was done."

Ogé was of no importance to him. He looked at me, and I at him; I could still see, in his face, the strange boy I knew so long ago, the one who had appeared detached, unfastened from affairs, the first to show me how he is make man.

"Dutty Boukman is not dead, Marianne," he changed his tone, suddenly earnest. Boukman? We had no idea of whom he spoke so reverently. "They killed him, but he is not dead, no, they took off his head, they put it on a post, high, for everyone to see." His eyes were wide open as if he was experiencing the miracle and the enigmatic power of the living dead, once again. I nodded, understanding what he meant. We had experienced that, obeah, together, long ago.

We later learnt that Dutty Boukman was the inspiration for the slave insurrection. He was executed by the Assembly in Le Cap Français a few weeks prior to our arrival. His head, placed upon a pole, had been carried to various parts so as to show the people that he was well dead, for true. This was after they had burnt the headless corpse in the public square and thrown the ashes into the sea so as to dissipate its spirit amongst the fishes, who, not being mammals, wouldn't be haunted by his ghost.

"Boukman is not dead, Marianne, he is not dead. No, he is alive and living in the hearts of all." Henri-Christophe had assumed a distant look, his thick-lidded eyes half closed. His face, darker than the shadow, was intermittently illuminated by the lamp's light as it swung gently with the ship's movement. I sensed, and thought perhaps the others did as well, that this was a performance for us to recognise him as an authority on the spirit world and to understand these events from that perspective.

"What was it like, when it all commenced, how did Boukman...?"

With a glance at the captain, he reached for the bottle of rum that stood on the table between us. With a wink, the captain pushed a tin tumbler towards him, he filled it to the brim. The captain placed more tumblers and another bottle on the table. After a deep draught Henri-Christophe's account of the start of the slave rebellion began. I recorded what he said to us that night as I heard it or imagined it over the next day or so. I have it here. Listen.

Imaginative and well spoken, he told us that from the very beginning there had been a beat, the heart-beat of the unborn, and the eye went in search of it and found it in the belly of a drum—the drums of liberation, Henri-Christophe said. I liked that.

There was a fire. Piled high, sparks streaking, bursting through grotesque, wind-formed smoke-shapes, rising. The woman Cécile Fatiman, her features grotesque, in black rags stiff with salt and blood, she put the knife into the heart of the biggest blackest pig that bawled and screamed like a woman in travail. Without hesitating, she dug out the guts and spread out the innards, arranging the liver, the heart, the lungs, and the kidneys. The torches bending close, brightening the blood-spread ground around, she plunged a long cutlass into the soft earth, making a mark with flour that was instantly washed away by the rushing rain. She made it again with a dagger in the blood and dirt and poured rum that she ignited; a blue flame shaped the véve's invisible power as it poured into the cosmos; now searching, peering at the augury, squinting for a portent. She mumbled omens that described what lay beyond the opening that is a gate. A boy they called Zinga brought a human skull. He placed

17: BATON CHANGES BOUT 1792

it carefully next to the upright cutlass. Another man came and sat down near to the fire, he had upon him the head of a freshly slaughtered bull, horns, everything, dripping blood down his body. Men sliced themselves with knives and swords to pour their own blood into a calabash that contained the blood of the beast. Men drank the blood and tore at the meat to swallow it raw. All the while, Dutty Boukman was jumping, bawling, prophesying. He said that Jean François, Biassou, and Jeannot would be the leaders of the rebellion. Take the swear, he said to them; take the swear, he said to all. Swear to kill the white man, to drink the white man blood, to kill the white woman, to drink she blood, to rip out the child in she belly, no more the race of the enemy to rule over we. Beat the iron, beat the drum, Bamboula! Bamboula!

In a high piping voice he sang: *Bon Dieu qui fait soleil. Qui clairé en haut, Qui soulevé la mer, Qui fait l'orage gronder,* . . .

> *Good Lord who made the sun*
> *Which shines on us from on high, Who raises the sea,*
> *Who makes the tempest roar,*
> *Hear you, people, the Good Lord is hidden in this cloud.*
> *From there he looks down on us*
> *And sees all that the white men do.*
> *The God of the white man commands crime,*
> *Ours solicit good deeds,*
> *But this God who is good orders us to vengeance.*
> *He will guide your hand, And give you assistance,*
> *Break the image of the god of the white man*
> *Who has thirst for our tears*
> *Hear in our hearts the call of liberty* . . .

Henri-Christophe showed us a tooth extracted from the sacrificed pig. He wore it around his neck on a thick gold chain. He said that it was for protection. Well, I would think to myself as the months went by, if all the people who said to me that they were there on the night of the 14th of August 1791 at Bwa Kayiman, had been really there, the crowd would have had to be bigger than the one that shared the loaves and fishes at that other inauguration. In any event, one week later, the gate opened and the revolution in Saint-Domingue commenced.

Henri-Christophe said he was there. Some years later, he became king of Saint-Domingue, by then called Haiti, so who can doubt the word of majesty. Especially as his mother, Marie-Hortense Saint-Cyr, had foretold it. I understood what Henri-Christophe meant by Dutty Boukman being a man of the book. Looking back, I have come to appreciate that the sacrifice at Bwa Kayiman had put an end to the slavery of the soul forever in Saint-Domingue and that a different struggle could now commence, one that would be for the mind.

He, like everybody in Saint-Domingue, understood that something had ended and something else, a new covenant, had been inaugurated. "What is man? What is truth?" He had asked us that, too, that night in the harbour at Le Cap Français; he said that Boukman was a Mandingo from Jamaica, a man who could read, who had a book, he was a man of the book, a Musulmán. A different kind of black. A book-man. I understood that. I looked at him, he seemed spent.

"Come," I said, standing, "come, let's get some air and you can tell me what you have been doing since we last met in Grenada so many years ago."

He rose and with a bow to all, followed me up the hatchway and out into the open.

Night had come quickly and the officer on duty was calling for the changing of the watch. All about, the red fiery glow and rolling clouds of smoke told of the war that was ravaging this island. From below us in the dark water came a low whistle that he answered.

"I have nothing to relate, Marianne. There is not much that your man can accomplish. This has to run its course. I shall come to

17: BATON CHANGES BOUT 1792

him when the leaders of all that," he waved a hand towards the land, "are ready to talk, it will probably be too late by then," he laughed his deep rumble, "but we shall see." And with a mock salute to the officer on deck, he descended into a waiting pirogue.

HE TASTED AN ACIDITY RISING as he rose from the bed and walked, unsteadily, towards an open window, picking up a glass of water from a silver tray that, illuminated by the moonlight, shimmered to a stark black and white. He yawned and his head hurt as he swallowed. Having been awake all night, he felt deeply weary. And there was she, Soubise, fast asleep.

The room darkened as the moonlight faded. A cool breeze entered through the opened window. Just a year ago, he had been a servant of the Crown. "Now you are in Saint-Domingue, representing a revolutionary faction in Paris that's attempting to control an uprising here," he murmured out loud.

An uprising that is going find a furious reflection of itself in all the islands of the Caribbean Sea. It would take them a year or two to get it started in Grenada, but once they had, it would spread and become a war to the death—as it would be here. He shied away from that thought. His effort to promote the acceptance of the Royal Cedula for the population of Trinidad amongst the French colons of the Antilles would save the lives of hundreds, perhaps thousands. Spanish Trinidad would be a safe haven. He smiled grimly at the thought, at least for a while.

Soubise, he saw her in the moonlight. Did we fall in love while pretending we were not ourselves? He had seen her confusion on meeting Stanislaus de Barras. He had assumed that the result would be something of a sordid and likely a deadly affair. He had chosen, purposely, not to notice her disarray. She and de Barras had once known each other in the barrack-yards of Soubise and Balthazar: who knows what had transpired there. If the truth be told, he depended on this ingenious girl. He needed her, there in Paris, and particularly now. He had already killed a man for such a thing. He had reasoned at the time that the death of de Barras by his hand could have meant his own, and possibly hers as well, at the whim of any one of the several extremists who ran that maelstrom of murder. Stanislaus de Barras was one of the elected and so, apparently was he. The revolution had given him a purpose in life and this place, here, these times, must be dealt with quickly so that he, they, could return to Paris, where everything was.

The air had grown colder. He inhaled deeply with closed eyes and listened to the far-away rolling throb of the omnipresent drum. This was punctuated by explosions, soft thuds of artillery, irregular but encircling, coming from beyond the city's walls. He felt alien to this island. They had to survive this.

Earlier that night, he had returned more than a little drunk from an excursion to the city. He had been unable to sleep and arose in the predawn chill with an undreamt dream of Belvédère. Walking away from the gayelle, and leaving the company of those who had fêted them, the dream returned to him. The shouts of the men, the screams of the whores, the smell of the cheroots, of the rum, and of the blood of the cock whose decapitated head was being eaten by the blinded victor—the events of the day were returning as an ebbing tide. He felt himself entering the floating calmness of the clairvoyant. He knew what was going to unfold here, in Saint-Domingue, for him, for them. But how would they leave?

Upon coming ashore the morning after they had dropped anchor at Le Cap Français, the ship's officers, resplendent and forming an honour guard, the three commissioners in full dress uniforms, were greeted by a large delegation of Assemblymen, officials and planters. These were eager to show respect and submission. They were received with military honours and led in procession across the town's main square to the Cathedral of Notre-Dame. There, the blessings of the Almighty were implored for the success of their mission. De Mirbeck announced, at the first opportunity given, that they were expecting the imminent arrival of a large contingent of troops which had already sailed from Brest.

This was followed by a feast at which he and Soubise were treated as a welcome novelty by a few, and as an abhorrent indication of the collapse of the status quo by the majority who immediately saw them as the indication of the intention of the revolutionary government in Paris with regard to civil rights being granted to *les affranchis* by the decree of 15th May, 1791.

Later that day, swept up by well-wishers who had been encouraged to think that they were men of power, de Mirbeck, Saint-Léger and Roume were taken on a tour of Le Cap Français, the colony's ancient capital. What he saw were public buildings and private mansions overflowing with refugees of all colours and conditions. There was a sense of unfolding chaos with every fresh alarm, or news of atrocities in the close by hamlets. The authorities appeared to have no solutions. This generated the anarchy, the ex-judicial executions in public parks, of dozens of people, mostly mulattoes who were perceived as dangerous by the terrified Assemblymen. The previous day, there had been other executions of people who had rioted for food. The bodies, not yet removed, teemed with enormous flies.

In the older districts, they came upon blacks shackled to the decorative iron railings of houses, which they would later learn were set on fire by men made mad with fear. They were informed of the outrages of the Petits Blancs, who now called themselves patriots, as they became bolder, challenging the authority of the military police who were deployed in the streets. As the people told them their fears, the commissioners could see that the town was patrolled by a nervous soldiery, these maintained artillery positions at intersections and at particular buildings.

There was hysteria amounting to what appeared to them as lunacy amongst the whites. A terror, visible in the faces of the women. Many of these, abandoned by their servants, had come in from the countryside. Some were convalescing after being raped. As the atrocities became known, there were men who appeared to rally and become strong, determined to hold what they considered theirs, while others, he was assured, were making arrangements to remove themselves to New Orleans with as much gold as they could carry.

What he saw in the sputtering flambeaux, as night came on, was a city under siege—a city that was barely defending its outer walls with heroic forays and with marksmen on the rooftops, so as to hold off black war bands coming in from the northern plains to test its defences. Rumours ran through the mansions of the urban neighborhoods claiming that the Petits Blancs, who had set up their own courts in Port-au-Prince, were already dealing out revolutionary justice to the titled, the rich, to known exploiters of the common people and that it would happen here in La Cap. All this was avidly discussed, only to be made more alarming as rumours of cockades made from the ears of nuns were passed around. It will not happen here, they were assured, by men who had only the day before broken into a jail and murdered all seven hundred mulatto prisoners.

Large crowds gathered wherever the commissioners were recognised. They lifted the spirit of all to whom they spoke, as they continued to give the impression that they were the forerunners of a mighty army now on the high seas.

Then the news of yet another uprising of the Petits Blancs of Grande Anse came to them. It was brought by a planter's son who had escaped castration after being shot in the face while attempting his escape. What he gleaned was that the Petits Blancs had broken into a powder magazine and had armed two thousand slaves in Les Cayes. Roume had no idea where those places were.

By then, he and the other commissioners were exhausted. Hungry, they were taken for a meal and refreshment in a public house, where there was rum and food and women with smiles, he thought, like barracudas.

17: BATON CHANGES BOUT 1792

Later that night, Roume found himself alone sitting on an iron bench. His fellow commissioners had moved on, taken along by an ever increasing crowd. Cobbled lanes with narrow Spanish architecture had led him to the little square with its shabby almond trees. It was dominated on one side by a miniature basilica and was illuminated by several bonfires. Looking about him, it appeared an old place, dating perhaps from the island's earliest settlement.

He was informed, in a casual manner by a pleasant voice, that the famous gayelle, El Chico, was just across the way. His informant was a young woman who, in spite of her appearing as a white person, was richly attired in the style and costume of a mulâtresse.

"A gayelle?"

"Yes, this is where the champions are tested."

"And you have knowledge of this sport?"

"Of course, the greatest cocks, some from as far away as Havana, come here to make a stand. It is a famous arena."

He glanced around him; the surrounding noise seemed to have abated and apart from a small gathering at the entrance to what he assumed to be the gayelle, the area was now almost deserted.

In his weariness, he had not realised that she had been sitting on the bench, or so it had appeared to him. She spoke good French into which she mixed a nuance of Creole Patois in a suggestive and coquettish manner. This caught his interest and amused him.

"What is your name?"

"Lys. Lys de Cayeux."

"I am Philippe Roume."

"I know who you are."

In the flickering cadmium light of the bonfires, she seemed to waver between illusion and reality. She smiled, her lips revealing perhaps her mother's identity, the trembling pins of gold in her small turban caught the fire and sent flashes of warm light into her eyes. He thought her pleasing, her appearance graceful, her face, not precisely pretty, but delicate and sensitive, with an odd charm of violet eyes, momentarily alight under black eyebrows. As he gazed at her, he felt that he might be ill and, passing his hand over his face, was surprised to find it covered in sweat. Cold, suddenly feeling faint, he put his head back against the back of the bench and breathed deeply.

He suddenly felt afraid and started to his feet. What had come to mind were the childhood tales of La Diablesse. He looked about. He was alone, the nearest bonfire had burned low. Mademoiselle de Cayeux had vanished, or so it seemed. The bench was empty and the place quiet.

"Come, let us join the game." She was standing behind the bench, he noticed her slim round arms and hands with soft fingers resting on its back. So young, her costume, madras and foulard with lace entrancing, and then came a cry, "Come, come!"

"The cocks' necks are being shaved," she smiled, "it is time to choose your champion! Come."

He took her hand, it was like a child's, cool and soft. They walked towards the small crowd that was illuminated by flambeaux at the entrance of a low arched passageway. He could feel the length of her legs moving in step with his. They joined a noisy company. He was known and recognised. He felt at ease. There was rum, it was mixed with coconut water, she told him to try it, he did. It was very good. He laughed aloud and looked about, all weariness slipping away. The close-packed gayelle, lit by flaming torches, wavered in magenta and burnt umber as if painted with a darker palette.

There were so many bloody encounters. In some he won what appeared to be fistfuls of money. In the excitement of the choice of a champion they had kissed accidentally and laughed. He was toasted. He toasted.

17: BATON CHANGES BOUT 1792

In the luminescence of his imagined foresight, as Lys de Cayeux smiled up at him and took his hand, the faces around him heaved and wavered as they rose to leave the cockpit. The faces appeared to him as from long ago, as they became looming, grizzled, grotesque and terrible in the overheated night that rumbled with unceasing drumming and the exclamations in Spanish and French Patois mixed with that of the African ritualists who shouted incantations to the strutting birds. Inhaling his own rummy breath, he experienced a stab of fear. A bugle had called. It was carried in the air. At a distance, a tocsin sounded continuously. He imagined a bent, wretched figure repeatedly tolling a desperate save-our-souls communiqué to an almighty unseen. He smiled to regain his sense of self and put his arm around her cool bare shoulders as the people parted to let them through.

The street outside was deserted, the fires in the square had all but died away. He tripped over his feet and laughed loudly and so did she. They staggered theatrically and stopped and kissed and laughed and entered a doorway that led into a small courtyard, a dog barked, she shushed it with a low whistle. There was a stairway that they climbed and a gallery that they walked along and then a room with a bed.

He could hardly remember coming back to the governor's mansion. She had awakened him gently and helped him into his clothes. There was a pony-drawn carriage waiting to take him away.

Turning from the window and returning to the bed, and lying quietly so as not to awaken Soubise he thought, in his sleep, that he may have dreamt of Belvédère. He had made himself indifferent to all news of his family's condition and of the fate of their former possessions in Grenada to a degree that selective amnesia had become, for him, one of his stronger attributes. He knew vaguely of a transaction that had taken Belvédère out of the hands of Samuel Bosanquet and André Fatio.

In any event the transaction had been long completed when he read with disbelief, in an out-of-date Royal Gazette of Grenada 'of the . . . conveying unto and to the use of the said Julien Fédon and his heirs and assigns forever a certain coffee and cocoa plantation tract and parcel of land on the island of Grenada in the parish of Saint John, called Belvédère . . .'

"Belvédère, Belvédère . . ." he whispered. That was the thought that awakened him, as he turned, making barely a sound in the sweat-soaked sheets. He knew that it was not a dream.

"Belvédère to them . . . the Fédons and the Cavalans." It was unthinkable. Black people were living in his house. In possession of his views. Commanding, in ignorance, the genesis of his memories. Insulting, while defecating in the foundations of his identity. Forever overturned, forever. They have arrived. He nodded. He understood. It was not the revolution. No. It was the English. They had facilitated this disgrace to insult his family.

Only the English would do that. To shame us, he thought, nodding. Allowing the niggers to take over Belvédère heightens the cruelty of the mockery. He felt it in his gut. Right there, where it tightened at the thought and twisted like a knife. They had lost Belvédère to Julien and Marie Rose Cavalan, the Fédons. Stanislaus de Barras, he knew, would by now be in Grenada as the idéologue, doing what he had been trained to do by Danton and Robespierre, which was to organise the revolution. With Victor Hugues, presently at Rochefort, his guillotine already packed and on board ship. He would not be far behind. As sleep came upon him once more, she came to mind, Lys de Cayeux. He yawned and smiled, that young girl, what a thing.

THE VERY FIRST PROCEEDINGS of the civil commissioners, after de Mirbeck's announcement that a massive armament was underway and would arrive presently, was to declare the colony's

17: BATON CHANGES BOUT 1792

new constitution and proclaim the establishment of the Legislative Assembly in Paris, as confirmed by the king. This was followed by the publishing of the decree of the 24th of September 1791, which decree annulled that of the 15th of May. This, naturally, brought comfort to the monarchist planters, the Grands Blancs of the local Assembly and to the Governor General de Blanchelande, while serving to anger the entire mulatto population of the colony, even though a mere three or four hundred free mulattoes would have actually qualified for the limited rights and privileges offered in the declaration of the 15th of May.

The response of the thirty or forty thousand free, mixed-race people, indiscriminately called here 'mulattoes', to these absurdities was to declare a general war. Under André Rigaud they formed an army and sought to establish themselves in the south and western departments of the island. Rigaud had proclaimed his support for the Legislative Assembly. He held that the Rights of Man was a guarantee for civil equality for all free people. Realising the lid covering the seething pot of their subjugation had been blow away by the French Revolution of 1789, and that the opportunity had arrived to implement what the middle-class lawyers, middlemen and merchants in France were doing, the mulattoes sought to seize a strategic position for themselves. They knew that they were outnumbered by the slaves and probably by the Petits Blancs, both of whom would exterminate them if they could, but they believed that they stood a good chance of capturing Port-au-Prince, or even Le Cap Français; this would put them in a strong position.

Reading from my Memoirs at La Fontenoy, Grenada, 1807

I SHALL NEVER FORGET THE SMELLS OF HAITI, for by that name it is now called. Saint-Domingue, for me, and certainly the city of Le Cap Français exuded the stench of death mixed with a stale, smoky, pistachio residue and the animal in man. At times, all this was overlaid by the fragrance of well-bred tobacco which was carried through the long, cool corridors of the elegant mansion in which we had barricaded ourselves.

I remember too the fragrances of the garden. One of these came before dawn, or at midnight with the rising moon. It was emitted by the most innocuous of blooms—a pale cream cluster of tiny buds. These poured forth such a flood of sad associations, all with morbid recollections of nightmares and haunting. It evoked memories of asafetida and red lavender, used by the spiritually desperate, and of aromas that could only linger in the tangled heaps of old wreaths, or in clothes worn to funerals, suffused with the perfumes of the bereaved.

As for the sounds, you only noticed the drums when they stopped. Then everyone would pause as though they had experienced the premonition of an earthquake. The drums of Saint-Domingue, slow and quick, deep and throaty, rapid, questioning, answering, telling, acting alone or in collusion with a spirit world, ever-present, knowing no other. They spoke of desires, of creatures, of lost and lonely beings engendered in the forest of the mind, occupying, not themselves, but remote ancestors who called out to the living and the dead through them. All this rhythm created a murmur, an ever present vibration, a backdrop to life, day and night, as news was passed, summonses issued, deaths foretold, mourned, grieved, or celebrated. An intricate network of communication from near and far. The drums rumbled or rang out, but it was in the night that they achieved the ominous quality of emerging from some omasum, some third stomach of a ruminant animal. This woke you with a racing heart.

From the kitchens, and there were several, would come a mixed bouquet that filled the air and timed the occasions for our meetings. Petit déjeuner was early here and sufficiently fulsome to last the day.

On the morning after our first full day in Le Cap, we walked the short distance to another mansion, the Assembly building, past the many outstretched hands of emaciated little children with extended

17: BATON CHANGES BOUT 1792

bellies. Philippe met with the other commissioners in a high, airy room that contained heavy furniture, shining silverware and the grim-faced portraits of austere men.

Tall white doors set in deeply recessed grey walls of dressed stone opened onto a wide, colonnaded verandah, paved with white and grey tiles, overlooking a rolling lawn, green and brilliant, with neglected flower-beds. There was now the smell of roses and stephanotis—a variety of blooms, overflowing, exuberant, and as vivid as the bird-song. From far voices of women were heard, singing shrilly a chant or work song in an African dialect. A call and response, rising, thrilling, now near, now distant.

Philippe, although encouraged by Robespierre to head this commission to investigate the slave insurrection and to restore order, had deferred the role of chief commissioner to Frédéric-Ignace de Mirbeck. Frédéric-Ignace was born into a family of notaries in Strasbourg. He had come to Paris some ten years before the revolution, where he became, I was told, conseiller d'état and had often been seen in the king's presence. He was never able to look at me; I never caught his eye. I could see he was a person long accustomed to authority and the company of men. Tall, dark and full-figured, with enormous calves bulging in his white hose, he had about him an overly sumptuous manner that was tiresome to endure.

Then again, there was our old friend, Doctor Edmond de Saint-Léger, a doctor of medicine, youthful despite his years, little, red-haired and freckled. He was a long time friend of Arthur Dillon's and had acted in Tobago as his interpreter. Gentle in manner, he had delivered our daughter Rosette. He was burdened by some nameless affliction, he would recluse himself at times for days on end; recovering from apocalyptic hangovers, I thought at the time. Philippe had asked the committee that adjudicated over these appointments to include Edmond, as it was hoped that Dillon would be sent to Saint-Domingue with his regiment.

I left the three men at the Assembly building when I saw the Assemblymen arrive. Subdued greetings all around, as the planters with worried expressions circled the commissioners while the Assemblymen arranged their countenances in a manner that sought to convince the commissioners that none of the possible choices was theirs to make.

Later, Philippe told me that the seeds of discord were sown that morning. Philippe had the impression that Mirbeck sought to create a division between himself and Edmond, which in a way he accomplished. Mirbeck, he said, had a clearly defined idea of what he perceived as legitimacy and had been sent to Saint-Domingue by the National Assembly in the interest of the moderate Girondists, whereas he and Edmond were seen as "old Caribbean hands" with experience in Tobago and other islands to see what could be achieved in the chaotic situation in Saint-Domingue. Mirbeck's mission was to re-establish the pre-revolutionary status quo of the lucrative slave colony, albeit with certain unavoidable alterations.

That morning, the kindly Edmond put forward the idea that everyone in Saint-Domingue who was willing to cease hostilities should benefit from a general amnesty. He was supported by the clever Frédéric-Ignace. Philippe, however, argued strenuously against the granting of pardons to people of all descriptions upon their laying down arms.

"Do you really believe that an amnesty will actually move them to give up their arms?" he asked incredulously. "Do you think that those people, those murderers of children, will give a damn about swearing oaths to the new constitution, to the king, to this local Assembly, to us, or to anyone? What do you think the planters will do? Men who have seen their wives, daughters, mothers raped, maimed forever, killed before their helpless eyes? Everything they have worked for gone up in flames?" He sceptically said to Mirbeck, "Do you actually believe that there will be no revenge? Look, there

17: BATON CHANGES BOUT 1792

is no black and white in Paris, but in the New World that is all there is!"

Philippe seemed to me to be more than merely indisposed to the direction that this—the first serious difference between them—was taking. I could see that he was torn between siding with the planters—he had been a planter himself— and supporting the notions of freedom and democracy that he had imbibed so recently and had expressed so volubly. He had been a royalist, and had been obliged to assume republicanism to save our lives. As for the slaves, no one thought of anything else but putting them back to work.

He threw up his hands and went along with the general pardon that Edmond and Frédéric-Ignace had proposed. The amnesty proclamation was dictated to the local Assembly, to be printed and published. As Philippe had predicted, it was the document that in one stroke lost the commissioners the confidence of the Grands Blancs, and even some of the Petits Blancs who had come out on the side of the Parisian sans culottes and imagined themselves as republicans, although they had no notion of what that meant. In truth, neither did I.

He had become distant to me. As I was to him: burdened as I had become by self-indulged delusions. I had not confessed. Aboard ship, he avoided any mention of Stanislaus, even when I would evoke our extraordinary conversations, saying his name in the context of elaborate reminiscences. Philippe, I loved him for it, did not accommodate the mad person's gift of collecting injustices. He did not enquire, but I knew that for the first time, we were estranged. I hoped that he was too distracted, even frustrated, caught up by this hopeless place, to be consumed with jealousy that would turn to bitter hatred over what had happened in Paris. I had no idea—he appeared so preoccupied—all I knew was that I did not want to lose him. Perhaps, because I was no longer immersed in that emotional storm, a great sense of grief would overwhelm me when I thought of Rosette. I had given her away, I had lost her.

Truly, we hardly spoke except for when he experienced crises of indecision. Then we somehow found our original selves and spoke without warning or preamble.

THE COMMISSIONERS were still in the Assembly building, some days later, when they came to understand that the Assemblymen had thrown out of the chamber two emissaries of the rebelling slaves— young men, well dressed, well spoken, with good French, who had come bearing a letter from the leaders seeking a reconciliation that would bring this catastrophe to a close.

"Get out! Get out!" the Assemblymen bellowed at the two unfortunates and threatened them with death.

"So outraged were they, hurling law books at them, calling them dogs and murderers," Philippe told me that evening, as I poured hot water into the copper tub in which he was sitting. "Then, when the fellows were fleeing, they ran after them, screaming like mad people."

"These people are stupid. They are outnumbered. The blacks will win," I said, glad that he was speaking to me normally. "Where were the emissaries by then?" I asked as I rubbed the towel up and over his body as if to bring it to a shine, and smiled crazily as he ignored my attempts at even more enhanced normalcy.

"They were trying to get out alive, downstairs somewhere trying to find the doors. 'Find them,' I told somebody, 'send for them, and I will hear what they have to say, do it, quickly.'"

I could picture them as they entered the room, tragic in their blackness, feeling that they were to be arrested, shot out of hand. Instead, the three commissioners met them standing side by side and bowed, then they were offered refreshments and comfortable seats near to the breezy window. A meeting was to be arranged with Jean-François, their principal leader. The letter which they had

17: BATON CHANGES BOUT 1792

brought for the Assembly was on the table before them; I imagined Edmond placing his hand on it and drawing it towards to him.

As we prepared for bed, a rainstorm came on, with northerly winds so ferocious that neither Philippe nor I heard the pounding on the main door until Desmaizeaux, the majordomo, came to whisper that there was a delegation waiting to meet the commissioners. Philippe, being the only one present, went down to receive them. I followed him, armed with a pair of pistols, primed and loaded, and waited just outside in the corridor.

I heard an angry voice shouting obscenities. The gist of it was that the white people were horrified, angry, moved with a deep sense of betrayal that amnesty should be given to the slaves and to the mulattoes who had taken part in the revolt. It was seen as a justification for their most heinous atrocities, while placing such a bad example before all blacks, especially those who had been loyal to the planters. To the delegation, this was an enormity beyond understanding. I agreed with the delegation. Every murderer should be hunted down and executed.

It took them all night and several bottles of rum to come to an entirely misunderstood understanding that was subsequently forgotten. It was almost dawn before they left. Philippe looked drained, poor man. I took him in my arms, undressed him and helped him into bed and loved him tenderly. We slept for some hours. By midday, the inevitable Desmaizeaux was whispering again. This time it was Henri-Christophe.

I watched him good. What a huge man. I had one of the pistols with me, loaded and cocked; he ignored me. There was something so indefinable about him.

That day he was being elaborately urbane. He was like a house-slave with invented etiquette. He had come to negotiate. Jean-François, who commanded the rebellious slaves in the north, would speak to the commissioners.

"How do you know this?" asked Philippe mildly, pouring a tall glass of Irouléguy and handing it to Henri-Christophe. It breathed such a rich, dark-red aroma into the room that I could feel it in my empty stomach, which growled appreciatively.

"I have come from La Grange," he replied, stretching out his huge black-booted foot before him, drinking deeply from the glass.

"And what would make him do that?" asked Philippe.

"Hunger," he replied simply, reaching for the decanter.

"May I, please?"

"Certainly. I must tell you, the house has a fine cellar. I would think that the capture and execution of Boukman and Jeannot has something to do with it as well."

"No," he shrugged and rubbed the palms of his huge hands together, producing a parchment sound. "They have done what their destiny compelled them to do and have gone their way. The revolution must now move to its next phase."

Philippe smiled encouragingly and, drawing up a chair, sat opposite his guest to afford him his full attention. I couldn't make out whether he took Henri-Christophe seriously or was playing a game. Perhaps a game? Well, why not. Look at where we were. At least we were speaking the Patois of Grenada.

Taking a dispatch from the desk, he said, "Jean-François and Biassou, who are the new commanders, want to negotiate while the Petits Blancs, having won the support of the regiments that have mutinied, have taken the city of Port-au-Prince. As I understand it, they are preparing for a long war."

My God! this place was worse than Paris.

"It is now, what, five, six months since the insurrection started," said Philippe, pretending to be rueful. "Yes, the slaves must be hungry."

17: BATON CHANGES BOUT 1792

"And scared," Henri-Christophe replied simply, still not looking at me and reaching again for the decanter. I saw that he had noted the hypocrisy in the other's tone.

"We arrived at Port-au-Prince," said Philippe, "in time to see the Petits Blancs, they call themselves patriots, I hear, consolidate their hold. There was a massacre, they killed hundreds of mulattoes who had become out of place as a result of the May 15th decree which gave a few of them a modicum of civil rights; they were holding some sort of poll. The point is the whites hold a defensive line that prevents the slave rebellion from entering the western provinces. They have formed an enclave at Gran Anse and established a line of fortifications that is called the Cordon of the West."

"These are pockets holding out," shrugged Henri-Christophe, "postponing the inevitable." He looked long at Philippe. "The uprising of the blacks here in the north has caused the governor to fortify the hills overlooking Le Cap so as to isolate the Plaine du Nord from those who seek freedom. They must not reach the white city, Le Cap Français." Henri-Christophe said this ironically, with a deprecating smile, "But seriously," he asked, "do you subscribe, in all honesty, to the principle that all men are created equal, citoyen Roume? As expressed in the Rights of Man. All men? Black men like me, and black women like Marianne, tell me honestly, before we commit ourselves to act in concert."

"Of course not. I am not a politician selling panaceas to the public, harping on their envy and their imagined rights; taking advantage of their desperation so as to stay in power, to stay alive. I am a realist, as you are, Henri-Christophe."

I regarded Philippe; he appeared calm. He was dressed—I hadn't noticed before—as he would have been at home, more like a planter about to ride out on the estate. Not like the other commissioners, who still wore their city clothes. Henri-Christophe's face was serious, but not unpleasant, waiting.

281

"Presently," Philippe continued, "I am employed as a diplomat. I am serving a revolutionary junta that is itself in transition; ruled by men who are influenced by the mobs from the slums of Paris, to support, by force, their faction in the Legislative Assembly. The point in time at which the mob will produce its own leaders and eliminate their present representatives is anybody's guess."

"You're here to perform a function."

"Yes."

"And. . . ?"

"My job is to bring this, rebellion . . . insurrection, to a close. In the hundred years that have passed since the Treaty of Ryswick, when Spain ceded this fertile half of Hispaniola to France, this colony has produced two thirds of the overseas trade of France. Some people have become immensely rich from the cultivation of sugar."

"And from the slave trade," I added.

"With this situation ongoing, the price of sugar has soared; only the English benefit," Philippe continued, sparing me the merest of glances. "The English hold Barbados and Jamaica and some of the Leeward and Windward isles, where sugar is thriving, while this colony, the largest producer, possibly in the world, has fallen into anarchy. The English are presently constructing, in London, the largest docking facilities in Europe to handle West Indian sugar with a storage capacity that will accommodate in excess of eighty thousand hogsheads."

"Have you ever heard of a man called Mackandal?" asked Henri-Christophe, interrupting Philippe, his bass voice casual, but containing a note that implied that what was being discussed had no relevance to him.

"No, can't say that I have. Who is he, a Scot? A Jamaican?" asked Philippe, his tone mildly curious, but I knew different.

17: BATON CHANGES BOUT 1792

"Mackandal, he was a noir," Henri-Christophe answered seriously, "some say he master-minded this slave rebellion, although he died almost forty years ago. He was a master poisoner. A maroon who created the first network of secret organisations amongst the slaves. An army within the plantations. This happened because of what you describe as the success of this colony."

"Henri-Christophe, like yourself and Marianne, I come from the same environment, although from the other side of it. I know about magic and obeah. I know that all this is about life, death, and misery and that to appreciate it, you must dish it out, or be on the receiving end of it. I understand that to change all this, and all this must change, it will take a war."

"Massacre," I said, "from massa to massacre!" I was ignored.

Philippe continued, "That war will enable English merchants—that is the City of London—to control the supply of slaves and maintain high sugar prices. They already control the slave shipping on the Guinea coast, all the French forts and trading posts have fallen to them. They have the slave trade in their hands, that is the supply of labour, new slaves. France's slave stock is tied up here in Saint-Domingue, its value incalculable. This rebellion must stop. The blacks must get back to work, whether as slaves or as free men. One thing that is certain is that the English will not free their slaves."

"The only way to win is to free the slaves," I said. "And you, Mister man," I watched Henri-Christophe good, "you captured Vincent Ogé, you held him, you delivered him to his executioners, you were there at his murder." Somehow, since the first time we had spoken, I had not been able to let go of the thought.

"Yes. I, too, do a job for money, I too have to eat," answered Henri-Christophe, "and you, Marianne—you do what you have to do as well, also for money, or whatever. Not so?"

I felt to shoot the black son of a bitch as he turned away from me.

"France needs the money from sugar," continued Philippe, ignoring us, "because although the income from the sale of the confiscated church properties over there will bring millions into the state's coffers, money must be generated from every source—and this colony is an important source—so that people will have money to buy the church property that the state has only just appropriated, so that the state will have money. The revolution must now stimulate the economy. The blacks must go back to work. The plantations must be cultivated, crops for sale and crops for food must flourish again. All this must stop, otherwise we shall all starve. The question of emancipation is entirely another matter."

Henri-Christophe laughed out loud, got up, and walked to the door that led to the verandah overlooking the lawn.

"Yes," he answered, "I understand that here in Saint-Domingue the planters maintain a yield of sugar almost two thirds more than that of Jamaica. The French get more out of their blacks than the English."

Philippe sat back in a big golden chair and put his booted feet upon a Louis XIV desk.

"Look here," he said, lifting an eyebrow, "I have a task to perform. I will do it to the best of my ability. I am not about to get into a discussion as to who are the most cruel slave masters, we or the English; that's for the historian who becomes a politician. The people who have sent me want a way out before they are murdered by the Parisian street. Name your price."

Henri-Christophe turned, the bright sunlight in the doorway framing him. He was dressed in white, as most men here are, his black skin in contrast with it, as much as his so obvious authority was, in that officious room. He laughed again softly, like some giant cat purring.

"Philippe, Philippe, yes, I need money, but I, we, Jean François, the *noirs*, we also need your support. The slaves are starving. They place themselves beneath the standard of royalty, even as they burn and murder, and destroy the very things that could give them sustenance.

17: BATON CHANGES BOUT 1792

Their regiments are called 'The King's Own'. They will live off the land, then take to the mountains. But without the plantations, tens of thousands will starve in the coming year. All they know is plantation life—it's cruel, but it feeds you. Jean-François has styled himself High Admiral and has appointed aides-de-camp, the others know this. It means nothing without organisation, otherwise all this is death."

"And this is why you are here," I said. "To act as Judas for a traitor who will double-cross those blacks who have put their lives in the hands of those leaders who are now seeking to save their skins."

He looked at me, really looked, for the first time. I saw his eyes narrow for a brief moment and I felt a stab of fear.

"I am here to live to fight another day, Marianne. And, because I believe that he," he pointed to Philippe, "will ultimately stand by us, the *noirs*."

"If the revolution in Saint-Domingue," said Philippe, rising, his manner affecting indifference, and standing face-to-face with Henri-Christophe, "evolves into a Black Jacobin movement instead of another slave uprising, it will become, before long, a test of the ideology of the French Revolution, because it will radicalise the very idea of the slavery question."

"And will it force French leaders to recognise the full meaning of their revolution?" I asked. I thought that these two pragmatists should remember the ideals that perhaps had moved them once—although I was not even sure about my own ideals.

"The slaves who have made themselves free do not want the planters to take over here," said Henri-Christophe. "But the mulatto war that Ogé started has only just begun. The terrible speed with which the blacks have destroyed the sugar factories that would have given them sustenance in the future indicates the presence amongst them of an aptitude, superior to any they could possess."

"Is that aptitude supplied by the mulattoes?" asked Philippe.

"Of course. They organise the destroying gangs and give the directions as to what is irreplaceable," Henri-Christophe answered.

"The bastard and degenerate race strikes a deadly blow at their criminal parents, both black and white," I said with as much irony as I could muster.

"The mulattoes, many are slave owners, would destroy what the blacks cannot rebuild," said Henri-Christophe sharply. "The ones who can think know that this island can become theirs, the mulattoes', but only under the protection of France. What will happen to them if it continues under the rule of the local planters is 'au revoir' to their imagined freedom. And revenge? The blacks know that the planters will kill as many as they can and then restock the plantations at whatever the cost. No black man who has violated a white woman will be allowed to live."

"Will the slaves, the insurgents, give their support to the French forces and then go back to slavery? Or will they fight to the bitter end?" asked Philippe.

"Yes, the slaves will fight. Yet they believe that the king will save them. But there will be no more royalists here, I assure you, citoyen. You see, I believe in the Rights of Man; those high ideals of the Enlightenment, they mean more to me than to you. You have always had rights. I cannot afford your cynicism, although I admire your honesty."

My word—how superior he has become. "You have nobody's support, and we know that there is no French army on the way, Philippe. You alone must now play a significant part in all this. That is why I am here. Money. Yes. Five thousand Louis d'or, now, if you don't mind. And, we leave in the morning to talk to the leaders. You shall retain your position, and more." He was on the point of walking to the main door when he turned and said, "There is a man you should pay attention to. His name is Toussaint."

17: BATON CHANGES BOUT 1792

I MADE IT MY business to find out about Henri-Christophe, Mackandal, and this man, Toussaint. That evening, I inspected the kitchens and after a short and to the point introduction, I was able to gather around me the chief cook and one or two of her assistants. I had a bottle of rum. Henri-Christophe, they knew him only too well.

"He was a soldier in the Chasseurs-Volontaires de Saint-Dominigue," whispered Desmaizeaux, as a wiry, wrinkly-faced, red-skinned woman, who was apparently hard of hearing and smelled overpoweringly of carbolic soap took the bottle from my hand. She tipped the bottle and a few drops sprinkled the earth.

"And what is that?" I asked, handing her a cigar. I had taken to smoking these since our arrival. I found them comforting, and I knew that amongst the practitioners of the African rituals it was regarded as a method of summoning the 'old ones'. I also passed one to the cook.

"It was a regiment composed of *gens de couleur libres*," the cook said, taking a sip from the bottle. "He was not a soldier, he beat the drum, he was a boy. Brave. A brave boy."

"He was at the battle of Sa, Savannah," whispered Desmaizeaux, "yes, he was there, so was I." He had declined the cigar and the rum.

"You!" shouted the bottle washer, "Ha!" She had put her cigar into her sparse bosom.

"Quiet," ordered the cook, passing me the bottle.

"He worked for his freedom, saved his little money and his master freed him. By then he had been a sailor, a ship's carpenter and a billiard table maker. He worked as the maître d'hôtel in the big hotel here in Le Cap Français, yes." The cook had picked up, with her fingers, a red hot coal from the coal-pot to light her cigar.

She reclined upon the back stair upon which we were all sitting and exhaled a fragrant cloud.

"Yes," whispered Desmaizeaux, "that is where he learned the ways of... of sp, sspeaking and acting like a big man, like a . . ."

"A king," I said.

"What?" shouted the bottle washer.

"A king!" I hollered.

"Yes!" bellowed the bottle washer, "Yes, that self."

"He got that skill by imitating the Grands Blancs, of having dealings with them," the cook said, her eyes dreamy. "He knew his place as a *noir,* and he had a sense of humour, he could make them laugh, and he was smart, he could tell what they did not know." I took a sip. That too is special about this place, everyone loves to drink, but you never see anyone drunk.

"At a price," I said.

"Naturally," she replied.

"He has dig-dignity," whispered Desmaizeaux.

"Yes," said the bottle washer, only a little less loudly than before.

"Yes, true, true, but he was b-brave at Savannah, people know that, he did not flinch when called to beat the charge as he stepped into the f, f, fog. After the retreat, the commander, the Comte d'Estaing asked him where he was from; he answered, Gr, Grenada," whispered Desmaizeaux, "I was there."

"Ha!" said the bottle washer. "Monkey see monkey do!" The rum bottle was now substantially reduced.

"Now he is with Biassou and Jean-François," whispered Desmaizeaux, "he and Tou, Toussaint." His eyes were wide, his nostrils quivering in his old, coal-black face.

"Yes!" shouted the bottle washer, passing the bottle to the cook.

"Tell your master to meet Toussaint," said the cook.

17: BATON CHANGES BOUT 1792

"He is not my master," I answered, "I am a free woman. Who is Toussaint?"

"Toussaint is an educated black man," whispered Desmaizeaux, "a free man. He is a doctor."

"A doctor?"

"He has the knowledge of herbs, and he was trained by the priests in the Catholic school," said the cook.

"What?" shouted the bottle washer.

"He has the knowledge of herbs, and he was trained by the priests in the Catholic school!" repeated the cook loudly.

"No!" shouted the bottle washer, "it was Jesuit missionaries. I know that. He has money," she said. "Money."

"He is a Franc Maçon," whispered Desmaizeaux.

"No, never!" shouted the bottle washer. "Never. He is a devout Catholic."

"Where is he now?" I asked.

"He is with Georges Biassou," whispered Desmaizeaux.

"Biassou was prophesied by Dutty Boukman to lead the revolution, but it will be Toussaint who will win," shouted the bottle washer. "Tell your man, the Commissioner, that he must meet him."

"He is an educated house Negro, cool as punch," said the cook, puffing on her cigar, watching the smoke waft up. "He saved his white people from harm when the revolt started. He guarded them. Because he respected them. You see what a powerful man he is."

I nodded, "Yes," and drank deeply.

"Mackandal. Tell me, did you know him, Desmaizeaux?" I asked casually, making as if to leave.

"N, n, no, Madame, I never met him," he said, all a-quiver, his watery eyes as big as saucers.

"Mackandal is a houngan," said the bottle washer in what was for her a hushed voice. "He is still alive, my mother see him leap from the flames right here in Le Cap. They say he turn a bird, then a deer, and take to the high woods. None can hold him." She stared about her. "He come back now." She stared as if she saw him.

"The white people 'fraid he, he poison them, he make the poison, the spirits show he. He give it to the slaves. They put it in the food, in the water goblet; man and beast fall. They couldn't catch him." This the cook said while relighting her cigar with the piece of burning coal. She then passed the coal to the bottle washer who, having taken her own cigar from her bosom, lit it, inhaled deeply, and exhaled, the smoke rolling from her mouth and nostrils, the coal glowing sullenly between her fingertips.

"Here, light back up," she said passing it to me.

"Thank you." I took the burning coal from her and relit my cigar, blew upon it, and brought it to a charming red and then tossed it back into the coal pot.

The cook looked at me, then nodded gravely.

"He was the sèvitè of the spirits in the voodoo," said Desmaizeaux. "He served them. They come when he call them. They are tied, he and them, soul to soul."

The bottle washer continued, her eyes closed tight, "He raised the spirits because of the dishonour and greed of the white people. They dishonoured us, the children of Guinea. Not by enslavement, no, but by cutting us off from the ancestors."

"How did they catch him?" I asked. A battery of drums had started up close by, delivering a rolling bass, an undertow, like a current hardly felt at first, but pulling. Fatal news.

"He, he had only one, one arm," whispered Desmaizeaux hoarsely, "one arm, he lost it in a mill, so, so they give him light work, so he get, get away, and take to the hills, and maroon in the mountains, the blue mountains. Nobody could find he. But he had a friend."

17: BATON CHANGES BOUT 1792

"You see, friend does take you, but they don't bring you back!" shouted the bottle washer.

"Don't pay her any mind," said the cook, "listen to Desmaizeaux, shhhh."

"De, de friend, she make a child for a white man, the white man love the child, a girl, pretty too bad. The white man say, 'I shall free you and the child; what can you give me for that?' The woman say, 'I shall give you Mackandal.'"

So they took him one night when he came to her, I thought to myself.

"Dat, self!" shouted the bottle washer, staring at me and nodding, "Dat, self!"

"He was burnt alive," whispered Desmaizeaux, "in Le Cap."

"He not dead!" bawled the bottle washer. "It is when the wind blow that you see the skin of the fowl!" The bottle was empty.

THAT NIGHT I LAY awake, alone. Philippe, who had appeared distracted at dinner, suddenly departed for the Freemason's Lodge in Le Cap. The drumming, unabated since I had left them in the pantry, had not become louder, nor had it changed its purpose. It continued like a shading—slowly covering an empty space, taking up room, encroaching, spreading, filling in and up, until it was everywhere. It became as familiar as the wind, as unnoticed as the change of light, until it stopped. I lay and listened. A silence now occupied the night. I strained to hear a creak, a rattle, a small thump, and felt reassured when I recognised them, knowing that was how this house spoke to itself in its sleep.

Then the drums began again, from a distance. They gave a picture contained in the off beat, something glimpsed in the corner of the eye that is no longer there when one turns to hear, but returns as a hint to tease the pretended indifference of the listener. It is the power that lies hidden, the enigmatic guessing game that one plays as the senses slip away into another realm where things are suddenly realised before they vanish. Like a man on fire, he lights up the clearing between the buildings and smoulders until the sun comes up, then he no longer shines, but still burns. I turned over, leaving that alone to find him on the other side, but it is she who finds him, and she weeps as she believes him to be the person that she knew. Then the sky cleared. I am here. Philippe is there. We are all safe, for now. In the distance, the drums have quickened.

18: THE STIGMATISED

SAINT-DOMINGUE, 1792

He wondered, could this be a turning point? Beneath the anvil heat of noon they were riding out and across a dazzlingly brilliant countryside to the St. Michel plantation at La Petite Anse, a hamlet just some miles from Le Cap, to meet Jean-François. If some kind of arrangement could be reached, the inevitable might be averted, postponed, for a time. Which could mean an early return to Paris. For reasons known only to himself, Mirbeck, the third commissioner, had declined to join them.

As they clattered and jingled along with a detachment of lancers riding in close formation, he could see the destruction of the war and smell the reek of burnt cane fields and of human and animal rot. He had searched the city's streets for her, Lys de Cayeux, and had come away with the feeling that he had just missed her in the colourful crowds. Meeting her, and not quite remembering everything, had disturbed him.

The vastness of this island, its azure mountains, so lofty, in a distance not imaginable, and these rolling plains, savannahs really, seemed to belong to a continent. This had surprised him. The earth, so red. He said so; Saint-Léger said nothing.

The people in Saint-Domingue—earth-blue negresses, pungent as wood smoke, they seemed blacker than anyone in Grenada, with features that he could not recognise as similar to the faces that he had known on other islands. And so many! He had been taken aback by the crowds in the market as they rode from Le Cap. All dressed in vivid attire, predominantly red, and now the long lines of people walking in the country. Going where? There were no slaves in the fields.

The effect of more than a hundred and fifty years of racial mingling was evident in the varied skin-tones, the very physiognomy and hair textures of the people of colour. The cadence of their Patois, the languid sensuality, so casually displayed in a glance or an averted smile. He scoured his memory for hers. He was surprised at their affluence, so much gold. All this in contrast with the poverty, indeed decrepitude, of the Petits Blancs. So many cripples and amputees, both black and white, yaws that afflicted people of all sorts, and the children, covered with sores. He felt certain that there was leprosy as well. There was grim savagery here; this was a place as irrational as the nightmare.

Already, he was learning, despite the novelty of his surroundings, not to notice, not to see. He understood that. It was ingrained in the colonists from birth—not to notice, not to see the ubiquitous depredations of slavery. This practised indifference had shaped their character over the generations, trapping both the master and the slave in the same degeneration of the human spirit. This was his first experience of war. She was a spoil of war, he smiled. Beyond that, this was the unthinkable made flesh. This was, more than likely, a war to the death with France, as he was beginning to understand. The slave revolt beyond all control: the most primordial fear of all Antillean colonists since the beginning of European settlement.

Saint-Léger appeared indisposed, his hands were bandaged and he seemed pale behind his red-freckled face. In the immediate distance, from the rise that the company had gained, Roume could make out the burnt buildings that the night's rain had not quite extinguished. That had been Ville La Petite Anse, and closeby, the

18: THE STIGMATISED 1792

ruin of the mill at the Saint Michel plantation. These overlooked the wide, blue expanse of a moon-shaped bay that sparkled in the morning sun.

The red earth track along which they rode turned down and around between tall sugarcane, so intensely green in colour that it shone almost blue. Waving, these fields had obviously escaped the burning. Suddenly, he was alarmed to realise that they had been joined by a company of riders. Fear bit into his stomach as black men appeared amongst them—wild, stinking, some in dirt-encrusted rags, most barebacked, all armed with muskets strapped to their backs and machetes at their waists. There were shouts of alarm and cries for order in the formation, mixed with what was shouted in the Creole Patois of the island. He understood, as he controlled the dark bay stallion he had impulsively chosen for the expedition. This was an escort—irregular, but not threatening.

The sergeant in charge of the detachment, a grizzled veteran, maintained order in the column. The enlarged body continued on and down-hill towards where a large troop of horse and foot had gathered under a copse of immense châtaigne trees beneath which could be glimpsed sheds, where fishing pirogues were beached and, it would appear, constructed.

Still unnerved, his heart racing, Roume noticed that Saint-Léger was as shaken as he. He recognised Henri-Christophe at once—he was standing next to a tall, thin, very dark man who dismounted as they approached. Confident in the king's representatives, he thought. The man was dressed in an elaborate uniform that seemed to be comprised of a dragoon officer's blouse, combined with civilian clothes and an enormous tricorne hat, black with large white feathers. Around and close to them was gathered a company of equally bizarrely uniformed blacks, some of whom were mounted; all had sabres and some held muskets levelled—almost all were barefooted. Without hesitating or even glancing at Saint-Léger, Roume dismounted and started towards Henri-Christophe who, he noticed, had said something to the man whom he assumed to be Jean-François.

Then the tableau suddenly changed. From the shadow of the trees came a crouching figure—a man, a white man dressed in white, with a red face, running hard towards Henri-Christophe and Jean-François. In the man's hand was a carriage whip, which he commenced to wield, even from a distance; it caught Jean-François across the face with the sound of a pistol shot, causing him to cry out and stumble to the ground. That was followed by another lash that snapped in the air above the fallen man. At once, the white man was grabbed and thrown to the ground. Roume realised that the man was going to be killed, and stopped where he was.

Suddenly, Edmond Saint-Léger was walking towards the melée. He had dropped some bandages that appeared to be bloodstained. Jean-François, howling in agony, his body shaking, was being helped to his feet by Saint-Léger, who was holding out his hands as he said something quietly, so quietly that it caused both Jean-François and Henri-Christophe to bend forward to hear what he was saying. In the mid-day heat, the place had become still; even the beaten man had stopped groaning. Then, suddenly, Jean-François dropped to his knees before Saint-Léger and took both his proffered hands to his lips. Still the Irishman spoke, his words barely audible, as the rebel slaves and soldiers crowded round. Some began to drop to their knees.

"What in bloody hell. . ?" thought Roume.

Henri-Christophe beckoned towards Roume, he appeared sombre, chastened. "Come, Philippe, a miracle has taken place here." His deep rumble sounded shaken. "I don't know what to say. Come, let's go to the house, it is beyond the mill, over there; you will join Jean-François and your companion. What is his name?"

"Edmond Saint-Léger," answered Philippe, as they set off.

"A saint?"

18: THE STIGMATISED 1792

"No. Not like that." My God, these people.

Edmond now appeared quite ill. Arriving at the house, he lay down on a cot. Jean-François' wound was being treated by a woman with a paste made from crushed herbs. The attacker, Pierre Bullet, was trussed up like an iguana in the gallery, his feet and hands tied together behind his back, and suspended from a beam; he had either died or had lost consciousness. Roume heard a man say that his name was Bullet and that he was Jean-François' former owner.

"Philippe Roume, the king's commissioner, I present Jean-François, the leader of the independent north," said Henri-Christophe, this with a considerable formality in a booming voice that brought the room to silence. Roume stood forward and bowed to the man who sat at a dining-room table with a cloth held to his face. Upon the table had been placed several crystal wine decanters, full to their brims, and several glasses.

"Sit, Monsieur, your companion is resting. He is a holy one who has demonstrated that, like St. Paul, he bears on his body the marks of Jesus. This miracle has given us heart, hope and trust. You know what is written in Paul's Letter to the Galatians. Take refreshments, come, there are things that we must speak of, that I must speak to you about, because you come from the king."

Jean-François, his face swollen, the laceration now beginning to inflame his eyes, began to speak of the cruelty of the planters, the distress that knew no end. He spoke of the desperate plight of the blacks, of being trapped in hell, where, suffering, they prayed for death to the God to whom their destiny had been transferred. He was a student of the Bible, he said. Never having been taught to read, he had learnt by remembering what had been read and preached to him since he was a boy on the plantation where he was born. He was sold to Bullet when his master died—Bullet was a cruel man, a terrible man. When Boukman came to the Bullet plantation and prophesied freedom, Jean-François ran away and became a leader of a maroon band. When the conch sounded, he brought out his battalion to join the uprising. Revenge had been taken on Bullet, his wife and his children were dead, and he was there, trussed up, waiting.

The rebel slaves could no longer speak to the Colonial Assembly after their emissaries had been thrown out of the council chamber. Their only recourse was the king's commissioners. Jean-François wanted his wife returned to him and his mother set free from gaol. He wanted a ban on the use of the whip in the fields, and an extra non-working day per week, and freedom for the other leaders of the rebellion. He would bring in four hundred men, all captains of thousands. Fifty of these, he said, should be given their freedom, after they had persuaded the tens of thousands of slaves to return to their plantations. They would return all prisoners. Jean-François himself, with some others, should be allowed to leave the island.

Roume listened, paying close attention to this former slave, this African who expressed himself clearly and with sincerity in the French language. They all knew that the alternative to settling along certain terms would be a continued war that would bring with it the death of thousands, and then tens of thousands, through starvation. Roume agreed with all that was requested and pledged to move the Assemblymen to recognise that a fateful juncture had come to them all. A crossroads—an opportunity that should not be missed.

"You and your companion are the only white men that I have met who have shown humanity," said the injured man in obvious pain, his body trembling spasmodically as it dealt with the shock of the lash, his mind reeling at the miracle he had witnessed.

Later that afternoon, having toasted success and thanked the Almighty God for witnessing the miracle, Jean-François mounted the horse held for him by grooms dressed as bandmasters, and with considerable dignity departed, his retinue forming up behind. They cantered out of the plantation yard, taking Bullet, tied to the tail of an unbroken horse, with them, and disappeared into the cane fields, the setting sun turning everything to red and black.

18: THE STIGMATISED 1792

"ROBERTUS DE VILLAPARI SANCTO LEODEGARIO," said Saint-Léger, as if relating an often-told story, "also known to history as Sir Robert de Saint-Léger, was a Norman knight. Apocrypha has it that he rode with Duke William in the Conquest of Britain." He and Roume were sitting in the gallery of the plantation house at Saint Michel, having decided to return to Le Cap the following morning. The troop of lancers was setting up camp on the lawn.

"Sir Robert had stigmata. It has reoccurred in the family over the centuries. For some, it has been literally a blessing; for others, a curse. For me, it has been a burden, although, I must tell you, I have trotted it out on occasion. It happens at times of a great shock or some deep emotional upheaval. Or just in awkward moments. There was a woman, Irish, beautiful, redheaded like me—from Strangford Lough, very rich and titled in her own right. Every time we made love, it was terrible. I begged her to marry me, she said that she would not saddle her offspring with such a burden." He lifted his hands in exasperation, now again covered with bandages.

Two days later they entered Le Cap just after noon. In the town's square before the cathedral, members of the Colonial Assembly were gathered, along with a large crowd of people, black and white, slave and mulatto. All appeared in an uproar. Jean-François had allowed the white prisoners held by them to return to the city. There were about fifty or sixty bedraggled white men, women and children, who clung together, their clothes in rags, some merely tattered strips covered with dirt. They appeared as people returned from the dead.

The straw-hatted mounted rebel escort, themselves in ragged bits of uniform, was surrounded by a menacing crowd, in the midst of which was the president of the Colonial Assembly, who, refusing to debase himself by conversing with the blacks, had come prepared with a number of notes which he handed to the captain of the escort. He was answered in perfect French, Roume noticed. There was about this man, the captain of the rebel detail, a civility and an easy, confident manner in which he sat on his horse. Above the noise, Roume could just manage to hear the president say, "Continue to give proof of your repentance, demean yourselves, and inform those who have sent you to seek the advice of those commissioners, there, see them, there, it is not by their intercession that the fate of all you blackguards will be decided. It is by me, and by this Assembly."

"He seeks to give the impression," said Saint-Léger, "that we must answer to them."

"Who is the officer in charge of the prisoners, the captain? The one who is listening to the president?" Roume asked the sergeant in command of the detachment of lancers. Before he could reply, an old woman, whom he recognised as a part of his household, shouted:

"That is Toussaint!"

This caused the captain to look in their direction, their eyes meeting. Roume tipped his hat, in response Toussaint did the same.

"What has transpired?" inquired Roume, bending low to address the old woman.

"They tell the president that it is Toussaint who save them," shouted the old woman. "The president say he want more white people. Toussaint say it 'ent have no more. He out of white people. The president say 'get to hell out.' Toussaint tell him adieu. Look, look, they ent going."

A great wave of shouting arose from the crowd. People were grabbing at Toussaint and his men, holding them by their jackets if they were on foot, or by their ragged trousers if on horseback. About them a scuffle commenced, as the crowd swarmed and surged around, swords and cutlasses appearing to shouts of "Kill them before they kill us!"

"Traitors!" a hysterical voice screamed. "No mercy for the merciless!"

18: THE STIGMATISED 1792

Quietly Saint-Léger said to Roume: "Merde, they brought the prisoners to prove that they are serious about the terms, but these stupid Assemblymen are going to allow the mob to lynch them. A bit of a one-sided truce, wouldn't you say?"

Roume looked at Edmond for a moment, and then, on a sudden impulse, kicked the sides of the stallion and surged forward into the crowd towards the Assemblymen and the insurrectionists. Drawing his sabre, and holding it high above his head and still urging the horse forward, he stood up in his stirrups and began to shout in a voice that was hard and clear: "Toussaint! In the name of the king, halt! To all of you, stand back, stand away, I command you, all of you!"

Startled faces turned towards him as Roume brought the now skittish horse to a wheeling stop and commenced to jerk it around. This sent the crowd scrambling in all directions to escape the snorting, nervous stallion, who seemed to have his hooves everywhere, turning his sweaty backside one moment here, the next there, stomping, while his rider berated the onlookers in a mixture of French and Patois.

"Out of your minds! All of you! You have no right to proceed upon this path. Neither the laws of France, nor God's law permits a mob to overwhelm a herald, or those who have come to offer terms. You are no better than the pirates who haunt the bays! It is not you," he pointed the sabre at the Assemblymen, "who have the power to decide what happens to Captain Toussaint and his men. It is I, and only I, who will decide who dies here."

Already, there was a murmur in the crowd which rather resembled an understanding. Roume, eyes and sabre flashing, bellowing, the horse still stomping every which way, came evidently as a surprise to those who had been irate before, and were now curious. All present were apprehensive, weary, and desperate, and this was the behaviour of one who was not afraid. A man of vigour had taken command. A man to follow, who knew the law, thank God.

Roume now kicked his horse on towards Toussaint, who sat immovable on his own ragged mare. Drawing up at his side, he put the tip of the sabre on Toussaint's chest. Looking straight into his eyes, he said loudly and clearly in Patois: "Leave now, captain. You have made your proposal known to the commissioners of the king's National Constituent Assembly, you have taken the first step by freeing your prisoners. You have nothing further to say, so shut your mouth and leave." And then, loudly and in French: "In the name of the king, Louis XVI of the glorious fatherland, Vive la patrie! Vive la revolution!"

Toussaint, never breaking eye contact with Roume, backed his horse away and eventually turned and left the square briskly with his bedraggled escort, the shouts and jeers of the crowd following them with some hurling stones and pieces of wood, but they let them leave. Roume turned his mount, and glowered at the Assemblymen who were looking at him, some with disdain and others with amazement. They too had been taken in by his performance. The crowd, which had offered scattered applause, was by now thinning—the show was over, and the freed prisoners were being led away, to be taken care of in the houses of the town.

"We will deal with you tomorrow," said the president of the Assembly to Roume. "This will not be the end of this, let me assure you, commissioner. You speak Creole, but you are not from here, you and your fellows. You know nothing."

Roume sheathed his sword, ignoring the insult, and turned away affecting the most bored expression he could muster. The crowd was already rearranging itself into noisy, quarrelling segments arguing the inevitable and postponing all decisions. Saint-Léger had pulled up his own mare next to him. Roume looked around, and suddenly, he saw her in the crowd, she was looking directly at him.

"I see a person I must speak to, Edmond, we shall meet later at the house." Without waiting for an answer he turned away the stallion's head and made his way through the people, some of whom

18: THE STIGMATISED 1792

sucked their teeth and sneered, but mostly they nodded approvingly, while affecting an appreciation for his mount. He tipped his hat.

"M'sieu Roume." She made a little bob of a curtsy in the space allowed by his mounted presence.

Seeing his hesitation or indecision at how to speak to her in such a place, she smiled the smile that he would come to know. Whispering something to his skittish stallion, she took the bridle in one hand while passing the other along his soft nose. Glancing up she said, "Come, just follow me."

She led the way, he saw that some people were looking at them, he saw them catch her eye and step out of their way. The street noises faded from his mind. Now at his side, he saw that she held his boot just above the silver spur. He could not feel her grasp through the leather but he could feel her presence and glimpse her finely made shoulders as they emerged from a starched white blouse. The narrow street into which they turned was not unfamiliar, he saw the doorway and dismounted, she took his wide-brimmed straw hat and together they entered the small courtyard.

"Lys de Cayeux, who are you."

They were in a bed rumpled by the urgency of meeting again. The sheets smelled of vertivert, the small room that was painted a pale green had one window, which overlooked the street. There were shouts and cries of children coming from downstairs and the smell of chicken fricassee. A shaft of sunlight slicing through was lighting her delicate profile, her mass of brown curls, her turned up nose, her slim-built form and tiny, dark-brown nipples. What an enigmatic little woman; he was now imagining her as a fairy or as a nymph, her resigned lubricity. He could smell her, she smelled like a child, freshly cleaned and tidied.

"I am nobody, actually, M'sieu Roume." She said this smiling with lowered eyes, and looking up suddenly, even seriously, she bent forward and ran her fingers through his hair, her eyes, searching, not leaving his. She seemed to be examining him with much approval. He lay back, every muscle in his body relaxed, he took a deep breath, exhaled and closed his eyes. Even then he could see her, she was smiling again, he smiled in return.

She was somebody, as he would come to know over the following months. She was a planter's daughter, a child of the plaçage of Marissé de Cayeux and Madeleine La Chapelle, a free quadroon of this city who was now dead. She had been educated at the convent of the poor Clarisses.

"This house belongs to my father, they, below there, they are his tenants. I am a free woman."

"Woman? You must be sixteen."

"I am twenty on Christmas day next year, God willing." She was sitting up, her knees under her chin, "I chose you, M'sieu Roume, I selected you."

"Why?"

"Because I am a woman of means, don't smile, my father will leave me with a future that is secure. What we own here is modest compared to what we have in Cuba. You are a great man, and noble, handsome too, and I would want a man such as you to be my first son's father. I wondered if he would look like you, just now, when I looked at you."

He had to laugh out loud. She became serious as a shaft of sunlight brightened the room.

"Then come," he said, reaching out and taking her hand. "That is a big job, now, I must fulfil your every wish."

He found it hard to leave her, there was so much he would know; ". . . tell me, I know that I was not the first. . ."

"You were, could you not tell?"

"Your father?"

"He sent me to you."

18: THE STIGMATISED 1792

THE FOLLOWING EVENING they were in the long gallery at the governor's palace. Roume and Edmond Saint-Léger took turns reading the letter ostensibly written by Jean-Francois and Biassou, but more than likely composed by an educated person who succeeded in being both coy and ambivalent and, in so doing, proved his diplomacy.

"Clever fellow, this one," said Saint-Léger. "He starts by pointing out what a rich place this is, then he admits that they are involved in the killing and the destruction, but blame? No. Justice, he claims, will give to them what their situation merits. He points out that in France, there is one form of government, a republic in the making, that was created by people who rose up against tyranny, which is for everyone; but that in the colonies, egalitarianism is not shared."

"He is right," said Roume. He could only think of Lys de Cayeux, he imagined that he could still smell her youthful body, it contained the flavour of her childhood, clean linen and how she had tasted.

"But he is a slave," said the other, "he has no rights. He claims that they should share in the general pardon granted by the king, 'indiscriminately,' he supports the rights granted to the mulattoes in May and notes that the king grants us, commissioners, leave to pronounce on the status of non-free persons and the political status of the *sang-melés*."

"This man is correct," Roume said, regarding Saint-Léger as he thought again of Lys de Cayeux, a mulâtresse, no, more a quadroon, that skin, but one never knew.

"And informed. Look, he writes 'We defend the decrees of the National Assembly and your own, invested with all the necessary formalities, to the last drop of our blood,' and he puts it to us, 'should not such rights be the same for Africans?'"

"I understand what you are saying," said Saint-Léger, "but do you believe him when he claims that the revolted slave population would submit, with confidence, to the orders of the monarch, if a monarchical system survives in France? I think that this letter is a ruse to buy time. Written by a clever man who knows that his deception is seen through, but attempts it all the same."

"True, absolutely," said Roume, now paying more attention to the conversation, "but that does not take away that he is right."

"Listen to how he closes," said Saint-Léger. "'It would, in fact, be interesting if you declared, by a decree sanctioned by the local Assembly, that your intention is to take an interest in the fate of slaves. Knowing that they are the object of your concern and knowing it through their leaders, to whom you would send this work, they would be satisfied and that would help restore the broken equilibrium, without loss and in a short time.' Diplomatic, I would say."

"Yes," answered Roume, "but it is a betrayal; he betrays his cause, the cause of the slaves. The slaves whom he took to war."

"The very mention of the wealth of this place is a signal to the local planters to pay attention to their interest," Saint-Léger laughed ruefully. "He does not mention that the arrangements made just yesterday were to send the slaves back to the plantations. Jean-François promised that, my blood still on his mouth where he had kissed my hands. He writes that he will restore the broken equilibrium."

"Alea iacta est, my friend," Roume said. "There will be a war over the price at which they eat sugar in Europe. The blacks will fight for freedom, liberty and equality, and for the king. I wager that the author of this letter is that man we saw today, Toussaint. If he wrote this, he can lead them. The mulattoes and the poor whites will be his canon fodder."

"Add the English to your equation. Maitland is in Jamaica with the English squadron," said Saint-Léger, rising as Soubise entered the room. "My dear, can I pour you a glass of rum?"

18: THE STIGMATISED 1792

"Why yes, thank you, Edmond. I have been listening. The planters—don't you think that they will fight? All they have is here; most of them cannot go back to France. Their backers are dead, guillotined," said Soubise, taking the glass from him and seating herself on one of the ornate settees.

"England is their only hope. In the meantime, they will fight, their pride demands it," said Roume, his tone serious. "Obstinacy is part of their nature, they will fight everyone, including France, the Assembly should send a fleet with troops now."

"The accommodation that the rebelling slaves seek will be difficult," replied Edmond. "Jean-François came in desperation—their people are starving. However, will they be able to get the slaves to go back to the plantations? I'm not sure. A terrible war is upon this place in which everything could be destroyed—everything—all this could go."

The three sat in silence for a while. The potted plants exhaling the twilight smell of watered earth mingled with that of melting wax, as a long line of housemaids, like fireflies, dressed in white, brought lighted candelabra from the outhouse across the darkened lawn and into the rooms, there to light the tall candles in their ornamented sconces. Roume took Soubise's hand in his as a funereal smell of mourning arose from the garden and the crickets commenced a high-pitched, screaming overture. Lys de Cayeux. He could not think of anything to say to her, she may have noticed, he was thinking this, when she spoke.

"Have you noticed that all the drums have gone silent again?" Soubise was sitting up, erect, her head upturned to one side as if testing the air.

"Since when?" asked Roume. Her palm was cold and damp.

"Since just before sunset," she answered.

"By the way, what did you tell Jean-François when you showed him your stigmata?"

"I told him that you are an honourable man, Philippe Roume de Saint Laurent," answered Edmond.

ENCOUNTERS SUCH AS THAT had meant little to him in the past. Pretty girls, all in a row. This child, and he thought of her as a child, although clearly she was not, had stirred him, entranced him, captivated him. Entrapped him?

"Diablesse."

"Yes."

"When I am with you I am always afraid of being ridiculous."

"That is because I am lucky."

"What do you mean?"

"Because you are not sure if you are, or not."

"I will soon be gone."

"I know, and so will I."

At times, when they were together, it appeared to him that a glance from her, a movement that indicated something which escaped him, might have been an invitation to something just beyond his imagination. Just to think of her could make his pulse throb through his body, and he would hurry to her apartment praying that he had not missed her. Sometimes he had. He would wait in the only chair and she would arrive, the heat of the day upon her, sweat running down her pale neck, and he would make love to her. One night she said to him, "I am going to the country next week, shush," she kissed him, "you will not see me again, shush, I shall have a son and I shall call him Marissé Roume de Saint Laurent."

He knew that she would not be persuaded to stay. He had already seen the kind of woman that she was going to be and he approved of what he saw. My son's mother, he had to smile proudly as he suppressed a laugh.

18: THE STIGMATISED 1792

"Why Marissé?"

"It was my father's name. Remember."

"You will forget me."

"How could I?"

"Oh very easily, you shall get another man."

"Oh yes. But you shall be my son's father, Philippe Rose Roume de Saint Laurent, Commissioner to Saint-Domingue."

It was hard to believe that he would never see her again. Indulging in a nostalgia that was sweetly painful he returned, at first often, to the small room above the courtyard. He searched it for a memento of her, of their time together, there was none, he felt a loss. He would sit in the only chair left and look out of the window—if only for a short while, knowing that she had left the chair for him to do precisely this.

Reading from my Memoirs at La Fontenoy, Grenada, 1807

THE DAMNED. I instinctively stayed close to the house slaves during those months in Saint-Domingue. Looking back, it was Marianne, surely, who had returned, talking Creole Patois, walking barefooted, making obscene jokes with the plongeuse who also was the bottle washer, and listening to the cook. All the news came to them in much the same way, I suspected, that the news of what went on in the house found its way to the street.

I knew that I was not trusted. I knew, as well, that they were selective in giving me information. I did not care; it was the company that I needed—to be with women who, like myself, experienced what women alone can know. Whatever the hell that was. And it was hell. I lived in hell, the hell of guilt. The shame I felt only I could feel. I could not be alone. I have no words for it. Especially as I saw him get up every day stronger and more certain and face this terrible place, the people in this vile country, black and white, who had already been greedy and cruel before the uprising and who had since become desperate and vengeful. It became obvious, to me at any rate, that Philippe and Edmond Saint-Léger were perceived as being sympathetic to the Africans. This, naturally, generated greater animosity from both the royalist planters and from the Petits Blancs. Who knows what the mulattoes thought?

Fear now shaped and coloured all the actions of the royalists as they waited to take revenge on the blacks, because revenge must come first, then justice and, perhaps, a massacre; then a restocking of the plantations.

As for the blacks, Jean-François and Biassou, I learned, had returned to their armies that now numbered in the tens of thousands. Powerful, each in his own right, they fought like man rats in the same hole.

Desmaizeaux was a source of information during the humid wasteland of the day, between the end of siesta and the men's return from the Assembly, a time when his service was not in demand. He would enter whichever room I was in as silently as a moth and, in his black livery and crooked periwig, trembling all over, stand in the doorway, holding a silver tray. His entire being, long and angular, slightly bent, arranged in the habit of perpetual servitude, waiting. I only had to look at him and raise an eyebrow and he would stutteringly commence anywhere, at any point in a narrative that was forever passing through his mind. Like a conversation restarted, he would recommence with a slight stammer at the start, and then let go a flood.

There was always news of the mulattoes, I felt in deference to me.

"Beau-Beauvais, rich people. He was educated in France. Fought with us in Savanna."

Beauvais was a mulatto leader, together with Pierre Pinchinat who apparently hated the whites. "But, but a g-g-genius."

18: THE STIGMATISED 1792

He assumed that I knew of these people. And then he would go on quickly, for him, to the real substance, which was the rift and the inevitable split between Jean-François and Biassou. This he told against the background of growing mass starvation as a result of abandoning the estates. The leaders had come to an open quarrel, because both were now very powerful men. To feed their armies, their depredations increased and became more widespread as isolated plantations were burned and their owners killed, the women and girls violated. Increasingly, they sold the captured slaves—the very men, women and children they were fighting for—and, in some cases, their comrades in arms, to the Spaniards across the border in Santo Domingo.

"The armies have to be fed," he said, leaning forward, his lower jaw going into a spasm, his teeth chattering.

It was, however, the man called Toussaint who attracted my attention, because he filled Desmaizeaux with awe whenever he mentioned his name—which he did increasingly, with a respectful tone, a hushed reverence that implied the presence of something sacred. Toussaint, I gathered, reading between Desmaizeaux's whisperings, was now the aide-de-camp to Biassou, which gave Biassou a distinct advantage. This caused jealousy and a widening of the rift between the leaders to the point of open warfare.

But Toussaint was so intelligent, so gifted, so diplomatic, that he could soothe anyone into compliance. Toussaint alone was unsullied by the crimes of war. Toussaint ignored the dissensions and kept on excellent terms with both generals. The armies, seeing this display of duty, paid him respect and gave him the only thing that armies possess, which is trust.

"He was the only one to weep when he saw all hope of peace vanish," Desmaizeaux whispered, his teeth chattering, tears pouring from his supplicating eyes.

"Where did he come out from?"

"Toussaint, Madame Roume, is a great soul. His great-grandfather was king of the Arradas." My God, they are all kings here. "We are a proud and warlike people, we Arradas."

I could hear the plongeuse in my mind as she shouted, "Ha!"

But Desmaizeaux's account of Toussaint made me understand that this was no slave-become-general war-chief of a rag tag army of desperate, hungry men and women. No, this Toussaint was a free man. His antecedents were known, he was the grandson of a man named Gaou-Guinou, a prince in his own country who had been taken in war and sold to a ship bound for the west, where in this Saint-Domingue he became the property of the Count of Bréda, a nobleman of Brabant who owned a sugar manufactory. Fortunately for the kindness that followed this family, the son and the grandson of the prince of the Arradas grew up in what could be only described as an enlightened household. I had to contain myself, for instinctively I wanted to tell Desmaizeaux that I, too, had had a similar upbringing. I understood the difference implied. Here was a Creole like us, me and Philippe Roume. With a twinge in the pit of my stomach, I said to myself: like Stanislaus, but not quite.

But the story was continuing, I must pay attention because with Desmaizeaux there was no turning back. Toussaint, I gathered, was born in 1743, the same year as Philippe Roume; I wondered what month. They were both now nearly fifty. He grew up on habitation Bréda, which was then controlled by the Comte de Noé and managed by a Bayon de Libertat. As a boy, they called him fatras baton, Desmaizeaux said, tittering and weeping. Laylay stick, eh, swizzle stick, he must have been a thin boy.

It was his godfather, one Baptiste, a slave who could read, who taught him to read. Well, look at that. It would appear that his grandfather and father enjoyed a form of freedom on the estate. They had slaves in their employ. You see, everybody knew that he was a prince in Africa, and all and sundry treated them with respect.

18: THE STIGMATISED 1792

From what I understood, Toussaint did more than learn to read and write. He was educated. This too I understood. His mother and father died when he was a boy, leaving behind five children, of whom he was the eldest. He had a brother and three sisters.

He was a Catholic. He married a beautiful woman, his cousin—Suzanne Simone. Toussaint became a free man when he was thirty-three, but continued to work at Bréda as chief overseer. He had a way with herbal medicine; perhaps that was why he was in charge of the livestock at plantation Bréda.

"Yes," whispered Desmaizeaux, glancing over his shoulder, "he is a member of a fraternal order in Port-au-Prince. Since he was freed."

"Is he a fighting man?" I asked Desmaizeaux.

"He is a man of peace, mild in manner, of indomitable will, he will be terrible in war."

Today, however, he had something more to say. When I instigated the pause that was intended as a signal to end the conversation, which, as a good servant, he was aware of, I saw him hesitate in turning to leave, the silver tray pressed to his palpitating chest with both hands.

"Please, Madame Roume, there is more news."

"Yes, Desmaizeaux, and what is it?"

I felt my heart leap as I stared at this moth-like man who now appeared as an omen of some unimaginable doom. For such was the state of one's nerves in this madhouse.

"What the hell is it?"

Both he and I, alarmed by my alarm, moved towards each other.

"What?"

He was shaking, his mouth moving, I could hear his teeth click; he seemed about to weep again.

"What is it, Desmaizeaux? Tell me."

"Madame Roume, the general is going to start a rebellion today."

General? Which general? There were so many generals. "Which general, Desmaizeaux, one of the black ones or the white one, Sire de Blanchelande?"

"D-d-de white one, de Blanchelande, Madame Roume." Governor-General de Blanchelande was a person that I had not yet met. He was in command of local forces and had been in the Caribbean for some time. In 1781, as maréchal de camp, he had taken Tobago from the British and was governor there from 1781 to 1784. A Viscount of the old order. Philippe Roume had described him as a martinet, a strict disciplinarian.

"How do you know this, Desmaizeaux?"

"Please Madame, my b-b-b-brother, Sigismond, Madame Roume, he washes clothes for the officers and he overheard the general telling the others that he will take the place for the king, yes, Madame Roume, for the king."

"Are you sure of what you say?"

"Yes, please, Madame Roume."

Yes, he was. The brother—he must be interrogated, but there was no time.

"Thank you, thank you very much, this is good to know. I shall tell the Master, he may want to speak to you, I sure he will. Desmaizeaux, have you mentioned this to anyone else?"

"No, please, Madame Roume, only to you."

"Stay here, Desmaizeaux, stay here and wait for the Master."

"Yes, please, Madame Roume."

I too stayed.

Before Desmaizeaux could finish repeating his news, Philippe Roume was through the door with Saint-Léger at his heels. They had just returned from Port-au-Prince.

18: THE STIGMATISED 1792

Later that night I heard of the events of the evening from Philippe as he soaked in a tub of hot water. Apparently, commissioner de Mirbeck had escaped or deserted, in any event he was no longer to be found. De Blanchelande, always more than a little unsteady, had become alarmed by de Mirbeck's disappearance, which, as it would appear, had been occasioned by a near death experience. In the midst of an orgy, a mulatto boy had attempted to suffocate him with a pillow. This he survived, only to realise that he had been poisoned. It had taken the effort of both a surgeon major and an obeahman to purge him with laxatives. All this had been kept a secret.

De Blanchelande, who had been present at both the orgy and the purging, was being manipulated by the Colonial Assembly. They had declared for the king and were consorting with the English in Jamaica. The Colonial Assembly then invited soldiers loyal to de Blanchelande into the barracks. They were stationed at the fort along with the white militia and the inevitable mulatto opportunists. From the barracks, which was in the middle of the town next to the cathedral, they had started to fan out, taking with them artillery pieces, flags displaying the royal arms, and the regiment band. All this right under our noses.

"We were supported by a mounted detachment of hussars, small, only seventeen or eighteen, and a platoon on foot comprised of the household's sentries," Philippe related, "all men who had travelled with us from France." Philippe, dressed in his official uniform that he had had the wit to put on before he left the residence, rode into the barrack courtyard just as de Blanchelande was setting out. Galloping in, they went straight for the general. Already there were shots being fired outside the main gate as troops loyal to the commissioners, alerted by me through the good offices of both cook and bottle washer, had made their way to the centre of the city.

"Arresting de Blanchelande was another matter," he said. "His officers, alarmed by the galloping arrival of our horses, drew their sabres to repel the attack." With de Blanchelande in their midst, they put up a fight in which both Philippe and Edmond Saint-Léger were wounded on their faces and their arms, while from outside came the thunder of an artillery duel fought at close range. It was the militia, comprised mostly of Petits Blancs and a few planters, that gave way at the gate when put under pressure by the loyal troops. This served to tip the balance in the courtyard as those loyal to the commissioners streamed in. The fight continued in other parts of the building and in the city streets as the mulattoes, joined by a large contingent of the Assemblymen, held their own against the loyal troops who were still fighting, ironically, for the king.

De Blanchelande vigorously denied that he was involved in any sort of plot and in turn attempted to arrest Philippe. All this naturally came again to a fight. They were eventually separated and parted swearing revenge, but not before Philippe had taken written statements from several officers who were now trying to save their heads. Seemingly, de Blanchelande had indeed not been directly involved in the planning of a counter-revolutionary coup, but was invited to be party to the treason when the British from Jamaica had landed.

EDMOND SAINT-LÉGER LEFT FOR PARIS on the 1st of April, 1792. This itself caused much turmoil within the army and the Colonial Assembly and a degree of stability was only accomplished with the help of newly arrived troops, their officers responding to Philippe's command. He was the only remaining commissioner, the legitimate representative of the National Assembly of 1792.

The situation in the colony had deteriorated, if that could be imagined. Dismay and dread now prevailed throughout Le Cap; kidnapping became common because of the urgent need for gold. All the while, the armies of the blacks fought each other over those areas still producing food. This triggered a state of war between

18: THE STIGMATISED 1792

French Saint-Domingue and Spanish Santo Domingo. We received a dispatch that three new commissioners were to be posted to Saint-Domingue and that Philippe must report at once to the Legislative Assembly in Paris. Their identities indicated the mood that we were to expect on our return to Paris.

"Sonthonax, Polverel and Ailhaud. They are all Girondin abolitionists. This is an indication of what is to take place here," said Philippe. The emancipation of the slaves was still for him a step too far.

"And what's that?" I asked.

"They may have it in mind to free the slaves here in Saint-Domingue and in the Antilles."

"They are mandated to hold this place for France," I told him. He ignored me.

"I also understand that the Tuileries palace has been stormed by the Paris Commune, a mob, thousands of them. There is talk of a massacre of the Swiss Guard. There are rumours that the king and the royal family have been arrested and that the monarchy has come to an end."

I could see that this weighed heavily upon Philippe. To save his life he had turned into a black silk culotte-wearing republican, then a sans culotte revolutionary, but at heart I knew that he was still servant of the crown. God alone knows what he would now have to become when we returned to Paris and were forced again to face the dictatorship of the rioting mobs.

"Look," I was standing before him. He seemed tired, his head and face scarred, but recovering from his encounter with de Blanchelande. "Look at me, we could go to Trinidad. Ships are sailing for that island, the haven that you created for this very reason. Let us go there and get away from these never-ending wars. I miss my child." He did not look at me as he rose to walk to the bed.

19: THE SEPTEMBER MASSACRES
PARIS 1792-1793

HE COULD PLAINLY SEE THE fear of imminent death in the faces of those to whom he turned for an understanding of the tension that was paralysing the city. A Jacobin insurrection had thwarted the gestures made by the king. This was followed by the Jacobin's continued defiance of the Assembly. The mountain had moved. These events had mutated into a contagious and overwhelming fear in the minds of the Girondin faction. They had lost their nerve.

Favourable winds had brought them swiftly across the Atlantic. The royal family had been imprisoned on 13th of August 1792. The National Convention succeeded the Legislative Assembly, and had founded a Republic on the 21st of September. Roume heard, en route by coach from Le Havre to Paris, that a member of the new government had proclaimed, "If any attack is made on the persons of the representatives of the nation, then I declare to you in the name of the whole country that Paris will be destroyed." Roume took this to mean that the monarchy was finished and a new and different political contest was about to commence.

The Paris Commune, that is to say the municipality that controlled the city since 1789, had become insurrectionary in June of 1792. It no longer answered to the authority of the Girondin-controlled

19: THE SEPTEMBER MASSACRES 1792

Legislative Assembly. The city and its environs were dominated by the insurrectionary bands of the Commune, who in the journée of the 10th August had overwhelmed the Tuileries palace, aided by the National Guard. The king, along with his family, were compelled to flee the palace to the Legislative Assembly, seeking shelter.

Once again the people had seized the upper hand, their will expressed in the 21st September abolition of the monarchy. It was now to be expected that the armies of Europe would descend upon Paris to rearrange the affront to majesty. The people's fear was that while they were away meeting the invaders, the imprisoned aristocracy, some five thousand, breaking free from the dungeons, would join forces with the thirty thousand or more of their kind within the city, and enacting that age-old primacy would engender massacres on the people. Their revolution would fail. The leaders would face a horrible death.

Chaos had been incited by the conflicts between the two rival political factions. The radical Jacobins who, in the wake of the storming of the Tuileries palace had massacred hundreds of Swiss guardsmen and imprisoned the royal family, replaced the more moderate Girondin faction that had controlled the revolution from 1791. For Philippe it meant that his erstwhile superiors and protectors were now on the wrong side of history. He would have to change tack yet again to survive.

As he hurried through the crowd, breathing hard, shoving people out of his way, an irrational fury was rising in him; he hated them, these French people and loathed their vile city. Nonetheless, this was exactly where, more than any place in the world, he wanted to be: surviving, against all odds, at the very centre of this deadly revolution. This instinct drove his fury. He knew that his desire to be here was illogical. They should be in Trinidad which, as Marianne had rightly suggested, would have offered a safe haven, a haven of his own design and where his daughters Elizabeth and Rosette were, if they were still alive. The old world was coming to an end here, he told himself. You would have to be dead to this one, not to want to share in the creation of the next.

Knowing that his former friends no longer held the upper hand, he sought out Georges Danton who lived with Camille Desmoulins in the Cordeliers district of the old city, so as to clear himself with them of events in Saint-Domingue, whoever "they" might be at this time. Danton headed the ultra-radical faction of the city's Commune.

Danton, however, had no interest in Saint-Dominigue. "The slaves will be freed. That is inevitable," he said, not offering a seat to Roume who, with mounting anxiety, had burst into his apartment, declaring that he could not wait for the summons he was convinced was sure to arrive. "Here, take some cognac. The city's sections are demanding a war on tyrants and the extermination of hoarders and all aristocrats."

Danton's tall, burly form seemed to be bursting from his clothes. In his agitation he had spilled the drink as he poured it. The rooms smelled of boiled cauliflower and something else, like rotten leeks or very old garbage. Roume had seen the rats, now grown indifferent to human traffic, on the stairs and landings.

"Look here, Roume," said Danton, his coarse features more inflamed than usual, "you have a serious charge being formulated against you. It concerns Blanchelande and comes from citoyens Brudieu de Columbier and Simon-Armand Lignière."

"I arrested de Blanchelande for treason in Saint-Domingue," said Roume, his heart beating in his ears, his mouth dry. "He would have rallied the royalist planters and gotten into bed with the English from Jamaica. As for those two scoundrels, I ordered them deported."

"'Those two," Danton replied, pointing at the grimy window, "you should have executed. They are presently in the street below calling for your death as an aristocrat and a traitor to the revolution. Serious charges. You should have had them shot over there."

19: THE SEPTEMBER MASSACRES 1792

"Liars, they cover themselves," said Roume, the stab of fear mingling with the vile wine that was rising acidly in his throat.

"The political elite are no longer relevant to the people of Paris," said Danton. "The slightest hint of counter-revolutionary thoughts or activities will mean your death. Even my own. Had it not been for the German advance under Brunswick into the country and this ridiculous fracas, those two would be whipping up the mob to attack you and condemn you for treason as the scandal of the moment, without even bothering to bring you before the revolutionary tribunal."

This man is as terrified as I am, his only recourse is to distract the mob to even greater outrages, thought Roume anxiously as he watched Danton prime and load a pistol. The scars of some childhood accident crossing his upper lip and cheek had risen to red welts. He saw harsh resignation appear on the man's face, it was charged, it occurred to him, with the splendour of an approaching heroic death.

"Now that I command from this position, I shall demand the establishment of an enquiry before the Assembly into your matter," Danton said. "This may never happen," he continued, pointing the pistol at Roume. "The Girondins fear me and so should you. The national razor is waiting for you all," he made the motion of cutting across his neck. "If General de Blanchelande was a traitor," he stopped pacing and looked at Roume steadily in the eye, "you did the right thing in Saint-Domingue. Brudieu and Lignière are not the enemies of the revolution here, you could lose your life. We face invasion from Prussia and the damn Austrians. I am going to meet Robespierre and Jean-Paul Marat. You better come with me to the Hôtel de Ville. Marat has come back from London. You must prove your mettle to him, to me, to all of them."

He pointed again to the window with the pistol, where, in the streets below, the violent unpredictable masses were rearranging their anger. The pistol suddenly went off, startling them both. They stared at each other for a moment, and burst into laughter. Roume then realised that Danton, like himself, hesitated to ascribe any particular meaning to life.

They hurled themselves into the garbage-strewn medieval district, picking up followers as they went along the narrow lanes and alleyways. Roume, with fear for his life mounting, noticed that the Paris mob, which spoke for the Commune, had been joined by armed Bretons and Marseillais. These volunteers and other fédérés brought the numbers on the streets of the capital up to the hundreds of thousands.

Speaking from the portico of the Hôtel de Ville, Danton, standing in the blowing drizzle beneath a banner that read "The French people are standing up against the tyrants", commenced an address to the leading members of the Commune who had gathered around. Roume stepped forward and joined them, shoulder to shoulder, standing between the factions, Robespierre on his right and Marat on his left. He stared out at the vast, surging, hate-filled crowd. He could hear from the talk that arose around them that the death of the king and his family were now inevitable. They wanted to see their dead bodies, spit on them, walk on them as their blood flowed away.

"These people will not wait for legislative mechanisms. They want the royals dead," Roume said to Jean-Paul Marat. He sensed that Marat, hallowed by the charisma of the returned hero, plainly a very ill man whose popularity had mutated with the pace of the radicalised, would lead the attack against the Girondins. Marat, together with Robespierre, would compete for the implementation of the most extreme form of republicanism.

As Danton continued his harangue Marat murmured, "They will demand that a revolutionary army with a portable guillotine travel the length and breadth of France and execute every Girondin, and force every peasant to hand over his hoard of produce or take the knife right then."

19: THE SEPTEMBER MASSACRES 1792

"They are desperate," said Roume, "hundreds of thousands face starvation this winter."

"Sound the tocsin!" bellowed a gaunt toothless man, his voice louder than Danton's, his bald dome emerging from a dishevelled mop of dirty grey, his black clothes in tatters, his emaciated face and body scarred. He had fought his way forward to confront them. Shoving Roume to one side, he shouted into Danton's face, "Sound the tocsin! Or you die, Danton!"

Danton, without hesitation, swung about and struck the man across the face, sending him sprawling into the crowd below, which roared its approval.

"Take that fool away, I will die when I will die!" he bellowed, his voice rolling like thunder over the proletarian mass that was surging ever closer, as the rain began, many gaining the lower steps, barely held in check by sans culotte stalwarts and a small detachment of the National Guard.

"Citoyens! Citoyens!" Robespierre shouted above the noise, "Citoyens, the decision of the Jacobin faction is to dissolve this département of Paris, to dismiss Pétion, and to institute an insurrectionary Commune. It means that we who were at the Tuileries and took the king will carry the revolution!" This brought a great shout of approval. "Today we take the revolution to its logical conclusion! Today. . ." Even before he could finish this opening statement, Roume realised that Danton, Marat and the others were fleeing across the porch-way, running away from the excited crowd that was forcing them back into the building, reaching for them, pulling, snatching, seeking to drag them into their midst.

"Ah! Roume, just in time for the second act!" shouted Robespierre as they bolted through the tall doors that were slammed shut by guardsmen in the faces of the hysterical mob. Robespierre's red face, his dishevelled wig-less appearance and soiled clothes that no longer fitted him with the snugness they once had, spoke of the times in which the "Incorruptible" now moved and survived. He must envy Danton, thought Roume. Or fear him.

They gained the stairs and entered the council chamber. "Here it is, here is Brunswick's manifesto!" Robespierre said, picking up a large document from which hung several seals and ribbons.

"I know it, I have seen it, we all have," shouted Danton, walking away from them towards the rain-lashed windows which were reflecting the flames of the fire blazing in the council chamber's enormous fireplace.

"It is the eighth article," Robespierre was saying, "where it is said that the city of Paris and all its inhabitants shall be required to submit at once and without delay to the king. . . and if the Château of the Tuileries is entered by force or attacked or if the least violence be offered to the king, the queen . . . or . . ."

"What? What? Vengeance will be visited on the city? Robespierre, the time for what you call sober reflection is past. We are here to make decisions!" Danton declared.

"That was a challenge!" said Marat, looking disdainfully at Danton.

"I submit that citoyen Roland be Minister of the Interior and you, citoyen Danton, should head the council," Roume said this quietly, almost to himself. "It will appeal to the people, with whom you appear, at this moment, to be popular."

"I agree to that." They had been joined by Jean-Lambert Tallien, a known supporter of Marat, a deputy and a vigorous Jacobin.

Danton appeared startled, his disfigurement now even more apparent across his wide flat face. He sensed that this could mean his death, thought Roume as Danton's eyes met his own.

"Il dado è tratto," laughed Marat, Roume thought he appeared relieved. "The Girondins shiver when you pour scorn on their self-seeking. What do you say to that, Robespierre? And you shall enrage the populace to regicide."

"It is the only way that the armies of the Duke of Brunswick can be met, and be defeated by the people. The king, at the hands of the

19: THE SEPTEMBER MASSACRES 1792

people, must be brought low and must die." Again, Roume said this quietly, though loud enough to be heard above the surrounding commotion coming from outside the room.

"I am not Julius Caesar," growled Danton, his rough voice a harsh whisper from shouting. "A proletarian dictatorship is, comrade, a contradiction in terms. It can only be a moment in political time. Listen, the bells!"

From a distance, then suddenly from quite close, then from all around, came great pealing of giant cathedral bells, of iron and brass bells, brazen church, clock-tower and city-hall bells, chiming, tolling, calling.

"The bells of Paris, and the countryside. The tocsin sounds!" someone shouted.

Roume felt his stomach clench. Just then, a dishevelled woman, draped in the colours of the revolution, brandishing a cavalry-man's sabre, burst into the council chamber followed by a number of guardsmen and others, shouting, "Verdun has gone! The fortress has fallen! The Prussians are coming!"

They heard the shouts as the Hôtel de Ville was overrun by what he would come to know as the revolutionary Commune. Plainly, they had come to declare Georges Danton their leader.

"There you are Roume, your suggestion has been fulfilled by the will of the people," said Jean-Lambert Tallien, who looked at him approvingly.

"To the Tuileries!" shouted Danton, climbing onto a desk. "To the Tuileries and the king!" he bellowed as the first of the Parisians swarmed into the chamber and, seizing him by his collar and belt, presented him to the crowds standing below in the pouring rain.

Just as suddenly as they had burst in, they swarmed out and into the rain washed street with Danton on the shoulders of the foremost. Roume, acting on an obscure instinct, stayed in the rear of the noisy mass and as the last of them left, he closed the doors behind them. Standing in front of the dying fire, he nodded to himself, understanding that had he once again made the appropriate moves.

HE SPENT THE NIGHT in a corner of the council room and was awakened before dawn by a scruffy guardsman who came running into the building with the report that a party of priests had been attacked by a crowd outside the Abbaye jail.

"And? What? What has happened? Speak up, man!"

"They have been killed, some thirty or more," answered the guardsman. It appeared that he could not believe his own words. "And citoyen Danton calls for you to come at once."

Still befuddled by the sudden awakening, but relieved to have been summoned, Roume, in company with several mounted National Guardsmen, rode swiftly through the crowded streets in the predawn darkness to the site of the killings. There, a mob, maddened by the smell of ecclesiastical blood and caught up in the frenzy of anonymous murder, had broken into the adjoining Carmelite convent. Standing on a wagon at a street corner, he could make out Danton's towering figure. Arms waving, he was bellowing at the crowd. Some were paying attention, while others were apparently setting up some sort of podium, a makeshift courtroom as it would turn out.

"Citoyen Roume, where the hell were you? Get up here! Come along! Make room for the man, damn it!" shouted Danton.

Danton's command was abetted with pushes and shoves and not a few blows and kicks delivered by the ecstatic crowd. Gaining the top of the coach with the help of Jean-Lambert Tallien, Roume saw a sea of bayonets and pikes, hammers and axes glittering in the blazing torchlight. Patently the people of Paris had opened the armories and armed all the jailed criminals as well as the thousands who had come to the city from the provinces. From all around came the screams and cries of the aristocrats and their servants who had

19: THE SEPTEMBER MASSACRES 1792

been in hiding in the Carmelite building, as they were stabbed, shot or beheaded in the pastel light of dawn. Crowds had already entered the city jails and had commenced the killing of notables, priests and other ecclesiastics. They were doing this before setting out to meet the invading Prussian. He understood. They were thus engaged so as to safeguard their families before they left to face the invaders, convinced that if left in the jails the notables would somehow escape and stage a counter-revolution.

All over the city a great slaughter had commenced. Swiss-guardsmen, members of the Parlement of Paris, advocates, notaries and all former servants of the royal household were killed on sight. From his vantage place atop the wagon as it made its way through the narrow streets, where they had been joined by Robespierre, Roume could make out that more than one impromptu court was in session. He could see that the sentences being executed were for the benefit and even the entertainment of the people. Robespierre, stopping the wagon, would enthusiastically participate, holding high a severed head by the hair, sometimes two, one in each hand. Barrels of wine were broached as bonfires blazed and cups were handed about to those who had been set free. Already the self-proclaimed judges and eager executioners were leaving, going to the other city prisons, they said, "to La Force and then to the Conciergerie."

Caught up in this nightmare, knowing what they now had to do to survive, he, Danton, Robespierre and others led but mostly followed the mob to the jails. All around him in this hallucinogenic landscape a ghastly holocaust unfolded. He was drawn into the killing. They, the people, were all looking at him, at them. Afraid, he knew that the women would be the first to take him down. He came to himself, from time to time, during that apocalyptic day as it turned to night, blood-spattered, a sword in one hand, a club in the other.

As morning broke upon the smoldering city, the heavy smell of the abattoir clinging, he thought wearily of Marianne, at home in the rue Saint-Séverin, she must be going crazy with fear. There was no escape for him. He felt his own soul shrink and contract and a deeper, inarticulate anger beset him. Already the mad cohorts were dragging from the prison cells the women of the royal household. A princess was being beheaded in the street, someone said to him. He saw her head put upon an iron pole, while the dismembered naked corpse was violated by the street gangs. All before his eyes.

He could not step away. He found that he did not want to.

"Up there, up there!" A woman's voice, very near to him, was shouting above the noise, "Look the Austrian woman!"

Up above, in a stone tower, seen through a narrow window in the rosy light of another reluctant dawn, was a white face.

"The queen."

"The woman was her lover."

"What is this place?" he asked the woman, who held on to him, her face grotesque in the weird light.

"It is the Temple, the Temple of the Knights," she shouted, pointing at the huge stone building half obscured by the drizzle and smoke. "Tour de César," she cried.

Exhausted by the day, he fell into a sleep that seemed like the end of all things in an alleyway filled with garbage and stinking corpses. He awoke to find that he was alone except for those who now saw him as their blooded brother. He could not escape them.

OVER A MEAL OF stale bread and sausages followed by deep draughts of sour wine, which he shared with Tallien, news arrived that the lunatic asylum at Bicêtre, a place reserved for the daughters of the aristocracy, had been broken into. These tidings, like a magnet, drew him and his companions back into the crowded streets to join the rush heading to the hospital.

19: THE SEPTEMBER MASSACRES 1792

He saw them, the mad women of Bicêtre, pouring out, screaming, barefooted, running through the iron gates. Some were ancient hags, while not a few were children. Some looked wild and astonishingly beautiful in their chaotic dishevelment. Others were ranting and flailing, while many stood silently amidst the mayhem, a halo of innocence temporarily keeping the marauders at bay. Some were fighting off assailants with teeth and claws or anything that came to hand, as they stood about the fallen or already dead, defying the lust-filled to come closer and to pay with their lives.

Leaving Tallien behind and stumbling away, he got lost in the maze of the city's crowded, screaming streets and deadly alleyways. Hours later, captured in the swirling mass of howling people, he sought escape and paused to catch his breath. He had run away from the madhouse rape scene. He was startled to see a reflection of himself in a shattered pane of darkened glass. His face and head were bleeding from cuts and gashes he could not recall receiving. The shirt he was wearing was plainly not his own, it was ripped away at the chest, he had lost his shoes somewhere and wore wooden clogs. In his hand was a heavy sabre. Turning from the dreadful image reflected in that pit of a mirror, he lost himself once more.

He regained his self-awareness some time later, standing before the gates of the Châtelet prison. Looking up he saw thousands of white pigeons swirling in the iron-grey sky. Glancing about him he realised that he was surrounded by dead bodies who were mostly dressed in white underclothes. They were lying about in puddles of stagnant black water. They looked like victims of some appalling accident. He tried to move the fingers that gripped the blade's handle, only to discover that they were stuck to the hilt with blood, blood that had dried hard.

"Well done, citoyen," said a burly man. Roume recognised him as one of Danton's henchmen. The man placed a giant arm about his shoulders. "Now, from labour to refreshment."

As Danton, Robespierre, Roume and the other Jacobins gathered near the Pont-Neuf bridge, a man, he might have been a priest or a pious person, approached Georges Danton. He threw himself prostrate before him, then, scrambling up to his knees, he begged him to halt the slaughter, shouting, "Terribilis est locus iste!"

At first Roume, understanding what was said, thought that Danton or one of the enragés would kill the supplicant on the spot.

Beneath the tepid yellow lamplight Danton, who appeared as some weary overworked ox released from the yoke, turned towards the man, he raised his hands and waved away some others.

"No."

He looked at the abject figure at his feet and shrugged his wide shoulders: "It is a terrible place, and, it would be impossible."

He shook his head and turned to leave, the others following. Roume overheard him as he spoke aloud, perhaps to himself, ". . . a river of blood had to flow between the Parisians and the aristocracy who are now raising armies, the émigrés. The people are now pledged to the revolution." And to Roume, "Those volunteers who will be leaving to meet Brunswick at Verdun know that no mercy will be given to them."

"Yes, we shall be fighting for our lives," answered Roume. The man, still on his knees, was shouting after them, "Apage Satanas!"

Astounded, tripping over his feet, still caught in the vertigo of the bloodlust of the last three days, he wandered about in the darkness, mumbling like a madman. He had been called Satan. "Yes," he said aloud, "we have become as growths on this city, suffocating its past, making a corpse of history."

He came to himself as he sat between them later that night at a long table at an inn on the Seine. About him there were reflections of himself, some were women, he could see, for he could not yet hear, while others were boys and men. Outside the night had darkened. People were drifting away as torrents of rain poured from

19: THE SEPTEMBER MASSACRES 1792

an invisible sky onto the steep black roofs of the ancient timber-framed houses. High above, gargoyles spewed out a cold indifferent stream that mingled with the blood and gore, creating incredible patterns on the darkly lit cobbled streets. Hideous, they would rise as phantom shapes to haunt that city for generations to come.

Reading from my Memoirs at La Fontenoy, Grenada, 1807

TO WAR IN THE VENDÉE 1793-1795. Looking back now, I knew then that the killing would not end with the massacres of September. As for him, he was now a completely changed person. Philippe had become powerful. A blooded Jacobin. Violent, perhaps permanently deranged by the lunatic's blood-lust he had experienced. He knew how to hate. He had been a party to mass murder. He would be to regicide.

He, of all people, parroted the words of Robespierre, "Louis must die so that the nation may live." He had been in the Convention chamber on the day they abolished the monarchy, it was the 22nd of September 1792. He cheered wildly when the Republic was declared. Philippe was present amongst the delirious crowd, standing next to Robespierre, when citoyen Louis Capet was decapitated on the 21st of January 1793.

Louis, he said, like the fool he was, had attempted to address the mass of people. Standing out in contrast against the dreadfully erect black frame of the guillotine, he said he saw this portly, commonplace-appearing man try once more to be king, saying:

"Frenchmen, I die innocent; it is from the scaffold and soon to appear before God that I tell you so. I pardon my enemies. I desire that France —" as he said that, the cheering hullabaloo died away and the noisy crowd grew still. They began to pay attention to the king. In that instant General Santère, head of the Paris National Guard, call out sharply, his voice echoing in the freshly created quiet: "Tambours!" and the drums of the assembled regiments rolled and thundered, drowning out Louis' last words along with the hiss of the blade and the abrupt finality of its halt.

The severed head was held up by the hair for all to see, as an absolute silence spoke. The great mass of people continued to be so still that he could hear the sound of time passing, then the crowd silently started to sidle away as if escaping a thing too abominable to bear, not daring to look at each other, hardly raising their eyes.

He was just turning to follow the others with whom he had come when he saw a man rushing through the immobile mass. He lost sight of him. He was more conscious of the feeling that he did not care as much for what had happened here as those around him, when he heard me, my voice, in his head say in Patois, "You're Creole, boy. Just like me." Feeling differently, he peered about him and suddenly his attention was attracted once again to the man. He had forgotten him. He saw him plainly then. Dishevelled like a clerk in a rush. Or a student, late for class, bustling through. To his amazement he saw the man brush past those who were at the foot of the scaffold and take the stair with a leap onto the platform, next to the bloody guillotine. The man appeared like an actor on a stage. He had caught the attention of thousands of people.

He raised both hands high, his dark clerkish clothes tight on his thin frame, then, suddenly he bent forward and pressed both hands into the widening pool of blood that was still running out of the dead king's body. The man then sprang upwards and whirled his hands about, sending droplets of the dead man's blood onto those who were closeby. "Jacques de Molay, you are avenged!" the man screamed loudly, in a triumphant but anguished cry that echoed across La Place Louis XV, which had now become the Place de la Révolution. These words, Philippe said, were strangely held suspended, as if frozen for a spell before all other sounds resumed.

I hardly recognised him as he spoke of all this.

19: THE SEPTEMBER MASSACRES 1792

The struggles of 1793. Danton, he said, had made up his mind that all Girondists must be exterminated. The war was now between the bourgeoisie and the common people, rather than between the nobility and the bourgeoisie. Then what, war with England? War with Spain? Yes, but it also became wars waged in the recalcitrant provinces. Cities such Lyon, Avignon and Marseille would take up arms. In Toulon, he explained, as if I knew what he was talking about, a general, Paul de Barras and another, Buonaparte, a Corsican with troops loyal to the Convention, had successfully suppressed royalist insurgents. Over a thousand men had been killed there in one week. I had only to hear the name de Barras for my heart to leap.

"Who is he?" Looking across the table into his face, I saw his expression change. He grimaced, cynically, and sarcastically said, "They seem to be everywhere, don't you find, I'll get one in my soup next. Paul de Barras is Everard de Barras' nephew. The Vicomte Paul de Barras, now a democrat, has become the heavy hand of the Convention."

I saw in Philippe that night a man very different from the one who had sung to me in Tobago the lullaby: "Little lamb, who made thee? Does thou know who made thee, Gave thee life?"

"This former king," he told me, picking up his plate and rising to finish his supper in the pantry with the men who lived in the house with us, "has become in history simply citoyen Louis Capet. The Austrian woman Marie Antoinette née Hapsburg will follow him soon," he remarked casually, pouring a glass of wine for me, "then the Princess Élisabeth, to be followed by their entire cursed race. They will be joined by every aristocrat in the land and eventually in Europe. I hear that Sonthonax has arbitrarily freed the slaves in Saint-Domingue. That should make you happy!"

Léger-Félicité Sonthonax had been made the chief civil commissioner of Saint-Domingue in 1792. I had met him. It was said of him that he was a lover of African people because he had taken a black woman as a mistress. To survive and to secure the colony for republican France, Sonthonax had freed the slaves in Saint-Domingue. Le Cap Français had been burnt, destroyed. But Saint-Domingue was not on my mind in those days.

Anguished and unspeakably hopeless, despairing for my life, I went off my head when I heard that Manon Roland had been guillotined and that her husband, in desolation, had committed suicide as had both de Lannes, husband and wife, the couple who had befriended us when we first arrived in Paris in 1790. Manon's final words, I was to learn, as she faced the guillotine had been "O Liberté, que de crimes on commet en ton nom!" She had given me a little silver bell inscribed *Liberté*.

Every day brought news of suicides, murders and executions. Jacques-Pierre Brissot, along with twenty-eight other professionals, was arrested and guillotined. Jean-Paul Marat was assassinated by Charlotte Corday, a Girondist sympathiser. This woman surprised him in his bathroom and stabbed him to death with a butcher's knife. I felt such a profound sense of gratification. One murderer less. It allowed me to draw a deeper breath. Marat had stunk from his skin disease. I looked at Philippe, "Who will be next, eh? You?" He replied with a shrug and remarked callously that the Montagnards no longer needed Marat's support.

Robespierre was emerging as the leading figure of the revolution. He was in command of the Jacobin faction, which took its instructions from the monsters who listened to daemons possessing the souls of the damned who walked the streets of this city. They had killed all of Philippe's former friends, our friends, the Girondins.

Philippe, now affecting a wary indifference, had successfully distanced himself from them by his actions in the September massacre. He was now cold and clever and self-centered. He was by this time acting as an advisor to the Committee of Public Safety, speaking on their platforms, handing out pamphlets and badly

19: THE SEPTEMBER MASSACRES 1792

written feuilletons, participating in their barbarities. I no longer believed that this was meant for our survival. I realised what was the creature that he had indeed become: the loup-garou of our folklore, the shape changer, the night walker.

Yet I saw him falter one evening as we ate our frugal meal. I stared at him for a long time, studying those dark averted features that possessed an expression of abstraction. He raised his eyes to mine and we sat for a long time staring sightlessly into each other's minds. I saw him in pain, his heart breaking when he understood, without doubt, that our dear friend Arthur Dillon would surely face the guillotine. Dillon had been posted to the Army of the Ardennes by the Convention in October of '92. His recall to Paris would have only one result.

He said that "they" knew of his time with Dillon in Tobago, and that "they" were watching him. I searched his dark passionate face as it glowed in the soft light, it held a sort of sinfulness unconcealed. The notorious Law of Suspects was drawn up in the rooms of the house on the rue Saint-Séverin, which had become a sometime meeting place for members of the Committee of Public Safety. This harsh law empowered the Committee or its agents to arrest, without prior warning, anyone who displayed any indication of displeasure with or in opposition to the revolution. The age of dissent had passed. Thirty-one Girondins were executed one morning. I had met or had known every one of them.

The Revolutionary Tribunal now functioned like a well-oiled machine, generating death at the rate of between eight to twelve Girondins per day. These executions no longer drew huge cheering crowds. The people had become indifferent. There were actually more suicides than executions. The smell of decomposing corpses filled the air as despair overtook hopelessness and fear was an emotion that to my surprise I grew accustomed to.

The sound of a coach coming to a stop was a constant torment. People, unknown, could arrive at any time and take him away to be killed. Or me. The weather contributed to the dreadful misery. The rain was colder, then snow, and a howling wind. It entered my chest and I coughed my way through that terrifying winter.

He too was permanently feverish. His eyes bloodshot, his breath foul as his teeth fell out. He no longer exuded the odour of fresh milk and shaved and sanded cedar as he had done that day when we first met in Grenada. We were both grey-haired. I used henna, he seldom saw the barber. Our bowel movements stopped and our bones ached. Getting food was a daily problem. He did not complain and slept the sleep of the exhausted. I complained. The gloom permeated my soul and I am sure his own callous bravado. Tens of thousands of people were killed all over the country, the majority in Paris. I heard tell that many a rabid atheist republican revolutionary had returned to Catholicism.

That the western provinces and coastal regions of France had risen in revolt against the anti-religion laws and the levy demanding that men be enlisted in the republican army, came to us as a rumour. I understood that it was prompted by a disdain for the Jacobin party and was founded on an age-old loyalty to the Church and the feudal system. It was at first ignored. But when news came that Bordeaux and Lyons were in the hands of the counter-revolutionary movements and that the uprising had spread through the entire province of the Vendée in south-western France, involving tens if not hundreds of thousands of people, and that they were demanding a form of provincial autonomy, the Jacobins of Paris, led by Robespierre, understood that the rebellion in the west had to end.

These threats to the revolution had come after heroic battles had been fought and won by the desperate citizen army of Paris. They had defeated the invading German force at Valmy, where they had turned back the armies of the Duke of Brunswick and of the Prince of Saxe-Coburg-Gotha. Henceforth, it was believed that the revolution would enjoy victory in all its military conflicts. That the country could rise up against them was seen as betrayal.

19: THE SEPTEMBER MASSACRES 1792

This royalist reaction was a topic that they at first avoided. That the revolution could crumble into a civil war, that the Germans would return, the Austrians already being in the Alsace, became the abyss into which they all stared.

We met the new fire-brands who now spoke for the people. One I remembered from our early days in Paris. His looking at me had disturbed Marianne. Seeing him again I was attracted to his youthful body, long, slim and round-limbed, his very white skin, arms and long legs. A terrible beauty that festered. It was of the nature of an archangel fallen into hell. An enfant terrible. His name was Louis-Antoine de Saint-Just. He appeared in my dreams. To allay the fear-filled boredom of my days I allowed him into my imagination as a solitary vice. He was the youngest of the deputies elected to the National Convention in 1792. We were both twenty-seven in '93. He was a Jacobin of course, however, he had spurned both the Girondin elements and the extreme Montagnards. He sat alone. His first speech given at the Convention was a dramatic invocation of death. He frightened even them, the murderers. In him they saw their successor and their executioner. Several left the chamber, never to return. Even then few escaped him. He was a fanatic, a desperate man who was also an excellent soldier. He knew that certain death followed him closely as well. His devotion to Robespierre was absolute.

France did declare war on England, Spain and Holland in the first three months of 1793; Philippe had been right. The national army raised by the Committee of Public Safety rose to in excess of five hundred thousand men. Many were to be deployed under Saint-Just across the eastern borders to meet the Austrian invasion.

"Roume, you are to go with the army of the Committee of Public Safety to the Vendée," Saint-Just said to Philippe almost in passing, adding, "For revolutionists there is no rest but in the tomb. You must be harsh in the fullness of the authority delegated to you. The time has come to strike hard blows."

Saint-Just. I wanted Philippe to leave, to go into the Vendée, he was to be a *représentant en mission*, the eyes and ears of the Committee of Public Safety. The man whom Saint-Just, acting on behalf of the Committee of Public Safety, had ordered to lead this force was General Jean-Baptiste Carrier. He was a notorious Jacobin with a vile sense of humour who was a sometime operator of the guillotine. He entertained his comrades by mimicking the facial expressions he had seen on the decapitated heads as they lay in the basket. Carrier brimmed with enthusiasm. He had an eye on the future, he said to me. "Soon there will be too many people in this country. We therefore must quickly eliminate all nobles, clergy, religious people, commercial agents, notaries and former members of the Parlement of Paris."

Hard blows. Life had become a hard blow. I helped Philippe to pack. He was to join Carrier and a force of forty-five thousand who had been commissioned to carry out a "pacification" of the region. The revolt in the Vendée was now characterised as a Catholic and royal uprising that threatened Nantes. He saw my look of despair, despair for his soul, and he shrugged. He marched off, in the gilded uniform of a captain, covered with tricolored sashes, with the army of the Committee of Public Safety to put down the Catholic peasantry, returning émigrés and monarchists who wanted to reverse the revolution.

Life took an even more dangerous, and for me, exciting turn after he left. The people of Paris were rioting for food in the streets. He had left me with money, bags of coins looted from burnt-out commercial establishments that his band of robbers had occupied during the war on the profiteers. With the help of Jean Patience, a bodyguard whom Philippe had provided me with, I nailed up all doors and boarded the windows on the street level, and lived on the second floor where I kept a ladder. I would let down the ladder so as to venture out, which was rare.

By the end of 1793 the army of the Vendée was in the city of Nantes. Philippe, I heard, had been wounded in the battle for

19: THE SEPTEMBER MASSACRES 1792

Savenay and was recuperating in a dingy castle by the sea, looked after by an old crone with one tooth that wiggled when she spoke. He was to tell of it, of the war in the Vendée, some three years later when we were aboard the frigate *Immortalité* bound for Saint-Domingue, where he was once again to serve as a commissioner.

The frigate Révolutionnaire, in which Philippe Roume and Marianne made their final journey from Saint-Domingue to France where he died on the 29th of September 1805.

BOOK THIRD

20: MEETING CHADEAU
THE ESCAPE FROM GRENADA 1796

Reading from my Memoirs at La Fontenoy, Grenada, 1807

STEPPING AWAY FROM THE TERRIFYING TIMES we spent in France from 1792 to 1795 may now be timely. The chance meeting with an old man, Jacques Chadeau, who recounted to me all he knew of what became known as the Fedon revolution, should now be told. I will also give an recount of the final days and aftermath of the battle for Mount Qua Qua. This was related to me by one of the survivors of that awful war.

IT WAS IN 1806, HERE IN GRENADA that I met Jacques Chadeau. I was just thinking that I could write my name in the warm, humid air that had become as damp as an overheated bathhouse, when from beneath me came a rumble, then a shaking, which caused me to start to my feet; the earthquake was over before I could think of dying. I stood there breathless.

I stared about, looking for someone or something to share my fright, when I saw a dark form move in the shrubbery above and to the right.

"Who's that?" I called shrilly, my heart still racing, racing now even more, "Who's that?" I fumbled in the basket that held my étui,

20: MEETING CHADEAU 1796

my day's rations, various necessities and my Terzerol pistol. A tiny, deadly thing with twin barrels. It wasn't primed or loaded but. . .

"Get out here, now!"

Slowly, two hands appeared, then a face, then an emaciated, black as coal man dressed in rags slowly emerged from the bushes. Even from this distance, I could smell him.

"Don't shoot me, I just want food, food, please, Miss, don't shoot me."

"Who the hell are you? Eh! What you doing here—looking to thief—eh! Come out, come down here, on your knees, bend down, down, put your hands flat on the ground, put your head on the ground, flat, before I put a bullet in your ass."

With that, breathing hard, I delivered a kick into the emaciated rib cage.

"Don't move. What's your name, nigger? Where you come out from?"

My heart still pounding, I looked carefully at this grovelling form. Yaws, pian, as we know it, mapian as I could see, huge, yellow, swollen, oozing ulcers all over his back, arms, and body.

"Pardon, Miss, pardon, please, my name is Jacques, they call me Jacques Chadeau. Please, I beg you, charity, food, food."

I could see the lice and smell the sores, my God.

"Come, get up, up, walk ahead, up, up the hill."

He stank. This is how and when I met Jacques Chadeau, the last surviving revolutionary of the Julien Fédon revolution, at least here, in Grenada.

Thank God for the girl Vandelle, I would not have been able to deal with the yaws. She washed him in concoctions of herbal remedies. She made him soak for hours on end in a tub, into which she poured what appeared to be barks of trees and roots, ground down to their fibrous essentials. She sunned him and fed him bone marrow soup; but most of all, she sang to him, long-winded dirges of her own creation to which he reacted by becoming even more pitiable, acquiring the appearance of an overly chastised dog. The smell of his breath improved as his disease cleared up, leaving large white scars all over his emaciated body.

The régime, which lasted weeks, came to include long sea baths and walks along the beach. She cared for this derelict as he improved from a walking ghost to a shuffling old man, to some semblance of what he must have been when he took arms against the most powerful army on earth, the British, in 1795. As he improved and as I overcame my revulsion to his condition, I began to listen to his story. It concerned me to a deep and anguished degree, at times unbearable. I was also perfectly aware that I was harbouring a fugitive from British law, a former revolutionary. To me, however, Jacques Chadeau was a patriot.

He had been at Azima estate, close to the Grand Etang, and had heard the call to arms even before Julien Fédon and Stanislaus de Barras had stormed Grenville. He had been there. One day, several months later, I put a glass of rum into his shaking hands.

"Here, Chadeau, take some rum, here is tobacco. Now, tell me what you know about Julien Fédon's revolution. Where did it start?"

Swallowing the rum and pocketing the tobacco, he described the fires that burnt that night in Grenville to the music of a stiff easterly. It was March, and a hot night in the dry season when they started the fire. It inflamed the tops of the coconut trees as it jumped from estate to estate to take the château at Soubise with it.

His morocoy eyes came alive as he related how in February, he had accompanied Jean Pierre Lavalette and Charles Nugues, together with Julien Fédon, Joachim Philip, and Stanislaus de Barras on board the schooner *Diamond,* which had taken them to Guadeloupe to receive the flag of liberation from the hands of Victor Hugues.

20: MEETING CHADEAU 1796

My heart leaped. I had to know. "You knew Stanislaus de Barras?" I asked the old man. His expression changed to what appeared amusement.

"Yes, Miss. I knew him well, he was a commander. I followed him into war."

"Tell me, what you know of de Barras, we were children together in Grenville. When did he come back home, what happened?"

He must have seen my breathless desperation as his look softened; he took a drink of rum and related how de Barras' father had given him the overseer's house on Belle Vue estate upon his return from France. I calculated that it must have been in 1792. Chadeau said he told him to "settle down or go back to France." It was a case of out of the frying pan and into the fire, the old man said. Grenada had by then once more become a colony of England.

From what he described, I could see how Stanislaus, his republican heart burning, had arrived home with the fire of a Parisian revolutionary. This fervor had been stoked by his tutor, the Abbé Grégoire, his mentor Robespierre and his exemplar Victor Hugues.

Stanislaus had acquired the idealistic and inflammatory language of revolution. It had been the most active part of his vocabulary when I left him in Paris in 1790.

"He was a Jacobin noir, Miss."

"Yes, I understand. He was able to put the anger felt by the likes of Julien Fédon and others into the urgent need for a popular uprising against the English."

"Yes, Miss, he knew that Julien Fédon had strong personal reasons for staging the revolt."

This I knew from my own experience. Julien Fédon's uppermost purpose in life was to take revenge. For Stanislaus, the creation of a republican Grenada was a natural extension of the French republican revolution, it was the future, and it was also retribution for all those Sundays without sponge cake.

In 1794, France abolished slavery in all her possessions. Stanislaus commenced the role for which he had been prepared. Uncompromising and dogmatic, he became the revolution's main idéologue in the Windward Islands, after all, he had been there on the Paris streets with the grand masters of revolution. Victor Hugues, by February 1794, had arrived in Guadeloupe with the guillotine. It was natural that Stanislaus was the one who went there, together with Julien Fédon, to meet Victor, whom he knew.

"And you went with them, you saw Victor Hugues?" I asked Chadeau. "Tell me, tell what you saw."

He told me how he had lingered in a doorway, his huge bare feet suddenly an embarrassment. He had seen the gold epaulettes attached to their shoulders by Victor Hugues himself. They were given sabres, declared commissioned officers of the army of the Republic of France. Receiving these, they saluted.

They all returned to Grenada and sailed into Grenville Bay. They marched away from the French frigate's long boat that had been beached upon a moonlit curve of sand, then over the silent shore. He told how they danced beneath the diamond sky, celebrating, and then made their way through the sleeping town to take the forest trails, to find the high ridges that would lead them across the rooftop of the island's mountain ranges to Mount St. Margaret above the Forêt Noir and the Beauséjour valley to Belvédère, to Morne Fédon, as it would be known.

By this time, the talk was already in the air. Men knew what time it was. To take the place was the order of the day. As everyone was one in the Republic, nigger no longer meant slave. The army in the mountains reached five thousand. All had heard Fédon's call to arms. Yes, he had sharpened his cutlass long before.

They said to him, "Come, go."

20: MEETING CHADEAU 1796

He related that it was the fore-day morning of the 1st of March that they entered Soubise; the estate house was empty. They stayed in the deserted cocoa-field, the heat and pairs of small tiger-striped butterflies rising, and waited until night, then they set out for Grenville.

Midnight. He, Jacques Chadeau, had the fire—two flambeaux, one in each hand—and a cutlass in his waistband. Around him, almost one hundred men, all bare-backed, sweating murder, teeth and eyes white and grim, straining, running into the quiet street, mulattoes and black men together. Somebody blew a conch; at the blast, he said, he flung both flambeaux at a house, just as the white man came out. House and man burst into flames; he described how he saw Fédon run up and chop the flaming man in half, from shoulder to belt buckle, the equal sides falling away, blazing. More fire, as others ignited in their rage all that was about them. The white people came out, some with guns to fire into the fire, then to turn and run straight into the others who had come up from the beach.

The magistrate, M'Mahon, stepped outside his house and asked, "What is the matter?" Ventour said to him, "The matter is war, it is begun, the French army has landed, and you are my prisoner." A servant took the sword that the magistrate was carrying from his hand. M'Mahon had only a shirt on, no pants; they took him to the battery next to Doctor Hay's house.

Jacques Chadeau saw that Stanislaus had chopped the fat shop-man, the fat shop-man's wife, two or perhaps three children, and the Da. Then they went into the church swinging cutlasses, the people were hiding. The people who knew Stanislaus begged, "Oh God, oh God, oh. . .", wap-wap, wap, hand gone, head chopped off. By then, the others had arrived. Some were hurling big stones, some pelted fire. Stanislaus was the one who saw the priest. Fédon saw him, too. They ran after him, they held him, Fédon told him a thing or two, then chopped him in his head. Stanislaus, too, chopped again and again. The priest, he was old, he fell down

347

and disappeared into his black rags, only his white head and a pale bare foot remained. Chadeau said that they told him that the priest was called Peissonier. They burned down Mr. Nesbit's school. Stanislaus said, "Leave the house," Fédon said, "Burn it," so they burned it. Stanislaus burned it and Nesbit and all of them in it.

I looked at this decrepit creature as he spoke in the voice of someone who had told this story many times.

Coming back, Jacques Chadeau said, they made sure that everybody was dead. Some were chopped again, wap, wap-wap, arm gone, teeth flying. They were walking in the blood, he told me, when he saw a baby's arm and hand, white, perfect, like a doll's, dismembered, lying in the mud. The fires in the coconut trees, coconut branches travelling in the wind, blazing across the night sky. The conch blew again, everybody was to gather at Belle Vue estate. Stanislaus said, "To Belle Vue, to Belle Vue," Fédon said, "Open the flag, display the flag," it read Liberté, Egalité ou La Mort, they told him. Running through the almond trees, he described how certain of them stopped to throw torches into Soubise estate house and to fire the barracks. Where I was born. My heart was pounding as he spoke of this.

When they arrived at Belle Vue, he told how they killed the Scottish overseer, his wife, "She belly, big," he said, "they cut it open and take out what was inside, then they kill the little boy below the cart, where he went to hide. Then they burned down the old house, the barracks, the mill. Take the horses and the cows, kill all the dogs, was the command." I had seen this in Saint-Domingue.

Then to Balthazar plantation, there Wabo, the maroon, killed Mr. Ross, the overseer. Fédon told Stanislaus, "You kill your father, then we go to La Digue and you shall see me chop up that old bitch." They burnt down Balthazar when it was discovered that M. de Barras was not there. At La Digue, they found the old woman naked in a big bed. "A black nigger man, old too, was with her,"

20: MEETING CHADEAU 1796

Chadeau went on. "The man fired a shot, Fédon chop off his head and chop the old white woman in two, then they burn down the house. The conch blow again and we all left and returned to beyond Belvédère to Mount Qua Qua, where they had cooked an ox. The other war parties came back by morning."

The war parties had gone to Gouyave to burn the plantations. They returned with prisoners, many English, but French folk as well. Chadeau described old white women tied together, children, old men, young women, their mulatto servants—they were brought into the camp. Other white people came, men, they came in fear to the camp because Victor Hugues' proclamation had ordered them to, claiming that they were true republicans.

Jacques Chadeau described to me what he had heard of the capture of the governor, Ninian Home, by Jean-Pierre Fédon, Julien's brother. The governor and a party of his friends had been at Paraclete estate, about fifteen miles from Grenville, when news of the attack came to them. The governor fled to Sauteurs in the north, then took a sloop to Saint George's but landed at Gouyave where they were captured and taken to Belvédère, all fifty of them.

Grenada's plantation houses were burning, Chadeau said, he could see them from the heights. Cane fields blazing, fire in the mountains. News came that the governor of Trinidad had sent soldiers, and more were to come. Julien Fédon sent word to the president of the council in Saint George's that he would kill all the captives if the camp was attacked. In the meanwhile, the camp was secured and battlements were constructed with facines; fallen trees were arranged in lines of defence as reinforcements arrived.

By early morning, the first wave of attackers could be seen in open formation commencing the assault on the mountain, coming up through the forest that was thick with undergrowth and dangerously precipitous, climbing up towards the camp, just as a thunder-storm swept across the peaks. Chadeau said they had placed marksmen in the tall trees from the day before; these were now all hidden in the low-hanging clouds and lashing rain. As the leading English officers were shot, the soldiers ran, sliding down in the mud to fall into gullies where ambushes decimated their ranks; nearly one hundred lay dead by the afternoon. By the following day, they were stinking, he said, waving his thin hand before his face, grimacing in memory.

Chadeau related that when they returned to camp, it was to find that Julien Fédon had indeed ordered the execution of all the prisoners. Nearly all were dead, he said, there were some who had lost their minds and were mad with fear. Some others were killed while still bound to others in the stocks. They all died except for the magistrate M'Mahon, the doctor, Hay, and another man. Charles Nogues, the aide-de-camp and Fédon's brother-in-law, made sure of that. Jacques Chadeau said that Julien Fédon had ordered the killing when he saw his brother Jean-Paul's dead body brought back to the camp.

In the days and weeks that followed, small armies were dispatched to fight and hold different parts of the island. Some were successful, many failed. But the tenacity of the republicans grew with every success and even in failure men would say, "Tomorrow, we shall take Saint George's". Stanislaus de Barras was the one who talked, lifting the spirit, inflaming courage for the cause. I could well imagine that.

Chadeau described the men under Fédon and Stanislaus, who was his second in command, as made up of free mulattoes, the formerly enslaved, French men, white men who were true republicans from Martinique and Guadeloupe, and some from France who had come with Victor Hugues. Some had been in Sainte Lucie, where they had become famous as L'Armée dans les Bois, others had fought the English in St. Vincent and Dominica. They said that more were on their way from Saint-Domingue, that every republican in the Antilles was coming to free La Grenade from the English for the French Republic. Stanislaus, I know, wanted to make it clear

20: MEETING CHADEAU 1796

that this was not a slave revolt or even a mulatto rebellion, or some kind of local uprising. It was a republican revolution, its purpose was the creation of a democratic state in Grenada. Within months, Fédon's armies had overrun almost the entire island. The refugees, planters and mulattoes who had sided with the monarchists and the English had retreated and were besieged in Saint George's, which they stoutly defended.

"There was a battle here, Miss," he told me, "right here on this estate."

"Yes, I know," I answered, "go on, tell me what you did." From time to time, Chadeau said, he was sent with a party of patriots to collect the supplies that were coming in from Guadeloupe. At times, these were landed at Levera Bay in an area controlled by Louis La Grenade, a Free Coloured captain of the militia. The provisions dispatched by Victor Hugues, "that champion," as Chadeau described him, were of urgent necessity. They would be brought in by the Sainte Lucian Jean Baptiste Bideau aboard his schooner *Botón de Rosa*. Just managing to stay ahead of the patrols dispatched by Louis La Grenade, Chadeau made contact with Bideau's sailors, who brought the news that the governor of Trinidad had asked two British frigates to patrol the coast. The entire island, he said, was then mobilised for a sustained war.

From a carefully folded oilcloth, Jacques Chadeau extracted a tattered parchment—it contained a fragment of a printed declaration: Julien Fédon's summons to surrender, dated the 4th of March, 1796—and handed it to me. At a glance, I recognised the language of the Jacobin Club and could hear the voice of Stanislaus de Barras, who I suspected was the mind and hand behind this barely discernable declaration.

Without entering into any detail of our rights, we summon you, and all the inhabitants of every denomination in this colony to surrender to the republican forces under our command. We give you notice, that in case of your not submitting, as you are enjoined, you shall be liable to all the scourges of a disastrous war; and that all persons whomsoever that shall be taken in arms, or who shall not have joined the national flag in such time as we shall judge fit shall be punished with death, and their estates burnt, and the land confiscated to the use of the Republic.

"Did you think that you could win that war?" I asked him.

"Yes, yes," he said emphatically. "It was the supplies, the war supplies, that failed us." He leaned forward and then whispered, "The leaders failed us, Fédon came to distrust everyone, he quarrelled with de Barras frequently and came to distrust him, he fought with Joachim Philip and might have killed him. Hugues wrote them letters commanding them to cease the dissent as it was destroying the revolution. He pleaded with them, saying that he was pained to see how divided they had become; the enemy will hear of it, he wrote, and will take advantage of it to fall upon you and defeat you. I heard the letters read aloud by de Barras to the others. Hugues cautioned them, he said to let ambition give way to love of the Republic. It is impossible for all of you to be in charge. Hugues' advice was, hold together. But the weight of the war was too great," Chadeau said, shaking his head sadly. "They had become different men," he sighed.

It made no difference; they fought and quarrelled, got drunk and almost killed each other, but went out to fight the enemy as one the next day. But, he said, "I knew that they had given up hope when Charles Nugues sent his son to Hugues. Bideau took the boy aboard the *Botón de Rosa*. They had hidden him on Soubise Island. Young Felicien had him there in a hut." Yes, I told him, I had known his papa, I knew him well.

He went on to relate that the last shipment of arms and ammunition came aboard the *Modeste*, a schooner owned by the Irishman John Black, sailing out of Sainte Lucie. It brought the news that Morne Fortuné had been taken by the enemy. Captured by the British in May of 1796.

20: MEETING CHADEAU 1796

Philippe Roume and I had heard, while in Saint-Domingue, of the concentrated British assault on the patriotic camp in Grenada under British General Abercromby, which took place more than a year after the uprising. We heard of the massacre of the women and children, some thirty to forty, who were killed by Stanislaus and Fédon and the others with cutlasses, hacked to death as the final assault commenced. We heard that most of the leading men, some forty-seven, were captured and hanged publicly in Saint George's. But not Julien Fédon, and not Stanislaus de Barras.

"Where did they go to?"

"To Trinidad," Chadeau said, meeting my eye.

Jacques Chadeau left us as he felt strength return to his body. He said that he would try to make it to Guadeloupe where he knew that Charles Ventour, a former comrade in arms, had settled with his family; he said he knew them and that they would take him in. I gave him money for his journey, and asked him, once again, if he had ever heard anything concerning Stanislaus de Barras, even a rumour.

"No, Miss, not a word."

It was all the news when I went into Saint George's some weeks later to enquire at the port office as to whether there was any information from Trinidad concerning Rosette. I had put some money about in the hope of generating interest—there was no news. The news on the careenage, however, was that after ten years the last of the insurgents—one Jacques Chadeau—had been captured by a detachment of Black Rangers.

He had been sailing in a new dinghy. Making landfall at Mustique, he must have come ashore to rest. It was speculated that he had had accomplices who had provided him with the money to purchase such a craft. Brought back to Saint George's in chains, he was branded with the mark of a traitor and then hanged.

He was buried without ceremony in a pauper's grave. This saddened me immensely. I had given the old man too much money. I shall now relate the fate of the other Grenadian revolutionaries.

THE END OF THE GRENADA UPRISING, 1796. General Abercromby's assault had overrun the defences that both Stanislaus and Fédon had inspected the previous night. They had given hearty encouragement to the men who held these positions where cannons had been stationed. They both knew, even then, that their chances of holding the ridge were slim. The revolutionary companies from Guadeloupe, amongst whom Stanislaus found himself as the mad retreat commenced, had stood their ground, delivering a sustained fire on the advancing British regiment. All had died there. Around him, he could see men, their men, fleeing in all directions; some were throwing themselves over precipices, whilst others tried to escape down the steep hillside, through the tangled underbrush, and into the fire coming from detachments detailed to cut off the anticipated retreat.

As the final assault commenced Fédon led the prisoners out. They had been kept in an underground stockade. The state of hate that Stanislaus knew well and entertained on command for the French families could not be summoned in that morning's baleful light. With desperate fear mounting, he saw the sorry band of bedraggled people appear—mostly old women clutching children, little fair-haired boys and barefoot girls. This signalled the end of Mount Doom, Mount Qua Qua had fallen.

Slipping and falling over in the mud, they stared about. They had witnessed the horrible slaughter of other prisoners, of the governor and those in his party. Stanislaus, who had steeled himself, commanded them all to strip off their rags. He had no idea why he did that, he would later say. Naked, shaking, hiding behind each other, they huddled in the rolling mists that mingled with the gun-smoke. The English cannonade, exploding in the forest, was

20: MEETING CHADEAU 1796

coming ever closer, and bullets passed between him and them to shatter on the palings, the water barrels, the makeshift fortifications. They had begun to sing in prayer. He felt that he should die then, he was to say to me years later, as he tried not to listen.

Stanislaus related the fragmentary glimpses of the macabre scenes of dismemberment, of blood flying through the blowing drizzle. A boy's sweet face, so near to the head of an ancient hag, they seemed in conversation; he had laughed aloud. A woman's arm and chest cleaved from her still comely body, a hand that would reach into his nightmares for the rest of his life, causing him, even in his decrepitude, to be afraid to dream.

As the first of the red coats were seen coming through the shattered stockade gate, Stanislaus turned away from the slaughter. He was covered in the gore that the down-pour could not wash away. He bolted towards the rear of the encampment and took the trail that passed high above the ruin of Belvédère estate house. He was closely followed by Julien Fédon.

The two slithered into the mists and down the vertical side of the mountain to take shelter, about half-way down the precipice, where a fallen forest giant had created, not a cave, as much as a deep hole. This is where they hid for days—Stanislaus de Barras and Julien Fédon.

They were so close to the camp above they that could hear the English officers shouting commands, the grunts and moans of wounded soldiers, the cries of outrage at what was found on the cloud-covered mountaintop.

Night came and still more soldiers arrived. These, with torches blazing, were roped together and descended the sheer cliffs, shouting to their comrades, keeping contact in a darkness made complete by the mists and the misery. In their hole, Fédon and Stanislaus huddled, digging deeper, ever deeper, piling the mud and rock behind them, attempting to hold it all together with broken branches and the clothes that they had taken off for the purpose. The night was full of trepidation, but the day, when it bleakly arrived, was another thing in itself.

From a distance, they could hear the bark and howl of bloodhounds brought up from St. George's to ferret out the hidden, the runaways. Shots were heard, with sounds of engagement, sometimes cries of pain or terror; they saw a man go by, falling, so close to their hole that they recognised him—Jacques Chadeau—then another, Ventour, slipping, falling through the forest, through the undergrowth. These were followed by a party of perhaps a dozen St. George's militiamen who came by slowly, taking their time, talking, sure in their endeavour that they would catch their man sooner or later.

Night came. Fédon was caught in a spasm of trembling that he could not restrain. Stanislaus as well, cold and naked, shivered as water dripped and mud, dislodged from up above, fell into their hiding place now made near invisible against the rutted mountainside. Stanislaus prayed, he repeated Our Fathers, beseeching that the bloodhounds would not be brought to this side of the mountain, while making incoherent promises to Almighty God, to the blessed Virgin Mary, to every saint and martyr remembered from childhood instructions given by Father Peissonier, the man whom he had killed in Grenville the previous year.

In such a manner, the third day and night passed. Hunger was assuaged by eating the large cockroach-like insects and the fat worms with which they shared the hole in the mud. They drank the water that was wrung from their tattered garments. Then a day came, and then another passed, they heard not a human sound, no call or command. Cautiously, they pushed aside the dripping mud and peered about. The forest was full of light. There was an abundance of bird-song and the wind, rushing through the branches, possessed such an innocence and freedom that they wished they were not there, but in a place where the wind went, far away from what they had begun to sense, but had not yet realised as madness, a

20: MEETING CHADEAU 1796

nightmare in which they had moved and lived for so many long and hate-filled years.

Remorse and contrition were not yet emotions in their hearts. They had not arrived at a need to justify, even to themselves, what they had done. Guilt, a word as heavy as lead, had not even been approached. There was none of that as yet. They, however, knew that it had ended. It had ended with the familiar knowledge of failure. Of not accomplishing. This they knew too well, it had been with them all their lives. No hope. Even after this, the white man had triumphed. Notwithstanding everything, they had tried to free the people as well as themselves from a bondage so all-encompassing that it might as well be the ocean sea.

There was nothing else for it but to move away, higher, further up into the clouds, beyond the tall forest of great trees and massive tangles of vines to the other forest beyond, high above, the one of ferns, palms, lean tall growths and thick grass, which was always soaked by rain and by the moisture in the atmosphere that never changed, even on a sunny day.

They lived naked, wet and hungry for days. Shivering with the cold at night and hiding in the forest by day. Eating what could be dug out of the ground. They hardly spoke to each other. There was no need for words. To explain, to describe the nature of their death to this world. Nor were there words, or even thoughts, that could find an anchorage in minds as deranged as theirs. They survived in a cave on the eastern flank of Grand Etang and, like Adam and Eve, they no longer knew that they were naked. They acquired innocence and felt themselves like animals, redeemed of all sin, because the world had ended and they had survived to start anew. A slate washed clean with blood, with anger, and with the courage that they knew that they had possessed. They knew that.

From the mountaintop, in a distance hardly imaginable, they could see a vast expanse of ocean in which swirled, blue on blue, the tattoo shapes of mysterious currents. Like a mirage in the furthest distance appeared a shape, a paler blue, far paler than the brilliant sky, it seemed to float above the horizon. It was the mountains of the nearest island. Trinidad.

Behind and beneath them, rolling to the west, to the east and to the north, were the cloudy mountaintops of Grenada. They had murdered an old woodsman and his sons for the clothes that they wore. For the little wooden house, the iron pot, the fire, the salt, the oil, the chickens in the coop, and for the cassava and the yams that grew in their garden, which also contained pigeon peas, ripe for picking. They found a rough carving, Fédon said it was a charm, a *nkisi,* from Africa, they made a feast. Then they buried the corpses in the cesspit. Still, they hid and fled and climbed into the tallest trees where they spent their days on the lookout, returning to the little house in the clearing only when night came and promised rain.

Almost a year had passed since the taking of Mount Doom and the fall of fortress Qua Qua. There was something auspicious in the air. They had become creatures of the forest and, like them, their instincts were alive and fine-tuned and quivered, as the whiskers of a cat's would, at each and every change in the currents of chance. Each moved in his own spaces, delineated by lines of invisible avoidance. Not denial, no, not even postponement. It was that they, each of them separately, had created an other self. They had become simpler men.

They now kept to the north of the island as they had heard the rangers combing the high woods of the Grand Etang. Avoiding the remote, isolated estates, they followed the course of the Duquesne river to the sea, sleeping on boulders, swimming the mountain pools so as to leave no trail for the bloodhounds. The opportunity to leave Grenada came when they saw, from their forested hilltop hideaway, a corial pulled up on the sand of a small cove.

I WAS TO LEARN THAT IT WAS AGAINST HIS BETTER judgment that the Irish shipper John Black had taken on the cargo of horned

20: MEETING CHADEAU 1796

cattle at the port of La Guaira. He was bound for Port-d'Espagne, Trinidad. He smelled the storm in the morning's wind, two days out. His crew were up to it and the schooner *Swallow* was a good ship.

It was the wind's ferocity as it rose and came on in powerful gusts that sobered him, standing in her poop, looking at the heaving waves, the pulling water and low, intimidating sky. By mid-afternoon, the sea had become a cauldron, whipped by crosswinds that changed direction from hour to hour. He had reduced the sail to sticks and shrouds and had battened down the hatches as the ship became like a toy in the vastness of lashing rain, gusting wind and swirling water. The problem was the live cargo. He could hear them bellowing, sliding, crashing against the stanchions, destroying everything, including themselves, in the hold below. He prayed for the safety of the ship that night as, lashed to the helm, he endeavoured to keep her bow to windward.

The red and gold sky of the morning after found them adrift in a cold and angry sea, as errant easterlies whistled through the *Swallow's* denuded masts. He knew what he would find below and loaded the muskets himself. It took the entire day to clear away the carnage. Of the twenty-seven head, there were two heifers alive, a young bull, and four cows. He ordered all remains overboard. Then relented at the pleadings of the cook, to salt away as many carcasses as they could manage.

He felt ill, too much blood. The damage and the destruction below decks would cost a fortune. In the failing light, the wind now settled into a steady breeze coming from the east-south-east. With a bottle of Barbados in his hand, he sat amidships, watching the helmsman, and felt the *Swallow* settle under sail. They had been blown off-course, according to the compass; by how many miles? He had no idea. He would wait no longer for the stars.

It was the lookout's call that startled him from sleep. The night was clear, the stars had come out, the three quarter moon bright on the *Swallow's* phosphorescent wake that lit up the black waves.

"Small craft in the water off to starboard."

Plainly, there, gone for now, there again, between the rushing waves, a canoe with a lateen rig already falling astern. Faintly, shouts were heard above the wind. Nothing for it.

"Back sails! Prepare to come about. In irons, lower a boat! Take her about. Helmsman!"

These orders took the *Swallow* into a tight circle, crashing through the waves, her sails flapping impotently. That brought her bow into the wind, stalling her to pitch and roll, almost at a standstill, in the rolling sea. The wind had dropped from a regular easterly to a light breeze as if to accommodate his manoeuvre. The ship's boat, with four men at the oars, was lowered as she went about and was nearing the small craft that had lowered her sail. There were two men on board.

Captain Black inspected them. These are not sailors, he thought; refugees, no, fugitives. One, some sort of black man; the other looked French. They were both emaciated and frightened, the Frenchman obviously deranged.

"Get below and get some food into them," he said, signalling to the mate to take charge of the two. "We can't take your canoe with us, she is already adrift," he said to them. "Make ready to come about! Step lively there! Back out the jib! Put your backs into it!" he ordered, giving the impression of indifference to the strangers. I shall have a word with those two later, he thought, preparing to set a course for Port-d'Espagne.

Stanislaus and Fédon were guided below decks to the galley without a backward glance at the corial in which they had spent the preceding five days; the *nkisi,* taken from the house of the old man whom they had murdered along with his sons, still nailed to its floor.

20: MEETING CHADEAU 1796

SARUSIMA THE CARIB, grandson of the cacique Buchumar, sitting in the shade of a giant naked Indian tree on the hillside to the east of the port, was blackening his teeth when he saw the *Swallow* drop anchor.

She lay some four miles offshore. To him, the strangers reduced the possibility of opportunity. His people were not like the Guaran people, who were as abandoned children, left behind after everyone had eaten. He had shown the stranger, Roume, some things that only the Carib people knew; old things from the time of the weird people. The people who had left their marks on the boulders in the mountains and now lived as Zemies in stones of a perfect shape and weight, a weight that said that its purpose had been attained, a shape that echoed the perfection of completeness. He, his people, possessed these discrete attributes. They were complete.

The place now fairly teemed with strangers. If he could think of time, he would know that thirteen years had passed since Philippe Roume had sojourned here. Then it was complete. Everything was appropriate. The advent of the strangers had reduced this vital attribute.

AWAITING THE RISING OF the tide so as to send a boat ashore, John Black, sitting in the afternoon sunlight, regarded the emaciated appearance of the two he had rescued. He paid little attention to the croaking incoherence of these men who had grown unaccustomed to normal speech. He ordered that they wash and be given clothes and shoes, and he watched them eat and drink. It was a story that he had heard before. How could it happened that the French Republic could be possessed of such naïveté as to arm these half-breeds? They had been promised liberty and equality and had become inflated with ideals and hopes. These were dashed, of course, by the power of might. Cannon and steel. It had almost happened, they assured him, it had been within their grasp; they had failed because their leaders had failed them.

"Are you not the leaders?" he wondered aloud, mildly, stroking his beard.

"No, no, we are patriots, the betrayed, we cannot return to Grenada, the English will kill us."

Black doubted that the French had truly intended to give these mongrels anything. As someone who had lived amongst the French in these islands, he knew that they looked upon the mulattoes with suspicion and saw them as a degraded race. These people were treated with contempt, hardly different from the slaves.

He nevertheless explained that upon the sale of the cattle and the salted beef, he would be for Cayenne, where he would take on a cargo of logwood. There was nothing here in Spanish Trinidad. The island had become the home of the destitute, a refuge for outlaws and brigands that the English sloops of war raided at will. He indicated such a sloop of war with his thumb, from which he had anchored as far away as he could. Dangerous, this place, with people who held views deadly to each other. Treachery abounded in the squalor. It was a place where dogs ate dogs.

The emaciated mulatto, for such perhaps he was, begged that he be allowed to stay aboard. He said that he would earn his passage by work. Captain Black did not think that he could do much of that. The other had looked like a white man on the night that he was picked up from the sea; now that he could see him plainly in the light of day, John Black was still undecided, a *metisse* or *sang-melé* of some sort perhaps. He could hardly speak, and looked as though he had lost his mind. The man could not decide whether he would go with the mulatto, or stay in Port-d'Espagne, or make his way to the Main. They were both Grenadians. Fugitives, dripping with the blood of atrocious massacres, now fleeing from the failed rebellion.

Who was he to judge anyone? This was a voyage that had made a loss. He wanted nothing to cross him. From the archipelago of islands within the Dragon's Mouth to his lee, he could hear the sound of cannon fire. He had seen the two English sloops of war

20: MEETING CHADEAU 1796

earlier. He knew that they were presently engaging the flotilla of brigands that sheltered there under the command of Jean Baptiste Bideau, the Saint Lucian revolutionary who served Victor Hugues. He had a sense of sailing very close to the wind. If he was a superstitious man. . . but he was not.

A sudden land breeze carrying the smell of fish brought his mind back to the two. He had stopped listening. The tide had changed. It was rising. That would take the ship's boat beyond the shallow mud flats and past the stalking roots of the mangrove to the Rio Tragarete's mouth next to the redoubt and the short wooden jetty that jutted out to sea.

"Yes, I shall take thee to Cayenne," he said to Fédon, rising. His pipe had gone out. He knocked it on the gunwale.

"Go quickly, now," he said to the other, "the boat awaits." He would not be seen with this mad one ashore.

SARUSIMA, refreshed and repainted, Greater Ani feathers, long and shining black, worn high in his hair and confident of his smile, trotted past the toll-man at the gate and entered Port-d'Espagne. He was for a fête. The westering sun had set, the moody afterglow was now fanned by a cooling breeze. He liked rum and would get some tonight. And dance. Then he would go to the girl they called Louisa Calderon. She was Carib, and was a relative of his mother's.

Taller than most of his people, in fact, taller than many Europeans, he moved easily through the waterfront's shallow hullabaloo. Everything began and ended there.

The Spaniards knew it as Plaza del Marina. A Venezuelan, Farfan, had a grog shop there at its eastern end, close to a spring, it was called La Vantilla. There, for a bit of silver, he would get rum and find room for himself on the inside. The shed was crowded.

Black men laboured on a row of drums that spoke in a language that he did not know, while others, mostly women, sang shrilly, swayed and clapped their hands. He took no notice of them. He liked it better when an old black with something called an ekonting would join the dance and play an enchanting repetition of the same notes, over and over until it entered his mind as no other sound ever did. It was the one reasons why he came to take rum in Farfan's shed.

The old man arrived. Without waiting, he sat between the drummers and started to pluck. The swaying women went away. At once, Sarusima fell into the paradox of the spaces left between the notes. He listened for them, with eyes half closed; following intensely the short-lived drone produced beneath the two chords, so constant, while being thrilled when the player interjected with thumps, using the instrument as a drum; this he heard apart and separate from the ongoing rolling rhythm as played by the drummers.

Entering the trance, his consciousness suspended, he moved his body up and down as though making small bows, the blue-black feathers of his headdress emitting a dark shine. These movements were enhanced from time to time by hops, small, short but firm. Arms and hands always at his sides, he glanced unseeingly about him. He experienced himself becoming a Greater Ani, swaying forward and dizzily backward, as the big black bird would when balancing on a thin branch. Now croaking, gobbling, and calling loudly, kra-ani.

He was unaware that he had become the main attraction. He became lighthearted, dancing in the light of the flaming torches held high by some young black boys. He stamped out, with his big feet, his mating ground, while the ekonting player, moving in the enigma of his own magic, evoked images to himself of the village of Kanjanka in Lower Casamance, where he had spent his childhood near the banks of the Casamance River. Then, suddenly, Sarusima awoke with a start from the trance with staring eyes. The birds

20: MEETING CHADEAU 1796

had flown away and he was now alone. The girl known to the foreigners as Louisa Calderon, but to him as Cañari, was leading him away.

The following morning, the smell of fish baking and the sounds of women talking and laughing in a language that he knew made him smile. He was sitting on the earthen floor of a hut, the hammock cords, now at his feet, having snapped during the night, still in the position in which he had fallen asleep. Around him, the feathers of his invocation, and standing between them and staring at him with eyes like licked black stones was a foreign girl of about eight or ten.

"I am a rose," she said, in a language he recognised, "would you like to smell me?"

Not having any knowledge of roses and fully conscious that he was no longer the Greater Ani of the previous evening, he declined.

"Then come," said the child, with such firmness in her small voice that he obeyed.

Cañari awaited him in the manner of welcoming a bridegroom with orchids on the seashore. It was as he expected. He came to understand that the girl child called Rosette had been taken by relatives of Cañari from a Tobagonian woman, a peddler of embroidered appliqués.

At that same time, the *Swallow's* boat was landing a passenger at the short jetty that jutted from the of the dry river. Sarusima the Carib noticed the foreign man floundering, having stepped from the jetty's wooden planks into the mangrove's black ooze up to his knees. From a short distance away, amongst the ajoupa huts and towering ceiba trees, the noise of a great commotion was rising. This he ignored, as it rightly belonged to the other world.

Stanislaus de Barras, stumbled from the boat and gained a foothold on the boulder-strewn estuary of the dry river close to the redoubt. He glanced about him. He too had heard the commotion and immediately recognised it as the sounds of an insurrection. He approached cautiously. About him were people, some in groups, all were armed. Some had the blue, white and red tied as a bandana, others wore it as a sash, while others actually possessed the cockade of the earliest Jacobin revolutionaries. These were mostly blacks. He recognised a face or two in the agitated crowd. Grenadians. As he withdrew, afraid to show himself, behind a high root, he realised that there were several head of cattle about, grazing in the grass and stubble on the mangrove's edge. A body of English soldiers were attempting to form an irregular column under the protection of some Spanish soldiers. They were being shouted at by a sergeant standing near to two officers who had drawn their swords. All around them surged what he could easily make out to be sailors from the recently sunk brigand fleet.

Suddenly, a larger crowd appeared to be closing in on the column. From a window in a dilapidated wooden building, a person was haranguing those below in the Patois of Dominica, calling on them to kill, to exterminate, to boil these lobster-red vermin in oil.

"Pas des Anglais en la Trinité! No English in Trinidad!" commenced a shouted chorus. Something incomprehensible was bellowed by the hoarse voice of the woman in the window. From across the muddy street, from another house, came the cry "Aux armes! Aux armes!" It was a mass brawl. From what he could make out, the privateers were no match for the English swabs, who beat them bloody with a mass performance of fisticuffs.

The Black Jacobins, veterans of the brigand wars, were another matter. From the start, he saw the knives come out and long machetes sharpened on both sides. These entered the fray, slashing and stabbing. Before the English salts knew what was going on, the two officers were down in spreading pools of blood. The nature of the fight now changed. French planters were firing muskets indiscriminately into the melee. A party of English officers, all armed with pistols, emerged from a house across the way, and opened fire on the brigands.

20: MEETING CHADEAU 1796

The panicked crowd, comprised by now of the entire population of the town, surged for shelter towards the grove of trees in which Stanislaus was hiding. Several of the Spanish militiamen followed. Between them the cattle began to move. He stumbled, fleeing, trying to find shelter amongst the sea grape and manchineel trees that joined the mangrove's mud. The animals, lowing, some ambling, running clumsily, startled by the noise and the fleeing people, moved towards the water's edge and on towards the dry river's mouth. That was when he saw a white child—a girl standing in the path of the rushing mob that now contained even more animals, now crazed by the gunfire. Without hesitating, he scooped up the girl and ran with the crowd. Getting ahead of the stampede and through the undergrowth, he made for the redoubt close to the dry river bed.

Sarusima the Carib had just prepared the corial when he saw, running towards him, the man that he had seen earlier come ashore. The man was carrying the child, Rosette, in his arms. He was racing ahead of the others, all fleeing the charging cattle, the shooting and the uproar. Standing in the shallow water, he placed the last calabash in Cañari's hands, he would take this provisional Greater Ani that he had impulsively married to Güiria for a nesting. It was obvious that the man was coming directly towards him. Breathless and stumbling, he was about to fall at the water's edge, when Sarusima caught the child from the man and placed her in the corial. For a moment, they stood facing each other. The man was faint with the exertion of saving the girl who had been a gift from the embroidery peddler to Cañari. It meant something. Sarusima had had luck with foreigners. With a small gesture, he invited the man into the corial. The man did not hesitate; he waded into the muddy water and stepped carefully into the craft. Sarusima climbed in too and, pushing hard on the paddle, the corial was off. He handed the other paddle to the man and away they went into the hazy heat of the Gulf of Paria.

21: WAR IN THE VENDÉE

1793-1796

HE HAD BECOME A CREATURE OF THE CONVENTION. A représentant en mission, a political commissar. His prime function in the Vendée was to observe the conduct of the officers in the army of the new republic and to report to Louis Antoine Saint-Just.

The officer corps at this stage of the revolution was made up of men drawn mostly from the *noblesse d'épée* and still loyal to the previous regime. They were only kept in check by the sans culottes, the peasantry and members of the Jacobin Clubs in the ranks, who were all committed to the revolution.

The generals well knew that these citizen soldiers of the Republic would mutiny and kill them, as had happened to General Théobald Dillon. He had recently been murdered by his own troops outside the city of Lille. They were convinced that their defeat by the Austrians was the result of a conspiracy on the part of General Dillon, whom they called a "traitor and an aristocrat." Théobald had been Arthur Dillon's cousin, but Roume did not dare to make enquiries about Arthur's arrest and incarceration or its possible outcome.

The army with which he rode out of Paris was comprised of National Guard regiments that included veterans of the American war. There were several brigades of provincials under the command

21: WAR IN THE VENDÉE 1793

of deputies appointed by Saint-Just and battalions of peasants, farmers' sons, who were prepared to die for the Church property and noble land expropriated, which had now become their own. He rode with the ardent Jacobin patriots, who had been bloodied in the same massacres as he in September of 1792. He knew that they were watching him. In truth they were all watching each other.

Roume came to understand that this war in the western regions was a religious war. A contest between the Catholic faith and the newly established secular republic. Yet, he believed himself safer with the army in the Vendée than attempting to navigate the Parisian tempest. Soubise, he had convinced himself, would manage. She knows how to live, she will survive. In any event, he could not have declined. Robespierre was in control of the National Convention. His orders had been signed by Deputy Saint-Just.

Fervently Catholic, and inherently superstitious, the Vendée had been economically stagnant for a very long time. The ancient nobility still dwelt amongst the peasantry. They had over the centuries shared in the depredations of the religious wars, the misfortunes of country life, the poverty, the vagaries of the weather and the reality of famine.

These war bands were led by daring individuals, who at times were priests, acting as inspired by God, leading troops of cavalry comprised exclusively of the nobility, eventually evolving into an irregular body called by some the Red Army of the Vendée.

They went into battle with all the ardour of a crusade preached by some ghost of St. Bernard, armed with chivalric pennants, flags bearing the image of the sacred heart of Jesus, banners of various Catholic fraternities, relics of medieval saints, farm implements and trophy weapons taken off the walls of abandoned châteaux.

The entire province was in revolt. The countryside lay abandoned, the vineyards deserted. All around could be seen farm animals running wild, many starving, even more slaughtered and the remains left to rot. He noticed that people were removing the lead from the roofs of public buildings and churches, to be melted down for the production of shot. Poorly armed, they had as artillery the old long-barrelled culverins taken from castles and a few modern cannons obtained from republican positions that had been overrun.

As he rode now with the 2nd Carabiniers-à-Cheval, he imagined himself here at another time. Away from the dark chaos of Paris the charm of the countryside was pleasing. It saddened him to see how the French waged a war on themselves and were destroying a thousand years of history. The long months of the campaign had reduced the ranks of the republican army, and were eroding the fighting spirit of even the men from the political clubs of the city. He saw them slip away from the smoking ruins of small towns. Some had been intimidated by the presence of the relics of saints and the banners bearing the image of the sacred heart of Jesus.

Information arrived that the Vendéen army had crossed the Loire after being defeated by General Hoche at the battle of Cholet. It was now falling back on Grenville, a port city which overflowed with refugees, in the hope of taking it. They were expecting an English naval squadron, and a battle that would be a turning point in the war was anticipated.

The brigade of Carabiniers to which Roume was attached was ordered to reinforce the five thousand republican troops at Grenville under the command of Captain François Marceau-Desgraviers. From a hillside overlooking the bay he could see the Vendéen soldiery ranged for the assault. Then suddenly there came news that the English naval squadron had sailed away, and the besieging Vendéen army was fleeing. Fleeing only to fall into the hands of the brigade of Carabiniers.

Amongst the officers that Roume met at the siege of Grenville was General Paul de Barras, who had come as a representative of the National Convention and was its commissioner to the French Republican army in the west.

"Everard de Barras is my uncle," the rough, impatient young man informed him. Then, regarding Roume more closely, he said, "Yes,

21: WAR IN THE VENDÉE 1793

I have heard tell of you. They say that you are clever. Backed the right horse. Stayed alive."

The rain that had been threatening commenced in earnest. "Come, Roume, my tent is there. If survival is the test of worth, you are certainly amongst the most able. Come and meet Hoche, and tell me of my uncle and the islands."

They parted, saying that they would meet again in Paris. By the following day, the army was on the march again. Roume, as commissar, proceeded with his duties, which dictated that he remain with the Carabiniers. They were for the city of Savenay.

The Carabiniers had bivouacked in a dilapidated château which had but two or three rooms that were windproof, although the rain found ways to enter. Exhausted, he sat alone before a fire, still wearing his great-coat, his cuirass and helmet along with his sabre and a holstered carbine at his feet. A drop of water landed on his shoulder, he felt the cold splash across his cheek. The château's bare hall contained only the one chair. A fire blazed in the enormous hearth, illuminating him with dancing shadows that flickered about the room. Around him the debris left behind by the looters, scattered pages and rain-soaked books lay about the rotted carpet. Dark blue ovals and rectangles stood out from where pictures had once hung on faded azure walls decorated with a pattern of tarnished golden fleurs-de-lis. It evoked for him a vague despair that he attempted to distract by anticipating the drips that plopped and plinked on his armor plate that reflected the blazing fire. There was still beauty there, he thought.

The room, in its abandonment, appeared a metaphor of his existence. His melancholy engendered a nostalgia belonging not to him but to his forebears, he thought, speaking through inherited memories. The blood of the princes, he whispered, long dead. That he should be here, in France, now. He smiled sadly. From outside came the sounds of a commotion. Voices becoming louder, he heard his sergeant hiss, "He will not see you. . . the man is worn out, damn it."

Then came a shouting scream of something incoherent and the sounds of a scuffle. The door was thrown open and a dishevelled woman appeared, the sergeant's firm grip upon her arm. They struggled in the doorway. In his weariness, he recognised that he had seen this all before. Better to deal with her now than have her and her starving children throw themselves under his horse's hooves in the morning.

"What's this about?"

"This woman says that she is your wife."

"Let her be, Marsan. Come, citoyenne, come, tell me who has wronged you?"

"Wronged? Me? Philippe Roume, what have *you* become, a commandant in all of this?"

My God! It was Fanny!

"Fanny?" he said in disbelief as he stared in amazement at this antiquated version of the woman whose naked beauty he had once worshipped. She stood tottering before him, her ragged clothes and tattered shawl and large wooden clogs all steaming in the heated room. She swayed as if caught in the delirium of a dream and stared about her open-mouthed. He had recognised her eyes, although her face was as lined as a hag's from a folktale, and her hair had become the colour of tripe. Yet it was she. Her eyes, those were still her own.

And her story came, hurled breathlessly at him like boulders. Marsan brought in a chair. She ignored it. They had killed her grandfather and in their search for gold had destroyed everything that they could find.

"When?" he asked, not actually wanting to know, but attempting to slow down the torrent so as to catch himself. She went on, not noticing that he had spoken. Arguing her past. Moving relentlessly up and down and across her recent life like a spider repairing, reconstructing a vast web.

21: WAR IN THE VENDÉE 1793

"I returned from Trinidad and told my grandfather that I had found the gold stolen by. . . by that woman, your woman, the black one! The one who lives now in my house. Yes, Philippe, I found it."

"You found it."

It was unreal, this, it had happened too quickly. To talk about this, here, the gold, Soubise's gold.

"I found it!" she screamed shallowly, her hands held before her eyes as if seeing it. "I found it where they had hidden it in a cave on Gasper's island in Trinidad, Philippe. I am not worthless. No, no. I came back to him and told him, I told him, I said, 'I found your treasure.'"

Throwing the sabre that he had grasped when the disturbance began to the ground he made to reach for her, to take her arm, a drip fell on her dirty face and ran like a tear. She turned away with a grimace, avoiding his touch. Tottering and dragging her feet, she made a few steps towards the fire.

"All this," she waved her hand about, "was broiling to a head. He knew that it was time to leave. But he of course refused, until he had the right ship, the right men. I was afraid. There were no right men anymore. I left when I saw that they were coming from the mainland. I took a boat and sailed out. From out at sea I could see the house burning. Not the western tower-wing, I knew that he was there. All night, I waited, watched. The wind blew the fire away from it. I knew that they were looking for him. Then the wind changed. I saw it go. It went up like a candle."

"Sit, please, sit Fanny. Marsan! Some wine!"

"No. I want to leave this place."

"Where do you want to go?"

"To Trinidad."

"The gold, of course, I understand."

"I have a house there. I have nothing here, and yes Philippe, the gold, it is mine."

She sat heavily, her hands hanging on both sides of the chair. He waved Marsan away and poured a tumbler full and handed it to her. As she drank, he noticed her broken nails and dirty hands and glanced at her. She was staring up at him.

"Yes, this is what I have become. I took bread from a dead woman's hands this morning and ate it while looking at the flies that were coming out from her mouth. Help me to leave France, Philippe, please."

He took the cup from her shaking hands. "I can perhaps get you to England."

"To England, yes, André Fatio is there."

He saw that she was on the point of fainting, her body had swayed forward although her eyes, unblinking, had not left his own. Her stare was hard, blue orbs in a sea of blood. He leaned forward, he could smell her. She smelled of rot. He caught her as she fell.

"My God." She was all bones. "Marsan!"

She was dead. The Surgeon Major, young and matter of fact, told him that she had been repeatedly raped and mutilated. Septicemia. She had died of blood poisoning. He buried her in a field behind the château beneath a beech tree. He had stayed, caught up in the thought as to whether he should place a marker with her name on the grave. He was surprised at his indecision. In the far distance came a cannonade. That made up his mind. He turned and walked away, a dark and solitary shape against a sunset that looked like a blood-soaked cloth.

Late autumn weather was giving way to winter gales, which turned the roads to rivers of mud. Her face would not go away. He saw her everywhere in the starving ragged crowds of women.

The army, under Kléber, with which he rode was comprised of some eighteen thousand hungry men who all wanted to go home.

21: WAR IN THE VENDÉE 1793

Ahead of them was the well dug-in, and no doubt warm and well fed Armée Catholique et Royale. It was under the command of General Jacques Alexis de Verteuil, a veteran who had served in Canada and had been in command at La Rochelle at the commencement of the revolution.

The Battle of Savenay. Still haunted by the memory of Fanny and her horrid death, Roume heard the sounds of the opening skirmishes. The ordered sound of musketry and the reverberating echo of the defending cannon fire came rolling across the snowy fields that surrounded them. He also saw the retreating republican soldiers. What angered him was the state of the republican encampment.

With energy and command he and some others roused the soldiers to action and ordered their artillery to commence firing at Savenay's defences. Through the night, by the light of their artillery's now blazing thunder, they prepared for the battle that would commence with the rising of the pale winter sun. In fact it began before dawn. Roume with the Carabiniers charged the town walls where a breach had been made. From all around came the flash of explosions, walls tumbling and the cries of the wounded and terrorised horses. Dismounted and caught in the frenzy of battle, he fought his way towards the centre of the town, where the republicans had succeeded in turning a captured cannon on the defenders. This advantage was not to endure as a counterattack was launched by more than 600 Vendéens who swarmed in from the surrounding lanes and narrow streets.

The battle raged through the next storm-swept day and into the night. The following morning, Roume's position proved to be one of the few that had held through the night. By midday, they were in retreat. By afternoon, they were once more on the attack.

A steady fire from an artillery position kept Roume and the Carabiniers pinned down. The fire was coming from two pieces of ordinance expertly handled from the inside of a church. Roume realised it was meant to cover a retreating column that was making its way into a wooded area close to the town. He led a company of mixed troops towards the cannon. He felt a shot enter his waist just beneath his cuirass and the sensation of hot blood running down his leg. The other he did not feel.

The battle had been won. General de Verteuil's mangled body was removed from beneath the cannon that he had defended. The fall of Savenay signalled the beginning of the end of the war. The massacres of Nantes would bring it to a conclusion, but the injured Roume was not at Nantes where the mass drownings took place, the killing of prisoners of war and the extermination of tens of thousands of Vendéens, and eventually almost a quarter of the region's population.

CONSCIOUSNESS RETURNED painfully, only to vanish again into delirium and nightmares, to return with the fear that he had been captured. He saw Fanny in rags, her hair like cobweb that in a cosmic light turned to crimson as she removed her arms and torso and, standing on her rotted legs, handed them to him.

He thought that he was swimming upwards towards a light. He was so afraid. He made a massive effort, his prayers, to a world without end, Amen. But it was insufficient, he knew, yet he tried and when there was no longer any breath left he burst through the surface to look about him. He no longer was in pain. The bandages on his head were too tight. He made a mental note of that. A lilting voice declared, "Do not move, Philippe Roume de Saint Laurent, you have broken ribs and you have suffered concussion. Out of it for four days."

"Who are you? Where am I?"

"I am Laure de Girardin de Montgérald, once la Comtesse de la Touche, and until very recently the wife of a friend of yours." He was astounded. This woman not only spoke Patois, but did so with the broad accent of a Martiniquean fisherman.

21: WAR IN THE VENDÉE 1793

"Who are you?"

"I have told you."

"Where am I?"

"You are in my care and that makes me safe, for the moment. The Carabiniers who brought you are still outside. They have refused to leave. How do you feel?"

"I feel alive, I am very thirsty and this bandage is too tight, please come closer."

She did and stood near to a window where the pale winter's sunlight showed him a tall, slim figure, dressed in black, that bent towards him. The face he saw was very white, with dark thick brows and black eyes that regarded him seriously. Blue-black hair drawn away and pulled back so severely that it appeared to affect her expression.

"Yes, the bandage is tight. It has to remain that way, otherwise your brains might leak out. That would be a mess. Not so?"

"I beg your pardon. Do tell me, who was your husband?"

"Why, Arthur Dillon."

"Arthur Dillon."

"Yes, you served together in Tobago, and from what I heard of it, a grand time was had by all."

"Arthur Dillon."

"Yes, Arthur Dillon." She regarded him and smiled, he thought too brightly. "Yes, Arthur Dillon, for all I know I am his widow."

He had forgotten about Dillon. He suddenly felt ashamed. He had not even tried to help.

"Here, drink this, steady, do not try to rise, don't mind if it spills, drink. Someone will come to clean you up."

He drank the tumbler of cool watered wine and closed his eyes. Again he was overwhelmed by the sensation of falling backwards into darkness. When he next opened his eyes it was dark, except for a lamp that threw a shaft of light across the room towards a fire that burned low in a fireplace.

"You are at Château de Pornic. You have been asleep for a long time. The men who brought you would see you before they go. I have been assured that by virtue of who you are I too am safe."

He nodded. He felt clear-headed and looked around the dark room. He heard her rise and go to the door which opened into so bright a room that he had to turn away, but before he did he saw the shapes of the guardsmen fill the doorway. Yes, he was fine. Yes, he was starving. Yes, he was returning to join the regiment. Savenay? Taken, and Nantes. They were for Nantes in the morning. Yes, Kléber will be informed. And they were gone. He could hear them on the stair and later he could hear them in the courtyard below. Then he closed his eyes.

His Patois-speaking hostess, Laure de Girardin, had indeed been born in Martinique. Her father had been governor there in 1778. He knew her father, had met her mother, he may even have seen her there as a child. He had told her father about his plan for the resettlement of the colons in Trinidad. He had expressed interest. She was, like himself, a Creole of the Antilles. All this gave him a sense of ease. He could slip into Patois with her and talk about the war, the revolution, the awfulness of it all. They could make each other laugh, with the macabre humour that the Patois language facilitates. It had been created so as not to be understood by French speakers. They made fun of the death of the king, and laughed at the antics of the "Great Committee," its characters and the turn of events.

She told him that they were the guests of the Marquis de Brie Serrant, who had fled at the outbreak of the revolution to England. She had known him to be a friend of her father's and had made her way to the Vendée upon hearing of Dillon's arrest, having in mind getting to England herself.

21: WAR IN THE VENDÉE 1793

"I am known to the servants here at the château and they allowed me to stay hidden in one of the tower rooms. When you were brought, apparently dying, I was brought in, disguised as a maid by the gardener, to care for you."

"Thank you, I am very grateful."

Seeing his condition she had demanded that a doctor be found and brought. The men from the regiment saw to that.

"A représentant en mission arrived. A terribly important fop of a midget, name-dropping with every step, said he knew you, had met you with Danton in Paris, wanted to see you. To make sure it was you. He told me who you were, who you had been, before all this. Said he was on familiar terms with the man who sent you, Saint-Just, he said."

"Ah yes, Saint-Just," he closed his eyes, "l'éminence grise."

When he opened them again the room was full of light.

Outside, he could see through the window, the sun was out and had turned the snow-white countryside to brilliance. The doctor, a nervous man, came and did her bidding as best he could.

"Get me up fast," he told her, trying to appear as a man in a hurry. "Yes," she assured him, "you are already on the mend." She patted his arm and left the room with the doctor who explained that he had received a linear skull fracture and would need to rest quietly for several months.

His shattered ribs would mend over time, his head wound would heal more slowly. He had to be careful. He was not. His attempts to get out of bed caused him to faint with pain. She was there. She came and read to herself and to him when he was not asleep. He admired her lovely profile. She bathed him all over with soap scented with musk and cloves. She helped him with an easy familiarity, with such amusement that at times he had to beg her not to make him laugh, as he could not stand the pain.

He recovered his strength and with her help began to move about the room. Their closeness turned from kindness to intimacy into lovemaking even before spring came. He told her about Soubise and their life together.

"And Fanny?" This startled him.

"You spoke of her, called to her in a voice that seemed so desperate. As if she was far away."

"She is." He told her everything.

She told him of her marriage to Arthur Dillon, which had been an arrangement concerning property, and assured him that their affairs in Tobago were not her concern and he should guard against falling in love with her, as these were perilous times and he should be grateful to have found a woman who was willing to stay with him, seeing him safely through crisis after crisis, as he gathered position and power at every turn.

"And you stalk the dark streets of Paris, calm as the murderer you are. Lucky man, Philippe Roume. She is your luck. Do not lose her." And after a pause, "I too, am for Paris."

"Are you?" he said, sighing, his face buried in her thick black curling locks.

"My cousin is there, she is in prison."

"Your next adventure will be to free your cousin who has been put in jail in Paris. Who is your cousin?"

"Marie Josèphe Tascher de la Pagerie."

"From Martinique?"

"Of course, from Les Trois-Îlets."

"And she is in Paris, in jail, I am sorry for her."

"So am I, she is in Carmes prison, I must go to her."

"Don't be ridiculous."

"I must, she would do the same for me."

21: WAR IN THE VENDÉE 1793

"Don't be ridiculous," he repeated, cradling her beautiful head in his arms. "Paris is a deadly place."

Over time, he came to know more about Marie Josèphe Tascher. It would appear that Edmée du Plessis de Savonnières, the maternal aunt of both Laure and Marie Josèphe, had been the mistress of an elderly nobleman, the Vicomte François de Beauharnais, and had arranged for François' son Alexandre to marry a niece of hers. The niece was twelve and not in very good health, because she died even before she sailed from Martinique for France. The importance of this connection—it had to do with money, and the Tascher family had none—was such that one sister was replaced by another and Marie Josèphe eventually married Alexandre de Beauharnais.

He told her that he had met Joseph-Gaspard Tascher, Marie Josèphe's father, during one of his visits to Martinique.

"Hurricanes destroyed their plantations in 1766 and again in '81. They were ruined. I told him he should take advantage of the Royal Cedula for the creation of a population and go with his family to Trinidad. He wouldn't hear of it. It was different with your father, he listened, he liked the idea."

"He did nothing either, now he is dead and my, my. . . mother, as well as my brothers." He saw that she was crying quietly, tears streaming down her face.

"Marie Josèphe is all I have now. I must go to her."

PHILIPPE ROUME and Soubise had corresponded via the dispatch riders of the army of occupation in the Vendée. He had read her fear-filled letters that told of life in Paris during the opening months of what became known to the world as The Reign of Terror.

Their friends Robespierre and Danton had not forgotten her. She made sure of that. She had written saying that favourable dispatches came to the Committee of Public Safety concerning his tenure with the army of the Vendée. His popularity with the men, his gallantry in battle. The manner in which he enforced the principles of the Republic, its goals, its ideals, its triumphs. Soubise appeared to know everything about him. In one of her letters he read with relief that she had decided not to come to him when she heard that he had been wounded at Savenay. The Reign of Terror, however, had kept her in the house in rue Saint-Séverin. She was well, as well as might be expected. When was he coming home?

Reading from my Memoirs at La Fontenoy, Grenada, 1807

CITY OF DREAMS. I hardly kept up the diary in those desperate and morbid times, and when I did it was from a distorted reality. Robespierre came no longer as often as before and when he did, it was to escape the upheavals that swirled in the city's streets, political clubs and of course the Convention chamber. Safe here from assassins he would often sleep for several hours on a daybed close to the window that overlooked the rue Saint-Séverin. Sometimes he would bring Desmoulins with him. I discovered that they were childhood friends. Danton did not visit me in their company. He arrived at odd hours. Desmoulins published pro-Dantonist circulars. These excited the sans culottes and created the necessary political tensions—the daily distractions that revolutionaries require to stay alive. Saint-Just sometimes would arrive together with Robespierre. But increasingly, Saint-Just came alone.

When I did not see any of the deputies for a day or more I would be reduced to a state of hysteria, hiding, or walking endlessly up and down the dim icy corridors and surreptitiously peering into the devastated streets. One evening Jean Patience, the man that Philippe had set in place as my servant and bodyguard, came to say that citizen Saint-Just had come up the ladder. He had been at the trial of Marie Antoinette, the death sentence had been handed down.

21: WAR IN THE VENDÉE 1793

"When?"

"She will meet the executioner on the sixteenth of Brumaire." There is to be a new calendar, Saint-Just had already started using it. He had declared the date of this woman's death in a flat voice while stamping his feet and shaking loose his wet hair before the fire. "I have a letter. The letter she wrote to Élisabeth, Louis Capet's sister. She won't have time to read it either."

He fell exhausted into a chair, the letter, I could see, contained some scrawled words. He held it loosely between his long fingers, his legs sprawled out before him. The crackling fire from the hearth shone through the yellowish paper. He let it slip. A draft from nowhere lifted it as I watched, it seemed to pause between me and the flames, then, it floated forward and landed at my feet. I looked at him.

"Read it," he said and closed his eyes. He was evil, so young and beautiful and yet so deadly. The first moment that we found ourselves alone we gravitated. Then levitated. Afterwards he said that I was now and forever his Bathsheba. I had no idea who that was. He told me a story. It was about the Biblical King David, who had sent his general to war after seeing his wife Bathsheba bathing naked. "You sent him to the Vendée?" I had asked, incredulous. "And I had not yet seen you naked," the wretch replied. His presence would cause a rush of blood that excited me beyond endurance. The simple beauty of his shameless arrogance.

He had seduced me in my imagination long before his pornographic stories of the depravity of nuns. For some reason this excited my passions. Their debaucheries, carried on behind bath screens while dressed only in wet linen; how they prayed and yodeled as they had their way with one another, made me mad with desire. He had spied on them, he lied. He told how they had discovered him and punished him with enforced sex. He whispered all this in the obscene verse that he had committed to paper as we made love in front of a long mirror so that he could admire himself and see me in my mad disarray. He saw me looking.

"Weakness, not vice, is the opposite of virtue."

He said that he had been in jail. That he had stolen his mother's possessions, her valuables, all her money, to be in Paris with Robespierre who had taken him in, and elevated him to power because he was brilliant, stern and ruthless and brought fresh energy to the revolution. He said that the revolution was in constant need of people like himself so as to be original every day. A revolutionary government is in a hurry. The process from tyranny to freedom is urgent. It must only operate under emergency measures until victory is achieved. He could accomplish those things. From royalty to republic. Fascinated by his aura of death, I saw in him the revolution's ultimate end.

One night, I told him about the Society of the Friends of the Blacks. About Ogé and Victor Hugues, Stanislaus and Philippe Roume. He found it all irrelevant but amusing, and laughed aloud at the idea that blacks in the west could ever be free.

"They are foreigners who live in our world. They wear our clothes and use the things we make. How on earth can they ever be free. For them to be free they would have to return to Africa."

"Democracy is evangelical," I said to him, "essentially it is driven by love."

He laughed again, cruelly, and said, "I have no time to preach to heathens."

"Then what do want from me?"

"Nothing, I was curious."

He had just returned from the war against the Austrians. Upon his arrival in Paris he had gone directly to the Palais de Justice. He saw the queen, ashen grey, emerge from the Conciergerie. She had testified for eight to ten hours every day for five days before the Revolutionary Tribunal with Antoine Fouquier-Tinville as chief prosecutor.

21: WAR IN THE VENDÉE 1793

"Who is he?"

"A relative of Desmoulins," he said and shrugged. "She had disabused them of the idea that she had intercourse with her son, they would make it a charge against her. She shamed them. It was at this remark that she rose to her feet and addressed the jury. She told them no mother would do such a thing, the people agreed, they had gone too far with their allegations. The market women who would have killed her last month spoke up for her."

He smiled. "That appeals to you. After the sentencing, Fouquier-Tinville intercepted the letter to her sister-in-law and took it to Robespierre. Read it."

I picked up the sheet of paper, it was cheap, of the sort, I suppose, that people in prison used. It said simply: "My son must never seek to revenge my death."

I felt such a pang of guilt, it spread through me like being immersed slowly in some hot cloying liquid. I choked. Rosette!

He laughed, he always ridiculed my confusion. He always left me tinged with disgust.

After seeing Jean Patience reading Philippe's letters and knowing that he was privy to my affairs, I denounced him as a spy in the pay of the English. He was taken away that day. Some weeks later I heard that he had been guillotined at La Place de Grève. I then lived alone. I was no longer afraid of the people who had stalked us in the hope of taking me. I somehow knew that they were all dead, like all the other people in my past.

Robespierre's success seemed unlimited. His influence now lay with the Committee of Public Safety, which dominated the Convention chamber. His facility for information gathering and quick decision making kept him ahead of the others. His power was also founded on the victories of the revolutionary armies on several fronts and the emergence of the new generals, François Kellermann and Jean Baptiste Kléber who defeated the counter revolutionaries in the Vendée. They were perceived as the sons of the revolution; their loyalties lay with the Republic. What's more the levy had produced an army of well over a million men. We heard of two generals in particular, the Corsican, Napoleone Buonaparte, who would gallicise his name and become Napoleon Bonaparte and, increasingly, that one called Paul Barras.

I avoided leaving the house in those days. Outside, mass murder was being committed on a scale, they all assured me, that Europe had not witnessed since the Thirty Years War.

The Reign of Terror. It commenced in September of 1793 and would only end with the death of Robespierre, Saint-Just and the others in July of 1794. By then they would all be dead. It would take the lives of perhaps thirty or forty thousand people, including some four thousand Parisians. The vast majority of those executed were aristocrats. The cause of la Terreur? I believe it had to with the many fears that haunted the men who came to the rue Saint-Séverin. Fear of the nameless, faceless Parisian mob and fear of fear itself. There is a word for it, Saint-Just calls it, phobos. They were afraid of what they had done. Murdered majesty, condemned religion, destroyed feudalism, the very way of life for a thousand years. All Europe would now come to them for retribution.

As the Prussian army advanced through the provinces, a ferocious gaiety, matching the depth of the crisis, gripped the Parisians. The restoration of feudal rights filled them with the fear of massacre. Across the country there was only anarchy as the old regime collapsed and people, often very stupid people, took charge of the distribution of food, of what little that was left. The entire country was consumed with the fear of starvation. The war in the Vendée had become a slaughterhouse that could spread. This thought filled Robespierre with fear of a counterrevolution.

I received Philippe Roume's letters. They were written in the manner of reports with little personal reference or expressions of care or concern for me. I seldom replied. Where would our divergent

21: WAR IN THE VENDÉE 1793

lives take us, I wondered. The revolution appeared to be failing as the ideals that once sustained us gave way to survival.

The winter of 1793 promised to be the worst remembered. The streets of Paris growled with hunger, scowled with anger and thought only of murder. Danton, his ferocity often a farce, reasoned for an end of The Terror and peace with England.

Danton had grown in popularity, he had vast support amongst the people of Paris. On one occasion the way he spoke made me wonder if he sought to overthrow the "Incorruptible."

"Do not speak in that manner, do not do that," I cautioned him. We were sitting in our overcoats in the pantry at the rue Saint-Séverin, quite late, over a bottle of cognac. He shook his tired head. I noticed that he had winced at the execution of the queen. The Terror disgusted him.

"Robespierre has refused to entertain any idea of reducing la Terreur," he said sadly. He seemed like a man haunted by premonitions.

"He will intensify it," I told him, "on the grounds that the revolution is still bedevilled by saboteurs."

"Desmoulins has written a long article in *Le Vieux Cordelier* calling for its end." He drank deeply from the glass, and wiped his mouth on the tablecloth. The candle had burnt low and he knew it was time to leave.

"Kindhearted," I said, "they want to open the prisons. The priests, the speculators, the aristocrats, and if they are released. . ."

"They will reverse and destroy the Republic," he said ironically, finishing my sentence, and rising, "I am seen as indulgent. They would have my head. I told them leave something to the guillotine of opinion."

"Robespierre will use you as a cat's paw against anyone he believes to be the enemy. I suspect that Robespierre is planning your arrest.

Attack the Committee of Public Safety before the Convention!" I said seriously. "Do it tomorrow."

"If I thought that he had even an idea of that, I would eat his heart out!" he growled.

But what I saw before me was a man too weary, too worn away to engage in the historic dramas that had made him a legend.

And then more truthfully he said, his voice heavy with the cognac and his feelings, "I would rather be guillotined myself than to see any more people trundled away." He stood at the window about to descend into the dark where the wind was whipping the snow. "I am sick of the human race."

I heard from Saint-Just that Danton and Desmoulins, together with a number of other Jacobins, had been questioned by the Committee of Public Safety. They were convicted of embezzlement, of all things that were unlikely and preposterous. I sent a note to Danton begging him to flee, then experienced a panic that dissolved into diarrhea in anticipation of the summons to appear before the Committee. The following day he was arrested.

Incognito I went to witness his death at the Place de la Révolution. Of the group of fifteen who were guillotined together on 5th April, 1794, Desmoulins died third and Danton last. I believe to this day he looked at me and recognised me in spite of my blackened face, bonnet and old person's frock. He said, "I leave it all in a frightful welter. Not a man of them has an idea of government. Robespierre will follow me. He is dragged down by me." He was reported to have told the executioner, "Show my head to the people, it is worth it." He was thirty-four years old. Robespierre then proceeded to send everyone who crossed him or challenged the Committee of Public Safety to the guillotine.

22: THE FALL OF THE INCORRUPTIBLE

1794

He sincerely wished he could remain forever at Château de Pornic with that lovely woman, speaking of everything else except the war, avoiding all news, not ever mentioning the revolution and postponing all decisions. He was prolonging a recuperation that had slid into a form of domesticity he had never before enjoyed. He was dreading the prospect of the inevitable return to Paris and to Soubise.

News did arrive, it was brought by a young man who, incognito, was fleeing to England. He appeared at the château's kitchen window and carried an anonymous letter that urged Laure de Girardin to come to Paris where her cousin Marie Josèphe was in dire need of her. He told them of the execution of Arthur Dillon. This had taken place some months earlier, in April of 1794. He related that Dillon had mounted the scaffold with the shout "Vive le roi!" This brought tears to Philippe's eyes. Taking the young messenger into the garden that was exploding in wild summer blooms, Roume urged him to tell all he knew of the most recent events in the capital.

The situation in Paris, he related, had assumed an other-worldly atmosphere with the execution of almost all the deputies of the Convention. This was when Roume heard of the deaths of Danton and Desmoulins. It shocked and saddened him especially to hear of Danton's death. Danton, by his protection and patronage, had saved his life and Soubise's.

That the Committee of Public Safety, after Marat's assassination, dominated by Robespierre, had effectively become the government of France held a sense of doom. He knew what a self-righteous little man he was. With the silencing of all dissent, the ban on all political entities with the exception of the Jacobin Club and the strict censorship of all presses, the Incorruptible was creating a dictatorship. While this was taking place, the young man explained, all over the country people were rebelling against the closing of the churches and the killing of priests. Increasingly, ordinary people were returning to their age-old beliefs and habits, going to church on Sundays and taking part in the Blessed Sacraments.

Robespierre had taken the decision that the time had come to reunite the revolution with the religious philosophy of Rousseau, and that belief in God and an afterlife, along with civic and social virtue, were all necessary to the foundation of the Republic.

Roume laughed out loud. "He hopes to appease the pious and mitigate the horror of The Terror?"

"But still no one can touch him," said the young man.

"Why?" Roume asked, assuming a naïvety that he hoped would cause the young man to speak plainly.

"His real political power lies in the Jacobin Clubs, Sire, and the support of the new generals. An attempt was made on his life, Sire, a young woman tried to kill him," the young man breathed quietly, glancing about.

He had to think of Soubise.

"Heads are falling like slates from a roof, No one goes to executions any more. No one goes out. No one. Everyone stays at home. The taverns are empty. No one speaks, or if they do, they watch every word they utter. The majority who are now executed are the common people."

22: THE FALL OF THE INCORRUPTIBLE 1794

"And the war? What of the Germans?"

"They say that there is an army poised to enter Paris. And the English have blockaded all our ports."

By this time they both spoke in whispers.

"What of the Convention? Do you have an idea of what the people know of what is taking place?"

"No Sire, except that it is said that France is being run by three: Robespierre, a man called Couthon and another known as Saint-Just. Now I must go, thank you Sire."

"THERE IS CONFUSION and turmoil in the National Convention. The Terror is over!" Roume could not believe what he was hearing.

Just weeks following the young messenger's visit this was the news brought to them by François Marceau-Desgraviers, his comrade in arms from the Vendéen campaign who was on his way to join his regiment at La Rochelle.

There had been a revolt in the Convention chamber that resulted in the execution of Maximilien Robespierre, Louis Antoine de Saint-Just and a number of others on 28th July, 1794.

"I saw this degeneration last year, that's why I was glad to join the army of the Vendée," said Roume, putting an arm around Laure's soft round shoulders. This feels so right, he thought, remembering her taste, he could smell her, her perfume, chèvrefeuille. She smiled up at him. "Tell us everything, François."

"There were too many people around him who felt convinced that they would be his next victim," said Marceau-Desgraviers. "Then there were others who thought to avenge his killing Danton."

"That I can imagine, Danton saved my life," said Roume, remembering the forceful personality who, at times, seemed to have single-handedly overthrown the monarchy.

"People on the left had come to see Robespierre as a traitor for his rejection of atheism," continued Marceau-Desgraviers. "Circumstances arranged themselves with no little help from him, when he rose in the Convention chamber to introduce a motion reinforcing the continuation of The Terror. Draconian measures, death sentences for trivial or even vague matters such as the outraging of public morality. The fall of the Incorruptible commenced when one of his supporters shouted, 'I am certain that in a revolution all who appear before this tribunal ought to be condemned.' This caused those present to be convinced that another terror within The Terror was taking shape."

"Awful rabid people," said Laure, fearing for her cousin, Marie Josèphe, the anonymous letter's urging a haunting thought.

"It was the terrorists themselves, many returned from the provinces, men like Fouché, Fréron and Tallien, who then and there decided that their lives depended on the elimination of Robespierre. He had recalled them to Paris. Within six weeks of their arriving almost two thousand people were executed."

"Not one of them were of the nobility from what we have heard," said Roume, alarmed, he could be recalled, even now . . . everything has changed, I must change with this change. How? He saw that Laure was looking at him, their eyes held for a moment.

"Exactly. It was in the Convention's Hall of Liberty, as Saint-Just was presenting a report, that Tallien interrupted him," Marceau-Desgraviers continued. "Tallien may have felt that his own time had come to face the guillotine and jumped to his feet, pushed Saint-Just to the floor and bellowed, 'I ask that the curtain be torn away!' Whereupon he produced a knife. He proclaimed that he would kill himself if the Convention was not prepared to support him in denouncing Saint-Just and Robespierre. I was not present, however, it became common knowledge that Billaud-Varenne, another deputy, intensified the attack, which was supported by Fouché. This succeeded in silencing Saint-Just. In the confusion

22: THE FALL OF THE INCORRUPTIBLE 1794

Robespierre rose to speak against cries of 'Down with the tyrant! Arrest him now!' Robespierre called on the deputies to hear him out, shouting 'President of Assassins, will you give me leave to speak?' The entire room shouted its disapproval."

"He addressed the speaker as the President of Assassins?" asked Philippe, his disbelief moving him to laughter. "He of all people?"

"Yes he did. But let me continue, 'No, no,' cried several voices and one deputy shouted above the rest the fatal words 'I demand the arrest of Robespierre!'" Here Marceau-Desgraviers paused to look at them all in turn.

"That was when the Convention voted to arrest Robespierre and Saint-Just and take them under guard to the Hôtel de Ville. The Paris commune was not taking the arrest of their leaders lightly and sent their troops who freed them. The Convention responded by calling on Paul Barras and a force of gendarmes to rally men loyal to him in the defence of the Convention and to rearrest Robespierre and the others whom the Paris commune had set at liberty. This was done. It was on the night of the 9th Thermidor that Robespierre, held in custody, tried to kill himself. Well, the following day seventy members of the Paris commune met their end. This was followed by the executions of Robespierre, Saint-Just and sixteen others to shouts of 'Down with the maximum!' as his draconian laws were known. When Robespierre's head was held up for all to see the crowd cheered."

"My God. Could this really be the end?" exclaimed Laure.

"No," answered Marceau-Desgraviers, "I am afraid it merely marks another beginning. Les dieux ont soif, as Camille Desmoulins had written, in condemnation of the Jacobins."

"The gods are ravenous. Revenge killings will commence. Most likely they have started already," said Roume thoughtfully, remembering Soubise with a twinge of shame admixed with remorse. He looked at Laure and knew what had come to her mind, she nodded and smiled encouragingly.

"You will come with us to Paris, Philippe?" she enquired gently. "I am sure that you have matters there to attend to."

"Yes, I certainly do," he answered, he appeared sad. She took his hand in hers. They all sat silently for a while, each knowing that in these fateful times different futures awaited them all.

Roume grasped that these events would usher in a new regime in Paris, the shape of which would determine his own and Soubise's future. His relationship with Robespierre was well known. His actions during the September massacres had earned him the regard of the sans culottes, the followers of Danton and of the extreme left within the Jacobin Club. All these were now discredited. The fall of these men meant that he was without protection. They had been frequent visitors to his house. He had left Soubise in their care. He must have garnered any number of enemies, people jealous of his position, people whose relatives he had killed or had caused to be executed, who would use the existing state of confusion together with the attitude of the Convention towards extremists and identify him with the perpetrators of all heinous crimes committed in the streets of Paris.

"The men who will be in power, the men who brought down the regime, and I am only guessing here, will be Paul Barras and Jean Tallien," said Marceau-Desgraviers, rising. Smiling sardonically he added, "And perhaps Fouché, the butcher of Lyons. Barras protects him. He is a killer. He struck down the Rolands and the other Girondist friends of yours. He ridiculed Robespierre and defied him openly and plotted his overthrow. As for Tallien, another mass killer, he was on Robespierre's list for an early execution. His voice in the Convention chamber tipped the balance of power."

Roume nodded, he understood. "I have met Barras. I knew his uncle in Grenada."

"You may want to go to him. I gather that he is ruthless," said Marceau-Desgraviers. "Barras served in India during the Second

22: THE FALL OF THE INCORRUPTIBLE 1794

Anglo-Mysore War. Seen as unscrupulous, he was cashiered upon his return for conduct unbecoming of an officer."

"His relatives are notorious," said Laure. "He is a close relation of the scandalous Marquis de Sade. And my cousin, Marie Josèphe? How. . ."

"While in prison she, ah. . . became romantically involved with General Hoche. Her husband, Alexandre, was guillotined on the Place de la Révolution, just five days before the fall of Robespierre. When Tallien arranged for the liberation of his mistress Thérèse Cabarrus, she too had been imprisoned on Robespierre's orders, he also freed Marie Josèphe. They had become friends in Carmes prison. They are presently at a house provided by Tallien. I understand that your cousin Marie Josèphe has recently formed another attachment, to Paul Barras. Her situation is difficult, her husband's wealth was confiscated and then there are the children."

IT WAS TO PARIS THEN, a return to a civilisation turned sick by fear and brutality. He felt safer riding with the baggage wagon. There was an air of relief in every village they passed through. Some were holding celebrations with music playing and outdoor feasting. People were relieved, some delirious that the regime in Paris had fallen, that The Terror was over, that the Incorruptible was dead.

Now what? There was no question of returning to pre-revolutionary times. All they really wanted back was food and the certainty and comfort of religion. As he was thinking this, they passed a large party of nuns piled onto oxcarts, old ones, young ones, waving, the wind lifting and blowing their white habits like laundry on a breezy day.

During the four-day journey from the Vendée to Paris, he witnessed revenge enacted upon the Jacobins in village squares. A reaction had set in. That this would sweep through the country was a thought that made his stomach clench with fear. Their party heard of an emigré attempt, joined by certain royalists in Paris, to storm the Convention chamber. This had been put down by the artillery directed by General Bonaparte. Cannonfire unleashed upon a mob, that would have saved the old regime, he thought.

He also saw Laure de Girardin gradually become a different person. She treated him increasingly with the amused but affectionate offhandedness of a person who, having enjoyed a vacation with strangers, sincerely hoped that they would not take seriously the invitation to come calling.

Their entry into Paris was delayed for several days by food riots that swept the city. In the distance, they could hear the ordered regular fire of soldiery overwhelming the scatter-shot of irregular and random shooting. There was the very obvious presence of artillery regiments. A profusion of officers, resplendent in uniforms that reflected the change of regime, clattered by, drawn sabres flashing in the afternoon sunlight. All so young, he noted.

As they made their way through the dirty streets and narrow lanes towards the heart of the old city and the Hôtel de Ville, they saw more summary executions taking place of those who were now called terrorists. The petite bourgeoisie were taking revenge on the common people, the sans culottes. All Jacobins were in hiding.

They parted company close to the church of Saint-Jacques-du-Haut-Pas with the amused affection of people who had shared perilous times. It had become their style. He decided to make his way, a short distance, to the rue Saint-Séverin on foot. No longer in the uniform of a commissioner representing the Convention, unshaven and shabbily dressed, he blended into the wild-eyed, hurrying mass that was consumed with the all-important hunt for their daily bread.

22: THE FALL OF THE INCORRUPTIBLE 1794

Reading from my Memoirs at George Street, Port of Spain, Trinidad, 1810

I NEVER UNDERSTOOD HOW those who had been able to escape the charges that they had been blooded Jacobins, were able to purge themselves of the cult of permanent revolution and the habit of dealing in death, and be accepted into the next phase of the revolution, which was called the Thermidorean interlude. This lasted from 29th July, 1794 to 26th October, 1795.

Philippe Roume was one of those. The Convention, upon the deaths of Robespierre and Saint-Just, had managed to reassert itself and turn its freshly revitalised vigour upon the Paris commune, executing close to one hundred sans culotte activists and other rabble-rousers. The Jacobin Clubs were closed throughout the country by the middle of November of 1795. The undecided members of the Convention, the Plain, the middle of the road deputies, moved smartly to the right. This meant that the Girondin faction on the right, or what remained of it, was again in power. As for me, I was glad that Marianne was now free of Saint-Just, but it was difficult to resume being Soubise. As for Philippe, his coming reincarnation would take him full circle.

23: HEART'S CUT

PARIS 1796

He arrived at the rubble-strewn rue Saint-Séverin and entered it with caution. All about him in the smoke-filled air were the signs of recent fighting. A battle had raged. The burnt buildings with gaping holes where doors and windows had been, the furniture and household things mixed with the wreckage of wagons and carriages that had formed hurriedly erected barricades, all spoke of many a last stand. The rigid bodies of dead animals were being removed.

Philippe Roume hesitated before the door that had been boarded up. Then, making up his mind, he pounded on the rough wood until his hand bled. He was drawing attention. An assortment of people gathered, ragged children, dirty women, a few men.

"She is inside!" a voice shouted, "she, the friend of the murderers."

"Shut up, you fool," said another, "you know nothing."

"They were there, Robespierre, and the other one, they came to her, the whore, the black whore."

Without a doubt in his mind, Roume turned from the doorway and plunged a blade, twisting it upward, into the belly of the one who had shouted in his ear.

"And now you are dead. Who's next?"

23: HEART'S CUT 1796

Already the crowd was backing away. They had seen all this before.

"Come, please, they will kill you. Laissez-aller, get away from here," said a low rough voice, "the street is full of lunatics."

He turned, there was a harsh hooded face from which an eye looked directly into his, a firm hand had him by the arm.

"Take him to her ladder," a woman's voice shouted, "that was her stairway to paradise."

"Get out of the way," said the stranger, showing the brace of pistols in his belt, the bleeding body was already being stripped of whatever things of value that it held.

The crowd parted and they walked away quickly as an even larger crowd was gathering, the shouts of a commotion commencing.

"Come, this is a dangerous street, luckily the one you killed was a stranger. The jeunesse dorée, young ruffians, they kill former Jacobins around here." He was being guided along an alleyway, they now walked in step towards a dead end.

"Here we are, go, up those stairs, you shall be safe, the door is unlocked. You shall meet her later, she is there."

Already his saviour was turning away. He took the iron stair in a few bounds, turned the handle and entered a narrow room. In the half light, he looked around. It was some sort of writer's studio or office. There was a desk, a hand press, books, papers, and a large black cat that regarded him impassively.

Through the afternoon gloom and into an extended twilight he waited, famished and extraordinarily weary. He fought the urge to sleep and lost. He did not hear the man's return.

"Roume, wake up, it is time to go." The man shook him by the shoulder and then again more roughly, "Get up Roume, destiny awaits."

He sat up and rubbed his eyes. He had forgotten where he was.

The man understood. "Rue Saint-Séverin. You are trying to find out if she is alive."

"Yes, yes. And who are you?"

"Like yourself, I am a person in transition, citoyen. Louis Fréron, at your service. I live. . ." He made an ironical little bow. He was tall, with narrow lips, a big nose and even, if somewhat harsh, features.

"To fight another day," said Roume, his own voice hoarse in his ears.

"Precisely. Now wash, over there, and here is something to eat."

They shared a meal of an indefinable meat that had been cooked with beans. The bread was fresh and the wine was good. "Cat or rabbit?" Roume wondered out loud.

"Hard to say. It might be rat, actually."

"Who is in charge?"

"No one. In any event, Barras knows where the cannon are and Bonaparte holds the keys."

"Paul de Barras, yes, I imagine he would."

"Now, he likes to be known simply as Barras."

"Yes, I understand."

"Come then, she is waiting."

The street, now lit by blazing bonfires, fairly thronged with people who had ventured out in search of food, in search of lost relatives, and to assure each other that they were still alive.

"Come along here. There is a bell, it is attached to this cord." They were standing in the lane that ran alongside the house; it appeared dilapidated, abandoned. "Ring it, you are home."

He pulled at it, and immediately a window was flung open and a ladder was being lowered by a rope. It was attached to a beam or some contraption that accommodated its raising and lowering.

23: HEART'S CUT 1796

"Philippe, oh, Philippe!" Soubise's voice, a hoarse whisper, came from above.

"Go," said Fréron, standing aside.

"Thank you, citoyen, thank you."

"Go, we shall meet again."

He grasped hold of the ladder and climbed towards the open window. They met in the unreality of an Armageddon recently unfolded. It was just past the end of times. The new era, not yet commenced.

He took her emaciated frame in his arms and looked into her thin drawn face at once terrible, yet still beautiful.

"My God, how did you survive?"

"By putting out fires. By staying inside, by waiting and praying that you would come home."

He held her close. She was unfamiliar. She might have been a person he had just met on the street outside. Her smell, her look was revolting. She was like a wild animal too long caged. He felt pity for her, and as she sought to find his lips with her own, he realised that he felt disgust. This he overcame and kissed her deeply and as the memory of Laure de Girardin came to him, he felt to flee.

They could not make love. They were both relieved. Instead they related the carefully expurgated accounts of the harrowing times that they had each experienced. He felt ashamed. This surprised him. He told her of meeting Fanny.

"She had seen the gold?" gasped Soubise, "she had been down there? The man, Shadrach Lazare, the first mate, had taken her? My God, is he really dead, she said that he died in there?"

"Yes, she said so. Is he dead, I don't know. She said that he had never left Trinidad. That he had waited in a cove on one of the islands in the Dragon's Mouth and seen you and your companion.

He knew where it was hidden. He had meant it for them, himself and Fanny. It was to be their future. He had no idea who she was."

She listened, nodding, thinking, that is my gold. It is still there. He does not think of it as mine. What was being related was like a dream.

"You saw Fanny before she died. How sad her story, terrible, terrible for her." She had to think of herself. Her situation. She heard a voice say, "That could have been you."

Her manner, careful, loving, embarrassed him. They were able to smile, finally, at the awkwardness in which they were marooned. The account of Fanny's finding of the treasure, her appearance on the battlefield, her tragic death and fumbled burial, all contributed to the accommodating of their rapprochement. She kept him in view constantly, he noticed. They watched each other in search of signs, seeking a place to restart. They spoke of Fanny often, he could not forgive himself for leaving her grave unmarked.

"You will go back there," she told him, "and find it." He knew that he could not leave her. Over the next several days, they moved about each other like stranger-moths without a central flame, their feats of deceit uppermost in their minds; while in the streets below daily life played with much false gaiety and forced bravado at a normalcy that had to be imagined, now that the "Incorruptible" was dead, and the Reign of Terror over.

They were on the verge of starvation, being too afraid to show their faces outside, when they were visited by Louis Fréron. Fréron came to say that since the Peace of Basel had been signed, there was a renewed interest in Saint-Domingue.

"And what does that mean?" she asked.

"It means that France, last year in May, made peace with Prussia, Spain and with the Landgraviate of Hesse-Kassel. This means that we have divided the allies of the coalition that has stood against us."

"And?"

23: HEART'S CUT 1796

"And, Spain has ceded the eastern two-thirds of the island of Hispaniola, Santo Domingo, to France in exchange for keeping Gipuzkoa."

"Gipuzkoa?"

"Gipuzkoa," said Roume, he was already thinking what this could mean for him. "I think it is the seat of one of their great trading houses, where is it?"

"A region in Spain, I am not sure where, in the Basque country, I think," said Fréron, regarding Roume and smiling grimly. "I was sent by Barras to meet you and to keep you out of their hands," he gestured towards the street. "You have very influential friends, Barras, amongst others, it would appear. The white terror, they are calling the revenge killings, and I imagine that you, both of you, are high on someone's list," he regarded Soubise, "the Reign of Terror has not ended, it has just changed hands."

"Barras? You said Barras?" Soubise gasped, and looked at them both in the manner of a person who has lost the trend of a conversation.

"Paul Barras, formerly le vicount de Barras," Fréron answered.

"He is the nephew of Everard de Barras," Roume explained mildly, seeing her alarm at the mention of the name. "Don't you recall? I told you that."

"He is a general," said Fréron, glancing from one to the other, "and a commissioner to the Army and one of the five directors who presently control the executive of the Republic."

"And he wants you to go to him?" she asked incredulously.

MUSIC AND LAUGHTER could be heard coming from the Faubourg St-Antoine. A massive fortress in the heart of Paris, older than its neighbour, the Bastille, it was where the last of the previous regime's most radical supporters had held out and eventually died.

The courtyard, full of carriages, fairly overflowed with enthusiasm. There were shouts and greetings, hurrahs and congratulations as the returning moderates, Girondin survivors of The Terror and other massacres, greeted each other with genuine surprise that they were still amongst the living. There were many faces in the crowd that turned towards them as Roume and Fréron made their way through the crowd towards the main entrance. He heard his name called and there was a scuffle as men who yearned for retribution called for his blood. As they gained the entrance, a woman burst through the phalanx of National Guardsmen who were opening a way for them, losing her head scarf, her blouse torn away, and with a face distorted, swung a long blade with all her might at Roume shouting, "Kill him! Kill Danton's dog. His woman, Saint-Just's bitch." The knife grazed his cheek and would have entered his shoulder had it not been deflected by the heavy leather jerkin that he had on impulse put on before leaving the house with Fréron.

The uproar only increased as others, drawn by the smell of blood, sought their own revenge. The guardsmen held their ground long enough for Roume and Fréron to gain the main hall where they were met by officials sent to receive and conduct them to the apartments shared by Paul Barras, Jean-Lambert Tallien and Joseph Fouché, the three most prominent figures in the running of the country. It was the very equinox of the revolution that would see the return of moderates to power. These leaders were buttressed by men of action, who until recently had been extreme Jacobin radicals themselves. They would eventually under this alignment devise a new government, the Constitution of Year III, the Directory.

Bleeding from his cut cheek, Roume was instead taken by Fréron into a room just inside the main entrance, where he was attended to by a flock of nervous women, some of whom were domestics, as he could see, while others appeared to possess some sort of authority. To his surprise, he saw a face he knew.

"Once again, Philippe Roume, I see that you shall be my patient," Laure de Girardin smiled gently, taking his hand and leading him to a window-seat. "You look much worse than the last time I saw you. In hiding, what?"

As he caught himself, Laure, who wore her blue-black hair loose about her shoulders, told him that she had indeed made contact with Marie Josèphe de Beauharnais, her young cousin, who had become, for a while, it would appear, attached to Paul Barras. And had made the acquaintance of Marie Josèphe's former prison companion Thérésa Cabarrus, who was now known as Thérésa Tallien due to the relationship that she enjoyed with deputy Jean-Lambert Tallien.

"It is ménage à quatre," Laure whispered, and smiled demurely. "Marie Josèphe now calls herself Joséphine, a name given to her by her Corsican general; Napoleon Bonaparte, a friend of Barras. She is a gift to Bonaparte from Barras for services rendered."

Later that day he was received by the ménage. His eyes were immediately drawn to Joséphine de Beauharnais, who stepped forward and took his hand.

"Philippe Roume de Saint Laurent, what a pleasure to meet you," she paused, perhaps a trifle too dramatically, "again." She spoke to him in Patois.

He remembered her as a child, very attached to her father. She was now tall and languid, dark-haired, with a playful, perhaps mischievous light in her eyes. She ducked her head and smiled up at him in a manner that he recognised as typical of the saucy mulâtresses whom he had known all too well. He took her hand, and lifting it to his lips, kissed it, while smiling into her laughing eyes. Already, they were acting as though they had a secret.

"Ah. . . la petite mort," said she, pretending to be faint. "Take care, Roume," bellowed Paul Barras, getting to his feet, "you are not the one to go home with her."

"You better let me help you," said Laure de Girardin, "your bandage is becoming undone." While doing this, she whispered, "He will not be the one either, he has been overly generous."

"And your companion, the lovely, or perhaps, I should say, infamous Soubise, she does well?" inquired Jean-Lambert Tallien.

"Frightened. Waiting to hear what the result of this meeting will mean," answered Roume, regarding Tallien, a man whom he had met in the company of Robespierre and other Jacobins.

"Well to be wary in these times, Roume," said Tallien. His sunken eyes and emaciated features, drawn and grim, spoke of his own miseries. "Especially for the likes of us, we who have experienced the rigours of the September slaughter. There are those who care only for revenge."

"Enough of that," said Barras, "I don't care. And that is what's important. Sit down, Roume. We have all bloodied our hands, this is a bloody business. You are here because you come from that part of the world. And you have gained the trust," he waved his hands in the direction of Tallien and the women, "of these desperadoes. I don't suppose you have been following events in the Antilles, in Saint-Domingue?"

"I must say I haven't," replied Roume, settling into one of the several gilded Fauteuil chairs that stood about the room.

"The English want it. The Spaniards dream of it. The blacks control half of it, the mulattoes the other half. Have you heard of Toussaint, leader of the blacks?" Barras, who appeared shorter and heavier than when last Roume had seen him, was pacing the room, his hands clasped behind his back, pausing from time to time to rise up on his toes.

"Yes, I have."

"Interesting man. Mentally superior for an African." He had stopped in front of Roume and turned to face him. "And Rigaud?"

"Yes, Toussaint commands the respect of the other black leaders," said Roume steadily, meeting his eye. "Two years ago, he had the command of well over two thousand well-armed, well-trained troops. The best of their soldiery in the north of the island, it was

23: HEART'S CUT 1796

said. As for Rigaud the mulatto, I never met him. He too was a force in the west and south departements."

"You know that? Yes. He was given substantial powers by Commissioner Étienne Polverel. Toussaint successfully mounted a cavalry charge against British guns at a place called Petite Rivière at the beginning of the year. With the slaves free, miracles can happen. Expelled the Spanish forces from the Plaine du Nord, this while defeating various attempts by local chieftains to take away his ascendancy. Our man General Étienne Laveaux has his confidence. He made him a colonel. I trust Laveaux, trained to the artillery, good man. The black soldiery under Toussaint are fighting for the French Republic. What do you know of him?"

"Toussaint is far more intelligent than the average European officer. A natural tactician and a clever politician. He is a Franc-Maçon and holds Enlightenment views. I imagine that by now he sees himself as a republican patriot. A liberator, walking in the footsteps of General Washington, I expect. He wants absolute freedom for the blacks, although he may have held a contrary view earlier. I believe he would want to be allied to France and would not be easily seduced by the English. He would want to free his country."

"Free his country?" Barras appeared genuinely surprised.

"Naturally, wouldn't you?"

"That cannot be his decision," answered Barras, moving off, "we must control the place, the wealth. He has broken the Spanish hold and has challenged the English with success. He now embraces France. I want you to go there. You are to keep him that way inclined."

"His enemies are within," said Roume confidently, his voice unwavering, his eyes never leaving Barras, "the war lords, the poor whites who imagine themselves to be sans culottes, the mixed-race people called mulattoes under André Rigaud, and the royalists."

"Toussaint has made an accommodation with Rigaud," Barras was pacing the room. "He appears to control the turmoil. I have heard that he and Laveaux entered Le Cap together and at an assembly of a great mass of the people, including hundreds of mulattoes, Étienne Laveaux named Toussaint assistant to the governor, that means a general of division. I can't imagine a black in that position. Laveaux has committed himself to consult him on all important matters. 'Spartacus', they, the blacks, called Toussaint, with shouts and hurrahs. He is said to have turned to them and said pointing, 'After God, Laveaux!' or some rubbish of the sort."

"I can't think that Rigaud and the mulattoes were too pleased, neither the French residents, for that matter," Roume said, reclining in his chair. He admired Barras' energy, he saw that Barras noticed and that it pleased him to be admired.

"Rigaud and the mulatto population are terrified of the blacks. Good, that's how we want it. Toussaint has restored Saint-Domingue to France. We must keep it that way. I want you to keep the Spanish part of that place separate at all cost, and not be drawn into whatever erupts in Saint-Domingue. Can you manage that?"

Roume shrugged and said, "One can only try, there are many forces at play on that island, not the least the remnant of the royalist-minded planters who court the English based in Jamaica. And there is Rigaud, who actually needs the English, if he hopes to win." He rose to join Barras at a table where a large map of Hispaniola was displayed. "Toussaint's dream of independence may work for us," said Roume, lifting a heavy brass magnifying glass to his eye and studying the islands of the Greater Antilles.

"You'll have to do better than try! I am pleased to hear you say that his dream of independence will work in our favour. There are others who would not. That zeal will keep the English out and save the place from the royalist planters as well. The mulattoes must not get the upper hand. I want you to go there," Barras pointed at the map, "to the Spanish half of the place and hold it. The Peace of

23: HEART'S CUT 1796

Basel makes this possible. Get there by May. Sonthonax will return with you. He like yourself is a survivor, recently acquitted from serious charges. There will also be Giraud, Leblanc and Julien Raimond the mulatto. You shall sail with close to two thousand regulars, the appropriate armaments, all that is necessary to hold the colony. You are once again a Commissioner of the Republic of France, this time a High Commissioner to Santo Domingo."

"HE IS IN SUPPORT OF YOU," said Laure de Girardin, regarding Philippe Roume with such a mocking smile that it made him laugh out loud, "we all are." Laure had signalled to him that he should wait upon her in the anteroom, which he did.

"We convinced him," said Joséphine, "we must stick together, all Creoles, yes. Not so? And when shall we meet your Soubise? Your beautiful darky? You are ahead of your time: Philippe Égalité, I shall call you."

"Your Soubise is an asset," said Laure, tucking in his bandage. "She, together with another sang-melée, Léger-Félicité Sonthonax's lady, with whom he has had a long relationship, will place both of you in an appropriate light with those whose interest must be kept close to our own."

"Ladies of colour, what a delight that must be, such a novelty for you, Philippe Égalité, not so?" Joséphine giggled. She of course, coming from the islands, was being sarcastic. They were joined by Thérésa Tallien, who appeared on the arm of a young officer.

"Ah, at last, Thérésa. Allow me to present our newest High Commissioner to Saint-Domingue, citoyen Philippe Roume," said Joséphine in a laughing voice that carried more than a hint of her Creole origins.

Roume took the hand of the beautiful blonde woman who stood a head taller than all others in the room and kissed it.

"And, allow me," said Thérésa, "to present the celebrated hero of the siege of Toulon and the saviour of the Republic, Brigadier General Bonaparte."

Catching Laure's eye, Roume bowed with just a hint of reverence. He had heard of the celebrated hero of the battle for Toulon and had paid attention to what was said of the action taken by Bonaparte in October of the previous year, when royalists in Paris had staged a rebellion against the National Convention, laying siege to the Tuileries Palace. Bonaparte had defended the Convention chamber by ordering heavy cannon loaded with grape shot to fire on the royalist insurrectionists, killing some one thousand four hundred, thus turning the tide of history.

The general barely noticed Roume, sparing him merely a curt nod, having eyes only for Joséphine de Beauharnais. The republican moderates and the rising bourgeoisie had no need for the streets of Paris, now that they had won the support of the young generals.

"Fortune favours the brave," smiled Laure.

That was indeed the thought that had crossed Roume's mind as he looked upon the elegant scene in the high-ceilinged, brightly lit, gold and white rococo drawing room of the old palace. These beautiful women now influenced the most powerful men in France, and the youthful general, already with the aura of la gloire worn carelessly was in hot pursuit of l'amour.

"Les fêtes de l'Hymen et de l'Amour begin afresh I see," said Philippe, he suddenly felt lighthearted and, taking both her hands in his, smiled into her earnest dark eyes.

"Are you being prophetic, Philippe?" Laure asked seriously, as Bonaparte, resplendent, haloed by the lights of the chandeliers and reflected to infinity in the gilded mirrors, could be glimpsed raising the hand of the languorous Joséphine to be kissed in tribute to an allure as incomprehensible as it was compelling.

"Plus ça change, plus c'est la même chose," Roume said, also raising her hand to be kissed.

23: HEART'S CUT 1796

One ruling class being replaced by another, he thought. Time for a change, once more. So, it would be Hispaniola again, for him and Soubise.

From outside, the rain battered the diamond-shaped panes of the medieval window through which he could barely make out the empty grey courtyard below. Santo Domingo. "Yes." He smiled.

Reading from my Memoirs at George Street, Port of Spain, Trinidad, 1810

RETURNING TO SAINT-DOMINGUE, 1796. Once again, we were aboard a ship of war, battered by the Atlantic gales, with Marianne crucified on the crossbeams of shame and guilt. Her guilt, my shame.

Philippe was a changed man, again. Throughout his life it seemed he must engage in hazard. It appeared to suit his fickle personality. This was not a choice, he explained. It was a necessity in those revolutionary times. "Res, non verba. Deeds not words," he said, swinging his legs out of the narrow bunk, the night's stuffiness in the cabin not yet dissipated. He wore his grey hair and beard in what he believed to be the Spanish style—severe and disapproving. His physique, as he shrugged off his night-dress, was strong and sinewy. He held himself erect, no longer was he slouching and showing his remaining yellow teeth like the vermin in whose company he had became indistinguishable.

He rose to pace the windy quarterdeck of the frigate *Immortalité*, which was sailing westward beneath a blistering sky. This he did on a morning, early, a step ahead of her captain. He had also taken to inspecting the equipage, the men, their quarters and to visiting the horse lines below deck, so as to appraise the condition of the mounts. He had brought aboard a magnificent Andalusian stallion, black as night, whose untrimmed mane and tail he groomed, whispering endearments, to a high blue-black gloss. To the regiment that would be under his command, he wanted to appear a serious man, a careful man, a dangerous man.

After one hundred and twenty days at sea, we were in sight of land, whether it was Saint-Domingue or Santo Domingo I couldn't say. The canvas, braces and sheets that had been trimmed and set fifteen days out of the Azores for the long traverse without landfall were being rearranged aloft. Breezily swinging in the topgallant skysails and swaying yards the sailors sang shanties and shouted Huzza! in the brilliant tropic light, crystal clear to the horizon. It raised my spirits and brought out the long-forgotten sailor in me.

I wandered round the deck at night and thrilled at the smells brought by the wind and at the sight of the vast phosphorescent ocean. By day, I felt comforted at the sight of the first wreaths of yellow sea grapes tossed about between glistening shoals of flying fish, bunches of coconuts and gigantic Amazonian driftwood that carried as anxious passengers families of iguanas and once a solitary boa constrictor. These were mindlessly accompanied by battalions of Portuguese man-of-war diligently drifting, trailing their will-o'-the-wisps like iridescent and very poisonous tentacles.

The commissioners, Sonthonax, Giraud, Leblanc and Raimond had embarked prior to our departure from Bordeaux, bound for Saint-Domingue and Le Cap Français. We came ashore at noon the following day and were met by them in that devasted city for the commencement ceremonies. It was the 8th of May of 1796. Sonthonax was a chubby man with a tiny nose and a cherubic appearance that belied his ruthless character. A rehabilitated Girondin, he inaugurated the proceedings by declaring that colonists no longer resident in French territories would be seen as enemies of the state and that their property would be seized and sold before the doors of the court. He made much of declaring that to suggest that the freedom now enjoyed by the former slaves could be revoked, or that it was legal to own human beings, would be punishable by death.

23: HEART'S CUT 1796

Philippe was drawn immediately into the quagmire of the island's internecine wars. Everywhere we heard of Toussaint. Philippe became furious at the Vicomte de Rochambeau's inability to occupy Santo Domingo. Rochambeau, assigned to establish French authority over the Spanish half of the island, had failed in the face of an unrelenting insurgency mounted by the Spanish ranchers as well as the resistance of black war bands that had become affiliated with the English and were stubbornly loyal to the Spanish Crown. From the inception of their war for freedom the blacks had expressed loyalty to the principle of monarchy. A king, any king, was perceived, in the delusion of their confinement in the nightmare's nest, as the font of ultimate power and the purveyor of cosmic justice.

The city of Le Cap Français, in spite of it having been burnt and fought over, still retained the atmosphere of vibrant trade and exchange. It wanted to be gay, the women, wanton as ever, were brilliantly dressed, the men, sly, and on the lookout for what they could get for free. The drums, ever present, were those I remembered from three years ago. The nights, hot, were underlined by their vibration, as near and far they spoke and were answered, stubborn in the persistence of this meagre freedom. From the city slums came the cries of those who would evoke deity and command the observance of ritual ordinances. The feral dogs, as ever, howled their doleful chorus. Roosters called eerily in the pre-dawn stillness that overlaid the nightmares of those so recently unchained in truth nothing had changed. Except that the name Toussaint was breathed, inaudibly in and out, like the wind. He was waiting. Then suddenly dawn would streak the sky with red warnings, signals of tragedies as yet undreamt. I longed for my childhood and wondered where my daughter could be. Had she too waited for the sunrise?

TOUSSAINT STOOD ALONE. I watched from the sidelines and listened to what the people said. He had joined the French Republic in early May of 1794 at Gonaïves where he raised the republican standard. The men closest to him were his brother Paul, his nephew Hyacinthe Moïse, Jean-Jacques Dessalines and, I was not surprised to learn, Henri-Christophe.

Toussaint's subordinates did not dare cross or step upon his shadow. I stood in the crowd and looked at him. His air of majesty came from a stillness that surrounded him alone. It also emanated from the fifteen thousand men under his command with whom he entered the city of Le Cap Français. There, he freed General Étienne Laveaux who had been imprisoned by Jean-Louis Villatte, thus halting an attempted coup mounted by Villatte and others.

In appearance he was a less than medium-sized black man in the uniform of a French Republican general, not handsome, but fine-boned and sharp-featured with a well-shaped head. When smiling his ruined teeth were hidden by a graceful sleight of hand, which only seemed to enhance his attractiveness. He gave the impression of being about his own affairs only just briefly detained by French officialdom. Toussaint greeted Léger-Félicité Sonthonax like a long lost friend, paused to regard Raimond as though inspecting a horse and nodded briefly to the other commissioners. Of the thirty thousand muskets being unloaded from the *Immortalité* by far the majority would pass into his hands. I understood that they would be used to keep Rigaud's mulatto armies in check and to maintain an ongoing resistance to the English who controlled some towns and strategic positions.

Toussaint was here to receive the citation that elevated him to the rank of général de division. France had kept him close as the wars in Europe generated by the revolution would drain her of manpower. The ceremony of investiture was performed with elaborate attention to deference. I had the sense that they were asking his permission to bestow it. I felt that I must meet this new Caesar.

That evening I did. Dressed in my finest, wearing the emeralds of my pirate past, I stood beside Philippe, along with the other commissioners. The mistress of Sonthonax, Madame Villevaleix, a

23: HEART'S CUT 1796

small black person with a strong resemblance to a type of toad, was on my right. In the fading light that still contained a hint of gold, the wide curving stair at the entrance to government house, where we had sojourned some three years ago, was crowded with expectant lobbyists. I was on the lookout for some old friends.

A dissonant blast of trumpets announced our important guests. The shiny black carriages drew up, the splendidly conditioned horses stamped, jingled and snorted in their traces, the resplendent coachmen, footmen, factotums and functionaries made way for a company of gorgeously attired mounted officers who reined in their mounts in the nick of time. My word, what a fabulous collection of black men. They looked like Polish Hussars or Cossack cavalrymen with Toussaint in their midst, he upon the great grey stallion, Bel Argent. Magnificent they were, with bearskin shakoes and covered in gold epaulettes, braid, embroidered collars, red and green fitted tunics trimmed with galloons in metallic gold thread, all booted and spurred. They tossed their reins to the hurrying grooms who themselves bustled about in brand new livery.

The party of officers, led by Toussaint, mounted the wide stairs. They paid scant attention to those who bowed and smiled: a confused mixture of blacks and whites, men and women, who had tried their hardest to keep their white gloves spotless for this very moment. Outside, the evening had grown dark. Inside, a golden brilliance illuminated the white walls of the foyer, the entrance hall and ourselves. With hearty voices the arriving party called out to friends, stamped about and rattled their sabres, their high shiny boots creaking with newness. They were above protocol. How did they know to behave like princes?

"Madame Roume?"

A white-gloved hand was before me. I placed my own in it and involuntarily curtseyed.

"No, no, not at all. That is not for us." I was raised to high heaven.

"Your thoughts, they appeared to have taken you away. . ."

"I was thinking of the last time we were here. Now, it is so different."

"I hope it meets your approval."

"It is beyond my imagination."

He had a thoughtful expression, Toussaint. No malice there or guile. I glanced at Philippe, he was grim-faced, stern and distant. He had been that way all across the Atlantic and even more so since discovering that there were insufficient troops available for him to enforce his position as High Commissioner to Santo Domingo.

The great ballroom doors opened and we followed the crowd that was hurrying in. In our time here, I had not seen it lit. It was magnificent. There was Toussaint again, trim and erect; appearing taller, he strode to the centre of the floor, the crowded room hushed. I could not take my eyes away, what a cockerel. With one hand on his hip he glanced about and then briskly walked towards me. He stood there, one gloved hand out-stretched, and theatrically, he bowed. I took his hand and as if on cue the orchestra commenced a bourrée, and away we went. Then there was a Spanish chaconne, that made me breathless.

"Would you like to take some air?" he asked, I nodded, the music stopped, he waved towards the orchestra and it recommenced. All around us couples were dancing but keeping a distance. "Come, we shall stand on the terrace." On his arm, with the company parting before us, we passed through the tall doors and into the cool night. The sound of the orchestra seemed to come from afar as those standing about the wide gallery bowed and stepped away. My God, this man was like a king! As if reading my mind he looked at me, there was a twinkle in his eyes.

"I must behave this way, otherwise they would never take me seriously. What shall I call you?"

I hesitated for a moment, I saw that he had noticed.

23: HEART'S CUT 1796

"I am Soubise. Everyone takes you seriously. I hear that you win battles and show no mercy."

"Ah, on the contrary, I show too much mercy." A quarter moon illuminated his profile, highlighting his fine head and shoulders.

"Then, as they say, 'blessed are the merciful. . .'"

"For they shall obtain mercy. Soubise, I take this happen-chance to say that I shall need the support of Roume to bring, all this—" he waved his hands like a conductor signalling an ending, "—to a close, we cannot endure endless war. And to achieve this, my instincts tell me I shall need his support and your own. Wait, let me finish, I know something about the two of you, where you are from, who you are and who is Philippe Roume de Saint Laurent."

I had to think of Henri-Christophe.

"They, in Paris, have sent him, they want me to stay within the Republic, their republic. . ." He appeared to pause.

"And you would have a republic of your own?" I asked.

"Of our own," he answered. He had become tense. He looked at me, and I at him.

"Yes."

"We can bring the best of this new thinking that is sweeping the world to our people. We can lift them from servitude and ignorance, educate their children and place them on the path to freedom. First, there is a war to be won. André Rigaud will compromise the revolution and sell it to the English. We must resist the English, and the mulattoes under Rigaud. To halt that we must unite the entire island under one flag." He smiled a rare smile.

"And you imagine that I can persuade Roume to break his word to those generals in Paris, which is to keep Saint-Domingue for France, while keeping Santo Domingo separate?"

"No, perhaps not. For that he will have to make up his own mind, but you can encourage him to see a future for you both, here.

A future in which he will be amongst the founding fathers of the second republic in the New World after the United States." He took my hand, through both gloved fingertips a warmth passed. I looked hard into his eyes. He is taking a chance with me, but then, we are in his power here.

"You believe that they, they in France, will give this up to you? All this wealth without a war? These are terrible people. Their greed, boundless. Their capacity for cruelty, as unimaginable as their power."

"I believe that we shall win. We are here. They will have to come here and fight here. Everything will fight for us. The weather, the terrain, the diseases that afflict them. The powers that we possess, these come from the very heart of our suffering. We shall win. We have no other choice." The moon of the first quarter slid behind a cloud. An owl hooted and was answered by its mate.

"What role can Philippe Roume play? He is a white Creole, do you think that he will give them up and join you?"

"I believe that he is a realist first, and as a Creole, he will select a future in which he will benefit by way of fame and, yes fortune. As he has always done. I saw him take control of a crowd in Le Cap, he may have saved my life. Over there, in France, he is no one, here, he will be remembered, accorded a place, a home for you both."

"Yes, I remember, it was in '92. I'll think about what you have said. Look, there is a crowd gathering, waiting for you."

"Then come, we must return or we shall be a scandal." The music had started a passepied.

"Please, spare me this one," I begged, "my skills are limited at best." He laughed softly, he was good natured, and believed that I could alter events, and there was Philippe.

"Roume, forgive me, but I had to steal her for a moment."

Philippe bowed. "By all means, citoyen Toussaint, I am much obliged that you have returned her intact. Are you intact, Soubise, or was it Marianne who danced with the general?"

23: HEART'S CUT 1796

"Ha, I see that you have learned to become someone else as needed. Tell me, Roume, do you as well have several selves into which you can step as the occasion demands?"

I saw that Toussaint was serious, in spite of the levity in his tone. My heart gave a deeper thud and then raced.

"Yes, Toussaint, I too have had to change with the times, or perish."

"So have I. We just discussed this, Soubise and I, the possibility of change. We have stories here of the shape changer, the loup-garou. We share an experience then, you and I."

"We, too, have heard the sound of the jumbie bird," I said, taking Philippe's arm just as the owls called once more.

"Roume, please, come to me in the morning, early, we must begin. I have little time and events are on the move. I have asked," Toussaint searched my face for a moment, "Soubise to help me win your trust, that was what our tryst was about, now I ask you, trust me, and I shall trust you." I could see that his candour had touched Philippe, it had surely touched me.

"Yes, you have my word, we shall work together, in trust, both Marianne and Soubise will keep us in check."

"Good, thank you Roume, now we rejoin the dance, shall we?"

Stepping away from us he was immediately surrounded by those who stood and waited. I looked up at Philippe, he appeared sad.

"Come, let us walk in the garden, it is cool." I removed my gloves and took his hand, it was hot, and raised it to my lips. We descended the broad stairs into the soft night and, for the first time in a long time, we kissed. I tried not to let him see that I was crying, but he saw, he gave me his handkerchief.

"What did he ask of you?"

"That I convince you join him in this great enterprise."

We could hear the orchestra, it was playing a moody overture to some unknown piece. He didn't answer. I hadn't expected him to. Our embrace turned into a dance, I put my face against the gold brocade of his uniform and closed my eyes, we swayed a bit, I must have fallen asleep, because Philippe was laughing softly, and there was Desmaizeaux. As moth-like as ever standing in the shadows. I saw that his teeth were chattering and that he was trembling from head to foot, he held a silver tray precariously, it contained two glasses of wine. He smiled a quivering smile with his very old eyes, stuttering.

"M, ma, Madame Roume, welcome."

I could see that he was overcome with the anxiety of me remembering him. I placed my hand on his shuddering arm and thanked him for the wine.

A mazurka was ending as we entered the great room, the crowd milled, the tinkling sound of broken glass came, a girlish shriek, someone laughed out loud, the music started, something brisk and we danced. Later that evening, I found them waiting in the commodious pantry.

"So, tell me everything."

"You have to sleep with fowls to know if they snore!" shouted the bottle washer, nodding her head knowingly.

This of course was sage advice. The city of Le Cap Français had in effect become the stronghold of republican interest. All because of Toussaint L'Ouverture.

"L'Ouverture, is that what he is called now?"

"Yes, yes he is an overture, an opening movement, a beginning," Desmaizeaux said without stuttering.

"He is for France and the Republic so long as the people are free," said the cook seriously, shifting her weight on the large chair from which she presided. "This is no slave uprising."

23: HEART'S CUT 1796

"The people must wo, wo, work, p-plant food, for people to ea, eat," Desmaizeaux said in a conspiratorial whisper.

"The French generals are worried that Toussaint L'Ouverture's black soldiers are only for him. Would die for him. Not for them," said the cook.

"True, especially that one, Desfourneaux," shouted the bottle washer, "the knife alone knows what is in the heart of the pig!"

THE TERRIFYING SCARCITY of food drove almost all decisions. We were relieved when Sonthonax finally made the decision to arrest Étienne Desfourneaux, commander of the forty-eighth Infantry Regiment stationed in Le Cap who instinctively distrusted the ascendancy of the black officer corps. Toussaint then became the highest ranking officer in the colony. This was followed, on the day of our departure for Santo Domingo the following year, by Toussaint L'Ouverture being named Commander-in-Chief of the French Republican army in Saint-Domingue answerable only to Philippe as the plenipotentiary of the French Republic. He and Philippe had spent hours talking the night before we left, walking in the garden of the palace. He did not say what about, and I did not enquire. It appeared that even without my intervention concerning what Toussaint had asked for at the ball, Philippe and he were in agreement, and yes, perhaps Philippe had indeed fallen under the spell of this charismatic soldier cum hero.

Does the knife really know what is in the heart of the pig? I wondered to myself as we embarked the *Perseus* to take advantage of the falling tide so as to make the cape of the Cap before sunrise. Toussaint had sent a detachment of cavalry to escort us to the docks. I could see them as they departed, catching the last of the moonlight on the gold and silver of their uniforms.

By late afternoon the following day I plainly made out the plantation houses and cultivated lands from the deck of the sloop-of-war. We were for Santo Domingo, the Ciudad Colonial of the former Spanish half of Hispaniola. The aromas coming to me over the choppy dark water told of a great old forest. Later, the forest smell commingled with the more nostalgic Caribbean odours of wood-smoke and fish pots. In the early dawn, upon the tree-bare ridges, I saw the outline of factories and distilleries.

The long run to the Mona Passage that separates Cabo Engaño, Santo Domingo's furthest eastern point, from the island of Puerto Rico was accomplished by the *Perseus* in spite of contrary winds in under three days. The seas through the passage were kind as we stood towards the island's capital. The sun set quickly behind a lightning-streaked storm that enveloped the distant mountains. We were standing on deck amidships, the wind racing by as Philippe explained that it was the oldest town inhabited by Europeans in the New World.

"It is where Bartolomeo Columbus built a fortress on the banks of the Ozama River," he said.

"Who was he?"

"The brother of Christopher Columbus. On his third voyage he sailed directly from Trinidad to Hispaniola, having mistaken the Venezuelan mainland for yet another island. There," he said pointing, "the cornerstone of the New World."

"Who did?"

"Pay attention. Christopher Columbus did. The bones of the Admiral of the Ocean Sea lie there, in the crypt of the Cathedral of Santa María la Menor." I could barely understand his Spanish.

"Whose bones?"

"Pay attention. Christopher Columbus' bones."

We disembarked at the Atarazanas docks in Santo Domingo with the drum-corps of the forty-eighth. The regiment had been loaned to us by Toussaint. Their thunder woke up the city even

23: HEART'S CUT 1796

before the golden dawn, which characterised that side of Hispaniola, faded into the pastel heat of a dry season day. Philippe entered the walled city via the Calle Damas, resplendent in the official uniform of a High Commissioner of the French Republic, mounted on the black Andalusian that caracoled upon the dew-covered cobbled streets with the clatter of a virtuoso castanet performance. He rode on ahead, alone, through a gate of ancient masonry, in advance of the massed infantry and grenadiers of the forty-eighth marching in close formation with regimental colours displaying ribbons that spoke of honours achieved at Basel where the Prussians had been reversed in '95. I followed in a closed black enameled coach drawn by matching greys, as people, in various stages of undress, looked down from iron balconies. I had to think of what Philippe had so vividly described of the vision he had received from Doctor Mesmer that night in Paris. Remembering it, in the dawn light of this city, gave me a such sense of déjà vu that I had to shake my head, to clear away what I had already seen in my mind's eye that night in Paris.

We were nearing the great Fortaleza Ozama fortress as the sun cleared the surrounding mountains, and to the sound of a thunderous cannonade fired from the battlements in salute to the High Commissioner, we took the winding stone road through the desuetude of narrow streets that spoke of the declining population of this once prosperous colony.

Occupying the fortress, raising the French Republican flag with pageantry and military show, was only the beginning of a month of celebrations, the highlight of which was the ceremonial planting of the tree of Liberty in the main plaza. There Philippe declared the end of all vestiges of anachronistic feudalism, condemning these in an address to the assembled disbelievers as being as dreadful as they were meaningless. We moved into the viceregal residence, the Casas Reales, a morbid place whose rooms were hung with ancient tapestries and dark Moorish carpets and crowded with the gigantic carcasses of ghastly furniture.

Philippe was supported by a slowly increasing coterie of inconspicuous men who stood about him at all public occasions. They were mostly black men, some were soldiers, others individuals who were trusted in their communities. The old Spaniards resented this. Philippe's support of Toussaint in all his undertakings had been noted by his fellow commissioners in Saint-Domingue, Raimond and Michel, as he had written to them frankly expressing his admiration for Toussaint.

News came from the Lesser Antilles. Victor Hugues, who had retaken Guadeloupe for the Republic in October of 1794, had exported the revolution to the neighbouring islands of Dominica, Saint Martin, Saint Vincent and Sainte Lucie. And from Grenada, that Julian Fédon had raised the flag of Liberté there in 1795 and had made it clear that his was not a mulatto uprising or a slave revolt. It was a war against the English for the establishment of the French Republic in Grenada. This, of course, had sent tremors through the imaginations of those who sought freedom in Saint-Domingue. We were now hearing that the English had landed troops on Grenada. Philippe and I did not speak of Stanislaus de Barras, but we both heard his loud voice in our minds, haranguing, compelling us to join him and Hugues in the creation of a Caribbean republic. I had to think of my conversation with Toussaint.

Philippe commenced an exhausting counter-insurgency by siding with a junta of desperately ambitious merchants and shopkeepers who inhabited the city of Santo Domingo. By separating the interest of the remaining grandees from the rebellious blacks, the tobacco farmers, the hidalgo ranchers, horse thieves and part-time bandits of the countryside, he was able to bring calm to the city. Leading the forty-eighth into the hinterland, he confronted the enemy. In a series of battles he defeated first the blacks, driving them over the border into Saint-Domingue where they were met by forces loyal to Toussaint and were forced to submit. A great many did this, while others, escaping, joined bands of the marooned in the mountains above Jacmel. The counter-insurgency against the ranchers proved to be far more difficult. To achieve just a modicum of success, Philippe had to change tactics and become even more subversive and cruel than they. It was only after the burning of several of their homesteads and the slaughter of their wives and children that they came in from the mountains to lay down their arms. All of this took a toll on him.

Philippe opened the port to ships flying the flag of the United States and accommodated the corsair and brigand captains who were challenging English hegemony on the high seas. He was not able to curtail the trade in slaves, in fact it increased. This was where we met Jean Baptiste Bideau, the Saint Lucian captain, swashbuckler and companion of Victor Hugues. I would come to know Bideau, hold him in high regard and be forever in his debt. He too was one of those eggs laid in the nightmare's nest.

Philippe inaugurated the first commercial club and commenced the propagation of the ideas contained in the manifesto of the Society of Friends of the Country, as they applied to agriculture and trade. Commerce quickened as warehouses that had been shuttered for years reopened and the opportunities for Santo Domingo's exports of smoked beef, hides, mahogany, sugar and tobacco were seized, resulting in increased shipments of these goods to France. The circulation of money rose dramatically. In spite of all this the Spanish grandees continued to manipulate, for their purposes, the men in key positions in the administration of the colony.

He financed fandangos and bullfights and on one starry night, the opera of Tomás de Torrejón y Velasco with a libretto by Pedro Calderón de la Barca was performed by a troupe left stranded in Santo Domingo. It was very impressive as it stressed patriotism and heroic loyalty for the values of the Rights of Man and the Citizen, for democracy and for the ideals of the Republic. These vital principles, so foreign in this Spanish culture, were to be inculcated in the population, as Philippe proclaimed on the night of the premiere performance. 'The Republic of Santo Domingo', now independent of Spain. It became a topic hotly debated in the commercial club, the newsroom and the counting houses, which were draped in the revolutionary tricolour, as were all public places throughout the city.

IN SANTO DOMINGO, our conjugal life resumed at last in the vastness of the viceregal palace. It was fostered by the whispering wind that had rediscovered Marianne in the red-tiled courtyards where fountains blew a cool mist to the strum of invisible guitars. With rum concoctions at dusk, it assumed an indelible presence which was shaped by Philippe's ever increasing role of 'El Caudillo'.

With an entourage of mestizo beauties dressed in radiant silk, I took to wearing a huge red turban and walking barefoot in billowing skirts of a light white cotton with little or at times nothing beneath. My neck, ears, wrists and ankles dripped with gold. I encouraged the gallantry of brilliant officers and went riding out with them. I planted evidence of what I wanted him to think were surreptitious liaisons and would vanish for hours on end to appear glassy-eyed, smelling of the sea, of fishing nets and of the dark rum enjoyed by the Spanish peons. When he came to me, I ravaged him with unfamiliar caresses. That made him think twice. What else could I have done? We were going to be here for a damn long time. As nature would have it, I became pregnant.

I ACCOMPANIED HIM TO Les Cayes where he was to meet Toussaint. A terrible massacre of whites had occurred at the hands of blacks on the instigation of the mulattoes. The brother of Rigaud had inflamed them with lies that their return to slavery was imminent. It was a ghastly experience and I saw that it had a very bad effect on Philippe. This place would frighten anybody, even hardened Jacobins.

23: HEART'S CUT 1796

The duplicity of the mulattoes, the opportunism of the English and the bewildering complexity of this unending conflict had deepened the bond between Philippe and Toussaint L'Ouverture but it had also created a dependency, one upon the other.

"You have come to rely on him, depend on him. I would not do that, if I were you," I said as we were leaving Les Cayes. The bumpy road, the heat of the lurching coach and the anticipation of the long ride to the ship that would take us back to Santo Domingo had tired him.

"He is a good man, and there is no other," he said and removed his hat. His hair, white and thinning, was plastered to his head with sweat. "I shall support him," he said wearily.

"Yes, but will he support you?" Or will your dependence on him for your life, make you an easy foil? I wondered silently.

It was simplistic to say, as some did, that Toussaint recognised in Philippe a man who liked the black people of Saint-Domingue. I for one knew, as they both did, that black people, like all people, came in a variety of types of which a great many were despicable. But there was a common understanding that brought Toussaint and Philippe together. Perhaps they both shared the same republican ideals expressed in the Declaration of the Rights of Man and the Citizen. I was not altogether convinced that Philippe was a true republican but, I believed the he was against the perpetuation of slavery. What was important, was they both believed that a Caribbean interpretation of the republican ideal could be arrived at. This belief had at its centre the certainty shared by them that the African, slave or free, educated or primitive, atheist, animist, Christian or Moslem was a complete human being in possession of choice, free will and an immortal soul. This understanding had meant a great leap in Philippe's growth as a person and had come about, overtime, during our lives together. They had discussed, the night before we sailed for Santo Domingo, the high-flown notion of *prohairesis* through a long night, Philippe explaining the subtle distinctions between Aristotle's and Epictetus' interpretation of *prohairesis* or moral choice; Toussaint responding with an explanation of the Yoruban concept of the ori, a mediator between body and soul, which distinguishes humans from other creatures.

"It is known even by the children," Toussaint said reassuringly, "there cannot exist slaves on these islands, servitude must be forever abolished. All men who are born here must live and die free and French."

They both foresaw that the domination of the New World by the European powers was drawing to a close. This was due to the people of the New World coming of age, they agreed, rather than simply the precedent of North American independence. The shocking misery of the slave economies could not endure. No amount of money made as a result of wanton cruelty and suffering could maintain the old order. The crime had become too heinous, too enormous to be sustained by the human condition. The rank evil of it stank of the pit, the inferno, and the daemon that dwelled within.

We spoke of the patriots, Manuel Gual, Francisco de Miranda, and others in Venezuela who were struggling for the freedom of the southern continent. An impulse had been stirred.

"You, Toussaint, are the essence of it, my friend." He looked away into the distance of burnt cane. And then back again at Toussaint. I could see that he felt old, although they were both the same age, Toussaint was possessed of a vigor that made him appear younger, a power that seemed to overshadow Philippe. I felt a pang of fear. Taking a breath that was released as a sigh Philippe said slowly, "There is an urgent need to take your freshly incubated destiny in hand and escape this nightmare's nest, as Soubise calls it, now and forever. Create the Republic."

"It is an idea shared by the thinking people as well as by the most ignorant black," said Toussaint. "This island must be as free as the United States is."

23: HEART'S CUT 1796

Toussaint would come to us in Santo Domingo accompanied by his close friends. He enjoyed the difference in the Spanish atmosphere of the old viceregal palace and would sit and listen to Philippe as he spoke of Paris, the revolutionaries and the wars in Europe, his small thin frame erect, his eyes never leaving Philippe's face, serious and intense except for when his laughter, which was that of a larger man, erupted at some creole witticism in our shared vernacular. One evening, late, I was already nodding off, I heard him say to Toussaint, "I will ask her now, and you will be our witness. Soubise, Soubise!"

"Yes, my love."

"Will you marry me?"

"Of course I will marry you, but first you must divorce your Fanny." I answered. Yawning and bidding them both a good night I went to bed, only to discover the following morning that he had been serious and that with Toussaint's flair for organising, the event was already well in hand. We were married a few days later in the chapel of the old palace, by the same judge who had signed his divorce decree and who had only recently held the position of Clerk of the Peace at Laborieaux, in the presence of Toussaint L'Ouverture, Louis Beauvais and Paul L'Ouverture, who all three gave me away. Me, as they say, great with child. Within weeks I was brought to bed. I named her Manon for Manon Roland and wept a little, remembering Rosette.

BEFORE LEAVING FRANCE, Paul Barras had instructed Philippe to seize any opportunity to encourage Toussaint to consider an attack on Jamaica. The purpose was to tie down Toussaint's resources and cause him to make a clean break with the English. Even as this was discussed Philippe knew that Toussaint would not risk it, as French staff officers loyal to him, such as General Agé and Colonel Vincent, cautioned against it. In any event he would not do France's bidding to serve their ends. Roume agreed. It marked the deepening of an understanding that would shape their relationship.

Because the forces on loan to him would be returning to Saint-Domingue shortly, Philippe declared the emancipation ordinance that had been promulgated in the other half of Hispaniola, Saint-Domingue, knowing that he could hardly enforce it here in Santo Domingo. To do so would mean a campaign against the big land owners, and that would ensure the destruction of the colony's economy.

He did march against rebellious maroons, who were supported by the English. They had created a situation where Spain might attempt to regain control. In battles, mostly unrecorded, fought in places that possessed only colloquial names, Philippe defeated those who stood against his authority and earned respect for himself. I could see the effort it required for him to stay in the field for months, the effect that fevers, contracted in the foul swamps had on him, how they drained him. How they returned to weaken him even more. He was fighting to hold this place, this other half of hell.

He supported and endorsed the commissioning of black officers. We invited them and their wives to dine at the official residence. Some Spanish servants, footmen and the like, who would not serve them were jailed. Most importantly, the blacks in Santo Domingo saw him and me in the hospital, a dreadful place, almost every week, improving the conditions of that hell hole. It was the black people of the city who said that Philippe was a friend of the blacks and made the point of saying that he was not a Frenchman, but a Creole from Grenada. For Philippe his loyalties were becoming increasingly clear, as he was to write to Barras: "The merit of Toussaint is so excelling that I have difficulty in understanding why some people do not find qualities in him to praise, but only to criticise and malign. . ." These views were duly noted by some of the members of the Directory, especially as Toussaint, having dismissed its other representatives, had so obviously decided to work with Roume.

23: HEART'S CUT 1796

We heard that a vast sum had been paid to Toussaint by the English in compensation for materials seized by them, which were entrained to Toussaint. It was with pleasure that Philippe showed me a letter from Toussaint in which he praised and thanked Philippe for his support in deciding against the attack on Jamaica.

"A million and a half francs. For what?" I asked.

"For arms and munitions taken by the English, and returned to Toussaint. And to compensate for any ill feeling. He does not want war with England, even though the English are in Saint-Domingue."

"What does he want?"

"Freedom for his people. He has embraced the Enlightenment and the republican system. Laveaux too calls him 'The Black Spartacus'."

"Who is that?"

"A slave. He led a rebellion and challenged Roman rule."

"And?"

"He was killed in the final battle."

"And you support him?"

"Of course. Rigaud has a saying, I hear, 'how terrible is the rage of the people;' it is his latest profundity. And he is right."

"Yet, Rigaud has almost defeated the English."

"Toussaint wrote to me in July demanding that I authorise an invasion for the purpose of the annexation of Santo Domingo. He too wants to harness the people's rage."

"Why?" We were lying in bed. He was relaxed and happy. "The pretense is I have not been able to end slavery here. The Spanish ranchers are raiding Saint-Domingue so as to steal blacks and sell them as slaves to the big land owners in Jamaica."

"They have been doing that for years. Toussaint's own people do that. They sell slaves over the border to here, to Jamaica, to anybody," I told him, thinking to myself what we both knew, that Toussaint wants the whole of Hispaniola for himself.

He understood that saying, "It is pretense, he wants to take this place to show that he can rule the entire island. I can't allow it. My orders are clear."

"Time will tell," I said as he turned towards me, taking me in his arms more tenderly than he had done in years. "Wait for the change of events in Paris before you decide," I breathed into his ears. "They always change over there, you know that. Change with change. Wait for news before you say anything final, Wait."

I awoke before the dawn and lay quietly for a long while close to him. I had dreamt of Rosette. I searched for the flavour of the dream and not finding it, thought sadly of her. "No one can serve two masters," I murmured, looking at him asleep, still wrapped in his rumpled dreams, "either you shall be devoted to the one and fear the other. You cannot serve these two powerful personalities, Barras and Toussaint. You must make up your mind, are you of the Caribbean, or do you belong on the other side, the Atlantic."

I then thought of the old Patois proverb, that went: The cockroach must be very careful when he is invited to a party of fighting cocks. He did look, in his sleep, very old and white. White cockroach, I thought rising, and banished the thought.

24: THE ADMIRAL'S BONES

1797

He saw plainly that the people sent out from France were the primary sources for the confusion generated amongst the men vying for power in Saint-Domingue at this crucial time.

The Comte D'Hédouville was such a one. He had been dispatched to Hispaniola by the Thermodorian generals in Paris and naturally had gained the attention of the island's planter interest. He arrived as sole Agent for France in 1798 in the wake of commissioners Sonthonax, Leblanc and Giraud's departure. This island was not for everyone, this Philippe had come to understand.

D'Hédouville's instructions, he was to confide to him, were to subdue the blacks by reducing the status held by Toussaint and secure the deportation of André Rigaud.

"That was doomed to failure," said Philippe, affecting an indifference that he did not feel. He had listened in silence to D'Hédouville's complaining voice, which appeared to be the rehearsal of what he would report to Paul Barras and to the men of the Directory, his head throbbed, it wearied him.

Interrupting, Philippe said somewhat languidly, "Toussaint L'Ouverture has a philosophical turn of mind. He is by nature a legislator. As a general he is exemplary, as professional as any in Europe. But most importantly, he has an understanding of the meaning of freedom. He achieved legendary status a long time ago. It borders on the supernatural. As for Rigaud—his position for various other reasons is as firmly entrenched."

D'Hédouville, unable to comprehend the meaning of things, had apparently worsened his own untenable position by treating with Toussaint as if he were a minion. Then, he had apparently proceeded with the mandate given to him by the generals and proclaimed that all blacks must contract themselves to plantations for a period of three years. Toussaint's reaction, working with Hyacinthe Moïse, was to raise the former slaves in the north to an even greater state of revolt against the proclamation, claiming it was an attempt to reinstate slavery. This uprising forced D'Hédouville to escape from Saint-Domingue to Santo Domingo and to seek out Philippe Roume.

Toussaint's position had moved beyond his successes in the field. Once negotiations with the English for a complete withdrawal from Saint-Domingue had been achieved, he was beyond the authority of an agent from Paris. However, long before D'Hédouville's arrival in Santo Domingo, Toussaint, trusting Philippe's discretion, had sent Colonel Henri Vincent of the engineer corps to him. Vincent had shown himself to be a friend.

They met in one of the vast echoing rooms of the palace. With considerable tact Vincent revealed that the Directory, uncertain of D'Hédouville's reception, had entrusted a member of his staff with a sealed envelope. His instructions were that this was to be opened in the event of D'Hédouville's death or enforced departure from Saint-Domingue. He handed it to Roume, Philippe opened it, it contained his appointment as D'Hédouville's successor. He was now Agent for the entire island of Hispaniola as well as High Commissioner of Santo Domingo, answerable only to the French Directory. Vincent regarded him closely, what he saw was a man

24: THE ADMIRAL'S BONES 1797

whose hands shook a little and a person who made a pretense of briskness.

HE FOUND THAT HE RESENTED having to discuss the destiny of the remains of Christopher Columbus in the presence of D'Hédouville. The Spanish envoy Don Isador Avalar's small black eyes regarded his discomfort coldly. Roume's resentment was founded on the certainty that D'Hédouville was sitting there, pretending to the Spaniard that he was adjudicating Roume's handling of the affair. Avalar's deeply engraved features reminded him of José de Gálvez, a man he had never met.

Avalar was saying, "It is imbedded in the Peace of Basel, the remains of the Admiral are to go to Havana." Yet Roume was undecided. This was a political issue. Many of those who were his allies here in this city believed that Columbus' remains should be forever kept in the cathedral at the city's heart. It was a matter of prestige—ultimately his own.

D'Hédouville appeared to be on the point of interrupting when Avalar suddenly fell off the tall chair in which he had been sitting and landed on the stone floor. Both Roume and D'Hédouville rose to their feet, there had been hardly a sound, as Avalar's thick black fur-edged doublet and velvet plus fours had cushioned the fall. He was dead. His hat had rolled away and was retrieved by Roume who covered the Spaniard's face with it.

He left the room to the undertaker, with D'Hédouville, recounting misfortunes suffered at the hands of Toussaint, walking on his heels.

Ignoring the talkative guest who rode at his side, he entered the old inner city of Santo Domingo through one of its many gateways, his magnificent Andalusian drawing scattered applause. In the harsh light of noon he saw a walled town of the Middle Ages set in the tropics, overflowing with carriages and donkey-carts, with what he recognised as an architectural influence left in Spain by the Moors. Flocks of gaudy parrots flew breezily through shadowed arcades crowded with a miscellany of vendors, fortune-tellers, letter-writers, haberdashery enthusiasts and schoolgirls seeking to escape the watchful eyes of nuns whose medieval bonnets gave them the appearance of sea birds. This made him smile. There were large shade trees and tall palms everywhere, these conveyed the impression that the place had been built in a primeval forest at some unimaginable period, whose roots had lifted the streets and unbalanced the houses. The level of noise increased to a pitch as he approached the central market, it assailed the ear in much the same manner that the eye was overwhelmed by the cornucopia displayed and the outrageously cosquel costumes of the black women. Capuchin monkeys and a variety of unidentified rodents appeared as pets. These were lovingly caressed by long-nosed sloe-eyed Criollo beauties who gazed languidly at him through iron-grilled arabesque ornament. He fancied them wearing nothing but their starched lace white mantillas, held high by combs made from dark honey-coloured turtle-shell, decorated with pearls. Into their small ears, he could imagine the whispered warnings that came from the cracked lips of doncellas, withered hags wearing mourning since the massacres of the previous century. He could live in this city, he thought to himself.

Leaving the old town behind he rode on through the cloying humidity that drained his energy and promised a midday deluge. Somehow reluctant to return to the viceregal residence, he gave way to an urge and halted before the fortress-like structure of the old Cathedral of Santa María la Menor, where the bones of the Admiral rested. Dismounting, he motioned to D'Hédouville that he should wait, handed the reins to his retinue and entered its great doors. In the cool darkness, gold glistened in shadowed alcoves where the eroded likenesses of mitered bishops carved in sandstone looked down. He stood still, entranced amidst a silence that contained traces of incense trapped, he imagined, after hideous exorcisms, or following the interrogation of men who broke as they falsely

24: THE ADMIRAL'S BONES 1797

confessed to crimes that in their simplicity they could have hardly imagined. He conjured the rant of their insane revelations echoing as he moved forward into the gloom. Seen amidst the forest of tall pews were figures, forms draped in black, like shadows detached from their human companions who were there praying for those who had been submitted to the rack, the garrucha, the auto-da-fé; their inquisitors, having concluded that they were in possession of insufficient testimony to further torture their bodies, had sentenced their souls to perpetual cross-examination.

He resisted the urge to leave, being drawn towards what the low-vaulted gloom of the side chapels might contain. Through the darkness, to which his eyes had only just grown accustomed, he could make out such a chapel, it yawned a deeper shade of night. This tunnelled deep into his imagination and he could see them dressed in the san benitos, the yellow cotton sacks that bore front and back the red Saint Andrew's cross. He could hear the weary drill, the dragging feet, as they were rehearsed for the morning's meeting with the scaffold. He turned away at the vision of those weak from torture or crippled by it, who were stretching out thin dirty arms for the cup of wine at dawn, the chunk of bread fried in honey, that would be their last memory of the sweets of this world. This filled him with the premonition of his own end.

Turning, he met an elderly black-robed Dominican who held a tall staff tipped with an ornate gold crucifix. The man stepped aside to let him pass, but Roume could not move. The priest indicated a massive confessional, carved like a reliquary that might have contained the bones of Goliath. Philippe Roume reeled away, feeling for the edges of pews now invisible, and did not open his eyes until he found himself standing before the altar. It towered above him aflame in red-gold-leaf and blazing with the fire of dozens of votive candles, crowded with figurines and the miniature statues of saints. From the very heart of all this glamour rose the blue and gold draped statue of the mother of God. Her sad Botticelli eyes upturned and her delicate Florentine features evoked a profound despair. She reminded him of the young Soubise, the beautiful adventurous girl whom he had taken on this macabre journey that he thought of as his life.

The tolling of an iron bell reverberated deep within him and brought him to his knees. Rising, he felt himself unsteady and believing that he would fall, grasped the cold edge of the altar rail, crumpling the lace cloth with his fingers. A hand steadied him, and a kind voice said "Come, ancient lives tend to have an unnerving effect on some, especially on those who have strayed."

The voice belonged to a priest with the physiognomy of a bullfighter. In the flickering red-gold light his habit, a brilliant white, appeared to Roume to glow. He shook his head to clear away the vision and rose to his feet.

"Perhaps your Excellency would like a drink of water? Sometimes the air in this old place becomes stale, please, do step this way."

Roume was guided gently through a small door just off the high altar and along a passage into a lofty, well-lit chamber that smelled of bees' wax and clean linen.

"Please sit," said the priest, indicating a chair that was obviously as old as the cathedral itself. "Here, refresh yourself, I assure you it is the holiest of waters, as it is drawn from the oldest and deepest well in the New World."

"Thank you," said Roume and drank deeply. "Thank you, you are very kind, for a while I felt quite beside myself."

"Forgive me, Don Felipe, permit me introduce myself. I am Father Isobar of the Resurrection, and I suppose that you have come to visit our crypt and to see for yourself what you shall soon have to decide upon. An awkward choice."

"Indeed."

"Come then, Don Felipe, with me, for a visit to the house of the dead."

24: THE ADMIRAL'S BONES 1797

Unsteady on his feet, a whirling giddiness coming upon him, Philippe Roume was led by Father Isobar into the undercroft of the cathedral. The low fan vaults echoed the rustle of their clothes and their shuffling footsteps, giving Roume the impression of the presence of a large whispering and disapproving crowd. Ahead, in the shadows, a low Gothic door studded with iron bolts gave way to a spiral stair that descended into a pool of darkness that appeared as a solid mass of an unimaginable depth. Not even the pitch-burning brand with its wavering orange light penetrated for more than a foot or two.

As his eyes became accustomed to the dark, around him emerged the grinning faces of hundreds of skulls. He gasped as a vision of hell sprung to his agitated mind. *I must not fall over before this priest.*

"The first ossuary in the New World," said Father Isobar, holding the torch to another which burst into flame, illuminating the vastness of the crypt. Moving forward with a shuffling step, his mind wary of some pitfall, some gaping chasm through which he might vanish, Roume caught sight of the outlines of huge iron sarcophagi, four, perhaps five, that loomed out of the darkness in the encroaching glow. He stood before them, overwhelmed not so much by their antiquity but by a significance that he was only now beginning to appreciate.

"Who are these people?" His whispered question was repeated in the lowering ceilings as though from one phantom ear to another and yet to another. He started and looked up and about him.

The priest laughed softly, "Our echoes reverberate to the ridiculous," already his last words were joined by his first which in turn were repeated and then repeated and then repeated like audible reflections contained in opposite mirrors. He pointed at one of the caskets.

"This," whispered the priest, "is the casket that you seek, and that is his son Don Diego's, and these are those of Doña María Álvarez y Toledo, Don Diego's wife. The others are of Diego's sons and other members of the family of the great Admiral, including that of his brother Bartolomeo Columbus."

"How long have they been here?" whispered Roume.

"Don Christopher's from 1537, when María Álvarez y Toledo, the widow of Diego, caused the bones of her husband and his father to be interred in this cathedral, which was founded by her illustrious family. Now come. We shall converse more comfortably with less of an audience," the priest said, raising his hands to the ceiling, where already the reverberating echoes were conducting an animated account of what had been said by them both.

"These islands carry forward into history sagas both tragic and apocalyptic," the priest said, when a little while later they were sitting in a pleasant atrium surrounded by the sounds of running water splashing against masonry, shaped by its passage for over three centuries. Around them a variety of blooms in large pots dazzled the eye, while the scent of oregano filled the air.

"Yes, for some, as the tragedy of discovery unfolded, what you call God's will became indeed an apocalypse. Their world ended," said Roume ironically, indicating the servants standing, waiting, who were by and large all of Taíno heritage. His eyes never left those of the priest, who maintained the stare.

"That is so, Don Felipe, it was an ending. We shall never know what was lost to the world with the passing of those civilisations."

Roume was mildly surprised by the priest. He had expected the self-righteous defence of the indefensible: the elimination of entire nations and the imposition of a religion and a culture so alien that it could be only responded to by the mass suicides that characterised the first settlements.

"The skulls and bones you see below in the crypt are the remains of the first colonists who were massacred in the early 1500s when the Moorish slaves rose in rebellion."

24: THE ADMIRAL'S BONES 1797

"Who in turn were hunted to death by mastiffs," said Roume dryly. It occurred to him that he had not spoken to a priest in decades. He restrained the urge to laugh, while he understood that the priest wanted to convey the notion that all who came paid in blood one way or another. Good. "Please continue, Father."

"Thank you." It was obvious to him that the priest thought him cynical. "The crypt also contains, as you have seen, the caskets of several members of the family of the Great Admiral. His own were first interred at Valladolid. As you know, that city is where his patrons, Queen Isabella of Castile and King Ferdinand of Aragon, were married in 1469. Christopher Columbus died in 1506 in Valladolid. His catafalque was then removed to the monastery of La Cartuja in Granada, where he stayed, lived and worked when planning the voyages to the west. By the will of his son Diego, who was governor of Hispaniola, his bones were transferred here in 1542."

"Quite a tour de force for a bundle of bones, don't you think? I do, however, understand: as a relic it symbolises both the historical and sentimental right of Spanish possession of these lands. And Havana can play but a secondary role in all this."

"The power of relics has resonated through millennia," said the priest calmly. "Have you not heard of the man, long dead, who was brought to life as a result of his dead body coming into contact with the bones of Elisha?"

"Of course," said Roume, "in second Kings, chapter thirteen, verses twenty to twenty-one." His memory often surprised even him, he smiled, and held up his hands as if to say, what can I say.

"Ah," exclaimed the priest in surprise, "you do understand. In 1795, when France received authority to rule the entire island of Hispaniola, the news of the order to remove the remains of Columbus was deeply resented by the population of this city."

"You mean by the descendants of the conquistadors, the land owners, on whom I rely for stability in these unruly years."

Father Isobar, a member of the Scolopi, Escolapios, was an educated man. Born in Santo Domingo, he was a teacher and a descendant of several of those whose bones surrounded the sarcophagi of the Columbus family in the ossuary below. As a Creole, he felt deeply for the unique history of his city as the founding place of western civilisation in this hemisphere.

"Under the terms of the Peace of Basel, Columbus' remains are to be taken to Havana. This has to be complied with," said Roume. He had the sense that the priest had something else in mind. "What are you suggesting father, a little pious fraud?"

Father Isobar sat back and, looking at the man who maintained his gaze and smiled blandly, opened his hands as though he was framing the globe.

"Don Felipe, as a man of these times you know well the need to keep the peace on the border between the French and Spanish sides. You have been sent to govern here and to keep that peace. Let us work together so that all parties are pacified."

As Philippe Roume rose to take his leave, a wave of wariness surprising him, he said, "I shall not be returning for some time as I leave for Le Cap in the morning. I expect that you shall see that the terms of the treaty are kept in word and in deed. Thank you Father, it has been an interesting experience."

The sun was setting as he stepped out into the warm twilight. He could see his party, much as he had left them, in the shadow of the fountain. In the middle distance stood a woman with a boy at her side. He recognised her immediately.

"Philippe Roume de Saint Laurent." She smiled.

His heart's thud sounded in his ear.

"Lys de Cayeux."

"I am now Lys Duarte Azusa. This is your son, Marissé, greet your father."

24: THE ADMIRAL'S BONES 1797

A boy of six, perhaps seven, stood calmly, his dark eyes bright in the glancing light. He put out a slim hand and, taking Roume's, he bowed, "I am happy to meet you, Father," he said as if he had been rehearsed, and then he smiled and looked up at his mother and gained her approval.

"I thought you two should meet before we left for Cuba. We live there, my husband is a rancher."

Taking her hand, which was soft and familiar, he raised it to his lips and kissed it. They looked discerningly into each other's eyes as the last rays of the sun crossed the square, illuminating them for the briefest moment.

"Good-bye, Papa."

"Good-bye, Marissé, fare you well, Lys."

He rejoined D'Hédouville and the party of horsemen who had waited patiently in the plaza outside the cathedral. "D'Hédouville, you stayed. Please excuse my impulse, I felt compelled to see for myself, if you understand what I mean."

"Indeed I do not, Roume, pray tell me."

"A remarkable deception is about to unfold. In the weeks to come, in the gloom of the mausoleum beneath the cathedral, the bones of a father and of a son will be mingled in such a manner that they will remain locked in an embrace both paternal and filial, for all time."

"Remarkable that, Roume," said D'Hédouville, "as I was. . . "Come, Soubise awaits us with lechazo, it has become her favourite dish, it is made from the flesh of unweaned lambs."

FATE'S FOLLY: Having succeeded D'Hédouville as the Directory's agent, Roume diligently reported all developments to a Paris growing increasingly remote. Addressing his missives directly to

Barras and receiving no response, he addressed other members of the government, men he hardly knew, Lazare Carnot and Étienne LeTourneur. Toussaint's increasing autonomy was realised by Philippe Roume with mixed feelings, not the least being whether he possessed the strength to deal with what he had come to believe to be inevitable.

Toussaint had dealt with the Directory's men, from Sonthonax to Laveaux and now D'Hédouville, by simply sending them back to France, while personally negotiating an agreement with the English under General Maitland to withdraw from Saint-Domingue, in return for which he promised amnesty to all partisans. This was to Roume's thinking not only dangerous, but an act that clearly challenged his own authority. It had crossed his mind that he might be the next victim of the man's growing independence and not knowing what was the true situation in Paris, he was loath to leave the frying pan that he had grown accustomed to. In discussing this with Toussaint, he had assured him of his continued support. They both knew that these arbitrary decisions violated the Directory's explicit orders.

That Toussaint had arrived at an accommodation with John Adams, President of the United States, with regard to trade, in spite of France being at war with its former ally and with Maitland threatening to blockade the harbours, appeared to Roume as a reckless and dangerous action that flew in the face of the dictates of the regime, which, although far away, could still reach out and strike with deadly force. Yet, he could not bring himself to object.

In the quiet of his own mind he knew that his inaction was based on his inability to call upon troops to support of his authority. He was, too, he had to admit, somewhat in awe of the sheer energy of the man. Was he in fear of crossing Toussaint? He understood that in this situation, his life, hers, could be ended as abruptly as the extinguishing of a candle.

24: THE ADMIRAL'S BONES 1797

With regards to Saint-Domingue's perpetual state of internal war and its attendant Byzantine-like politics, which was beyond understanding, Roume made every effort to keep himself apart. In truth, he doubted that anyone truly understood its several layers, including Toussaint himself. This revolution, war, whatever it was, had become a dragon, breathing fire and death whereever it turned its dreadful head.

Against it all, one thing was plain: the mulattoes, despite the gallantry and the genius displayed by Rigaud's generals in the south, possessed insufficient resources in terms of treasure and manpower to sustain a protracted war. The contest had only quickened when Toussaint dispatched an army of over forty-five thousand well-equipped, well-trained men who swept into the south.

When news arrived that Toussaint had narrowly escaped two attempts on his life, Roume felt afraid for himself and for Soubise, keeping the information secret from her. The messenger who brought that news also carried a summons. The following morning, Roume prepared to set sail for Jacmel in Saint-Domingue.

The small city had become a key defensive position in what was to be known to history as the Battle of the Knives. There, André Rigaud had brought up an army of some thirty thousand. These were supported by flying cavalry columns and batteries of heavy artillery on the surrounding hillsides. From there, Rigaud's second in command had been able to strike out and enter the town of Jacmel and was holding out with considerable success.

Roume joined the siege and was received by Toussaint, Henri-Christophe and other members of the general staff. The final battle for the southern peninsula was about to commence. Roume had come, ostensibly in support of Toussaint, but he knew that the vexing question of Santo Domingo and his role as agent of the Directory as well as his position as high commissioner, would be at issue and was likely to assume a significance even greater than the outcome of the impending battle. Without much ado the subject was broached by Toussaint as Roume entered the tent where the generals were pouring over a plan of the town. Toussaint dismissed them all with a wave of his hand and pointed to a chair.

"We must now occupy every part of this country, my friend, the remaining enslaved people, over there, in Santo Domingo, must be freed and I must protect my flank in the event of an invasion," said Toussaint.

"This, you know, I cannot assent to."

"This I need for you to do now," replied Toussaint. Rising from his camp chair and walking to the tent's entrance, he pointed to the rain-washed encampment. "I must demonstrate to all of them, here, and also to those over there that I can liberate this entire island. I must now enforce the decree of 4th February, 1794. This calls for the implementation of all the clauses of the Peace of Basel. I need to do this, otherwise my army will fade away. They are tired of this war. And Rigaud will win here. The English will return."

"I have supported you, I have believed in you, God knows, but my orders from the Directory, from the Republic, are that I must hold Santo Domingo for the French Republic."

"You are the Directory's agent for both parts of this island, friend. Shall you lose one to save the other? Or lose both to the English? General Agé is poised to cross the border. . . Santo Domingo will fall before the end of the week. Please my friend, this is the hour of destiny, your own."

For a while, only the drumming of the rain falling on the canvas above them could be heard. In the glow of the oil lamps the two still figures, resplendent in their uniforms, appeared as a painting of a historic moment captured by an invisible master and saved for an unknown posterity.

"Toussaint, those epaulets and insignia you wear, that define your rank and place, are there by the leave of the Republic of France. You command the army in the name of the Directory. Both you

24: THE ADMIRAL'S BONES 1797

and I have a duty to follow. What you demand could trigger an invasion and be the end of all that you have made. Would you take that risk?"

"To be plain, Philippe, all that hardly matters, not now, not at this stage of my life." He shrugged, the gold of the epaulets sparkling in the lamp-light. He passed his hands across the plain blue tunic he wore and lifting his chin, said, "I need another groundswell of support now, another mass movement, of people, men. These must come from Santo Domingo. Fresh, en masse, to join this war and to face the English, and the French, for they will come and, we must win. They must make this land their own, for all time. Please, sign the order, that I may take possession of Santo Domingo."

"No, I cannot."

"You must know that you are little more than the official French Resident here, you have no power. In fact you are in my power." Toussaint said this flatly, his tone had hardened. "The Spaniards never really left. Sign and I will drive them out, to Cuba, to Mexico, to Spain."

Toussaint held out a quill in one hand and an ink bottle in the other. On a table before them was the order paper. Outside, the sound of rain had stopped and another noise had arisen in its place. It was the sound of angry men. Roume regarded Toussaint, he understood.

"Why do you need me to sign, you have the power, invade, just do it, give the command and it will be done."

"There is great danger here for you, my friend," Toussaint said sadly. "For your life to be spared, for you to leave this place alive, today, those out there must be convinced that you have joined them in the fight for the freedom. If you are perceived, for one moment, as one who stands against the liberation of Santo Domingo, I cannot guarantee your life. In truth I will have to let them kill you, so that I do not appear to shield you, a white, a massa, a traitor."

ROUME DE ST. LAURENT ... A MEMOIR

And all the remaining whites at Le Cap will die. That was the unspoken thought that crossed both their minds, as they looked at each other.

"Clearly you do not understand why and how the situation has changed. Do you want their blood on your hands? The tide has to be turned. I shall enter Santo Domingo over your corpse and put it to the sword. Sign now or die here."

"I demand that I be given leave to return to France," Roume said, knowing that this demand was hollow and that he would have to face a Directory that would condemn him to death for giving up his charge. Time, he needed time, there was no time. Outside, the partisans, their anger at him heightened by the haranguing he could plainly hear, were demanding his life: which was in the hands of this man. He straightened up to hide the painful twist of fear that had bitten into his stomach. From where he sat he could see Hyacinthe Moïse and hear Henri-Christophe pretending to control the angry men. For Philippe Roume it had become clear, he would have to do this.

"My choice is plain. France will condemn me if I am forced to choose between your interest and that of France."

"Stay and this nation will honour you in our pantheon of heroes. You will stand, an equal, with the men who have liberated the New World. See this as your time, come, join with us. Live with us."

Roume rose. A sense of unreality, of doom and the ending of things enveloped him, so overwhelming that he could barely walk. Taking the pen from Toussaint's hand, he dipped it in the inkwell and signed his name to what became known as the order of the 27th April, 1800.

The following morning, as they sat at breakfast in the morning's soft light that belied the rolling thunder of an artillery barrage, the news arrived that the Corsican general, whose acquaintance he had barely made in Paris in 1795, had assumed the powers of First

24: THE ADMIRAL'S BONES 1797

Consul of the French Republic. The Directory had ended. For Philippe Roume, this signalled a profound change in the status quo in France, one that, while placing him outside of events, caused him to understand that he had acquired a new master. He was to say, later, that he remembered then the words spoken by Soubise when she cautioned him that things in Paris could change and that he should be cautious with his decisions.

On the table before them was a Carib zemi made from obsidian crystal in the shape of woman, or so its appearance suggested.

Toussaint, indifferent to the news from Paris, was saying, "This brings good fortune, I am told."

"I shall now return to Santo Domingo, I must see how things go," said Roume, he was not sure why he said that, perhaps because he sensed a change, a different drum, a new beat, an unfamiliar rhythm, he searched for it. Careful, "And would be honoured to serve you, if you would have me."

"This I shall gladly do, my friend. We shall meet there, God willing, after this battle which appears to begin without us."

"How may I be of service now?"

"Give this zemi to Soubise with our compliments."

Reading from my Memoirs at George Street, Port of Spain, Trinidad, 1810

HELD HOSTAGE BY TOUSSAINT, 1803-05. He returned from Jacmel and the 'Guerre des Couteaux' and brought me a gift from Toussaint, a zemi, an ancient female figurine. To this day, every time I look at it I remember the old palace and how zemi made me feel.

His decision did not came as a surprise, but mostly it added more fear. I watched him closely over the following days. I could tell that he had altered something in the administration of the place as there was a presence, subtle at first and then more obvious, of Toussaint's people. When Toussaint, along with his brothers and other officers, arrived it was plain that the protocol had changed. The black and Spanish officials who had stood by Philippe melted away. Some left the island for Cuba, while others simply returned to their fincas in the countryside. The bonhomie surrounding Philippe's decision to allow Toussaint to occupy Santo Domingo evaporated, even as the messenger galloped into the courtyard of the palace on the night of a pyrotechnic display celebrating the union of the two halves of the island. As the explosions and showering lights fell to earth, he reported breathlessly that a party of emissaries from France had arrived at Port-au-Prince and were aboard a battleship anchored in the harbour. It was led by General Michel who was accompanied by Colonel Vincent and the mulatto Raimond. They had with them instructions for Philippe from Napoleon Bonaparte, now the First Consul, that the two parts of the island of Hispaniola must at all costs be kept separate. This, of course, did not prevent the occupation of this half of the island by forces dispatched by Toussaint.

Within months another upheaval was occasioned when Philippe met with General Michel here in Santo Domingo aboard the battleship. His decision to change his mind and break his commitment to Toussaint and rescind his order of 27th April was declared and published.

"You let them sail without us! Are you stupid? Toussaint will kill you! You could have explained yourself to Bonaparte, presented an invasion plan. Your friends, they could have helped us." I was beside myself, angry and desperate. Manon's birth had been an easy one, thank God, and there was only one thing on my mind now. To leave this place and to find my other child. My anger, I could see, dismayed him.

"What is the matter with you?" I shouted, but even as I did I could not help but see that he was not himself. "Philippe, are you ill? What is it?"

24: THE ADMIRAL'S BONES 1797

"General Michel's instructions came from the Consulate, from Napoleon himself, he demanded that the order be rescinded. Here, read it yourself. I had no choice. France is under a new administration, look, they left this with me."

He opened a large package that had arrived together with his sealed instructions. Wrapped in oilskin, it contained his new uniform, sash, sword, and hat, a bicorne with a general officer's plume. He was being refitted.

"Colonel Vincent will meet with Toussaint, something will be arranged. . ."

A cold dark fear descended upon me. This is the end. That he had made the wrong choice by reneging on his word to Toussaint was obvious to me. He argued that Napoleon Bonaparte was the power that now controlled France. That he was a servant of that power and so was Toussaint. But this I could not support.

"Look, we should have left aboard that ship. Bonaparte is in France, this man Toussaint is here. Either you beg his forgiveness and join in with him or we must leave at once, before it is too late."

Even as we argued late into the night, it was plain that he had made up his mind to stand the consequences here. I lay awake, the child at my breast, he sitting in a chair that he had brought close to a window that overlooked the courtyard. I thought to speak to him about Rosette, she had been on my mind, but I did not. He was staring into the night. I could see that he had lost something, the something that he called *prohairesis*—his volition to make the right choice. It had shaped and informed his instincts in the past. But now the shape changer, who had slipped from one role to the next, always in keeping with events and often to his own surprise, was, when he returned from Jacmel, outside of events. I felt so sorry for him. I awoke to find him standing at the foot of the bed. The morning sunlight seemed to have taken away the gloom of the previous night from his brow. The maids were bringing in breakfast. Outside, I could hear a bustle of activity. He was wearing the new uniform, it appeared huge on him.

"I am going to Toussaint, he is besieging Les Cayes. It will fall. This is Rigaud's last stand. I must be there. You shall be safe here. There is no need to worry."

He sat on the bed and with a finger pulled aside the sheet that covered the child. Her little face twisted into a smile or so he thought, as he too smiled. He was tired, I could see. He was going to Toussaint to try to extricate himself. He had made the wrong choice. The shape changer instinct that had landed him on his feet in the right place at the right time had betrayed him. Caught between identities Creole and French, he had chosen Napoleon the Corsican instead of Toussaint the Creole. He would not be remembered as a part of the wars of independence that brought the New World republics into existence.

I had no faith in a reconciliation. To me, events had taken a turn that possessed a quality of inevitability. These men, Toussaint, Henri-Christophe, Dessalines and all the others, were entranced with destiny. They were waltzing to a great and terrible melody that was only the overture to a fantastic drama. Philippe and I were no longer to be a part of that future.

There was much to do. Not trusting those around me, I made every effort to prepare secretly for a swift departure. I began by sewing all the jewels that I still had from my pirate past into my clothes. There were quite a few precious stones left, which I had prised out of their settings over the years so as to sell the gold in which they had been set. Several small diamonds, a quantity of good-sized ones, a few sapphires, small but good, the emerald necklace and what went with it. Some gold, small bars that I had had made for me upon arrival in Santo Domingo, all these I sewed and fitted as best I could into the dresses that I packed into one strong case. He had nothing, just clothes and boots.

24: THE ADMIRAL'S BONES 1797

I was watched each time I went out, which I did whenever the weather allowed. I went into the city market and took rides into the countryside and waited. I received a letter from Philippe, it was pathetic. He had had, he described, a great falling out with Toussaint. This had been occasioned by the arrival of a minister from France, a person called Forfait, with clear instructions from Napoleon to Toussaint not to enter Santo Domingo. This Philippe supported. It ended in something of a brawl in which Philippe was arrested by Hyacinthe Moïse, Toussaint's nephew, who placed him in a chicken-coop where he spent an indeterminable length of time. My God, what was happening to us? He wrote that Toussaint himself had released him, after a very long wait, and that he was coming to me.

He arrived. He was as a shadow of himself. His fine uniform filthy, they had not even given him the chance to clean himself. They had simply put him on a ship and sent him back to Santo Domingo. I bathed him, shaved him and cut his hair, which was now so thin and white that I could see his scalp, old and white. I told him what I had done in preparation for our departure. I told him the packed trunks were already aboard a schooner. He had hardly any interest in all this, saying that he was blamed by Toussaint for the failure of General Agé in his attempt to pacify Santo Domingo. He said that he had a report to write and left me. I found him asleep in his chair at his desk and helped him to bed.

The following day, news arrived that Toussaint had sent an army into Santo Domingo and would be entering the city within days. I pleaded with him to leave. Outside in the streets the people were in an uproar. Blacks were being attacked and killed by Spaniards, entire neighbourhoods were being looted. His orders to the garrison had been ignored.

I told him again that I had transport arranged, the wagon loaded, a horse. A schooner, a captain, to whom I had given gold, was waiting to take us.

"We must leave or they will arrest you. Toussaint has no choice, he has to arrest you when he enters the city."

"Leave me now. I must write a report. I must tell Napoleon that he should not enter this place. Leave me, please."

As I left him, his account of the vision that Doctor Mesmer had evoked that night in Paris returned to me with all the force of the supernatural. I stood on the stone verandah of the viceregal palace. Déjà vu overwhelmed the present. From then on it was like revisiting a dream.

I glanced up into the morning's light where, rising with the thermals, a vast congregation of vultures swirled and glided in a vortex of hot air. I looked across the wide lawn towards the main gate. There was a commotion taking place beyond it, shots, musketry and the flash of arms in the sunlight. A body of horsemen were coming at a rush. I turned and ran to the bedroom. The door was locked, I hammered on it and shouted for him to open. I could hear the footsteps of the men on the carriageway. I ran to the rear of the building that was now deserted. The staff had all left. I had anticipated this. I had already sent Manon ahead with the young woman in whom I had placed my trust, promising her a gold bar. The smell of smoke, hot and choking, came to me. My God, they have set the place on fire. Sure enough, I could hear the crackling sound. My heart racing, I ran panting round the verandah to the side where I could look through the tall glass doors into the bedroom. He was not at his writing desk. Horses. I thought, I must get horses. Running down the steps and into the garden I saw them, the five or six mounts that had brought the intruders. Mounting one and taking another by the bridle, I rode up the steps of the verandah and, picking up a flower pot, smashed the glass of the tall doors that led into the room just as the men started battering at its door.

"Come, come," I shouted, he stood in the middle of the room, "Come!" he hesitated and put a hand to his brow, what the hell was he thinking. "Come on, man!"

24: THE ADMIRAL'S BONES 1797

The horses were rearing and skidding on the stones, I felt that I could fall. "Philippe, come!"

He turned and looked at me. He was calling my name over and over again. This man is lost! "Come!"

It was then that he stumbled through the broken door and, taking the reins, mounted the nervous animal. As we turned I could see the men inside the room, some were on the terrace, one was levelling a pistol. I heard the shot as we bounded on to the lawn and galloped towards the gates.

It was not to be. Even as we drove the horses we could see the great iron gates swinging shut and the tall shape of Henri-Christophe standing before them.

It was now one humiliation after the next. Henri-Christophe was kind. He said he had set sail for Santo Domingo as soon as he heard that Hyacinthe Moïse had received instructions to arrest Philippe Roume. He had decided to come as quickly as he could, as he knew that it could mean Roume's death as well as my own. Nevertheless, the orders were the same. We were to be taken to Dondon in Saint-Domingue.

The wagon with our things, together with our child, had been intercepted.

"Everything will be taken there."

"There? What do you mean, there?" I screamed. I was completely out of my mind, mad, mad, mad. "My child. . ."

Henri-Christophe put his huge arms about me, Philippe was simply standing by.

"They were already on board the schooner that you hired. They have been taken off and put aboard the sloop that brought me here. I shall escort you to Dondon."

And so our retreat from Santo Domingo commenced. First the long journey which reversed the one that we had taken five years before.

Some days out, sitting in the shadow of the foresails, Philippe told me of his experience in the office. It was, he said, indeed a case of feeling that he had already experienced that situation, déjà vu. He had seen it all before with Doctor Mesmer, when he had been told that he would face a choice of life or death.

I told him that I too had that sense of the rewinding of the present. That I felt that everything was happening at the same time, then and now. "Did you face a choice?" I asked, for me there had been no choice.

"Yes. I did. With Mesmer, I experienced death. I knew that it was that all over. I might as well have died there, were it not for you and Manon."

He paused and looked at me with such love that it broke my heart to see him old like this and so pathetic.

"And Rosette, we shall find her when all of this is over."

When all of this is over. It was all over. We were kept aboard for some weeks after our arrival, anchored in the harbour road and finally came ashore at Le Cap in the dark of night. The docks were deserted, the oil lamps casting the barest of damp yellow light. I found myself listening to the soft lap and splash of the water on the quayside. I felt so alone. Without delay, we were put aboard the wagon that had been landed and harnessed to a team of sleepy mules. Holding the child close, I took his hand. Under a mounted escort we set out for Dondon, which lay about twenty miles inland. We were met there by Toussaint and Hyacinthe Moïse. I could not bring myself to look at them. It was all very official. There was something to sign. Toussaint claimed that he required Roume's authority to send more troops into Santo Domingo. What a farce. Philippe of course signed. It was the last official document that he put his hand to.

Dondon was a dilapidated old place. The prison in which we were kept was an abandoned distillery. We did well there. He slept

24: THE ADMIRAL'S BONES 1797

better and brightened. He spent time with his daughter. She was a lovely baby, she had his colouring, and bright eyes that I thought looked like my own. It was said at first that he had been detained for his safety, as there were some in the military who wanted to bring him to trial. We understood from Henri-Christophe that Toussaint had written to Bonaparte, asking approval for his imprisonment of Roume and for invading Santo Domingo. I almost lost my mind on hearing this. He then accused Philippe of plotting against him and impeding him at every turn. We learnt that he wrote: "Having decided to take possession of the former Spanish colony by force of arms I found myself obliged before setting out to invite citoyen Roume to desist from the performance of his duties and retire to Dondon until further orders. . . He awaits your command. When you want him, I shall send him to you."

ALMOST ONE YEAR LATER, an order from the Ministry of the Marine arrived. We were to be deported. The very next day, we were once more jolting along the road that led to Le Cap Français. It was a sullen little party led by Hyacinthe Moïse that gathered to make certain that all orders and instructions were obeyed and nothing would gainsay the inevitable. We were departing not in secret, but under a cloud.

The cloud was anonymity, which is somehow worse than disgrace. The sky above, the sunlight, the green of the countryside, all appeared to conspire in the sundering of the three of us from all of them and from this place. Around us the city that had been looted and plundered, bombarded and burnt, still managed to hum with the noise of commerce and the clatter of reconstruction. In between the ruins, people had erected shacks and tents and stalls. Houses were being constructed from the rubbish of war. Already I was disconnected from all this. As for him, he moved in the uncertain world of the aged. I would now have to mind him. Literally keep him in mind.

The wharf at Le Cap had been partitioned. We were to have a great space about us. A company of soldiers stood manfully in lines, keeping the curious at bay. We entered the long boat and it pulled away. There had been no one to say good bye to. In the bright heat of noon, the 110-gun ship of the line, *Révolutionnaire*, appeared as if painted on an enormous canvas. I saw that he was looking sadly at the mountains behind him. These were sharply etched in a paler blue than the sky. He tipped his hat. That was his goodbye to Saint-Domingue.

Philippe Rose Roume de Saint Laurent's outstanding career was now over. Napoleon, choosing to ignore his failures, had granted him a pension of three thousand five hundred francs a year on eighteenth Germinal, an. XI or, the eighth of April 1803. This ceased on his death, on that day in Paris, as he lay in my arms, our daughter Manon asleep beside us.

I was 38 years of age when we were married in 1799 and he, 56. He died on the 29th of September 1805. I had great difficulty in obtaining a pittance for myself and the child. I made several appeals to the Ministry that had commissioned him, in 1783, Commissary-General in the Ministry of the French Marine Royal and in the administration of Tobago as ordonnateur, commissioner to Saint-Domingue, high commissioner to Santo Domingo and finally, agent responsible for the entire island of Hispaniola. At one point, Napoleon was reminded, "Your majesty had refused this application because this woman is coloured." The note, however, continued, "but she dies from hunger and a pension of four hundred or five hundred francs is recommended." Napoleon ordered that a pension of six hundred francs a year be paid to me from the Naval Pensioners' Fund. He initialled the decree himself.

Saint-Domingue was a genie that would never return to its bottle. We would hear of how Toussaint in 1801 had promulgated an autonomist constitution for the colony, with himself as governor for life. The civil war that followed lasted over a year, with the

24: THE ADMIRAL'S BONES 1797

defeated Rigaud fleeing to Guadeloupe, then France, in August 1801. General Leclerc, Napoleon's brother-in-law, went with an army in February of 1802. This ended in his defeat. Leclerc's death signalled a final victory for the blacks, but not before Toussaint was arrested and deported to France where he died in prison on the 7th of April 1803. Napoleon walked away from the New World. He even sold La Louisiane, now called Louisiana to the newly constituted Republic of the United States. The great days of the French were over in the west.

25: FINDING CALYPSO

1793-1796

Reading from my Memoirs at George Street, Port of Spain, Trinidad, 1810

I HAD SPENT SEVERAL months at Jean de Pontieux's residence in St. George's on account of an illness that had finally taken my old friend to his grave. He had left me as the sole heir of his estate, which was considerable. I now possessed a townhouse, a country estate with several dozen slaves, comprising several domestics, and a quantity of praedial hands. I offered all their freedom, just thirteen actually accepted.

Caught in the mist of nostalgic reminiscences, as I prepared to return to La Fontenoy, I was informed that a stranger had come to the house and was waiting to see me in the sedan porch. Upon coming downstairs, I saw what appeared to be an elderly Carib man with a dark, expressionless face. He was taller than the average savage and was dressed in an ill-fitting suit of clothes, with alpagatas on his very large feet. There was a quantity of black feathers hanging in a bundle from the inside of his wide-brimmed hat. In imperfect French, mixed with Spanish and accompanied by odd gestures, he explained that he had come for the money.

"What money?" I asked, my heart in my mouth, as I knew that this had to with my daughter Rosette.

Refusing to sit in either the sedan porch or even the inner courtyard, he explained that his name was Sarusima, the Greater

25: FINDING CALYPSO 1793

Ani, and that he had been told that I was the mother of his adopted daughter and that I was offering a prize for information concerning her whereabouts.

"Yes, yes! Where is she, is she here, with you?" I asked breathlessly.

Apparently not. She had been "in his nest, but had flown away."

"Flown away? Flown away how? To where?"

To Tucapita perhaps, it would appear. "Tucapita? Where is that?"

"Amacuro. She is with the Warao people."

Whereupon he spat on the floor.

Ignoring that, I asked "Where is Amacuro?"

He explained that it was behind God's back somewhere in the Vice Royalty of New Granada. In the jungle, in the heart of the Orinoco delta. My God. I had seen the maps, it was an area as vast as the Low Countries. When, how?

I had last seen her in Tobago when she was two years old and I had left her in the care of Decima. That was in 1789, nineteen years ago. She was now an adult. I had always thought of her as a child. Here was a person who had seen her grow up. There were so many questions.

But this man! It was like talking to a stone effigy. At times I could swear he seemed like a giant bird on the point of losing its balance. With a lot of coaxing, accompanied by fruit offerings and finally rum and coffee, the old Carib agreed to sit with me at the cast-iron table in the inner courtyard.

I ordered my purse brought to me and placed several coins, a few silver and four gold, discreetly within his line of vision. Yzore Delpeche, the dwarf, seemed to alarm the savage, so, dismissing him, we were served by the hysterical kitchen maids who had never seen a Carib.

It would appear that Sarusima was a man of several worlds. He had travelled to many distant domains and not merely seen a great many marvels, but had become a marvel himself. His life experiences included being some kind of rodent before he became a full man, having passed a period when he was a fish in a river or perhaps it was a cougar on a cliff, I wasn't quite sure. He had also been a matamata, a type of turtle, but that was a while ago. At long last he had become a bird, a Greater Ani, I knew the bird. Large, blue-black, a cross between some sort of crow and a black parrot.

"A bird, eh?" I asked. At first I could not bring myself to believe what he related, especially because of the manner in which it was told. I had to pay very close attention. I knew that as a savage, he was speaking from an understanding of the world that was not shared by myself. I was very anxious, as this might be some sort of joke or hoax or just nothing at all.

Well, as it turned out, it was just after he had become a bird that he had decided to join a flock in Trinidad that was known to his people. He was familiar with Trinidad and proceeded to tell me all the famous men he had met there. He could not be hurried, so I ordered more coffee and waited as he listed their names. Suddenly I heard him say Roume.

"You met Roume, Philippe Roume?" I asked incredulously. He apparently had, and had been his guide, and at another time, he would tell me more of those meetings. Which he eventually did. But with impatience mounting, I probed him to continue with the story of Rosette, the version that would take us to her whereabouts. It would seem that Sarusima, having become a Greater Ani, started to build a nest in a naked indian tree on a hillside overlooking Port d'Espagne. The object of his utmost attention was a pretty bird of an indeterminable species, but was known to him to have connections with his mother's people who lived in the Tamana tepui. Her name was sometimes Cañari or at other times Louisa. As was common with the Greater Ani, where several females live communally and lay their eggs together in the same nest, his chosen one Cañari had an egg laid in her nest, and when it hatched it was a girl whose name was Rosette.

I almost fainted. I felt the blood leave my head as my heart pounded and I knew that I must have become very pale, as a cold sweat enveloped me from my hairline to the palms of my hands.

"How did she come to be in Cañari's nest?" I asked carefully. She had been given in exchange for a life, I gathered. A life? What could that mean? A woman had come to Cañari's family tree, where they all nested, and was dying. She was from another island, called Tobacco by some people, he knew it as Cohiba. She was a peddler of embroidery. She had a child with her, the child looked like a Spanish child. This child was all she possessed and she would exchange her for her life.

It was apparently not difficult for Cañari's people to postpone this woman's death. The arrangement was kept. The woman departed still alive, the child stayed.

"What was the woman's name?"

He did not know. What was she like? What kind of person, white, black, brown, like me?

He pointed at me.

Decima. Decima de la Forêt. That bitch had given away my child to the savages. I felt such a rage. I had to get up and stamp about, shouting for the wrath of hell to fall upon her and kill her dead. Sarusima regarded me with interest throughout my outburst.

There was more. I sat back down, breathless. The child that had come into the nest was later saved by a man who had come from a ship at Comucurapo, when a stampede of cattle occurred and he and Cañari were just about to embark to the mainland. Miraculously, it would appear.

The strange expressionless man explained that, being at the point of commencement of his mating period, when all occasions were propitious, he had no choice but to take the man who had saved the child with them to their new nesting ground across the water and to the Uaipán-tepui deep in the forest of Auyán, the home of the Caribs. This was where the man and the child continued to live as she grew. Because they were not of the Greater Ani people, she was brought up as a common song bird. They married each other and had their own nest until the war came, and then they left for the Amacuro. No, he did not know where in the vastness of the Amacuro they were, but he had heard that I had offered a prize for anyone with news of a young bird by the name of Rosette, and he had travelled all the way from the Uaipán-tepui to Grenada to tell me this story in exchange for gold. He pointed at the pile of coins. I passed them to him. He extracted the five Louis d'or and put them into a small bag that he wore around his neck.

"Who was this man whom she married?" I asked incredulous.

"The one who saved her," he said simply.

"What is his name? Tell me, who is he?"

"Stanislaus, the outlaw," he said, rising.

I saw nothing. Black. When I revived, I was lying on the flagstones at the feet of Sarusima with the house servants in even greater hysterics. Yzore Delpeche held the flintlock, longer than he was tall, cocked and loaded, and levelled at Sarusima's stomach.

I could not digest that Stanislaus de Barras had married Rosette. Stanislaus, the outlaw? Yes, Sarusima explained, he had been a fighter here in Grenada, and when the war against the English was lost, he and another man had run away. My daughter! Married! It must be another Stanislaus! Married! What the hell did that mean—in the middle of the bush?

My first impulse was to go to Venezuela with Sarusima. I was, however, persuaded by him that this would be impossible, as he could not accept responsibility for me, being, by my own understanding of his telling, well in excess of one hundred years old. I accepted

25: FINDING CALYPSO 1793

the absurdity of the idea as he, with his bird's eye view, brought home to me the sheer vastness of the wilderness of the continent. I had my own idea of this, as a result of my sailing experience. I had seen the bewildering medley of estuaries, the several caños or mouths of the Orinoco delta. His absolute unwillingness to help meant that this would necessitate the mounting of an expedition. In any event, there was a war raging in the eastern region of that country, where revolutionary fighters were attempting to dislodge the Spanish colonial establishment with a view to creating a republic.

It was just absurd. The idea that Stanislaus de Barras had married Rosette! My child. Philippe Roume's child. That wretch who had almost ruined my life! It made me ill. I drank rum, far too much, and actually became quite ill. I contracted a fever which took me to bed, where I remained for several weeks. The servants thought that I would die, I was prostrate with grief as though someone had indeed died. I had died. Rosette had died, and as for Stanislaus de Barras, he was a dead man. Of that I had made up my mind. Dead.

I DECIDED THAT I WOULD travel to Trinidad. Philippe Roume's Cedula of '83 had saved some French planters from the wrath of that maniac, Victor Hugues, who had guillotined the royalists in Guadeloupe and Sainte Lucie and other places. He had set himself up as despot in Guadeloupe, I heard, and was eventually sent to Cayenne.

Fédon and Stanislaus' massacres here in Grenada had displaced even more people to Trinidad, a mixed crowd of the survivors as well as the murderers of the survivors' relatives. These upheavals had increased and altered Trinidad's population. Until the English conquest in 1797, Trinidad was in a state of upheaval. The Spanish governor could not control the population, they mostly ignored him. Then it got the governor it deserved, an Englishman, a Colonel Picton. A roughneck, as murderous as the population,

465

who instituted public death and the exportation of the criminals, of which there were legion, to the Mainland.

There was another reason for my going to Trinidad: my share of the treasure that had been hidden away in the cave at Winn's Bay on Gaspar Percin's island. Over the years, I had not so much forgotten about the hoard of gold coins that Jean-Saint-Paul Funillière and I had hidden away on the island, as postponed thinking about it. I knew that gold attracts murder as caca attracts flies. So even to think about it was a dangerous business. I might talk in my sleep and be overheard by one of the servants, Vandelle for example. Or even Manon, who might tell of it. There was buried treasure all over these islands.

TRINIDAD IN 1807 was a hellish place and yet, like hell itself, more and more people arrived daily. The British occupied it since 1797 and have ruled over it with military rigour, while maintaining the cruel laws of Spain. This was understandable, as this island has been the recipient of the human debris of the revolution, the slave uprisings, massacres and all the dreadful happenings that have overtaken these islands in recent years.

There was no society. Everyone had just arrived, strangers to the place and to each other. Seeds of wide variety flung down that would all grow in the same furrow, unknown and alien to each other. With the exception of less than half a dozen Spaniards of long-standing residence, a few French families and the *gens de couleur libres* who formed the majority of free people, the place was awash with thousands of refugees of every race and distinction.

Trinidad was also on the periphery of a revolutionary war, a continental war that was being conducted, organised and implemented from here. In Trinidad, they raised battalions that crossed over the Gulf of Paria and entered the jungle to go in search of the Spanish army.

25: FINDING CALYPSO 1793

There was a frenzy of construction taking place day and night. Large wooden buildings were going up at a pace, haphazardly built, crooked and dangerous. Unlike in Grenada, there was no authority here that would condemn faulty construction, people simply did as they pleased. I had purchased a property towards the eastern end of the Plaza del Marina, the main square, close by the mangrove shore. It was almost a complete house. It had a stone floor that was raised a foot or more from the ground— that made it a mansion, I was told. I had with me Manon, who was eight and growing to resemble Philippe more with each passing day, the girl Vandelle, Delpeche, to whom I had given freedom, and three strong men, all slaves. I was expecting, hoping that Sarusima would come with news of Rosette from the down the Main.

Settling in, one night I was haunted by a sense of unease. Invasion? Earthquake and tidal wave? What? Vandelle arrived with a decoction of lime-bud tea. It was meant to relax us and put us all to sleep. It worked on them. I was haunted and I must have looked the part, as I startled Delpeche out of his wits when I appeared on the back gallery where he was sitting smoking his pipe.

"What are you smoking in that?" I asked. "It does not smell like your usual black tobacco."

"It gone out, Miss," he answered, rising on his short legs and pointing outside at the sky. "Something burning, look!"

He said this with such alarm in his voice that it made my heart leap. We both hurried to the side of the house and looked up into the sky, to the north. There it was, a huge, black-red billowing mass of smoke, with sparks and burning cinders rising. "Fire!" we shouted in unison, "Fire!" Then I heard it, suddenly, like a roar, like a grinding groaning wind that was filled with a sharp crackling, snapping sound.

The great fire of Port of Spain—as the town's name had been rendered by the English—of March 1808 was the turning point in many lives. It was certainly so in my own life.

Almost the entire place, some seven or eight blocks, including my own "mansion", were burnt to the ground that night.

WE WERE UNDER SAIL, saved by a man whom I had met in a chance encounter more than twelve years before in Saint-Domingue. Jean Baptiste Bideau, a Saint Lucian mulatto, republican patriot and skipper of the two-masted schooner *Botón de Rosa*.

Delpeche had acted with alacrity. He had roused the men who lay sprawled about their quarters in the sleep of the exhausted, while I shook Vandelle awake and took the money belt from beneath the mattress and tied it round my waist. Rousing Manon, I ran out towards a track that led to the water's edge, the fire was already quite close. The shifting wind was taking it in several directions and it was propelled by explosions coming from gunpowder stores in different parts of the town. I could now hear and see the towering flames clearly and felt the heat on my face. In the distance, along the muddy shore, I could make out the redoubt and the black outlines of its guns, the hut used by the soldiers and the flagpole. Manon and I ran towards it. I knew that I must leave this place or be drowned or burnt to death. This was when I made out the towering form of a dark-skinned man, who stood head and shoulders above the rest. I knew him, I knew that man!

"Hey, hey! Captain Bideau, captain!" I shouted, I saw him turn towards us. "Captain Bideau, it is I, Soubise, Philippe Roume's wife, this is his daughter, please help us, help us, we must leave this place, please."

His response was immediate. He took the child and called sharply into the darkness around him, and at once there were several seamen about us with flambeaux lighting darkly our faces. Delpeche appeared with the men carrying our boxes he had had the wit to pack with the few possessions that we had brought with us to Trinidad.

25: FINDING CALYPSO 1793

"Come, Soubise, look, we can only take two or three aboard the long boat, as we came for stores and we are loaded to the gunwales."

"Please, this is my maid and the dwarf is as a child, please."

"Alright, one box, alright two."

I dismissed the young men, telling them that they were now free. Already there was a curious crowd gathering around us, red wavering flambeaux sent reflections across the black water. We made our way through the sucking mud, our naked feet assailed by the spikes of sea eggs, painful as sharp needles. After we were hauled quickly on board the overloaded boat was pushed out and away, as the sailors swinging aboard took to the oars and pulled towards the shapely silhouette of the *Botón de Rosa* which was anchored in the stream.

We were soon far out on the rolling Gulf, the night sky illuminated by the gigantic bonfire blazing high. I had settled the child and her nurse below decks in the tiny space that had been assigned to us by the captain. Later I stood beside him on the poop deck, he at the wheel, coaxing the rising wind into her sails. In the east behind us the sky was showing the first hint of a pewter dawn.

"Güiria?"

"Yes, the war for the freedom of this continent commences. Spain has fallen to Napoleon. Her colonies will now break away." He spoke above the wind. "Francisco Miranda and the English are preparing an invasion of Terra Firma and we shall be there."

"Who is that?"

"Miranda? The great man of the Americas!"

"Oh for God's sake, not another one."

"Come Pedro, take her, take the wheel," he called to the coxswain who had come up with steaming mugs of coffee, "take her, keep her bearing north-north-west." He pointed, "Here, there," at the compass. I was admiring a small cannon, an Italian swivel gun, bolted to the transom.

"Nice little gun, got it in Grenada from Signor Commissiong, a Genoese sail maker. Come, you and I shall talk awhile." We settled amidships and sat in the wind upon the crates and bundles that had been loaded the night before. I explained to him the need to find Rosette. As expected, being at sea had a rousing effect on Marianne. Jean Baptiste Bideau was a handsome man. A fine-featured mulatto, dark, graying at the temples, with a commanding personality and nice manners, I liked him. "I must find her. You can put us off at your next port of call."

From what he said, I understood that he was indeed bound for the coastal town of Güiria. He was taking arms, ammunition and a variety of items that included clothes, cooking pots, rum, guns, axes and smoked meat to rebels who were attempting to divert Spanish troops towards the eastern coastal regions. "Wonderful," I said sarcastically, taking strands of hair out of my mouth while holding down my nightdress that the wind had gotten into.

"I have all that coming out of my ears. I lived, breathed and almost died of it," I told him, sipping my coffee.

"And you?" he asked. "Güiria is primitive. You shall need bodyguards. I noticed the money belt."

I had thought about it. Fate had sent that fire and this man into my life, here I was being taken to the wild coast of Venezuela. I told him something of what Sarusima had said. He listened carefully, curious, and did not pry, but seemed to think that this story was not a remarkable or unusual one. The upheavals of the times bred separations, deaths, unknown and unrecorded. Loss was the lot that was expected in those times and in these places.

"Luck, however, has a hand to play," I said, the morning sunlight now hot upon us. I noticed that my night dress was even more inappropriate by day than it had been in the night when I climbed

25: FINDING CALYPSO 1793

aboard. I said that, rising, steadying myself on his tough shoulder. "With your permission, captain, I must retire."

That evening I joined the captain at his table. We were within sight of Güiria, but would not enter its harbour until daybreak.

"It is a dangerous place," he said, "and I have no idea who is in control. I think you better stay aboard for the time being."

During the night there were explosions and the sound of musketry coming from the town. By morning I could see spirals of smoke rising in the still air.

"The patriots have held off an attack. We shall set about getting the supplies ashore," he said, clambering down a ladder into the ship's boat. Later that morning, I was half dozing in the shadow of a furled sail amidst the crates, barrels and various tools lying about. Manon and Vandelle were looking at the hands aloft in the rigging, making ready to sail with the changing tide, when I saw a large outrigger canoe under sail rounding the point and quickly making towards us.

"Sail, sail, off your larboard bow," I shouted, "enemy sail, look, look!"

The men above were already lowering themselves and others were coming up on deck.

"Look, another," I shouted, and to Vandelle, "take Manon below and stay there. Lock the door, go, go."

"Repel the boarders!" I screamed at the top of my lungs. Already I could hear the thud of the outrigger against the hull. The first garabato, an iron hook, hit the deck and was being dragged towards the rail. I grabbed an axe and chopped at the rope, which snapped away. Seizing the large grappling hook I ran to the gunwale and hurled it overboard. I heard a howl as several other garabatos attached themselves to various parts of the deck. The crew were ready to attend to this attack and several of the boarders were engaged with pistol, cutlass and sword. I seized a cutlass from the hand of a dead sailor in time to bring it down hard on the head of a boarder and turned to run up to the poop deck so as to get a better view. In the middle distance, to westward, a sloop flying the Spanish ensign was bearing down hard on us. From shore, the *Botón de Rosa*'s boat with the captain aboard was coming as fast as the six men on the oars could manage.

"Sail abeam!" I shouted, but I could see that they had about as much as they could handle. A gun, I must get a gun. And there was one. The swivel gun mounted on the transom rail, grapeshot, powder. Flint? It was all there. To do this now? But it all came back to me. I got the first round off just as the sloop was drawing abreast. Even as the smoke enveloped the poop I could see the devastation that the swinging iron balls connected by short chains had wrought on the boarding party, with the sloop's captain in its midst. I could hear screams and shouted commands. They would have to catch themselves to make a return run. Already I was reloading. What a handy little gun. On deck the fight was going our way, some were leaving, overboard. I reloaded and fired, I saw the grapeshot rattle over the Spaniard's stern and into her bridge. Aboard the *Botón de Rosa*, the boarders were being finished off with a pistol shot or the swift stroke of a sharp cutlass. God damn it, I loved the action.

The captain was aboard. Already I could hear my praises shouted by the excited sailors. I stood there looking down, one hand on the still hot barrel, and waved.

"Welcome aboard, Captain Bideau!" I said with a mock salute. This brought a wild cheer from all on deck. I had not been this pleased with myself in years.

We quickly prepared the *Botón de Rosa* to sail westward, hoping not to meet a Spanish coastal patrol. Bideau told me that in Güiria, a woman with whom he did business had said that there was a rumour of a white man and a child who had been taken in by the Warao people in the Amacuro delta. But there were many similar stories and this was ten years ago or more.

"Well, ten years ago would be about right. Where are these people? I must get to them."

"These people do not live in one place. And there are many of them scattered all over the delta. The area is enormous, it is huge, about half the size of France."

"What am I to do? Look at where I am, put me ashore, I have to make a start."

I looked at him. This man can help, can help me. I saw that he was thinking about it. After all, I had saved his ship.

THE TUCUPITA ADVENTURE, 1808. I had no idea of what it would take to go there. I had money, gold, and more at home in Grenada buried under the floor at La Fontenoy, and even more in a strong box in the Registrar General's office in Saint George's. Not to mention what might still remain in the cave on Gasper's island.

"I have resources. Look."

"Put that away," Bideau said sternly.

"What does it take?"

"It takes time."

"And you are busy with a war to change the world."

These men. Why do I always have to meet men who are busy trying to change the world. But I understood. It would take time mounting an expedition. Sarusima had explained the nature of the environment, the dangers which were legion, in his way, which I suppose was correct.

We were beating up the Paria peninsula in a stiff breeze, making for the Grand Boca en route to Margarita. Bideau was quite surprised by what I had to say about myself. He had had entirely the wrong impression when we first met in Santo Domingo; then he believed that I was some sort of camp follower. Roume's woman. Well, that was true in many ways. But, on the long tack north of the Paria coast I gave, for the first time to anyone, an account of the last twenty years of my life. I could see amazement in his eyes as I related how Funillière taught me the use of weapons and how to sail. I described Tobago and my life with Philippe Roume, then the barbarity of the mass executions I had witnessed in Paris. That I, in my youth, had been a corsair, an outlaw, was to him, I could see, unbelievable.

"You knew Toussaint then, you say you met him, he spoke to you?"

His incredulity was as touching as a child's.

"Yes, I danced with him, he was the witness at our wedding."

Bideau sat in silence for a long time and listened as I spoke of Philippe, his achievements, our adventures.

"Just a few of the people in Trinidad know of his existence," I told him, "only the French families from Grenada, the Cedulants, as they call themselves. And his mother's relatives of course. He has already been reinvented by them, turned into a sort of redeemer, a person too good to be true. He was not like that at all."

"What was he like then?"

"People said he was fickle. I came to know that he was a man who could reinvent himself. He was a man who lived in the present. He was not fastened to the past, which is like nature, fixed, forever repeating itself. He understood that the present, at any given moment, determines the past and the future. He was a New World man, like yourself."

All this appeared to consume Bideau, as he took on a look of reflective astonishment. His astonishment stayed with him for days. Naturally I had left out all compromising aspects of my past, such as my relationship with 'the white man who had been taken by the Warao people,' and his relationship with my daughter as related to me by Sarusima. Neither did I mention the treasure in Winn's Bay.

25: FINDING CALYPSO 1793

"I shall take you to Tucupita."

I felt so relieved, so overwhelmed that I had to pretend that my hair had fallen into my eyes. All I could do was nod and smile. He had the grace to look away.

"I shall take you there, to Tucupita. However, before that, arrangements must be made with regard to your child. She cannot go on that river. Death stalks at every bend, strange currents that could carry a boat away, to waterfalls or sandbars. You get stuck, you die. Hostile savages and every imaginable misery. You will have to dress like a man." He laughed, a deep rumble.

"I shall, I have done that before. From tomorrow I will work the foredeck, I need to put some strength into my back. How's that?"

"Please yourself. By the day after tomorrow, we should be in Margarita. I shall arrange something. I have an old friend, a comrade from another time. You shall need to establish a household, get the right people around you, in the meantime, be my guest." He pointed at the rigging and the foresails.

The following morning, in spite of my years, I was barefoot and aloft, to the delight of all hands. It was not easy to become familiar with the ropes, after all, it was more than twenty-five years since my pirate days. I had all my teeth, and I was able. Marianne was returning, I noticed, when I sat down to share a pipe of tobacco with two grinning swabs, my mates on the *Botón de Rosa*'s foredeck.

I was the first to see the castle of Juan Griego at Margarita, a massive fortress overlooking the bay that was so blue that it gave the impression that the sky had fallen. This fortress was a place of some consequence in the Americas. I heard it had been destroyed by successive earthquakes, fires, and pirate attacks in the past. Yet it had always been rebuilt by the enthusiasm of the gold speculators. From the *Botón de Rosa*'s lookout it appeared dazzlingly white and charmingly European after the filth of Port d'Espagne and what I had seen of Güiria. Captain Bideau took us into the harbour and dropped anchor about half a mile from the quayside. He wanted to make certain that there were no bad surprises awaiting. After his scouting party returned with the information that the town was empty of those who would wish him captured or dead, we came ashore to meet Bideau's friend Pedro de Sucre and found him in his herb garden.

By late evening I was, along with Manon, Vandelle and Delpeche, comfortably ensconced in a newly built, inside and out whitewashed, house. Quite small, it was adjacent to the main house, which itself was situated on a bushy hilltop overlooking the wide bay. We were conducted to it by Antonio de Sucre, the teenage son of our host.

A few important things had been agreed upon, not the least of which was that Manon would be placed in the care of the extended Sucre family. Our departure for the Amacuro delta was imminent. I noticed that Bideau looked closely at me as I attempted to hide my feelings. I had left a daughter behind once before and when the discussion focused on the likelihood that Rosette might not want to be rescued and that her husband or companion might forcefully resent an intrusion into their affairs, I suppose I became hysterical.

"She is my child and I will kill him," I screamed, I was shaking, my entire body was twitching and jumping like a fish out of water.

"She means it, my friend," Bideau said seriously, "this is no ordinary woman. I had not known her a week and she saved my ship from the patrol."

I offered him money. He replied that I could give what I chose to. I gave him half of all I had with me. He smirked and pocketed the gold. I kissed and hugged Manon and took away with me the memory of her fragile and iridescent smile.

Botón de Rosa sailed from Juan Griego bay. We were bound for the delta of the Amacuro and the Caño Manamo, a major branch of the Orinoco.

25: FINDING CALYPSO 1793

Bypassing the coastal hamlets and evading the Spanish sloops of war, we, early one morning, silently entered the gossamer vastness of the delta. I stood upon the *Botón de Rosa*'s bowsprit as she was drawn forward, inexorably, by an invisible force that lay beneath the glass-like surface. By midday, the vast estuary had brightened and something of its boundlessness could be imagined. About us an invisible horizon belied the fact that we were now several miles inland. As twilight fell, we watched as the first stars appeared.

The approaching night contained the fleeing yells of unseen animals and the howls of troops of monkeys, telling of bedtime escapades, of contentions for the comfortable branch or fork or hole, as rain would surely fall before the dawn. An intermezzo followed; this featured an à capella performance, a royal croaking, a bass chorus of toads. All competed for encores as the curtain of night was flung: bellowing, whistling and pinging in accompaniment of independent soloists, all chanting as a trope to plainchant. A silence suddenly spoke after a guttural snort, followed by a low snarl, turning to a frightening growl, then into a terrifying roar. Human shrieking followed, to the echo. Then, a slow and menacing quiet. We all turned our heads and peered into the darkness.

From far away something laughed hysterically. This laugh was taken up and carried abroad, then, startlingly close, as though the laughing creature had come amongst us, invisibly. Men sat in silence, refusing to allow their most primaeval fears to penetrate an already threadbare sanity. Thank goodness for the swarming mosquitoes and their string assemblage, as this sent us all off to bed.

It was not until the following fore-day morning that we could see, rising from the rolling mists, a distant shoreline, outlined by the black silhouettes of gigantic growths that towered above the dense jungle.

We travelled beneath a hot mother-of-pearl sky, taken upstream by the current and propelled by gentle puffs that billowed the mainsail's canvas from time to time. These puffs, inundated with the river's warm mammalian smells, breathed like the slow exhalations of some gigantic antediluvian creature into whose maw we had inadvertently entered. We would have appeared as tiny and insignificant to the high-flying birds that circled far above, as they to us were mere specks in a vastness of sky and air.

And still the great river turned and meandered. Bideau, feeling for the current, threaded his way past gleaming white sandbanks and forested islands. Huge drifts of floating vegetation and gigantic half-submerged logs went slowly by.

Never was a person in sight, although I observed rafts and canoes drawn up alongside broken piers, black and rotted, lonely reminders of men abandoned to die of solitude.

Bideau appeared impervious to the change of scene and spent his days overseeing repairs. He established a routine and worked the men in shifts. I would come to understand the reason for this.

At a distance, hard to gauge in the shimmering heat, the river narrowed, to curve again. The wind had picked up; we set a twenty-four hour watch for treacherous sandbanks and the sunken carcasses of giant trees, and anchored at night, huddling and sweating, as swarms of mosquitoes devoured us in the airless humidity. Then the nightly jungle nocturne commenced, its overture an ear-piercing aria, as millions of insects, singing as one, establishing a sonic barrier against the bats that swarmed in their millions and swooped in ominous moving clouds over the river.

Sleeping was more like hiding from the night, which carried, along with its raucous cacophony, a damp and clinging heat. One prayed to sleep the night through, because to be awakened by an unidentified sound would mean listening to the river. This could easily draw the imagination to out-do even the wildest dreams, as images of forms, swift or lugubrious, tentacled or fanged, with eyes just upon the still surface, long necks submerged that could recoil and strike with claws and tear this ship apart, floated in the mind's eye.

25: FINDING CALYPSO 1793

There were creatures in the water, I had seen them, river dolphins, giant otters, the sirenia manatees on the sandbanks wailing, calling like a stricken woman, nursing their young from their pendulous breasts. There were huge turtles and giant crocodiles in droves with mouths open wide, catching yellow butterflies or simply basking, to slide suddenly in a deadly slither through the mud and into the river to devour a victim quite unseen, as the flocks of parrots screamed to fly away, repeating in a deteriorating doggerel all that they had seen and heard.

Bideau organised hunting parties to go beyond the mangrove swamp that lined the river to raise morale and to resupply the stores with fresh meat. They came upon deserted villages with smoking fires, the smell of their recent inhabitants lingering. We realized some weeks before that we were being watched day and night. That we saw no human being was one aspect of the macabre world in which we moved or stopped.

It was with great relief that I saw the wavering reflection of the settlement of Tucupita appear. Some had started to doubt its existence, as increasingly members of the crew slipped into a forgetful form of melancholy: a state of nostalgia, inculcating brooding silences that maintained longings, wistful or suicidal, as they gazed into the glass-like surface of the changeless river, becoming convinced that there was to be no tomorrow and that they would be trapped perpetually in today.

Built on stilts in the shallow water, Tucupita was hugged into the humid armpit of a bend in the river, from which scores of children dived into the still water, while their elders slowly waved, not entirely sure whether we were illusions generated by their boredom. Behind these water dwellers and wrapped in a cloud of river mists and cooking fire smoke were more palm-covered shacks, haphazardly placed. These were scattered along the shore to dwindle away into the thick undergrowth. Mangrove, fern and palm forest met the high woods here. High in the branches of the towering trees that emerged between the hovels and improvised lean-tos, I could see large cages that contained the grinning skull boxes and bones of now forgotten conquistadors in their rusting armour.

Curious and gaping the people began to gather, hardly daring to come closer. I could smell them, they smelt like crustaceans, like crabs or fresh-water fish, like what we call wabeen, sort of dank, not yet stink. The children, all with enormous eyes, shy yet curious, naked and so identical. Some held sakiwinkis, little monkeys, squirrels, and other forest creatures. They were tiny, the children. And yet others emerged, slipping from the hovels like the resurrected dead at the end of days. They stood about, many of the women were almost naked, some men wore tattered clothes, rags, their feet bare, their arms hung listlessly at their sides. The women were the strangest, as there was a remoteness in their expressions, while the men appeared as freshly awakened from a collective stupor. They commenced, I saw, to slip into the present, as one would into working clothes. They were all Caribs, although some were mixed.

A white man appeared, perhaps a Spaniard, he may have been always there, as the crowd had simply parted, leaving him to stand alone. Behind me I could hear several clicks as primed flintlocks were cocked. Bideau, who was the last to come ashore, made his way briskly forward, his hand outstretched.

"Hello my friend, I greet you well," he boomed, using a Spanish Patois of the Mosquito Coast, "we are here in search of someone who came amongst you some years ago, a Frenchman and a young girl. We hope that you can be of assistance."

The man hesitated, then took Bideau's hand and replied in what I recognised as unaccented Spanish, "Welcome to Tucupita, friend, please tell your men that there is no need to have their weapons at the ready as there are no outlaws amongst us. I am Father Ibaiguren."

The encomienda of Tucupita had been established in a past so remote that it defied history, by the ones in those baskets high above in the giant trees, five Franciscans and three Spaniards of

25: FINDING CALYPSO 1793

noble birth. They had given their lives in defence of this outpost of civilisation at a time when Philip of Spain was contemplating marriage with Mary of England. He said this with the simplicity of someone who might have been there.

"Saints in heaven all, they have always interceded on our behalf with the merciful Lord of Hosts."

There came a mumbled "Amen" from the assembled inhabitants of Tucupita.

"The ones you seek were here last year, at the end of the rainy season. He inhabits the Brazzo Macareo water and lives there with a woman and a child, a boy of three years, and some other outcasts."

Coming forward I said to the priest, "You saw them, the woman and the child, here?"

"Yes, here," he pointed to the ground, "they are white, he is French, he is an outlaw, she has become one of them. They have taken the ways of the Warao. The woman knows no other way."

No other way.

"How far away is the Brazzo Macareo water?" asked Bideau.

"Your ship will not take you there. This is as far as you can go. Beyond are the rapids, then the falls. The Brazzo Macareo water lies overland, it is a lagoon. Five, perhaps six days' journey away."

"Five days away," I gasped, I could hardly speak, he looked at me.

"She is your child?" He asked this simply and smiled sadly.

I nodded and restrained myself, yet the tears came. I did not want them to see me weep, so I turned and ran away blindly into the swirling mists. I heard Bideau say, "Leave her alone, she will catch herself."

I did, after I had stumbled and fallen on the rocks along the river's bank and staggered about with my fist in my mouth, biting on it hard.

We set out at dawn the following day. The track almost immediately gave way to a thick undergrowth through which the men hacked with machetes, hardly clearing a way through masses of what they called, bejuco de cadena, the travellers' vine. All around the jungle screamed and wailed, yelled, croaked, and fluttered; creatures bolted at our approach, to stand still just some paces away to stare at us, so unused were they to humans. We walked, we camped. I ate what was given to me. I had seen the thick snake hacked to chunks and thrown into the pot and the iguana eggs, these were devoured with hot peppers.

One morning I lingered in my hammock, staring through the entrance of the shed that had been built for me the night before, when I saw a familiar figure standing amongst the large wet shiny heart-shaped leaves. It was Sarusima. Ageless. Immobile, as if cast in bronze, black feathers and all. He was ignored by the Carib porters who passed to and fro before him, perhaps he had assumed invisibility. He was looking directly at me. I rose immediately and went to him, even as I walked he turned away. I hurried, being afraid that he would vanish, he didn't. I could see the black feathers moving steadily on.

"Hey, hey, wait up," came a shout from behind me, it was Bideau. I could not answer, I had no words, I hardly touched the ground as I sped along behind the clutch of black feathers. On and on we went, at quite a pace, the cold morning air shaping my hot breath. Bideau had caught up with me and we began to run, so swiftly did the old Carib move through the undergrowth. I noticed that the vegetation had changed, this was a mangrove swamp that we were now entering.

The Carib kept a pace, always staying on a narrow dry track that wound about the tangled mangrove forest. Only once did he pause, I saw it almost instantly, a viper on the path, coiled and erect, swaying in its own deadly wind. He whispered and it turned away. And so it continued for more than an hour until in the shifting

25: FINDING CALYPSO 1793

dappled light I could make out what looked like a body of water. A lake, misty-green, still and dull, surrounded by the forest.

Out of breath, Bideau and I caught up with the Carib who stood calmly on the shore. So still, this man. He seemed like a tree. Through the light haze that hovered over the water I could make out an island. As the air cleared I realised that it was in fact a raft, huge, made of gigantic logs lashed together. These, over time, had taken on the look of an island because it was covered with shrubbery and a few trees, some large, in between the lean-tos. I could make out a hut or several huts and a thin column of smoke that rose pale blue to curl an arabesque in the morning air. Then, to my surprise, I saw her, she appeared out of the water and with practiced ease, gained the raft and stood there in the sunlight, tall and slim and shimmering white. Rosette.

I caught my breath, to call. Bideau placed his hand on my arm and motioned silence and signalled wait.

God damn it! What was there to wait for! There she was! Then I saw a man appear, tall and gaunt, grey hair down to his waist. A beard, grey, he had a clutch of feathers in his hair, black, like Sarusima's. Stanislaus! He was as naked as she. He held the hand of a small boy, whose voice I could hear coming across the water. A child's enquiry. Asking, what? It broke my heart, I wept, silently, in Bideau's arms as Sarusima stepped out into the water. To our amazement he did not sink, but strode briskly out towards the raft, the water splashing round his feet as though he was walking upon a rain-washed pavement. In fact he was. A path made of stone lay just beneath the surface of the water. A long narrow way, made of a single giant slab of rock. Seeing him approach Stanislaus lowered a wooden bridge, which fell with a splash before the Carib who calmly climbed onto it. The two men stood there, the morning sunlight green and gold about them, talking for some time. We waited. I could see Sarusima tottering forward, tilting back, balancing on the moment as he spoke. The woman, Rosette, my child, was occupied with the things that occupy women who are concerned with the fire, the child, the arranging of life, on this so small floating world of theirs.

Stanislaus turned and said something and together with Sarusima descended the plank. They walked in single file across the water towards us. I felt faint as they neared. I could see him clearly now, his features gaunt and drawn with sunken eyes. I could see him search me out and find me standing next to Bideau in the thicket of ferns and prickly shrubbery. My heart was racing, I felt Bideau's arm around me as my knees gave way. He held me up and as Stanislaus drew closer he released me.

"You know him?" I nodded. "Yes."

He stood before us, naked, with an array of black feathers in his hair and something that hung from his groin, a wooden tube of sorts that contained his privates. I looked at it, at him, into his eyes, yes, it was he. Stanislaus de Barras, grown old.

"Marianne, is that you?" His low voice was thickly accented.

"Yes. Stanislaus, it is me. What have you been doing, living here? Is that Rosette, my daughter Rosette?"

"Yes, she was Rosette," he said, as if recalling a thing long out of mind. The bitch. I flung myself at him, catching him across the face and chest with the stick that had aided me throughout this trek. I struck him again on the head, he did not move, then again across the shoulders, hard and again. Bideau grabbed my arm and took the stick away. I was out of breath and falling over. No one said a word. On the raft I could see Rosette and the child standing, looking towards us.

"Come," said the Carib, teetering over, almost losing his balance, "come and meet the bird that came into my nest and then flew away."

He said this quietly, now teetering backwards, in a voice that came from somewhere inside his body as I did not see his mouth move. I nodded, breathing hard, tears pouring. He took me by the

25: FINDING CALYPSO 1793

hand and I remembered another hand, that of another old man, who had taken mine in his so many years ago. It felt the same, like holding a plank of wood. I found that all the rage, all the turmoil in my mind had left me. I just wanted to make sure that it was she, and see her.

We walked on the water swiftly towards the raft that rose up gently on the still water, the two figures becoming clearer, plainer. She was so beautiful to see. Her body was nude except for some string about her waist, from which hung a small apron, covered with a pattern of beadwork, and there was an amulet around her neck. Her features were so fine, her eyebrows, black, thin and arched; her eyes were dark and large. I could see her father, when he was young, in her face.

"Rosette," I croaked. "Rosette."

She stared at me with a swift jerky movement of her head, slightly tilted to one side, so quick. And just as quickly towards Sarusima. She clucked several times and glanced at me without moving her profile away from him. He answered slowly, deeply, movingly in a tongue so strange it may have been the low murmuring, the lowering of some old beast. I stood there looking at her, her long black hair hanging straight partly down her shapely back and partly across her round shoulders and over her small breasts. She listened, I could tell, intensely, quickly glancing at me, her eyes, black, bright and unblinking. With her round face and pointed chin, she appeared like a bird. Of course she did. She was raised as a bird. I felt mirth, an urge to laugh, I suppose I did. This was incredible. I looked around towards the far shore. Between the ferns I could see Bideau and Stanislaus standing apart from the porters who had all sat down and had started a fire. They carry fire in a stone jar with them. To cook a snake, I thought, and felt hysteria rising once again as my stomach tightened to repress laughter.

And yet these two before me spoke, making little clicks, and peeps and muttering long sing song monologues in what sounded vaguely like French Patois. She whistled softly sometimes as if confiding a confidence. It must be a very slow language, I thought. Suddenly she turned her body towards me and moved her head in a small circle never taking her eyes away, her little mouth pursed as if to kiss. I understood the movement, it was her beak. Oh, what a beautiful little bird, I could see her now, see the lovely perfect bird that she had become, oh dear, oh dear. I held myself as still as I could manage as she made a little hop and with her pretty hands flat along her body she brought her face up close to mine, her large bright eye looking directly into mine. I could smell her, she smelt like a flower, strange and undiscovered, I felt her nose, small and pointed, along my cheek as it went into my ear. Oh, my god, I could have died of love. I heard her click and click again and thrill, so softly into a low sweet whistle. I heard her say something in a low whisper, it may have been French. I nodded and nodded, I could hardly see her, my eyes had overflowed. She glanced up at me, her lovely head tilted to one side, I could see the bird, oh, I held her, I could feel her shiver, flutter in my arms, I could feel her arms around me holding me as close as I held her. I could feel her little heart beating at a rate. This wild child, this beauty that Philippe Roume and I had created so long ago on the leeward coast of Tobago.

The wind came and blew about us, lifting the dry carat leaves of her nest. She glanced swiftly about her, the boy was sitting at our feet, looking up at us two. He smiled, his eyes as bright as licked stones. I could see myself in them.

"HE WAS ONCE YOUR LOVER?" Over the flickering firelight, Jean Baptiste Bideau stared at me, incredulous. Evidently I continued to amaze him.

"Yes, when we were young, children, in Grenada on the plantation. Then I met him again in Paris during the revolution."

25: FINDING CALYPSO 1793

"You were lovers again there. Did Roume know of it, the affair in Paris?"

"Yes, I think so. It was a dangerous time and he, Stanislaus, were close, very close to the men in power, Robespierre, Danton, all of them."

"Roume could do nothing eh? I would have killed him."

"Easier said than done. I did not love him. It was the times, the revolution, it brought out the devil in you."

"Do you think that they," he glanced across the black stretch of silent water, "will leave here?"

"I don't know."

"Do you hate him, Stanislaus?"

"No, no, strangely no, I do not."

"The man you did not love, but did whatever with, has mated with your daughter, married her in a pagan ceremony that turned them into birds and they have produced a child. And you do not hate him. I would."

"No, Bideau, I do not. Left to me, I would take them all back to Grenada. I have a big house, means, they can make a nest there, if they choose to."

"He is a criminal, a murderer."

"Aren't we all, Jean?"

26: L'ANSE MITAN, TRINIDAD
1820

Writing my Memoirs at L'Anse Mitan, Trinidad, 1820's

PERHAPS IT WAS THE END OF TIME. Or, maybe he had been waiting for an excuse or a reason. I have no idea. When I told Stanislaus de Barras that I would be happy if he, Rosette and the boy would return to civilisation with us, he immediately agreed.

"Yes?"

"Yes."

"Not to Grenada," I told him. "They will hang you there." I said this with some glee. He seemed even more hopeless.

"We will go to Trinidad," I said. "I have property there, in the town, a horrid place, and an estate at L'Anse Mitan above Carenage Bay. You can live there quietly, anonymously. I shall not trouble you." He appeared grateful.

"I understand it is as yet difficult for you to speak, don't mind, you will relearn the art with practice. Explain all this to Rosette for me."

He nodded. My God, he looks like a bird as well.

I had joined them on the giant raft. With gentle undulations, its gradual rotation brought around new forest vistas which were reflected in the mirror like surface of the lake. The effect was pleasing to the eye and produced a sense of being adrift in a floating bubble.

26: L'ANSE MITAN 1820

Jean Baptiste Bideau couldn't stay any longer in the wilds of the Orinoco and neither could I endure the solitude and the insects. The return voyage commenced within days of our reconciliation. Sarusima said farewell to Rosette with a ritual of elaborate formality, sitting, facing each other high in the branches of a giant Brazil nut tree. Later on she was told by Stanislaus and Sarusima that a new and different nest awaited her in Trinidad. I was there when they spoke to her. They all sat around a small wooden stool, carved with bird-like motifs. It had a seat made from what looked like the down found in hummingbird nests. No one sat on it or touched it or, I think, looked at it. It was just there.

Sarusima clicked and squawked and made peeping noises, Stanislaus did the same, adding words in Spanish and French. They both pointed, I supposed in the direction of Trinidad. She said little, only looked quickly from one to the other, her pretty face tilted that way and then this way. So beautiful she was in the shafts of sunlight that slashed across her, her features round and fine, her black eyes bright and shiny. Her little mouth and fine nose like a little bird's. The rest of her, as she sat there erect and attentive, was the form and body of a beautiful young woman. Her light creamy skin firm and flawless. It was not as difficult as I thought it would be to get her to wear clothes on coming aboard. I suppose that she might have seen them as new feathers.

Stanislaus adapted quickly to civilisation. At first they lived quietly in the rooms that I allotted them. He cut his hair and shaved his beard. I gave him money. He found that he could not stay on the estate in Carenage and sailed with the fishermen increasingly into Port-of-Spain, pretending to be one of them, always on the lookout. He saw people on the jetty, in the streets, he told me, whose relatives had died on Mount Qua Qua, killed by him or by Fédon and the others. He knew them, could call their names. There was no remorse, none that I could see. Both he and Philippe Roume had committed terrible acts and so had I.

Stanislaus took to calling the boy, their son, Julien. I thought he did this in memory of Julien Fédon. I never broached the subject but he, on an evening, would relate to me the terrible events that he had been a party to. Stanislaus appeared to me to have become quite a different person, whether as a result the harrowing events of the Grenadian war or the years spent in the deep forest with Sarusima's people, I was never sure. I was pleased to have him about as he made himself useful, becoming in his manner somewhat servile. When he wanted to set up himself in the town, I gave him the money he needed to buy a parcel of land to the east of Port-of-Spain and enough to purchase a pirogue. The land that he bought became known as Stanislaus' Place. Rosette did not follow Stanislaus into the town. She could not bear it—its smells, the noise, the perpetual confusion of the place was more than her nerves could bear. She stayed on the estate with me and Manon, appeared not to have noticed when Stanislaus stayed away for months at a time and was indifferent when it became apparent that he had left for good. I had the boy baptised at the church in Port of Spain and taught him to speak good French and to read and write. He went to school at the chapel in Saint Peter's Bay. Julien grew into a lovely child and a handsome lad.

I loved the house on the estate. Large and simply built, it was set high on a hill and surrounded by old trees. It overlooked the grand sweep of the Gulf of Paria and its scattering of green islands—in one of which lay a treasure in gold. This I had kept to myself, never uttering a word to a soul. I knew well what gold could do.

The true treasures of my life, my joy and reason for being, were Rosette and Manon, who had been brought to us from the Sucre house at Margarita where we had left her. Vandelle and Delpeche also returned to us. They all became quite attached. Indeed, it was Manon who encouraged her sister to try putting on pretty clothes. As I looked on, it came to me how Philippe Roume would speak of his young days and his schooling with Everard de Barras. One

26: L'ANSE MITAN 1820

of his stories was how he was fascinated with Trinidad, seeing it as the legendary Utopia, the mythical paradise inhabited by the nymph Calypso, a pretty naked girl who lived in the wild.

As Rosette settled into life with us she became somewhat less bird-like but was always quiet and gentle as I could wish her to be. She remembered more of the French Patois of her childhood. Simple words, expressing childlike thoughts. This made her more endearing to us. To speak a little French with her funny accent gave her pleasure, as it made us laugh. We learned the language of the birds a little as well and this made her laugh. Her beauty and her original personality naturally attracted the attention of the young men in the area, particularly Maurice Noel, the eldest son of a planter whose estate was close by. He has become a regular caller in spite of his father's disapproval, as we are not a part of the island's aristocratic society that had been created by her father.

Growing up close to L'Anse Mitan, the fishing village on the Carenage estate, Julien became quite a good boatman and sailor and fell in with the families of the area, later becoming engaged to marry a Tardieu girl, Anita, daughter of Honoré Tardieu and Marie-Amélie Tetron. I enjoyed their company, and would sometimes go boating with them to the fishing bank, Trou Tazar, to catch the large red fish and cavallie that swarmed so abundantly in the Gulf.

Sitting in my windy garden above the bay, I would see the men put to sea on a morning to fish or hunt the whales that nursed their young in the still waters around the rocky islands of the Gulf of Paria. My gold, my treasure, was still a secret. I had not told a person. I wondered if it was all still there, if Funillière had come back for his share or had taken it all away.

In 1824, I was approaching my sixty-third birthday. On the whole, my health was as good as could be expected at that age and my memory was as ever. Soubise had left me and I was once more at peace with Marianne who maintained, in good grace, all her nostalgias. One Sunday morning, I said to Julien, "I want you to take me out to Gaspar Percin's island."

Willing as ever, he was pleased to oblige and answered that he would get the men to ready the pirogue.

"No Julien," I said to him, "just you and I, a quiet outing, perhaps we shall bank off the whales' point." It was a quiet day, just the blue sky and the placid sea. Julien handled the oars and I sat in the shade of my umbrella.

"Should we drop anchor here, grandma?" he asked, the pirogue drifting comfortably in the tide that was just going out.

"No," I said, "we go to Winn's Bay."

"Winn's Bay?"

We made the southern side of the island in about half an hour. The sea, as noon approached, was picking up an easterly breeze. It sparkled green with just a little chop. I could taste it on my lips.

"Take her in and put out a stern anchor, there, then make fast to that tree, there, on the little islet. We shall go ashore on it. There is something there that I want to tell you about. And to show you."

"Yes grandma," he answered. He is such a good boy.

FINIS

Glossary

Absinthe: Is an anise-flavoured spirit derived from botanicals, including the flowers and leaves of Artemisia absinthium ("grand wormwood"), together with green anise, sweet fennel, and other medicinal and culinary herbs.

Acadian: French colonists who settled in Acadia during the 17th and 18th centuries. The colony was located in what is now Eastern Canada's Maritime provinces (Nova Scotia, New Brunswick, and Prince Edward Island) as well as part of Quebec.

Adraskan: Is an old town in western Afghanistan where the most exotic and distinctive oriental rugs are woven.

Ajoupa: The native South American and Caribbean name for houses built from mud and thatched with grass.

Alizé: A French word meaning "trade wind".

Alpagatas: Footwear made from leather and colourful woven thread.

Anoto: Amerindian term for a botanical that produces a red dye.

Apage Satanas: Away Satan.

Aparche: First fruits are a religious offering of the first agricultural produce of the harvest. In classical Greek, Roman, Hebrew and Christian religions, the first fruits were given to priests to offer to God.

Aperçu: Perceived, to become aware or conscious of.

Arrière-pensée: An ulterior motive; concealed thought, plan, or motive.

Asiento: Permission given by the Spanish government to other countries to sell people as slaves to the Spanish colonies, between the years 1543 and 1834.

Auto-da-fé: Was the ritual of public penance of condemned heretics and apostates that took place when the Spanish Inquisition had decided their punishment. The most extreme punishment imposed on those convicted was execution by burning.

Balisier: Heliconia bihai (red palulu) of the Heliconiaceae family is an erect herb typically growing taller than 1.5 m. It is native to northern South America and the West Indies.

Boucan: The native South American and Caribbean name for a wooden framework on which meat was slow-roasted or smoked over a fire. Spaniards called the same process "barbacoa", later "barbecue". The term "buccaneer" for pirates or privateers is said to be derived from buccan.

Bumboat: A small boat used to ferry supplies to ships moored away from the shore.

Caciques: Leader of an indigenous group, derived from the Taíno for the pre-Columbian chiefs or leaders of tribes in the Bahamas, Greater Antilles, and the northern Lesser Antilles.

Cadet gentilhomme: Young men of noble families who enlisted for military training.

Cambion: Most often depicted as the offspring of an incubus or succubus and a human.

Carmelite: Roman Catholic religious order founded, probably in the 12th century, on Mount Carmel, hence its name.

Cataplan: Parochial term in Trinidad meaning flat or spreading.

Cedula: Official document or certificate issued by Spain.

Chabine: (fem.) Light-skinned, mixed-race person, with yellow or reddish hair and Negro features.

Cheroots: Comes from French cheroute, from Tamil curuttu, roll of tobacco.

Chevrefeuille: A scent derived from the honeysuckle. These are arching shrubs or twining vines in the family Caprifoliaceae. It is a symbol of love.

Cocott: Patois term of endearment.

Cocoyea: The hard spine in the leaves of a coconut leaf.

Commère: Patois term for Godmother.

Commonplace book: A book of blank pages. Used to compile knowledge. Such books were essentially scrapbooks filled with items of every kind: medical recipes, quotes, letters, poems, tables of weights and measures, proverbs, prayers, legal formulas.

Compère: Patois for Godfather.

Conseiller d'état: A French Councillor of State, a high-level government official of administrative law in the Council of State of France.

Conseillier de Roi: King's Councillor, a general term for the administrative and governmental apparatus around the king of France during the Ancien Régime designed to prepare his decisions and give him advice.

Cornet: The third and lowest grade of commissioned officer in a cavalry troop, after captain and lieutenant, today's second lieutenant.

Cosquel: Patois term for vulgar.

Culverins: A relatively simple ancestor of the musket, and later a medieval cannon, adapted for use by the French in the 15th century.

Da: Patois term for a nurse or nanny.

Daub: Wattle and daub dwelling construction technique and materials, using woven latticework daubed with a mixture of sand, clay and/or dung.

Dirk: Long thrusting dagger.

Doncellas: Young girls of noble birth.

Dragoon: Originally meaning mounted infantry, the name is derived from a type of firearm (called a dragon) carried by dragoons of the French Army.

Ekonting: Folk lute of the Jola people, found in Senegal, Gambia, and Guinea-Bissau in West Africa. It is a banjo-like instrument with a skin-headed gourd body, two long melody strings, and one short drone string, akin to the short fifth "thumb string" on the 5-string banjo.

Embonpoint: Plump, hourglass figure.

Ezulie, La Sirène, Yemanja: West African goddesses.

GLOSSARY

Facines: Long bundle of sticks bound together, used in building earthworks and batteries and in strengthening ramparts.

Fanega: Spanish unit of land measure, equal to 8.81 acres (3.57 hectares).

Fédérés: Refers to the troops who volunteered for the French National Guard in the summer of 1792 during the French Revolution.

Filles de joie: Ladies of the night.

Gayelle: Ring or cockpit for cockfighting.

Greater Ani: Large bird in the cuckoo family. It is a breeding species from Panama and Trinidad through tropical South America to northern Argentina. It is sometimes referred to as the black cuckoo.

Hogsheads: Very large wooden barrel. These were used in colonial times to transport and store tobacco, sugar, rum.

Habitation: From the old French via Latin. A term used by French colonists to describe a plantation.

Houngan: Male priest in Haitian Vodou.

Ingénue: Girl or a young woman who is endearingly innocent and wholesome.

Intendente: Holder of a public administrative office.

Irouléguy: Wine made in the Pyrénées-Atlantiques department in south-western France.

Jarvey: The driver of a jaunting car.

Jean Breeches: Breeches were normally closed and fastened about the leg, along its open seams at varied lengths, and to the knee, by either buttons or by a drawstring, or by one or more straps and buckle or brooches. Jean fabric; the French word for Genoa, may be the origin of the word "jeans".

Jeunesse dorée: Gilded youth; name given to a body of young dandies, also called the Muscadins, who, after the fall of Robespierre, fought against the Jacobins.

Jourinée: The journée of the 10 August 1792 was one of the defining events in the history of the French Revolution. The day resulted in the fall of the French monarchy after storming the Tuileries Palace by the National Guard of the Insurrectional Paris Commune and revolutionary fédérés from Marseilles and Brittany.

Jumbie: Type of mythological spirit or demon in the folklore of some Caribbean countries.

Kalendé: Head-tie used by black women in the French Antilles.

La Manche: The English Channel (French: Manche, "Sleeve").

Lodestone: Naturally magnetised piece of the mineral magnetite.

Madras & Foulard: Madras is a plaid cotton fabric that was used for head-ties. Foulard is the word for a scarf or neckerchief.

Majordomo: Maître d'hôtel, butler or steward. A person who speaks, makes arrangements, or takes charge of another.

Maroon: Fugitive slave, which could be a corruption of Spanish cimarrón, meaning a household animal (or slave) who has run "wild".

Mauvais garçon: Bad boy.

Mosquito Coast: An area along the eastern coast of present-day Nicaragua and Honduras.

Nankeen: A kind of pale yellowish cloth, originally made at Nanjing from a yellow variety of cotton, but subsequently manufactured from ordinary cotton which is then dyed.

Nègre de la Côte: A native of the west coast of Africa.

Noblesse d'épée: Nobles of the Sword are the noblemen of the oldest class of nobility in France.

Noblesse de robe: Those holding certain official positions, such as maître des requêtes, treasurer or president of a parlement.

Ordonnateur: An agent of authority at the head of a department with the jurisdiction to handle public funds.

Paisley: Design using the boteh or buta, a droplet-shaped vegetable motif of Persian and Indian origin.

Parlement: Provincial appellate court in Ancien Régime France. In 1789 there were 13 parlements, the most important of which was by far the Parlement of Paris.

Parvenu: A relative newcomer to a socioeconomic class. The word is borrowed from the French language; it is the past participle of the verb parvenir (to reach, to arrive).

Peccadilloes: Derived from the diminutive of the Spanish language word "pecado" meaning small sin, especially sexual misconduct.

Petit déjeuner à la fourchette: Is the first meal taken after rising from a night's sleep.

Petit po-po: A lullaby.

Phrygian caps: A symbol of revolutionary France. It was first documented in May 1790, at a festival in Troyes adorning a statue representing the nation, and at Lyon, on a lance carried by the goddess Libertas.

Plaçage: A recognised extralegal system in French and Spanish slave colonies of North America (including the Caribbean) by which ethnic European men entered into the equivalent of common-law marriages with women of colour, of African, Native American and mixed-race descent.

Plongeuse: Female dishwasher (male: plongeur).

Poor Clarisses: The Order of Poor Ladies are members of a contemplative Order of nuns in the Catholic Church.

Pot-au-feu: Pot on the fire is a French beef stew.

Ramier: Tourterelles (turtle doves) are two kinds of pigeon, one rusty red the other slate grey.

Remous: Currents that run in the Gulf of Paria alternating with the rising or falling tides.

Retroussé: French for the stern, the back or aft-most part of a ship or boat.

Sachet: French for a small scented cloth bag filled with herbs, potpourri, or aromatic ingredients.

GLOSSARY

Sakiwinki: A small monkey.

Seine: A fishing net that hangs vertically in the water with its bottom edge held down by weights and its top edge buoyed by floats.

Schnaps: German for a strong alcoholic drink made from wheat, sometimes flavoured with fruit.

Seigneurie: Was the property or rights granted by an overlord to a vassal.

Sèvitè: Patois, in vodou "servant of the spirits" (French: serviteur).

Shako: Tall, cylindrical military cap, usually with a visor, and sometimes tapered at the top.

Sirenia manatee: Is an order of fully aquatic, herbivorous mammals that inhabit rivers.

Succubus: Female demon or supernatural entity in folklore that appears in dreams and takes the form of a woman in order to seduce men, usually through sexual activity, for example the "La Diablesse".

Sycorax: From the play "The Tempest", a vicious and powerful witch and the mother of Caliban, one of the few native inhabitants of the island on which Prospero, the hero of the play, is stranded.

Tafia: Cheap rum made from sugarcane juice.

Tasso: Dried or smoked meat.

The Tempest: A play by William Shakespeare. It is set on a remote island, where the sorcerer Prospero plots to restore his daughter Miranda to her rightful place using illusion and skilful manipulation.

Trivium: Systematic method of critical thinking used to derive factual certainty from information perceived with the traditional five senses: sight, sound, taste, touch, and smell. In the medieval university, the trivium was the lower division of the seven liberal arts, and comprised grammar, logic, and rhetoric (input, process and output).

Vendée: Originally known as the Bas-Poitou, and is part of the former province of Poitou.

Vertivert: A fragrant root.

Wanga: A curse.

Wabeen: Colloquial name for a fresh water fish.

Warahoon: Colloquial name for Warrao tribal people on the Gulf of Paria.

Wattle: Woven strips of wood forming panels used for fencing or for walling.

Yaws, pian, mapian: Is a tropical infection of the skin, bones and joints.

Zemi: Deity or ancestral spirit, and a sculptural object that houses the spirit, among the tribal people of the Caribbean.

THE ROYAL CEDULA
FOR POPULATION OF 1783

Translated into English by Governor Don José Maria Chacón, the last Spanish Governor of Trinidad, under whom the Cedula was promulgated throughout the Caribbean as a result of the endeavour of Philippe Roume de St. Laurent. Source: Prof. Carl C. Campbell, Cedulants and Capitulants, published by Paria Publishing Co. Ltd. in 1992. P.P. House of Commons, 1826-1827 (428) =II, Report of the Commissioners of Inquiry into the subject of Titles to Lands in the Island of Trinidad, pp. 191-194.

Whereas by our royal instructions given the 3rd of September 1776 to captain of foot, Don Manuel Falquez, at that time governor of our island of Trinity to windward, and by our commission afterwards granted to Don Joseph de Abalos, when we conferred on him the general superintendency of the province of Caracas, we thought proper to form rules and grant various privileges for the population and trade of the island afore- said; we have now resolved, in consequence of the representation our said intendant, as well as at the desire of some inhabitants already established there, and others who are anxious to become inhabitants thereof, to form a system of colonization and trade, by the following articles:-

Art. I. All foreigners, natives of nations and states, in friendship with us, who would wish to establish them- selves, or are already settled in our said island of Trinity, must make it appear, by the means prescribed by our government of the island aforesaid, that they profess the Roman Catholic religion; for without this indispensable condition, they cannot be admitted to settle there. But this justification shall not be required from the subjects of our own dominions, as no doubt can be harboured with respect to them on this head.

Art. II. Of foreigners who are admitted agreeable to the foregoing article the governor will receive the oaths of allegiance and fidelity by which they will bind them- selves to observe and abide by those laws and ordinances of the Indies to which the Spaniards are subject: in virtue of which oaths, we will in our royal name, grant unto them gratis and in perpetuity the lands they many be entitled to claim by virtue of the following regulations.

Art. III. To each white person, either sex, shall be granted four fanegas and two sevenths of land (equal to ten quarrees French measure, or thirty-two acres English measure) and half the above quantity for every negro or mulatto slave that such white person or persons shall import with them, making such a division of the land, that each shall partake of the good, bad and indifferent. And these distributions shall be recorded in a vellum book of population, specifying the

THE ROYAL CEDULA FOR POPULATION

name of each inhabitant, the date of his admission, the number of individuals of his family, his quality and rank; and every such inhabitant shall have an authentic copy from said book for the parcel of land allotted to him, which shall serve as a title to his property in the same.

Art. IV. The free negroes and mulattoes who shall come to settle in the said island, in quality of inhabitants and chief of families, shall have half the quantity of land granted to the whites, and if they bring with them slaves, being their own property, the quantity of land granted to them shall be increased in proportion to the number of said slaves, and to the land granted to said negroes and mulattoes, this is, one half of the quantity granted to the slaves of whites; and their titles shall be equally legal and granted in the same manner as to whites.

Art. V. After the first five years establishment of foreign settlers in the said island, they shall, by obliging them-selves to continue therein perpetually have all the rights and privileges of naturalization granted to them, and to the children they may have brought with them, as well as those that may have been born in the island, in order to be admitted in consequence to the honorary employments of the public, and of the militia, agreeable to the quality and talents of each.

Art. VI. No capitation or personal tribute shall at any time be laid on the white inhabitants; they shall only be liable to pay one piece of eight yearly for each of their slaves, of whatever cast, and that only to commence ten years after their establishment in the island, and this tax shall never be increased.

Art. VII. During the first five years the Spanish and foreign inhabitants shall be at liberty to return to their native country or former place of abode; in which case they will be permitted to carry with them such property as they brought to the island free from any duty of exportation, but on the increase during such time they will be liable to the payment of ten per centum: and it is to be understood that the lands which have been granted to such inhabitants as voluntarily quit the island shall devolve to out royal patrimony, to be disposed of for the benefit of others, or as shall be found most convenient.

Art. VIII. We grant to the old and new inhabitants that shall die on the island, without having apparent heirs there, the power of bequeathing their fortunes to their relations or friends, wherever they may be; and if their successors should choose to settle in the island they shall enjoy the privileges granted to their constituents: but should they prefer carrying away the inheritance, they may do so by paying upon the whole amount fifteen per centum duties of exportation, where the testator has been five years established, but if he died before that period, only ten per centum, as provided in the foregoing article, and as to those who die intestate, their parents, brothers, or relations shall inherit, even should they reside in foreign nations, provided they are Roman Catholics and settle in the island; but in case they cannot or will not become inhabitants, they shall be permitted to dispose of their inheritance by sale or gift, agreeable to the rules prescribed in the two foregoing articles.

Art. IX. We also grant to all the inhabitants of landed property in the said island power, agreeable to the Spanish laws, of bequeathing or otherwise disposing of their said landed property, without making any division thereof, to one or more of their children, provided that no injustice is done to the rights of the other children, or to the widow of the testator.

Art. X. Any inhabitant who, on account of a law-suit or any other pressing or just motive, may have occasion to go to Spain, or any province of our Indies, or to foreign countries, shall ask leave of the governor, and he will be entitled thereto, provided he is not going to an enemy's country or carrying away his property.

Art. XI. The Spanish as well as the foreign inhabitants shall be exempt for the space of ten years from the payment of tithes upon the products of their lands; after which period, which is to be reckoned from the first day of January 1785, they will only pay five per centum, which is half tithes.

Art. XII. They will be also exempt for the first ten years from the royal duties of alcabala upon the sale of their products and merchandizes and afterwards they will only pay an equivalent of five per centum; but when they ship in Spanish bottoms for our kingdoms of Spain they will be always exempt from any duties of exportation.

Art. XIII. Whereas all the inhabitants ought to be armed, even in times of peace, to keep their slaves in awe, and oppose any invasion or depredation of pirates, we hereby declare, that this obligation does not comprehend them in the class of a regular militia, and that they will acquit themselves of this duty by presenting their arms every two months at a review, to be taken by the governor, or by the officer he may appoint for that purpose; but in time of war or disturbance of slaves they ought to assist in defense of the island, agreeable to the disposition that may be taken by the commander-in-chief.

Art. XIV. The ships and vessels belonging to the old and new subjects, of whatever tonnage or build, must be brought to the island and registered there, with a proof of the property, and they will be made Spanish as well as those obtained from foreign nations, by purchase or any other lawful title, till the end of the year 1786, and they will be all exempt from the alien and qualifying duties; and those who may choose to construct vessels in the said island, government will permit them to cut the timbers necessary for that purpose, excepting only such timbers as may be necessary for the use of the royal navy.

Art. XV. The trade and importation of negroes into the island will be entirely free of duties for the space of ten years from the beginning of 1785, after which time the inhabitants and dealers in slaves will only pay five per centum on their current value on importation; but it shall not be lawful for them to transport said negroes from said island to any part of our dominions in the Indies

THE ROYAL CEDULA FOR POPULATION

without our royal permission, and a consideration of six per centum when thus imported into any of them.

Art. XVI. The inhabitants themselves can go (having the governors leave) with their own vessels, or freighted ones, being Spanish, to the islands in friendship with us, or to the neutral ones, to look for slaves, and take with them produce, effects, or any other property sufficient to pay for them, it being registered in the custom-house, and paying five per centum for exportation, which duty shall likewise be paid by the traders who with our permission shall bring slaves to the island, besides that which they will pay on importation of said slaves, from which we exempt the inhabitants, in order to encourage their cultivation and commerce.

Art. XVII. The course of trade between Spain and the inhabitants of Trinity, and that which they may carry on with such of their produce as is admissible in our islands and American dominions, will be totally free of all duties from the 1st January 1785, for the space of ten years and even at the expiration of said time they will be likewise exempt of all duties of importation into our kingdom of Spain, agreeable to the rules laid down in our last regulation of free trade; so that they can never be encumbered with any taxes other than such as will be fixed on the products of our other West Indian dominions.

Art. XVIII. In like manner Spanish and foreign goods and merchandize and also the fruits and liquors of this our kingdom, which shall be entered in our custom-house and transported to said island shall go free of all duties for the said term of ten years, and shall be in like manner introduced and expended therein; nor can they be reshipped for any other part of my dominions in the Indies; but in case it should be permitted on any urgent or just occasion, it shall be only such articles as are real Spanish, and on paying such duties as are provided by the regulation of free trade.

Art. XIX. In order to facilitate by every means the trade and population of the island, I permit for the said space of ten years, from the commencement of 1785, that the vessels belonging to the inhabitants of the said island, and likewise to my subjects of Spain, may make voyage to the said island, sailing directly with their cargoes from the ports of France, where my consuls reside, and returning directly to them again with the fruits and productions of the island, excepting cash, which I absolutely prohibit the exportation of through that channel; but with the indispensable obligation that my consul shall take an exact inventory of every thing that is shipped, which he shall deliver signed and sealed to the captain or master of the vessel, to be by him delivered at the custom-house in Trinity, and also with the condition of paying five per centum on the entry of the goods and merchandize, and the like quota on the exportation of the produce they shall ship in return to France, or to any other foreign port; but they must not touch at any Spanish port qualified to trade to the Indies.

Art. XX. Upon any urgent necessity, which may appear to the governor of the island, we grant to all its inhabitants, permission similar to that contained in the fore- going article, to enable them to have recourse to the French islands in the West Indies, under the indispensable obligation, that the captains or masters of vessels take exact invoices of their cargoes and deliver them to the officers of the royal administration, in order to compare them individually with the effects they bring, and exact the same contribution of five per centum on their current value in Trinity.

Art. XXI. In order to furnish my old and new inhabitants amply with what may be necessary for subsistence, industry, and agriculture, we have given effectual orders to the commanders of the province of Caracas, for the purpose of conveying to the island such quantities of horned cattle, mules and horses, as may be deemed necessary, at the charge of my royal revenues; and they shall be given to the inhabitants at the first cost and charges, till they can form a breed of them sufficient for their purposes.

Art. XXII. We have made the like provision for a sufficient quantity of flour for the space of ten years, and if through any accident there should happen to be a scarcity of this article on the island, the governor will permit the inhabitants to go to the foreign islands with their own vessel or vessels belonging to my subjects, to purchase as much as may be wanted, carrying for that purpose produce equivalent, and paying five per centum on the exportation thereof, and the same on the importation of the flour.

Art. XXIII. We have likewise ordered to be sent to said island from the manufactories of Biscay, and other parts of Spain, for the said space of ten years, all the instruments and utensils necessary for cultivation, that they may be given to the old and new inhabitants at the first cost; but after the expiration of said ten years, it will be their business to supply themselves; and if during said time, through any cause, there should happen to be a scarcity of said articles and expressing want of them, they shall be permitted to be sent for to the foreign islands in friendship with us, subject to the same regulations provided for flour.

Art. XXIV. We have also directed that two secular and regular priests, of approved learning and exemplary virtue, and well acquainted and versed in the foreign languages, shall go to Trinity to serve as pastors to the new inhabitants that may be there, and we will appoint a competent living for them, to the end that they may support themselves with the decency due to their character, and be no encumbrance to their parishioners.

Art. XXV. We permit the old and new inhabitants to lay before us, through the hands of the governor of the island, the regulations they may think most convenient and proper for the management of their slaves, and to prevent their running away; in the meantime, we have instructed our said governor as to the regulations he is to observe on that head, as well as with respect to a reciprocal restitution of runaway slaves from the foreign islands.

THE ROYAL CEDULA FOR POPULATION

Art. XXVI. We have likewise instructed our said governor to use the utmost diligence that the plague of ants be not introduced into the island; to prevent which all the goods and effects coming from such of the Antilles as have been infested with this vermin, must be individually inspected; and whereas the inhabitants are the most interested in this point, they shall propose to government two persons of the greatest confidence and activity to examine the vessels, etc., and carefully attend to the performance of this point.

Art. XXVII. When the sugar crops shall become considerable or abundant in Trinity, we will grant to the inhabitants the liberty of erecting refining houses in Spain, with all the privileges and exemption of duties which we may have granted to any of our natural born subjects or foreigners who have erected such; and we will likewise permit, at a proper time, the erection of a council board in said island for the advancement and protection of its agriculture, navigation and commerce; with immediate direction to the governor in his particular instructions, and to the other judges, to use humanity, good treatment, and impartial and speedy administration of justice to all the Spanish and foreign inhabitants, and not to trouble or injure them in any way whatever, which would be very much to my royal displeasure.

Art. XXVIII. Lastly we grant to the old and new inhabitants of said island when they have motives deserving our royal consideration, liberty to send us their remonstrances through the means of the governor and minister for the universal dispatch of India affairs; and in case the business should be of such a nature as to require a person to solicit it, they shall ask our leave for it, and we will grant it, if their demand is just. And in order that all the articles contained in this regulation should have their full force, we dispense with all the laws and customs which may be contradictory to them; and we command our council of the Indies, the chancellors and courts of justice thereof, vice-kings, captains and commanders-in-chief, governors and intendants, common justices, the officers of our royal revenues, and our consuls in the ports of France, to keep, comply with, and execute, and cause to be kept, complied with, and executed the regulation inserted in this our royal Schedule. Done at St. Lorenzo, November 24th 1783, Sealed with our private seal, and subscribed by our under-written Secretary of State, and also Secretary for the universal dispatch of India affairs.

We the King. Joseph de Galvez.

About the Author

Gérard "Jerry" Besson was born in 1942 at 50 Hermitage Road, Belmont, Trinidad and Tobago, W.I. He has worked in advertising as a Creative Director in all media and as a writer, publisher and social historian, he has specialised in the history and folklore of Trinidad and Tobago. In 2007, he was awarded the national award of the Hummingbird Medal (Gold) for Heritage Preservation and Promotion. Also in that year, he received the Lifetime Achiever Heritage Preservation Award from the National Trust of Trinidad and Tobago. In 2015, the University of the West Indies conferred upon him an Honorary Doctorate of Letters.

www.ingramcontent.com/pod-product-compliance
Lightning Source LLC
Chambersburg PA
CBHW021132230426
43667CB00005B/87